Migration

MIGRATION

Changing the World

Guy Arnold

PlutoPress
www.plutobooks.com

First published 2012 by Pluto Press
345 Archway Road, London N6 5AA

www.plutobooks.com

Distributed in the United States of America exclusively by
Palgrave Macmillan, a division of St. Martin's Press LLC,
175 Fifth Avenue, New York, NY 10010

British Library Cataloguing in Publication Data
A catalogue record for this book is available from the British Library

ISBN   978 0 7453 2906 2   Hardback
ISBN   978 0 7453 2905 5   Paperback

Library of Congress Cataloging in Publication Data applied for

This book is printed on paper suitable for recycling and made from fully managed and
sustained forest sources. Logging, pulping and manufacturing processes are expected
to conform to the environmental standards of the country of origin.

10   9   8   7   6   5   4   3   2   1

Designed and produced for Pluto Press by Chase Publishing Services Ltd
Typeset from disk by Stanford DTP Services, Northampton, England
Simultaneously printed digitally by CPI Antony Rowe, Chippenham, UK and
Edwards Bros in the United States of America

Contents

Introduction

For centuries the River Danube acted as the frontier of Rome. In 104 CE the Emperor Trajan built a great bridge across the river below the gorge of the Iron Gates to make possible the conquest of Dacia (modern Romania) and Roman military camps along the river later developed into cities. The Emperor Marcus Aurelius (161–80) spent eight bitter winters on the frozen banks of the Danube facing the barbarians who threatened Rome. The severity of the final winter killed him. The Empire faced the most serious threat to its internal security for more than two and a half centuries during the years 166 to 180, when Roman armies had to mount four campaigns – at huge cost in wealth and lives – to hold the frontier. These Marcommanic wars marked the end of a long period of relative peace and stable relations between the Roman Empire and the peoples of Central Europe and signalled the coming of two centuries of growing external threats to Rome. The Emperor Septimus Severus (193–211) controlled twelve legions along the Danube – nearly half the Empire's permanent regular army – when in 193 he made his bid for supreme power. The Emperor Aurelian (270–75) had faced the fury of the Goths many times as a general before he became emperor and his experience in the field persuaded him to reorder the Danubian frontier; he did this by relinquishing Roman control over Dacia, which he saw as a reasonable price to pay for peace, and a century of peace followed. However, in 376 the Emperor Valens agreed to allow Goths to cross the river to escape the pressure of the Huns, a move that proved fatal to Rome's control of the Danube frontier, for, once across the river, the Goths turned against the Romans and in August of that year a Roman army led by Valens was defeated at the battle of Adrianople with the loss of 20,000 men as well as the Emperor himself. Twenty years later, when the Danube had frozen over (394–5) the Hun cavalry crossed the river into the Empire. These and subsequent migrations in the fifth century brought an end to the Roman Empire of the West.

A NEW DIMENSION

In the last decade of the twentieth century and into the twenty-first century the world faced huge movements of people, both within and between countries, that were both proportionately and absolutely the largest migrations in history. Europe and the United States, which have historically long been migrant target areas, faced new waves of incomers but the scale of these was dwarfed by the massive internal movement of migrants inside China, as people moved from the countryside to the cities to provide workers for the country's huge industrial and commercial development revolution. The great majority of all these movers are motivated by economic considerations, the search for a better life. One non-economic result of these mass movements is the creation of huge social strains. In addition to the economic movers are the people who have been displaced by famine and war or those who seek political asylum.

The economics of migration are demonstrated by the example of Ireland. One of the poorest countries in Europe when it joined the European Union (EU) in 1973 it then saw its people, especially the young, migrating in search of work and it was a net loser of people up to 1993, when unemployment stood at 16 per cent of the work force. Then its economic recovery took off and by 1995 it had become a net gainer of people, many of them returning citizens. Ireland was to enjoy a decade of growth and near full employment as the Celtic Tiger. But the 'miracle' came to an end abruptly in 2008 when the country entered into recession. Depending upon how long the recession lasts Ireland may again find that it is a net loser of people. The Irish example illustrates how economic fortunes control migration patterns.

DEMOGRAPHIC PROJECTIONS

According to United Nations (UN) projections the world population is likely to increase by 2.5 billion over the next 41 years, growing from 6.7 billion to 9.2 billion in 2050. Most of this increase will be absorbed by the less developed regions, whose population is projected to rise from 5.4 billion in 2007 to 7.9 billion in 2050, while the developed regions will remain largely unchanged at 1.2 billion – and this figure will depend upon net migration from the developing to the developed countries, which is expected to average 2.3 million persons a year. The more developed regions will see a near doubling of those over 60 years of age from 245 million in 2005 to 406 million in 2050, while those under age 60 will decline from 971 million in 2005 to 839 million in 2050. Thus, while the global population as a whole is increasing, with virtually all population growth occurring in the developing regions, the population of the more developed regions will hardly increase at all. These predictions, however, will depend upon upward or downward trends in the fertility rate, which in 2008 stood at 2.55 children per woman.

Population ageing as well as reductions in fertility rates will have a significant impact upon the developed regions. At the present time 20 per cent of the population in the developed regions is already aged 60 years or more and by 2050 this figure is expected to reach 33 per cent. Moreover, by 2050 there will be more than twice as many older persons in developed countries as persons under 15. A number of the least developed countries will experience particularly high population growth rates: for example, the populations of Afghanistan, Burundi, Democratic Republic of Congo, Guinea-Bissau, Liberia, Niger, Timor-Leste and Uganda are expected at least to triple by 2050. By contrast, in 46 countries or areas that include Germany, Italy, Japan, the Republic of Korea and most of the successor states of the USSR, populations are expected to be lower in 2050 than in 2005. During the period 2005–50 eight countries are expected to account for half the world's population increase: India, Nigeria, Pakistan, Democratic Republic of Congo,

Ethiopia, the United States, Bangladesh and China. The world median age, which can be taken as an indicator of population ageing, is expected to reach 38 years in 2050, but in Europe, where the median age is now 39 years, it is expected to reach 47 by 2050. The higher the median age the greater the ageing that has taken place. These figures form a necessary background to the migration of people. The UN estimates that the net receivers of international migrants in terms of annual averages will be: the United States (1.1 million annually), Canada (200,000), Germany (150,000), Italy (139,000), the United Kingdom (130,000), Spain (123,000), Australia (100,000). The countries with the highest levels of net migration are projected to be: China (–329,000 annually), Mexico (–306,000), India (–241,000), Philippines (–180,000), Pakistan (–167,000) and Indonesia (–164,000).[1]

REPLACEMENT MIGRATION

Western countries must face the vital question of whether replacement migration provides a solution to population decline and population ageing. Replacement migration means the international migration needed both to offset declines in the size of population in the population of working age and to offset the overall ageing of the population. According to UN statistics, major countries that have large populations and below-replacement fertility levels are France, Germany, Italy, Japan, Republic of Korea, the Russian Federation, and the United Kingdom. The process of population ageing – the transformation of the age structure to relatively greater proportions in the older age groups – is brought about by declining fertility and increased longevity. In most cases, those populations that are simultaneously ageing and declining will experience severe reductions in the ratio of persons of working age (15–64 years) to older persons (65 years and above). In 1998, shifts in population for the following six countries between 2000 and 2050 were projected as follows. In 2000 Germany had a population of 82.2 million which is projected to have declined to 73.3 million by 2050, while the percentage of people of 65 years or more will have increased from 16 to 28 per cent. In 2000 Italy had a population of 57.3 million which is projected to have declined to 41.2 million by 2050, while the percentage of people of 65 years or more will have increased from 18 to 35 per cent. In 2000 Japan had a population of 126.7 million which is projected to have declined to 104.9 million by 2050, while the percentage of people of 65 years or more will have increased from 17 to 32 per cent. In 2000 the Russian Federation had a population of 146.9 million which is projected to have declined to 121.2 million by 2050, while the percentage of people of 65 years or more will have increased from 13 to 25 per cent. In 2000 Spain had a population of 39.6 million which is projected to have declined to 30.2 million by 2050, while the percentage of people of 65 years or more will have increased from 17 to 37 per cent. In 2000 the United Kingdom had a population of 58.8 million which is projected to have declined to 56.6 million by 2050, while the percentage of people of 65 years or more will have increased from 16 to 25 per cent. Among demographic variables only international migration could be instrumental in addressing population decline and population ageing in either the short or medium term. Longevity will increase even without new medical breakthroughs. The prospects of population decline and population ageing in the first half of the twenty-first century raises crucial issues about employment, economic growth, health care, pensions and social support services. Such demographic realities in the advanced economies will lead to reassessments of many established economic, social and political policies and programmes, including policies relating to international migration.

The number of migrants worldwide rose from 36 million in 1991 to 191 million in 2005. Migration has become increasingly important to the population growth of developed countries. In 2005 the United States took in 61 per cent of migrants compared with 53 per cent in 1990. Because of low fertility rates in the developed countries, net migration accounts for 75 per cent of population growth in those countries. Should present trends continue, then between 2010 and 2030 net migration will probably account for all population increases in the developed world. In 2005 64 million migrants lived in Europe, 44.5 million in North America, 4.7 million in Australia and New Zealand and 2 million in Japan. By contrast, the migrant population of the developing world has risen by only 3 million since 1990, totalling 75 million in 2005: 51 million in Asia, 17 million in Africa and 7 million in Latin America and the Caribbean. Family reunification accounts for a major part of migration to North America and Europe though both labour and skilled migration is rising. The net impact of migration is generally positive for host countries. There may be small adverse impacts on the wages of non-migrants or unemployment when wages are rigid but such effects are small at the national level. In 2004, official migrant remittances totalled $226 billion, including $160 billion that went to developing countries. Such remittances generally benefit low- and middle-income countries and may also ease foreign exchange restrictions. As Malcolm Todd points out:

> migration, of one kind or another, is a live and abrasive political and social issue in the present world, in Europe, Asia and the Americas. Refugees, economic migrants, asylum seekers and others seeking new homes for whatever reason have been a dominant theme of world history over the past decade in Europe since the collapse of the Soviet Union in 1989.[2]

AMBIGUITY

When the repatriation of refugees and the natural return home of guest workers (those who come to make money in a more developed country than their own but always intend to return home) are taken into consideration, it becomes clear that migration is by no means all one way. Attitudes towards migrants are ambiguous almost everywhere. Even as developed countries have tightened their controls on entry, exceptions are always made for skilled personnel, especially in health care, where insufficient investment in the health services has occurred. The steady growth of migration flows, both legal and illegal, from poor to rich countries – with the EU and the USA as the prime target destinations – had, by the beginning of the twenty-first century, developed into a major aspect of rich–poor or North–South relations. Much of this migration represents a 'brain drain' of professional and other trained personnel from the poor countries of the South to the benefit of the rich countries of the North. The fear in rich countries of mass migration from low-income countries is all too real. And, given the disparities in living standards and personal freedoms across the Mediterranean and between North America and Central America, these fears are probably well founded, if exaggerated. Such fears could prove a major factor in reinforcing inward-looking approaches to the world economy. Labour migration will increase and it is in everybody's interest to develop and strengthen the rules that govern it. Cycles of migration always leave the poorest, least developed countries worse off. Migration, legal and illegal, and the movement of asylum seekers became increasingly contentious subjects at the beginning of the twenty-first century. The EU and the USA, with their wealth and apparent job opportunities, were the principal targets for these migrants, but both worried over the political and social impact that too many newcomers would have upon their social structures. This has been especially the case in the EU, where the debate has centred upon how to control such inflows. The EU has long, complex and porous borders: there is no simple way of preventing migrants from entering the region.

Migration raises a variety of international, political and social issues. First are the compulsions to move and the actual movement of people, whether as economic migrants, refugees or asylum seekers. Next are the reactions of the new host countries: racism, xenophobia, new laws, inter-state quarrels, the construction of border walls, the emergence of inward-looking patriotism that is displayed, for example, by the idea of creating a Fortress Europe. Human rights abuses are a partial response to these attitudes and include people-smuggling and the international sex trade on the one hand, and exploitation of illegal immigrants on the other. In the end, however, the economic arguments prevail. Countries with ageing, static populations need new young immigrants to bolster their work forces. Developed countries actively recruit people with skills from developing countries, to the detriment of the development of the latter countries, since too many of their most professional personnel are lost in this brain drain. Some countries, such as the Philippines, have a positive policy to encourage emigration since the economy cannot provide a livelihood for everyone. Remittances, although important, do not compensate developing countries for the loss of skills. Despite the economic advantages to be derived from migration, the ramifications of mass migrations of the kind taking place in the first decade of the twenty-first century are politically explosive.

> Migration is, of course, by no means limited to the poor, and is increasingly characteristic of highly educated and specialised professionals, bureaucrats, technologists and technocrats who move about and serve the interests of the global economy.[3]

According to Jeremy Harding,[4] governments all too often pay greater attention to their minorities that are hostile to immigrants than to the majorities that are not hostile. The contribution of incomers to the economy, for example, was illustrated in the 1991 British census, which showed that pro rata a higher proportion of Bangladeshi, Pakistani, Indian and Chinese males held managerial posts than did their white counterparts. Processes to determine asylum claims reveal parsimonious haggling on the part of the rich world. The depth of the problem derives from the global divide between rich and poor and the economic dependency to which the North has reduced the South. Thus:

The problem for rich nations aiming at minimal immigration from poorer countries is obvious: in attempting to discourage migration by enriching the source countries, they can never rule out the possibility that they are stimulating the very phenomenon they wished to depress.

Trying to negotiate with poor countries the number of migrants that are acceptable to rich countries is, almost by definition, a wasted effort. Only a total reversal of the globalisation process might stop the flow. 'To inhibit immigration in one way is to encourage it in others. To deny it altogether, as Europe is now trying to do, is simply to invite a growing disregard for the law.'[5] As this writer also reminds us, refugees from Kosovo and Kurds were referred to in 1998 in the *Dover Express* as 'human sewage'. Unfortunately, such attitudes are on the increase. 'Migrants in search of a better life are now entering richer areas at faster rates.'[6]

NORTH AND SOUTH

Understanding the North–South relationship is the key to understanding migration problems.

There are numerous instances of the logic of exclusion informing North–South relations, including the increasing restriction of immigration from the South since the 1970s and the hardening of the international refugee regime ... Although some views of globalisation stress interconnection and integration, the movement of poor people from South to North, and even across international boundaries in the South itself, is becoming more difficult and contested.[7]

Now if such attitudes inform North–South relations they differ little from those operating in the North, for example between the highly developed countries of the EU and the new poor members who joined the Union as a result of the 'Big Bang' in 2004. In subsequent years there were dire warnings about the number of Poles and other East and Central European migrants who were entering Britain. These migrants, according to the media, were putting some of the public services under intolerable strain. However, by mid

2007 the number of such immigrants seeking work had fallen to its lowest level since the Big Bang. This reversal of popular perceptions illustrated the all-important fact that migrants follow market forces: they come for jobs rather than permanent settlement and when the job market dries up they return home.

The end of the Cold War provides a convenient but also a political-economic dividing line between types and perceptions of migration. In the 1970s revolutionary and liberation struggles led to large movements of people in Africa, Cuba and Vietnam. Germany and the United States censured the governments of both Cuba and Vietnam and this led to a debate in the UN Special Political Committee in 1980 to investigate the root causes of migration – but, in the context of the Cold War, arguments polarised. Socialist and non-aligned nations argued that historical and external factors were to blame: that is, colonialism and inequalities in trade were the primary causes of poverty and instability and, therefore, of migration. On the other side of the argument, the West emphasised the internal causes of conflict – poor governance and ineffectual economic policies as well as environmental degradation. These divisions continued through the first half of the 1980s. By the 1990s large-scale migration, especially from Europe's south Mediterranean fringe and from the Balkans, was seen as a particular threat. Chaos and decline in the Third World were seen to threaten the developed world in terms of disease, migration and trade.[8]

GLOBALISATION

Globalisation must lead to increased migration flows as travel becomes easier and cheaper and demands for labour vary between different regions of the world. The flow of goods and capital from rich to poor nations will not be sufficient to offset the needs for employment in the developing countries. Of crucial importance in an increasingly globalised world is the fact that while governments do little to control flows of trade and finance, they take increasingly tough action to regulate the flow of people. Globalisation, however, must also mean the globalisation of people. Regulations and controls will not stop the flow of people; instead, they will lead to a more complex process of movement. Thus, a commercial migrant industry has emerged to assist those who wish to move and this industry is paralleled by illegal people trafficking. According to the UN Population Division there are now almost 200 million international migrants. The Global Commission on International Migration (GCIM) released its report *Migration in an Interconnected World: New Directions for Action* in October 2005. The commissioners stated: 'The international community has failed to realize the full potential of international migration and has not risen to the many opportunities and challenges it presents.' The spread of capitalism is the primary triumph of globalisation because that is what it is mainly about. In both the United States and Britain privatisation, the hands-off approach by governments, the collapse of the manufacturing industries and the emasculation of the trade unions have contributed to make capitalism more blatant and less controlled or controllable. In such a climate migrants offer a convenient scapegoat while also providing a pool of cheap labour that 'liberated' industries and companies are only too happy to employ. Indeed, immigration is a convenient scapegoat on two counts: it diverts attention from the capitalist system and neoliberal reforms, which are the true causes of worker impoverishment; and it encourages the indigenous working class (many of whom are second- or third-generation immigrants themselves) to regard new arrivals as their enemies, thus creating working-class tensions. Capitalism is an exploitative and competitive system, which pits individuals and groups of people against one another.

Migration, therefore, has to be seen in the context of globalisation, which is mainly about the spread of capitalism. It is both unrealistic and hypocritical to push for the greater movement of finances, businesses, trade and investment but not of people who are and must be part of the same process. According to Robert Cox:

> Much of the world's population is irrelevant in the formal global economy and this is manifest in the shift from attempts to promote economic development in the South in favour of what can be called global poor relief and riot control.[9]

Another analyst of globalisation says:

> The postulate concerning the beneficial character of international trade makes a general principle out of the opening of economies and societies to all kinds of external exchange (commercial, financial, cultural, and so on – the implicit exception being migration); it sets maximum openness as a necessary condition for the maximisation of welfare or the general interest, for all members of these economies and societies.[10]

Despite such attempts to except migration from the process of globalisation, migration patterns are becoming, to an increasing extent, globalised rather than simply regional. Arguments for 'one world' would eliminate half the problems associated with migration, yet the fanatical supporters of deregulation do not see this applying to migration. There now exists, as the outcome of the huge growth of migration over the years since the end of the Cold War, a fundamental need to respect and recognise the basic human rights of immigrants and refugees. Ahmed Ben Bella has said:

> All these people, despite their differences, are affected by the fact that the world system, as it currently operates, does not work ... People realise that the problems are the same for the North and the South. People try to contain the invasion. But they won't succeed. The army has already been placed on the Swiss border. You cannot stop someone who is hungry and believes he can help himself.[11]

In study after study we return to a fundamental theme in all aspects of migration: poverty. The poor, if they can, escape their poverty by moving. Major diasporas, especially in the United States and the EU, will bring about major changes in the make-up of the political and social systems of these countries, and the larger a particular diaspora from a poor to a rich country, the greater their influence with both their home and host countries. Diasporas are coming to be seen as assets by their countries of origin. They represent their country of origin in their new host country; they assist their country of origin economically with their remittances while the countries of origin exert increasing influence through the export of their people.[12] At the end of the last century (1998) foreign-born people formed 19 per cent of the population in Switzerland, 9 per cent in Germany, 10 per cent in France, 4 per cent in Britain, 17 per cent in Canada, 23 per cent in Australia, and 10 per cent in the United States. An increasing and inevitable aspect of these diasporas is marriage with someone of another race (that is, someone of the host country).

MIGRATION POLICIES: THE UNITED NATIONS

Each state has its own migration policy and this depends upon the extent to which it is a sending or receiving country. Sovereign states expect to control populations that are relatively uniform – British, German, Indonesian – although once such a specification has been made the absurdity of such distinctions becomes apparent when one asks the simple question: who are the British? Nonetheless, migrants threaten such a concept of wholeness and therefore must be controlled. Too many migrants will upset the balance. This may seem a truism when related to a single state but what is it when discussed in relation to a conglomerate such as the EU? As a regional grouping, the EU has discovered that border control, no matter what laws are passed by its individual members, is becoming ever harder to maintain. What happens to the migrants once inside the regional borders is another matter. All countries would like to control immigration but in many cases they have neither the capacity nor the machinery to make such control possible. In recent years boundaries have become an all-important aspect of migration. Where land borders divide areas of co-habitation, they are crossed no matter what control laws exist. In other cases walls have been constructed to control the immigrant flow but, as those responsible for their construction are discovering, walls present a challenge to be overcome rather than a barrier that cannot be passed. As we are coming to realise, migration is a normal – and unstoppable – human activity and too many restrictions become violations of human rights. Thus, for example, many states have constitutions that guarantee the right to emigrate – an assumption that has a necessary corollary – yet no states have constitutions that recognise the right of migrants to enter. The right to emigrate from one state is meaningless without the complementary right to immigrate into another state. Governments always face the dilemma of domestic pressures to keep borders closed so as to maintain the national character on the one hand, while human rights concerns recognise the rights of immigrants on the other. It is becoming increasingly obvious that in a globalised world no country can isolate itself from migration pressures.

The more legal migration is curbed by laws, the more human trafficking and smuggling will grow, since these become the only routes for determined migrants to take. The protection of migrant workers is the duty of both the state of origin and the receiving state, yet the former has only limited powers over migrants once they have moved while the latter will place the welfare of migrants low on its list of priorities: migrants are either a useful addition to the work force or an unwanted liability. The International Labour Organization (ILO) has established a series of standards for the protection of migrants while in 1990 the UN adopted the International Convention on the Protection of the Rights of All Migrant Workers and Members of Their Families (the Migrant Workers Convention), which entered into force in 2003. The Convention makes it illegal to expel migrant workers on a collective basis, or to destroy their identity documents, work permits or passports. It also lays down that migrant workers are entitled to receive the same remuneration, social benefits and medical care as nationals; to join or take part in meetings of trade unions; and upon ending their employment to transfer earnings, savings and personal belongings. Further, the children of migrant workers should have the right of registration of birth and nationality and of access to education. However, many countries, including all EU member states, as yet have neither ratified the Convention nor changed their own laws in line with it. In 2000 the UN proclaimed 18 December as International Migrants Day (IMD), a step that at least recognised the developing problem.

By 2007, UN predictions posited an annual flow of 2.2 million migrants into the rich world every year until 2050 and, for example, suggested that Britain's population would rise from 60 million to 69 million over this period, almost entirely because of immigration. It also argued that the indigenous populations of most countries in the rich world would either stagnate or decline. Almost all increases in the world population to 2050 would occur in Africa, Asia and the Middle East while there would occur a steady depopulation of vast areas of Eastern Europe and the former Communist world, a process that would be assisted by emigration and birth rates declining below replacement levels. The gap in wealth and opportunity between the rich and poor worlds will act as the most significant 'pull factor' behind these changes.[13]

REFUGEES AND THE UN HIGH COMMISSIONER FOR REFUGEES

Since its creation in 1950 the UN High Commissioner for Refugees (UNHCR) has helped about 50 million people. Its most important function is to ensure respect for refugees' basic human rights, including their ability to seek asylum, and to ensure that no one is returned involuntarily to a country where he or she has reason to fear persecution. The number of refugees in any year varies: in 1992 the number of refugees worldwide stood at 17 million and there was a similar number in 2005. Of all the UN agencies, the UNHCR almost always works at grassroots levels in response to crises and more than

500 non-governmental organisations (NGOs) work as operational partners with the UNHCR. At the end of 2005 the global population of concern to the UNHCR was 21 million (estimated), including 8.7 million refugees; 773,000 asylum seekers; 1.1 million refugees repatriated during the year; 6.6 million internally displaced persons (IDPs) who were protected or assisted by the UNHCR; 519,000 IDPs who had returned to their place of origin during the year; 2.4 million stateless persons; and 960,000 others 'of concern'. The pattern changes constantly. By the end of 2005, Asia hosted 42 per cent of all persons of concern to the UNHCR, followed by Africa (24 per cent), Europe (18 per cent), Latin America and the Caribbean (12 per cent), North America (3 per cent), Oceania (0.4 per cent). Of these 21 million persons of concern at the end of 2005, 8.4 million (40 per cent) originated in Asia, 5.6 million (26 per cent) from Africa, 2.8 million (13 per cent) from Latin America and the Caribbean, and 1.6 million (8 per cent) from Europe. Afghans constituted the largest refugee population of concern with 3.2 million (15 per cent), Colombians 2.5 million (12 per cent), then stateless persons 2.4 million (11 per cent) and Iraqis 1.8 million (8 per cent). As always, the most durable solution for refugees is to see them return to their countries of origin and in 2005 1.1 million refugees did so. The countries that resettled the most refugees in 2005 were the United States (53,800), Australia (11,700), Canada (10,400) and Sweden (1,300). Countries receiving the most refugees in 2005 were Chad, Benin, Uganda, Ghana and Yemen, while the main source countries of new refugees that year were Togo, Sudan, Democratic Republic of Congo, Somalia, Central African Republic and Iraq. At this time Tanzania hosted the highest number of refugees in relation to its economic capacity: 868 refugees per $1 of gross domestic product (GDP) per capita. Over the years 2001–5 the United States hosted the largest number of refugees in relation to its total population: 80 per 1,000. The work of the UNHCR represents only one aspect of the total problem of the movement of people worldwide but, as migration in all its forms has moved close to the top of many countries' agendas, so it encounters new attempts by host countries to staunch the flow of refugees. Thus, in 2006 Britain, Denmark and the Netherlands tried to introduce a new European policy whereby asylum seekers would be removed to centres outside Europe while their cases were processed, but the move was defeated by Germany, France and Sweden. The High Commissioner, Antonio Guterres, launched a report, *The State of the World's Refugees* which stated: 'In the past few years, asylum issues and refugee protection have become inextricably linked with the question of international migration, particularly irregular migration.'[14]

Refugees may be pitied when first they flee from some catastrophe but, all too often, they come to be regarded as a burden. Those arriving in the West receive the most attention, perhaps because of the efficiency of the media, although the majority of refugees are created by events in the developing world and remain there. Mass movements of people are divided into refugees and economic migrants; the definition of refugees was laid down clearly in the 1951 Geneva Convention as people who have left their place of habitual residence, 'owing to well-founded fear of being persecuted for reasons of race, religion, nationality, membership of a particular social group or political opinion'. Since some 150 countries have signed the Convention refugees should be able to enter and stay in such countries. International law faces the task of defining the point at which the push factors that encourage people to leave their homes, often under enormous stress and fear, become so strong that their migration should be seen as forced. An even more difficult category to deal with is that of IDPs who, in effect, are refugees in their own countries. There are special cases, the most long-lasting and outstanding in this category being the 4.4 million Palestinian refugees and their descendants displaced by the 1948 Arab-Israeli war. States that have signed the 1951 Convention are legally committed to respect the rights of refugees and this includes not forcing them to return to a country where their lives or freedoms could be endangered. One result of this commitment has been the creation of refugee camps, in which refugees may spend years without any possibility of work or education; such camps become centres of despair, ill health and crime.

The UNHCR outlines three 'durable solutions' for refugees: local integration, resettlement in third countries, and, arguably the best, repatriation to their countries of origin, although this last solution depends upon changes that have occurred in the country concerned. In this new century an increasing number of countries in both the developed and developing worlds are seeking ways to limit their obligations under the 1951 Geneva Convention.[15]

INTERNATIONAL LABOUR ORGANIZATION

The primary reason that people move is to find jobs and earn higher pay, and differentials in payment for work are part of the story. In the present age, falling costs of transportation and increased speed of communication have changed the character of migration – some might argue for the better – since a move from one country to another is no longer seen as permanent, as would have been the case formerly. Since 1970 there has been a steady increase in the number of countries classified as major recipients of migrant labour and the number of countries designated as major suppliers of labour, while some countries have become both suppliers and recipients of migrant labour. Certain destination counties have become so attractive that people trafficking to them has become a highly lucrative business, now estimated to be worth at least $7 billion a year. Differences in living standards provide the key to economic migration: for example, in 2000 the GDP per capita differential between the United States and Mexico was 6 to 1, and between Germany and Poland 11 to 1. The rate of migration flows can change sharply as economic conditions alter, and such changes will vary depending upon the employment opportunities in particular sectors of the target country economy such as agriculture, construction or services.

In 2006 the ILO estimated that half the global workforce earned less than $2 a day and that robust economic development on a world scale had failed to generate enough jobs in poor countries to provide an escape from poverty with the result that incentives to emigrate to the richer countries of Western Europe and North America remained very powerful. There followed a worldwide flood of migration restrictions while, at the same time, local resentment at incomers remained a conspicuous part of the overall migration scene. For example, workers in the New Caledonia aluminium sector went on strike in protest at the employment of workers from the Philippines. Globalisation is bound to intensify migration as the freer flow of both goods and capital creates greater income inequalities while also disturbing traditional labour markets. Increases in trade and investment, which are the result of globalisation, will not offset the growing and often huge need for jobs in poorer countries. Economic restructuring, the result of globalisation, will create many social disruptions and lead an increasing number of people to desert their traditional communities and seek work outside their own countries. The increased movement of people will not depend upon any liberalisation of immigration controls (assuming that such a liberalisation is any longer feasible politically) but to growing labour supply pressures, rising income inequalities both within and across nations, and the revolution in information and communication technologies (the IT revolution). What has now become a permanent factor encouraging labour movement is the growing knowledge worldwide of earning differences between countries. Counter-measures to mass migration will grow in proportion to the growing volume of labour movement.

Migration is a link between North and South or rich and poor. The reluctance of the rich nations to meet the problems of the poor has encouraged increasing numbers of people from the South to take the matter into their own hands and emigrate, and by 2000 an estimated 150 million people lived outside the country of their birth. Approaches to immigration change, depending upon circumstances. In Europe, there has often been deep sympathy for migrants, especially those escaping hardship or political persecution. But cheap air travel, a feature of the 1980s, opened up areas of the world to migrants as never before. Rich countries in Europe began to close their doors and new, often deeply racist arguments were deployed to justify keeping out would-be migrants. A mentality emerged that 'thrives on the idea that refugees are helping themselves to scarce resources: welfare, the public health service, accommodation paid for or provided by local government, premium space in the classroom'.[16] In all the debates about migration almost all participants fail to see – or if they do see, they ignore for political reasons – the fact that migration has, and follows, a law of its own. Broadly, migrants can only fill spaces that are there. In other words, there are not too many migrants and those moving can be absorbed – they are needed. A majority of objections to them are emotional rather than rational.

RACE, IMMIGRATION AND ECONOMICS

Given the growing interface between Western countries and the Islamic world it is unsurprising that racists target immigrants from Muslim countries as especially unwelcome incomers. In 2006, a year that witnessed some ugly racial attacks upon immigrants in the UK, the Muslim Council of Britain said the debate about integration had become 'increasingly ugly and shrill'. Britain, for example, controls immigration by rationing entry according to country of origin, a policy that is inherently racial. By contrast, immigration into the United States is first and foremost about economics: what the immigrants can contribute to the economy. Canada's western metropolis of Vancouver, with a population in excess of 2 million, includes 300,000 Chinese and 200,000 Asians who between them have made a remarkable contribution to the city's economic growth. When Hong Kong reverted to China in 1997 Britain refused to allow more than a handful of its subjects who wished to emigrate to come to Britain. Instead they went to Canada: it was Britain's loss (for racist reasons) and Canada's gain. Both Australia and Canada use a points system that focuses upon what the country needs and what the immigrant might bring. Migration is almost always a touchy subject that can easily develop into a racist confrontation but immigration cannot be dealt with in isolation. In the host country it embraces such areas as planning and investment in public housing and social improvement projects that benefit both indigenous and immigrant peoples. To talk of diversity and integration as core aspects of policy does not make sense unless these other aspects of policy have been addressed. Although many incomers take low-paid jobs on arrival, many of them have been educated – in some cases to professional levels – by their countries of origin. Cultures are different. Thus, while multiculturalism sees differences as a source of vitality and renewal, racists see them as the origin of antagonism and conflict. Cultural differences arising out of immigration to countries that previously were – or thought they were – ethnically homogeneous are now portrayed in the new racist discourse as both naturally and inevitably leading to social disruption and violence.[17]

The present (first) decade of the twenty-first century will mark one of the greatest shifts in human history. As Professor Mike Davis put it in 2006:

> Sometime in the next year, a woman will give birth in the Lagos slum of Ajekunle, a young man will flee his village in west Java for the bright lights of Jakarta, or a farmer will move his impoverished family into one of Lima's innumerable *pueblos jovenes*. The exact event is unimportant, and it will pass entirely unnoticed. Nonetheless, it will constitute a watershed in human history, comparable to the Neolithic or Industrial Revolution. For the first time, the urban population of the earth will out-number the rural.[18]

This change will present incalculable consequences for the world at large since more people, the more easily, will wish to make a further move from the cities to other countries.

PEOPLE TRAFFICKING AND ABUSE

By 2000, people trafficking worldwide was estimated to be worth between $5 billion and $7 billion a year. It had become a major criminal activity. People trafficking must be distinguished from illegal migration or alien smuggling. Questions of consent and coercion separate trafficking from other illegal migration activities. According to the UN Protocol to Prevent, Suppress and Punish Trafficking in Persons, Especially Women and Children: 'The consent of a victim to trafficking in persons to the intended exploitation ... shall be irrelevant' where the victim has been subject to force or coercion. It is the use of coercion, both during transport and upon arrival in the destination country, that distinguishes trafficking from other illegal activities. Recruitment and transport in the trafficking context is undertaken with the intent to subject the victim of the coerced transport to additional violations in the form of forced labour or slavery-like practices. The key element in trafficking is the exploitative element, where exploitation takes place in the location to which the victim is brought. People trafficking is the worst downside of migration, but traffickers are only a reaction, first, to the persecutions and bitter conditions from which the migrants are fleeing and, second, the antagonism to them by officialdom as well as the ordinary populations of their target countries.[19] In the case of Britain, according to *The Times*, by 2007 between 500,000 and 700,000 people were trafficked every year, to earn criminals £10 billion. Most immigration crime groups prefer to work within their own ethnic and family backgrounds, and are mainly British-South Asian, Chinese, Turkish or Albanian ethnic origin. Criminals charge from £2,000 to £20,000 to bring someone into Britain. Typically, repayment for the journey or accommodation provided can involve long-term menial and low-paid labour. In 2002 the Nationality, Asylum and Immigration Act created a new offence of 'trafficking a person for the purpose of controlling him or her in prostitution' with a maximum penalty of 14 years imprisonment.[20]

Worldwide, migrants are subjected to abuse – human rights violations, exploitative working conditions, non-payment of wages, arbitrary detentions and illegal deportations. Countries listed by the UN where such complaints were made included: Australia, Japan, Indonesia, Malaysia, South Korea, Mauritania, South Africa, Canada, the Philippines, the United States and Spain. Other complaints include ill-treatment at border controls, deaths resulting from excessive use of force by police and security forces; summary expulsions; gender violence; forced labour akin to slavery; withholding passports; restrictions on freedom of movement; and denial of the right of association and assembly. Of 191 million migrants in 2006, about 115 million lived in developed countries and three-quarters of all migrants lived in just 28 countries with one in every five in the United States. In 2005 the United States was host country to 38 million migrants, equivalent to 13 per cent of the country's population. The UN said 'a major challenge is to prevent irregular or unauthorised migration' and pointed out that there were between 11 and 12 million irregular migrants in the United States, 140,000 in South Korea, 221,000 in Japan, 60,000 in Australia and 20,000 in New Zealand. There was growing concern at the number of migrants, mainly from Africa and Asia, who lose their lives at sea. According to the Migration Policy Framework, adopted by the 54-member African Union (AU) 'a growing concern for states is the rise of discrimination and xenophobia against migrants'. As the AU claims, xenophobia hinders the successful integration of migrants into host societies and prevents the enjoyment by migrants of their fundamental rights. Combating racism and xenophobia must be an essential element of comprehensive national policy on migration. The Geneva Conventions oblige signatories to offer permanent shelter to those with legitimate fears of persecution in their home countries. Peter Sutherland, the UN Secretary-General's Special Representative on International Migration and Development, has said: 'The international community has invested heavily in developing a system of asylum conventions, policies, and practices that give life to the promises made in Geneva in 1951.' It's not a perfect system, by any means, but it is being constantly improved. Since the late 1990s the EU has developed robust legislation to create a common approach to asylum and refugee policies. Since 1951 legislation has extended the scope of the Geneva Conventions so that, for example, the right to family reunification is accepted by most developed countries. There are also liberal regimes for students. However, and here is the crux, economic migration (possibly 90 per cent of the total) is not a right and nations retain sovereignty to decide which economic migrants enter their countries. Economic needs should prevail: that is, countries should be allowed to match up who comes into their territory according to how well these incomers fill gaps in the labour market. If countries are open and honest about who they let in and why – matching incomers to economic needs – then public support for immigration might increase. As it is, a great deal of public antagonism to immigrants arises from opposition to unregulated, lawless incoming of criminals and people smugglers. Selection of migrants should be based on their skills and not on race, gender, religion or ethnicity: selection systems can be helpful to both host countries and migrants.

Almost all debates about migration take as their starting point how to keep migrants out, or at least how to limit their flow.

The idea that aid can be used to address the root causes of migration and war is an old one. Aired first in the mid-1940s, it was revisited in the late 1970s and early 1980s in the context of UN debates regarding measures to address migration, and the potential role of aid in stemming these movements.[21]

The main thesis emerging in the 1990s was that the cause of Third World conflict and therefore the threat to international security was internal mal-development, which in turn required more and better aid. The alternative to aid is the erection of barriers.

A couple of years ago (2004), an ominous decision of the EU passed almost unnoticed: a plan to establish an all-European border police force to secure the isolation of the Union territory, so as to prevent the influx of the immigrants. *This* is the truth of globalisation: the construction of new

walls safeguarding the prosperous Europe from a flood of immigrants ...
The segregation of the people is the reality of economic globalisation. This
new racism of the developed world is in a way much more brutal than the
previous one. Its implicit legitimisation is neither naturalist (the 'natural'
superiority of the developed West) nor culturalist (we in the West also
want to preserve our cultural identity). Rather, it's an unabashed economic
egotism – the fundamental divide is the one between those included into
the sphere of (relative) economic prosperity and those excluded from it.[22]

REMITTANCES

For an increasing number of poor countries, remittances by their expatriates
have become a staple part of the economy and are factored into the annual
budget. Moreover, expatriates who are the source of these remittances are
encouraged to stay abroad while others are encouraged to leave. According
to Dilip Ratha of the World Bank: 'Workers' remittances have become a
major source of external development finance, providing a convenient angle
from which to approach the complex migration agenda.' Officially recorded
remittances received by developing countries exceeded $93 billion in 2003,
although the actual size of remittances, including unrecorded transfers,
is much higher. In 36 of 153 developing countries remittances are larger
than all capital flows, both public (aid) and private (business). They are
also stable and person-to-person so go directly to people in need. Arguably,
remittances are one of the best means of encouraging development: they go
to individuals and thence straight into the economy; they do not have to be
repaid; they encourage small enterprises.[23] Already, at the beginning of the
1990s, the International Monetary Fund (IMF) estimated that remittances
for 1989 from host countries back home came to $65 billion, exceeding by
$20 billion all overseas development aid (ODA) and that they had become
a crucial addition to the incomes of families in a range of countries. The
World Bank's *Global Economic Prospects 2006* stated that officially recorded
remittances worldwide reached $232 billion in 2005. Although the emphasis
is on remittances sent from developed to developing countries, there is a
significant South–South transfer as well. However, as encouraging as these
figures may seem, there is a negative side to this transfer of wealth because
it represents the steady brain drain, particularly of skilled workers, from
developing countries to North America, Europe and Japan. This has had
a particularly adverse impact upon health systems in Africa. International
remittances have a strong statistical impact in reducing poverty. On average,
a 10 per cent increase in the share of international remittances in a country's
GDP will lead to a 1.6 per cent decline in the share of people living in poverty.
Writing in the *New York Times*, Jason Deparle paints a global picture of the
remittance business.

The money crosses borders $200 or $300 at a time. It buys cornmeal
and rice and plaid private school skirts and keeps the landlord at bay.

Globally, the tally is huge: migrants from poor countries send home about $300 billion a year.

This sum is more than three times the global total in foreign aid so remittances have become the main source of money flowing into the developing world. Surveys show that 80 per cent or more of the money is immediately spent on food, clothing, housing, education or occasional luxuries – a beer party or television. The International Fund for Agricultural Development, an arm of the UN, and the Inter-American Development Bank have produced a study which shows that 60 countries received $1 billion a year or more during 2006 and, in 38 countries, remittances accounted for more than 10 per cent of GDP. Remittances have become critical to almost every developing country.[24]

According to Dilip Ratha, remittances have more than doubled since 2000 and the flow is set to increase further. Remittances are larger than direct foreign investment in Mexico, tea exports in Sri Lanka, tourism revenue in Morocco, and revenue from the Suez Canal in Egypt. The USA saw the movement out of the country of $41.1 billion in 2005 and Switzerland of $13.2 billion. From Poland to the Philippines, remittances are helping families to combat poverty while also helping to keep national economies afloat. According to the Inter-American Development Bank remittances to Latin America reached $62 billion in 2006 and were expected to top $100 billion by 2010. Mexicans send $22 billion home, mainly from the United States. India has become the lead country in the volume of remittances it receives: $23.7 billion in 2005, rising to a possible $40 billion in 2007. Albania, one of the smallest and poorest countries in Europe, received $1.3 billion in 2007, equivalent to 13 per cent of the country's GDP and enough to finance half the trade deficit.

Part I

The Americas

The Americas have attracted immigrants from the initial 'discovery' of the New World to the present time: the Spanish colonised the whole of Central and South America except for Brazil which went to Portugal; the British and French North America; while the Caribbean Islands were fought over and divided between the Spanish, British, French and Dutch. Today, apart from being the world's only superpower, the United States is also the world's most important destination for migrants. The other major destination for migrants is Canada, although Brazil's rapidly expanding economy is turning it into another target country. The Caribbean for years has been a source of migrants seeking a better life in more affluent societies than their poverty-stricken islands. However, there is another side to the story of American migration and that is the movement of Latin American peoples northwards to the United States. Mexico has become wedded to its northern neighbour as a source of cheap labour and destination for illegal migrants. In its turn, though it tries to stem the tide, the United States is now host to an estimated 23 million Mexican immigrants, both legal and illegal, and though it is erecting a wall or barrier to stem the flow from the south this seems unlikely to be effective.

1
The United States

The story of migration to the United States divides, reasonably neatly, into four phases: the colonial period, the mid-nineteenth century, the turn of the twentieth century and the period since 1965. Each of these periods attracted different and distinct racial and ethnic groups. Thus, the mid-nineteenth century saw an influx from northern Europe; the early twentieth century mainly from southern and eastern Europe; and the post-1965 period from Latin America and Asia and, more recently, Africa. Until the 1930s, the gender imbalance among legal immigrants was sharp, with a majority being male, but beginning in the 1990s women came to account for over 50 per cent of all legal immigrants. When he was president Bill Clinton said that while an influx of new residents from different cultures presented problems, 'the United States has always been energised by its immigrant populations'. Giving the 1998 commencement address at Portland State University, President Clinton voiced support for immigrants, including those from Asia and Latin America, when he said that: 'America has constantly drawn strength and spirit from wave after wave of immigrants – They have proved to be the most restless, the most adventurous, the most innovative, the most industrious of people.'

Prior to the arrival of commercial airlines, immigration was long, arduous and risky. Today it is much easier, except for illegal migration across the Mexican border, which remains difficult, expensive and dangerous. In the new century there have been increasing American calls for tighter controls along the 2,000 mile (3,200 km) US–Mexican border. During 2006 a number of public and congressional debates about controls made headlines, but few of the proposals to tighten controls have become law – although Congress did approve the construction of a partial border fence between the two countries. Strong arguments are advanced on both sides of the debate but many cities, including Washington DC, New York City, Los Angeles, Chicago, San Francisco, San Diego, Salt Lake City, Phoenix, Dallas, Houston, Detroit, Jersey City, Minneapolis, Miami, Denver, Baltimore, Seattle, Portland, Oregon and Portland, Maine have adopted sanctuary ordinances, banning police from asking people about their immigrant status. Contemporary immigrants (aged 15–34) tend to be younger than the native population and are also more likely to be married and less likely to be divorced than native-born Americans of the same age. They will also tend to move to areas (formerly called ghettoes) populated by people with similar backgrounds. US citizenship can be obtained through state-controlled admission and registration procedures. In America, a green card gives the immigrant the right to live and work in the United States permanently. After five years, the immigrant can apply for American citizenship. The possession of a green card, therefore, holds the promise of eventual unlimited residence status.

In his book *Who Are We?*[1] Samuel Huntington poses a number of questions about what he calls America's Great Debate. He provides estimates of the rise in the numbers of illegal immigrants from 4 million in 1995 to 6 million in 1998 to between 8 and 10 million in 2003. Mexicans made up 58 per cent of this number by 1990, while by 2000 there were an estimated 4.8 million illegal Mexicans – 69 per cent of the total illegal population. Apprehensions of illegal Mexican immigrants into the US by the US Border Patrol were 1.6 million over the 1960s, rising to 12.9 million over the 1990s. Estimates of Mexicans who do enter illegally range from 105,000 to 350,000 a year. About two-thirds of post-1975 Mexicans in the US entered the country illegally. In 1993 US President Bill Clinton declared organised smuggling of people into the US to be a 'threat to national security'. Mexico's President Vicente Fox described himself as president of 123 million Mexicans, 100 million in Mexico and 23 million in the United States, some of whom had been born there. Huntington went on to consider the US–Mexican border, which he suggested was becoming increasingly 'blurred', a process that had been enhanced by the formation of the North American Free Trade Agreement (NAFTA). An increasing number of US cities now have a Mexican-Hispanic majority. Today, the growing Mexican diaspora in the United States (of 20 million plus) is of increasing social, economic and political importance to both countries. Mexico, moreover, is pressing the United States to accept illegal Mexicans as a *fait accompli*. Finally, in reference to Cuba, Huntington claims that the irony of US policy towards Cuba between 1960 and 2000 is that it has encouraged a flow of anti-Castro Cubans to migrate into Florida and Miami, which has become the largest, most Hispanic city in the US.

Three-quarters of immigrants surveyed by Public Agenda said they intended to make the US their permanent home. Moreover, if they had to do it over again, 80 per cent of immigrants say they would still come to the US; 50 per cent claimed that the government had become tougher on enforcing immigration laws since 11 September 2001 and 30 per cent had personally experienced discrimination. Immigration has been a major source of population growth and cultural exchange throughout American history, while the economic, social and political aspects of immigration have caused controversy regarding ethnicity, religion, economic benefits, job growth, settlement patterns, environmental impact, impact on upward mobility, levels of criminality, nationalities, political loyalties, and moral values of work habits. Despite this, the United States accepts more legal immigrants as permanent residents than any other country in the world.[2]

Absorption and change is the natural outcome of any large-scale movement of people. In 1900, when the US population was 76 million, there were an estimated 500,000 Hispanics in the country. Estimates now suggest that by 2050 25 per cent of the US population will be of Hispanic descent. In 1910 nearly 15 per cent of Americans were foreign born, whereas in 1999 only 10 per cent were foreign born. By the end of the twentieth century it was clear that the ethnic make-up of the total population was changing substantially as a result of immigration; according to the 2000 census there were 28 million first-generation immigrants in the country. While this was the highest number in the country's history it was not the highest percentage of foreign-born in relation to the total population: in 1907 this was 14 per cent, whereas in 2000 it was 10 per cent. Legal immigration into the United States has increased steadily from 250,000 in the 1930s, 2.5 million in the 1950s, 4.5 million in the 1970s, 7.3 million in the 1980s to 10 million in the 1990s. Since 2000, legal immigrants to the US number approximately 1 million a year of whom 600,000 are 'Change of Status' immigrants who are already in the country. Legal immigrants are at their highest level ever at over 37 million. Since 2000, possibly as many as 1.5 million illegal immigrants have entered the United States every year, of whom 700,000 remain to join the 12 million to 20 million already in the country. The figures for illegal immigrants are necessarily imprecise. According to Pew Hispanic Data Estimates, immigration led to a 57.4 per cent increase in the foreign-born population from 1990 to 2000.

Although the great majority of immigrants to the United States during the nineteenth century came from Europe, today they are drawn from across the globe and most immigrants from Asia and Africa are people with education and skills who are likely to find jobs and not become welfare dependent. However, a quarter of all immigrants come from Mexico and many of these have few skills. Nonetheless, the people who choose to emigrate tend to have greater ambition and more education than their fellow citizens and the more difficult it is to immigrate the wider this skill gap is likely to be.

Distance of travel, opportunity, financial costs, and the size of networks of family and friends in the home country are among the factors contributing to immigration difficulty. For Mexico, the barriers to immigration are not high. Therefore the skill gap is the lowest.[3]

The author of the above quote, Jeffrey Williamson, goes on to argue that although employers gain from paying lower wages, the overall effect on the economy appears to be neutral. 'Immigration had no effect on the pay of non-immigrants with some college education, but reduced the average wage by 4.9 per cent for college graduates, 2.6 per cent for high school graduates, and 8.9 per cent for high school dropouts.' Williamson comes to a number of conclusions: one is that the greater the perceived threat to the wages of the native unskilled workers from both lower- and high-quality immigrants, the more restrictive the immigration policy; and the United States is a clear policy leader, showing no evidence of responding to policies adopted elsewhere.

Present immigrants to the United States settle predominantly in seven states: California, New York, Florida, Texas, Pennsylvania, New Jersey and Illinois. These are all high foreign-born population states, together comprising 44 per cent of the total US population. Of immigrants from 2000 to 2005, 58 per cent came from Latin America. US government statistics reveal that the population grew by 2.8 million between 1 July 2004 and 1 July 2005 and that Hispanics accounted for 1.3 million of the increase. Of vital importance to any forward population predictions, 45 per cent of children under the age of 5 years are from racial and ethnic minorities. In 2006 a total of 1.2 million immigrants became legal permanent residents of the United States. The top twelve migrant sending countries in 2006 by country of birth were Mexico, China, the Philippines, India, Cuba, Colombia, Dominican Republic, El Salvador, Vietnam, Jamaica, South Korea and Guatemala (seven of the twelve were countries of the Americas). Immigrants from Muslim countries were also increasing and 96,000 became legal permanent US residents in 2005, despite the negative impact of 11 September 2001.

According to *Migration News*[4] there were 1 million Asian-Americans in the United States in 2000. They have one of the highest median family incomes of any ethnic group – $60,000 compared with a national average of $39,000. About 60 per cent of Indian-Americans over 25 have a BA degree or higher qualification and an estimated 5,000 were professors at US colleges and universities. About 300,000 Indian-Americans were in Silicon Valley and 750 Silicon Valley companies were headed by persons of Indian origin. This scenario represents a remarkable achievement on the part of one immigrant group. It should also be understood that many Indians who achieve success abroad subsequently return home to invest their savings. A significant proportion of Indians who immigrate into the United States come from the booming Indian software industry that employs about 300,000 Indians in the USA. President Clinton visited India in 2000, emphasising the growing connection between the two countries. During his visit President Clinton said that Indians working in the United States benefited both countries. 'We're moving from a brain drain to a brain gain in India because many are coming home.'[5]

Another increasingly significant group of migrants to the United States are black African: for the first time more black people are coming to the United States from Africa than during the slave trade. During the 1990s up to 50,000 legal black immigrants a year were arriving in the United States and probably many more illegal immigrants. Writing in the *New York Times*, Sam Roberts said:

> With Europe increasingly inhospitable and much of Africa still suffering from the ravages of drought and the AIDS epidemic and the vagaries of economic mismanagement, the number migrating to the United States is growing – despite the reluctance of some Africans to come face to face with the effects of centuries of discrimination.[6]

Although New York State attracts the most African incomers, many others go to Washington, Atlanta, Chicago, Los Angeles, Boston and Houston. This new influx of black people from Africa is redefining what it means to be an African-American. African-born residents of the United States send back more than $1 billion annually to families and friends. Overall, the proportion of foreign-born black people rose to 7.3 per cent from 4.9 per cent in the 1990s, while in New York City about one in three black people are foreign born. According to the 2000 census the proportion of black Americans who describe themselves as African-born more than doubled in the 1990s. The ten metropolitan areas with the largest black African-born populations in 2000 were as follows:

Washington – 89,281
New York – 73,851
Atlanta – 34,302
Minneapolis-St. Paul – 27,592
Los Angeles – 25,829
Boston – 24,231
Houston – 22,638
Chicago – 19,438
Dallas – 19,134
Philadelphia – 16,344

The largest black African-born populations in the United States by country of birth were:

Nigeria – 109,198
Ghana – 50,649
Ethiopia – 47,791
Liberia – 30,577
Somalia – 22,646
Kenya – 21,576[7]

The terrorist attacks upon Washington and New York of 11 September 2001 inevitably had repercussions for certain classes of would-be migrants. There was a US clampdown on visas for the Middle East (other than Israel) and South Asia. Visas for migrants from the Middle East dropped by 52 per cent from 107,184 to 51,529 between 12 September 2001 and 31 March 2002 compared with the same period the previous year. For South Asia (Bangladesh, India, Nepal, Pakistan and Sri Lanka) the drop in visas for the same period was 30 per cent, from 207,936 to 144,661. South Asia had been a preferential region for migration to the United States because of the high computer skills and mathematical proficiency of those involved in the South Asia brain drain. The US State Department classified 25 countries as operational fields for Al-Qaida and potential breeding grounds for terrorists. The countries so specified were: Afghanistan, Algeria, Bahrain, Djibouti, Egypt, Eritrea, Indonesia, Iran, Iraq, Jordan, Kuwait, Lebanon, Libya, Malaysia, Morocco, Oman, Pakistan, Qatar, Saudi Arabia, Somalia, Sudan, Syria, Tunisia, the United Arab Emirates (UAE) and Yemen. Meanwhile, public attitudes about immigration were heavily influenced by the 11 September 2001 attacks. The number of Americans who told the Gallup Poll they wanted immigration restricted increased 20 percentage points after the attacks. Half of Americans said that to tighten controls on immigration would do 'a great deal' to enhance US national security, according to a Public Agenda survey.[8]

The 11 September 2001 attacks undoubtedly had a significant impact upon American attitudes towards immigration. The public was less willing to provide government services or legal protection to illegal immigrants. Current rates of immigration are seen as moderate even though the United States admitted more legal immigrants from 1991 to 2006, some 10–11 million (according to an NBC/Wall Street Journal Poll) than in any previous decade. In the most recent decade, the 10 million legal immigrants who settled in the United States represent an annual growth of only about one-third of 1 per cent at a time when the US population increased from 249 million to 281 million. By comparison, the highest previous decade was 1901–10, when 8.8 million people arrived, increasing the total US population by 1 per cent a year as the population grew from 76 million to 92 million.

Debate in the United States about immigration often leads to a conflict of interests between those determined to stop illegal immigration from Mexico and big business that welcomes such immigrants as cheap and manipulable labour. In 2005 President Bush wanted to replace an 'outdated' immigration policy 'unsuited to the needs of our economy and the values of our country' with one that neither penalised 'hardworking people who want only to provide for their families', nor prevented business from hiring 'willing workers' able 'to fill jobs Americans will not take'. This Bush line was not acceptable to those who wished to restore the integrity of US borders. One result of this debate was the emergence in April 2005 of an anti-illegal immigration group calling itself the Minutemen Project, which began to patrol the border. The group claimed to be a 'neighbourhood watch' for the nation and would report but not confront suspected illegal immigrants. The group was criticised for acting as vigilantes. The project emphasised the gulf that existed between the government's new approach to the immigrant problem and increasing popular opposition to the flow of migrants into the United States. Opponents of this cross-border flow saw the country's vulnerable borders as posing a threat to the economy, culture and security of America.

The year 2006 witnessed groundbreaking changes in attitudes towards immigrants. In Los Angeles the biggest public protest in its history occurred in March 2006 when hundreds of thousands of peaceful demonstrators of all races thronged the downtown streets to demand justice and legal recognition for the country's estimated 12 million undocumented immigrant workers. The protest march exceeded any earlier protests, either for civil rights or against the Vietnam War, and was a huge reproof for the anti-immigrant lobby. The crowds, variously estimated at half a million to more than a million, chanted workers' rights slogans in English and Spanish and presented the face of a multicultural America as opposed to that of the mainly white anti-immigrant lobby. As Antonio Villaraigosa, the mayor of Los Angeles and himself the son of immigrants, said: 'We cannot criminalise people who are working, people who are contributing to our economy and contributing to the nation.'[9] This was the largest of a number of demonstrations across America that month in protest against a bill passed in the House of Representatives in December 2005 that would reclassify illegal immigrants as criminal felons and call for the construction of a 700-mile wall stretching a third of the way along the Mexican–American border. The bill, though never likely to become law, had been drawn up by radical Republicans in the run-up to the mid-term elections to appeal to the growing fears of the influx of Mexican and other immigrants. Ironically, perhaps, President Bush emerged as a moderate on the issue as he supported a guest worker programme that would keep immigrants coming according to the country's economic needs: in other words, cheap labour for big business interests. Growing militarisation along the border and 3,500 migrant deaths over twelve years highlighted the explosive nature of the immigrant problem as 60 per cent of Americans called for tighter policing of immigrant flows, something that had proved impossible to achieve. There was a clear division between anti-immigration hardliners, who supported a closed border and the denial of health, education and other public services to immigrants, and big business apologists who saw immigrants as a vital source of cheap labour. Despite arguments that immigrants would take jobs from Americans, in fact all too often they filled job vacancies that Americans would not touch. Data from the National Academy of sciences suggested that immigrants, whether legal or illegal, were net contributors to the US economy, to the social security retirement fund and to the Treasury.

A driving force behind the mobilisation of the demonstrators was the Spanish-language American radio DJs who ignited a broadcasting war in support of the illegal immigrants and successfully confronted the right-wing opponents of the immigrant cause.[10] Spanish-language TV and radio stations with large followings of highly popular DJs upset the political scene by their capacity to enthuse and organise huge demonstrations. The size of the protests brought home to both political parties the growing importance of the Hispanic vote, which could not be ignored. During April 2006 an estimated 2 million people took to the streets in 140 different cities across the country and the National Day of Action took a number of forms, including consumer boycotts by immigrants and labour stoppages. As a construction worker, Celerino Lopez said: 'They want to have a law to make us all criminals.' There were no jobs or opportunities in Mexico. 'We come here to work, we are not terrorists. I want my child to learn English and get a job.' There emerged from these demonstrations a deep feeling that in a nation of immigrants it is wrong for millions of people, whose labour is essential to the service economy, to live in the shadows, many of them woefully underpaid and at constant risk of exploitation or abrupt termination.[11] Although in the end no agreement was reached, the reaction of the US Senate to the demonstrations was to consider more progressive measures that would meet many of the immigrants' demands.

Further demonstrations took place on May Day in more than 50 cities. In Los Angeles the fruit and vegetable market came to a standstill, as did the garment industry and some port operations. Banners carried by demonstrators said 'No human being is illegal', while others read 'Today we march, tomorrow we vote.' Marc Cooper, a border and immigration specialist with the University of Southern California's Institute for Justice and Journalism, said:

> There's no question in my mind that we are in the midst of an historic, new social movement ... It's taken decades to build and reach critical mass and it is still going to take years to mature and fully pay off. So far, the cool-headed long-term strategists have dominated.[12]

As of 2006 there were 41 million Hispanics in the United States, including 23 million from Mexico (some second or third generation), 2 million from Puerto Rica, 1.6 million from Cuba, 1.3 million from El Salvador and 1.2 million from the Dominican Republic. Together the Hispanics constituted the largest minority group in the United States and the fastest growing. As US Secretary of State Condoleezza Rice said that year:

> But I also hope that around the world it's noted that on matters of race, the United States is about 100 percent ahead of any place else in the world .... And I say that absolutely fundamentally. You go to any other meeting around the world and show me the kind of diversity that you see in America's cabinet, in America's Foreign Service, in America's business community, in America's journalistic community. Show me that kind of diversity any place else in the world, and I'm prepared to be lectured about race.

These demonstrations heralded a revolution in the United States and in its image of itself. The United States has always seen itself as a land of immigrants and a model of racial and cultural integration. It has absorbed wave after wave of European and Asian immigrants, to the credit of both sides, but it has projected this melting pot image at the expense of its black people who, even after the successes of the civil rights movement, still have a long way to go to achieve full equality with the white majority while Native Americans have been consigned to reservations. Many Hispanics have been accepted because of their hard work and willingness to do jobs that Americans are no longer prepared to do. However, in recent years as the Hispanic minority has increased its size and political clout, its members have begun to ask why they should adapt themselves so thoroughly to American ways. In an increasing number of towns and areas Spanish has become the predominant language. A conservative estimate suggests that Hispanics will make up 30 per cent of the population by 2060, and a majority in large parts of the southwest. Inevitably, this growth of the Hispanic population and the apparently unstoppable inflow of more immigrants every year has created an unpleasant and sometimes brutal backlash. The frontier fences, the way border guards interrogate new arrivals, the armed vigilantes who patrol the border areas are quite contrary to the image of an immigrant-welcoming melting pot country that Condoleezza Rice advanced. The many questions that surround the immigration debate produce sharp divisions that will grow as the demography of the country changes. What now seems unavoidable is that this migration will change the character of the United States forever. The growth of the Hispanic minority cannot be reversed and Mexican illegals moving into the United States now constitute the world's largest long-term undocumented migration flow.

Writing in the *New York Times*, Eduardo Porter advanced the view that America's rich ethnic, racial religious and linguistic diversity was a major reason why government spending on social welfare programmes was much lower than in the more homogeneous nations of Europe. According to economics Professor Alberto Alesina at Harvard University, 'Racial divisions and ethnic divisions reduce incentives for people to be generous to others through social welfare.'[13] Clifford Kraus, also writing in the *New York Times*, had a different perspective:

> First came a wave of immigrants from Mexico and elsewhere in Latin America. Next came tortillas and Spanish-language soap operas, made in the United States, for a growing Hispanic audience in this country. Now, there is a surprising, broadening surge of investment in the United States by an intrepid group of successful and suddenly multinational Latin American companies.

He then enumerated a number of companies from Mexico, Brazil and Peru. Investments following migrants will prove to be a powerful factor in their favour. He cites the Brazilian-owned steel company that, since 1999, had acquired an empire of 17 steel mills in 11 states, or the Mexican company, Cemex, which has become the top supplier of cement and ready-mix concrete in the United States, with nearly 10,000 employees across the country. Direct foreign investment from Mexico, Central America and South America rose from $8 billion in 1995 to $13.5 billion in 2000 but then jumped to $30 billion in 2005.[14] The number of persons naturalised in the United States increased by 58 per cent from 660,477 in 2007 to an all-time record of 1.04 million in 2008. Meanwhile, coping with the recession that began in 2008 added new strains to the immigration debate. Americans who cannot get jobs because of the recession question giving jobs to illegal immigrants: with 15 million Americans without work and 32 million living on food stamps the issue is potentially explosive. At the same time, Mexico receives $22 billion in cash remittances from its illegal immigrants in the United States.

Although the United States is the most important immigrant receiving country in the world and attracts migrants from every continent, it is intricately connected to its southern neighbour, Mexico, which is by far the most important country in relation to US immigration policies. The trek of Mexican migrants northwards into the United States is unstoppable and is changing the demographic, political and cultural make-up of the country. Thus, what Mexico does and how the United States responds will provide major lessons for the entire world. Mexican poverty and population growth are the driving force behind migration to the north. The American need for unskilled labour and the presence in the United States of a large and growing Hispanic population present it with an almost impossible dilemma. The US–Mexican equation must now be considered from the viewpoint south of the border.

2
Mexico

Americans may see Mexico as an immigrant threat, with its huge surplus population always seeking to cross the border and settle, to change the demography and culture of the United States forever, but Mexicans regard the two countries' relationship in a different light. In the first place, most of the southwest of what is now the United States was once part of Mexico. Second, poverty inevitably drives Mexicans to seek work and a higher standard of living in their richer neighbour where, in any case, both big business and the annual California harvest willingly employ illegal immigrants as cheap labour. And, third – a factor which will ensure permanent change – there are already some 23 million Mexicans settled in the United States to whom newcomers naturally attach themselves. While it is relatively easy for the United States to control migration from Europe, Asia or Africa this is not the case with Mexico, which shares a border with the United States. As a consequence, the American government is constantly seeking new ways to control the northwards movement of migrants, hopefully with the assistance of the Mexican government, although the problem is viewed in a very different light from the south.

In January 2004, for example, US President Bush proposed a new temporary worker programme that would help further the cause of safe, legal and orderly migration. The programme would match foreign workers with American employers when no American could be found to fill the jobs. Further, undocumented workers currently in the United States would be able to come out of the shadows and establish legal identities. Participants in the programme would be issued a temporary worker card that would allow them to travel back and forth between their home and the United States without fear of being denied re-entry in America. All those who participated in the programme would have a job or a job offer and the legal status granted by the programme would last three years and would be renewable but would have an end. Those who wished to pursue American citizenship would be allowed to apply in the normal way though they would not be given unfair advantage over people who had followed legal procedures from the beginning. There would be no question of amnesty since this was seen as encouraging a violation of US laws and perpetuating illegal migration. The programme might have worked had it been introduced in the early 1990s but by the new century immigrant pressures from the south had become more unmanageable, not least because the Hispanic population already in the United States was becoming a political force for change in the US–Mexican relationship.

In 2002, as in 2001, the leading source country for legal immigrants into the United States was Mexico with 219,380 or 20.6 per cent of legal immigrants into the USA (followed by India with 6.7 per cent and China 5.8 per cent). In 2002, there were 37.8 million people of Hispanic or Latino origin (13.4 per cent of the total US population) of whom 60 per cent were Mexican (23.9 million), accounting for 11 per cent of the US population.[1] By January 2000 the estimated total unauthorised population in the United States came to 7 million, with 4.5 million of them living in five states – California, Texas, New York, Illinois and Florida, and approximately 69 per cent of the unauthorised resident population being from Mexico. A profile of the Mexican migrant population in America showed that two out of three had a job in Mexico before migrating and had worked in the industry and service sectors, and that 52 per cent of immigrants came from specific Mexican states, 23 per cent from the north, 15 per cent from the centre and 10 per cent from the southeastern part of Mexico, with 55 per cent from urban areas. Four Mexican border cities – Tijuana, Ciudad Juarez, Nuevo Laredo and Piedras Negras – act as transit cities, where immigrants stay an average of two or three days. California is the main destination for 50 per cent of the immigrants but, as the border control of California has been reinforced, more migrants have headed for Texas.

Remittances have become a major source of Mexican income, reaching $13.266 million in 2003. This 2003 figure was greater, for example, than foreign direct investment in Mexico or revenues derived from tourism. Remittances were equal in value to 79 per cent of Mexican crude oil exports. The US–Mexico border is now the busiest in the world, with more than 1 million people crossing it every day. During the fiscal year 2002 193.1 million people crossed the border. The two governments agreed in November 1993 on various arrangements to assist communities on both sides of the border to coordinate and carry out environmental infrastructure projects. The agreement was designed to further the aims of the North American Free Trade Agreement (NAFTA), which came into operation in 1994. The US has nine consulates in Mexico (more than in any other country) and ten consular agencies. The trade and other relationships between the United States and Mexico are very strong and they are being made stronger by the presence of a steadily growing Hispanic population inside the United States.

During 2005 Mexico and the United States again failed to agree on a migration settlement that would give between 4 million and 6 million Mexicans, then illegally residing in the United States, guest worker status. Mexico had acted angrily to the formation of the 'Minuteman Project' and in response co-sponsored a UN resolution which urged governments to act against private individuals or groups that undermined or coopted a government's border control functions. In November 2005 US President Bush announced a series of anti-immigration measures that included 'constructing physical barriers to entry'. This followed earlier pressure in Congress to construct a 'sea-to-sea' double fence along the entire border. Bush did not support a sea-to-sea fence but did call for the expansion of fencing in urban areas and the construction of new patrol roads. Despite disagreement about these border measures, the two countries did agree to implement fresh law and order measures against drug-related violence along the border.

A report in the British newspaper, *The Independent*,[2] described some of the hardships that would-be immigrants were prepared to face to cross into the United States. In the little town of Altar small groups of men collect prior to crossing 90 miles of desert to the US border. They are lured by the prospect of a new life and obtaining jobs that will pay 10 to 20 times what they can earn in Mexico. Thousands of immigrants pass through Altar every year. In the summer months of July and August the numbers drop off since the desert temperatures reach 40°C and that hazard comes before the border guards with their trucks, helicopters and sniffer dogs. Many die in the desert: the 2005 death toll of 473 was a new record. They need guides for the desert (called coyotes) and have to pay $2,000 a head for their services. The scale of the migration is vast and may represent the biggest voluntary cross-border migration in history. According to the US Customs and Border Protection they made 1.1 million interceptions of illegal or undocumented migrants in 2005 and guessed that a further 500,000 migrants evaded interception and got through. The economy of Altar depends upon servicing would-be migrants and business has boomed, providing the migrants with such essentials as backpacks, running shoes, bandanas, gallon jugs of water and tinned food. The shops also sell toilet paper, phone cards, sweat shirts and thick coats for winter, when desert temperatures may fall to zero during the night. Through the day vans take migrants north through the desert to a little border village where the migrants and their coyotes disperse to hide until nightfall when they attempt to cross the border. The unfenced border, both in reality and symbolically, represents the divide between the developed world, represented by its richest nation, the United States, and the developing world. As migrants point out, the constant migration northwards is not taking place in a vacuum but rather against a backdrop of huge disparity between the United States and Mexico. It is one of the ironies of the situation that NAFTA, which came into being in 1994 and was supposed to make for greater prosperity for each of its members, has had the opposite effect by removing restrictions on trade to the disadvantage of Mexico. As long as there are such differences of wealth between the two countries, the migrants will get through or keep trying until they do, no matter how many border controls the United States puts in place. One effect of increased border guards is to force migrants to attempt crossings at increasingly remote places where their chances of survival are proportionately diminished. As Sheriff Joe Arpaio told the *Los Angeles Times*: 'We've got all this surveillance and vigilance on the border and they're still coming. I'm not going to let these people come through this county.'

Americans complain that there is hypocrisy on the part of the Mexicans, who call them xenophobic yet place daunting limitations upon anyone born outside Mexico. Non-native Mexicans are barred from thousands of jobs, even if they are legal, naturalised citizens. Thus, while Mexicans denounced American plans to deploy 6,000 National Guardsmen along the border they gave enthusiastic support to President Vicente Fox when he deployed Mexican soldiers on the country's southern border to keep migrants out.[3]

Immigration problems always raise awkward questions that may be described as unintended consequences. In 2008, as the United States began to survey where the border fence between itself and Mexico would be erected, Americans who lived along the border began to protest. The Proposed Tactical Structure, as the fence is euphemistically called, which the Department of Homeland Security was committed to build, has outraged many South Texans. One-third of the 595 km intermittent pedestrian barrier from Brownsville, Texas, to California will be in Texas. The proposal created widespread alarm among property owners, fearful of being cut off from parts of their own land or access to the Rio Grande for livestock and crops. Not that these opponents of the wall want migrants from Mexico to have easy entry to the United States; they argue that other means of control should be used. Valley officials and residents who denounced the fence said they were not soft on illegal immigration or blind to the dangers of drug smuggling and terrorism. 'Who doesn't want security?' said the mayor of McAllen, Richard Cortez, 'Our fight with the government is not over their goals, it's how they go about them.' Their alternative would be to deepen the river, clear the land for better surveillance and create a legal Mexican worker programme.[4]

Nothing stands still in the migration world and data released in 2009 showed that 226,000 fewer people emigrated from Mexico to other countries during the year ending in August 2008, which was a decline of 25 per cent. Almost all migration out of Mexico is to the United States. According to both Mexican and American researchers this decline, reflected in the decrease in border arrests, is mainly because of lack of jobs in the recession-hit US economy. The decline set in with the onset of the recession and provided new evidence that migrants are drawn by jobs and when these dry up they stay away. According to Jeffrey S. Passel of the Pew Hispanic Centre, 'If jobs are available, people come, if jobs are not available, people don't come.' In 2009 the flow of migrants was also affected by swine flu in Mexico, and the government's response in shutting down schools and cancelling public gatherings brought migration nearly to a halt, although this decline will be temporary. Mexicans account for 32 per cent of immigrants in the United States and over half of them lack legal status. Wayne Cornelius, the director of the Centre for Comparative Immigration Studies at the University of California, predicted that if the US job market revived, border enforcement would become much less of a deterrent. He added that Mexicans are 'not foregoing migration forever. They are hoping that the economy in the United States will improve'.[5]

It is impossible to talk about migration into the United States without Mexico coming at the top of the agenda, just as it is equally impossible to debate migration in Mexico without the United States dominating the discussion. The subject is volatile, rouses deep emotions and heated political arguments. It is, therefore, refreshing to read a paper by the former US ambassador to Mexico, Jeffrey Davidow, in which he sets out the main arguments on both sides of the debate. He begins with the 'push' and 'pull'. The outflow from Mexico to the United States – the push – will continue until the Mexican economy can provide sufficient work opportunities for a far greater percentage of its people, while the attraction of the US – the pull – will continue as long as wages in America are well above those in Mexico, so that people working there can enjoy economic security. He argues that draconian measures to seal the border are unlikely to be acceptable to the American public as well as important political and economic interests. On the other side, the Mexican government will not use force to prevent its citizens leaving the country. Given these conditions, the immigration problem cannot be solved in the near or medium future. Meanwhile, the immigration issue remains the most divisive in US–Mexican relations since there is a fundamental difference in the way Americans and Mexicans look at the issue of illegal immigrants. 'Given the Mexican perspective, which comes close to seeing the northward migration as a right, recent efforts to harden the border that have made the crossing more dangerous are perceived as noxiously hypocritical.' Tightening of controls around major ports of entry such as El Paso has simply driven migrants to try more dangerous crossings through the desert that have resulted in 400 or more deaths a year. Attempts by Presidents Bush and Fox to find common ground when they met in 2001 came to nothing. As Jeffrey Davidow argues: 'Americans continue to prize the openness of their society and do not wish to close their country to newcomers.' However, the heavy focus on security following 9/11 made life more difficult for undocumented aliens. Social problems have become of growing importance to Americans living along the border, where their communities have to face mounting financial pressure for more schools, clinics and other public services necessitated by the large numbers of undocumented Mexicans in residence. Despite the benefits brought by illegal immigration – a larger labour pool, lower inflation, higher levels of productivity – these are felt at the national rather than the local level. As Davidow points out:

> U. S. immigration policy is not working well. If the criteria for success is to keep undocumented aliens out, it is clearly failing. If the criteria for success are an orderly, just, and humane flow, the policy is similarly a failure.

The author concludes simply, 'Shorn of all complexities and nuances, the answer to the problem is greater prosperity in Mexico.'[6]

3
Canada and the Caribbean

CANADA

Canada has always been second to the United States as an immigration destination. Nonetheless, immigration forms an integral part of Canada's social, cultural and economic development and as the years have passed so has the character of immigration changed, according to new domestic needs and the growing movement of people worldwide. In the twenty-first century immigrants are accounting for an increasing proportion of total labour force growth. Immigrants who arrived in Canada during the 1990s, for example, accounted for about 70 per cent of net labour force growth between 1991 and 2001, and this proportion is likely to increase to 100 per cent over the next decade, mainly because of low rates of natural increase in the Canadian-born population.[1] According to the 2001 census, 2.2 million immigrants were admitted to Canada between 1991 and 2000, the highest number for any decade in the twentieth century. The majority of immigrants arriving in Canada during the 1990s were aged between 25 and 64 and increased the size of Canada's working age population by more than 1.1 million.[2]

Immigrants arriving in Canada today are better educated than were immigrants of the past and are twice as likely to have a university education than the present Canadian-born population. Despite this, many immigrants have difficulty in obtaining well-paid jobs and their earnings are likely to be well below those of the Canadian-born population. There has also been a change in the countries the immigrants come from. In the past a majority came from English- or French-speaking countries; now, however, they have been educated in languages other than English or French so they have an additional language hurdle to overcome as they attempt to integrate into Canadian society. Permanent immigration for labour purposes constitutes a category, the 'economic classes', as opposed to immigrants who come to join families or as refugees. The economic classes cover skilled workers, provincial and territorial nominees, investors, entrepreneurs and self-employed persons. These immigrants are selected for their skills on a points system that assesses education, language proficiency, work experience, age and potential adaptability. The department of Citizenship and Immigration Canada (CIC) is responsible for all types of immigration as well as citizenship.

Recent immigration has accounted for an increasing proportion of Canada's population growth between 2001 and 2006. During these years, the immigrant population grew by 13.6 per cent, while the Canadian-born population grew by 3.3 per cent. The 1.1 million new immigrants that came to Canada in that period accounted for 69.3 per cent of the population growth. In 2006,

6.2 million immigrants in Canada represented 19.8 per cent of the total population, an increase from the figure of 18.4 per cent in 2001. Some 85.1 per cent of immigrants eligible for Canadian citizenship had become citizens in 2006. The major regions of the world from which immigrants arrived between 2001 and 2006 were Asia (including the Middle East) 58.3 per cent; Europe 16.1 per cent; Central and South America and the Caribbean 10.8 per cent; and Africa 10.6 per cent. These figures represent a major change from the 1970s. In 1971 only 12.1 per cent of recently arrived immigrants were from Asia while 61.6 per cent then came from Europe. The trend in the twenty-first century is for immigrants to come from the global South, which means they mainly belong to radicalised communities. Data shows that race significantly informs differential experiences of participation in numerous aspects of Canadian life, including labour market integration, education, health and housing.[3]

Racism in a variety of forms is never far below the surface in any country that is open to widespread immigration. In Canada, the Colour of Poverty Campaign advocates anti-racist strategies and engages with other anti-poverty coalitions to adopt an anti-racist approach. Of immigrants arriving in Canada between 2001 and 2006, 70.2 per cent had a mother tongue other than English or French, while over 200 languages were reported by census respondents. Language groups that experienced significant gains over these years were Chinese, Punjabi, Arabic, Urdu, Tagalog and Tamil. The Province of Ontario attracts the greatest number of immigrants: it is home to 38.5 per cent of the total Canadian population; 52.3 per cent of newly arrived immigrants in 2001–6 chose to live in Ontario. A majority of immigrants go to Canada's three major urban centres (Montreal, Toronto and Vancouver) and 62.9 per cent of immigrants lived in one of these three areas in 2006, while 68.6 per cent of immigrants between 2001 and 2006 chose one of these three cities. In 2006 a total of 94.9 per cent of all immigrants lived in urban communities.

Toronto has long been a major immigrant city and in 2006 68.3 per cent of all immigrants in Ontario lived in the census metropolitan area (CMA), equivalent to 45.7 per cent of the total CMA population. While the City of Toronto had the largest number of immigrants, the growth of immigrant populations also occurred in surrounding municipalities such as Brampton, where the immigrant population grew by 59.5 per cent between 2001 and 2006. At 56.5 per cent, the municipality of Markham has the second highest proportion of immigrants of any municipality in Canada: only Richmond, in Vancouver, with a 57.4 per cent immigrant population, ranked higher. Hamilton has the third highest proportion of immigrants of any city in the country at 24.4 per cent, behind Toronto and Vancouver. Such statistics as these indicate the extent to which the immigrant and ethnic make-up of Canada is changing.

In an article 'Immigrants in Canada: Have Ph.D, Must Sweep',[4] Clifford Kraus examines the prejudices that face immigrants. In British Columbia a Sikh, Gian Sangha, wanted to work so badly that he cut his hair and removed his turban for job interviews despite his Sikh beliefs. He sent hundreds of resumés but a job eluded him, even though he was highly qualified, held a doctorate from Germany, had published two books and had university teaching experience in the United States. He ended up doing clerical work.

Earlier in the previous century, Canada had sought professionals from the developing world. Today, with a declining birth rate, an ageing population and labour shortages in many fields, there should be openings for many kinds of professional immigrant yet recent census data as well as academic studies show that income and job prospects for immigrants are deteriorating. The question is why? A growing number of immigrants have been forced to rely upon unemployment insurance and welfare, obliging some to return to their homelands or seek employment in the United States. According to the government 25 per cent of recent immigrants with university degrees can only get employment requiring high school diplomas or less. Over the decade up to 2006 Canada attracted between 200,000 and 250,000 immigrants a year, which as a percentage of the population was triple the rate of immigrants into the United States: one in every six people in Canada is an immigrant. Yet highly skilled immigrants, nearly half the total, end up in menial jobs way below their qualifications. Although there is public support for the government goal of increasing immigration, this could founder if opportunities for immigrants do not also expand. According to Jeffrey Reitz, a Canadian sociologist: 'The existing system is broken. The deteriorating employment situation might mean that Canada will not be able to continue this expansionist immigration programme in the positive, politically supported environment that we've seen in the past.' He estimated that foreign-educated immigrants earn a total of $2 billion less than native-born Canadians with comparable skills, because they work in jobs below their training levels. Discrimination appears to be part of the problem, while professional and provincial licensing agencies have been slow to recognise foreign professional qualifications. At the same time, Canadians are better educated than 25 years previously and able to compete better against immigrants. According to Canadian Minister of Citizenship and Immigration Joe Volpe: 'We have an arcane infrastructure of professional organisations that essentially mitigate against the immediate integration of these highly skilled immigrants.' He continued: 'It's a shame we have a shortage of doctors, and yet we have thousands of foreign-trained medical doctors and we don't recognise their credentials.'

Canada emerges reasonably well over the issue of asylum seekers. With a more obvious use for migrants than Britain, Canada can take a more generous view of asylum. In 1996 Canada deemed that 76 per cent of applicants from former Zaire, 81 per cent from Somalia and 82 per cent from Sri Lanka qualified for Convention status (the UN Convention of 1951). In the same year Britain only gave Convention status to 1 per cent of Zaire applicants, 0.4 per cent of Somali applicants and 0.2 per cent from Sri Lanka.[5]

As in other countries, immigration stirs political passions. In 2008, changes in Canada's immigration laws, aimed at reducing a backlog of applications, passed the House of Commons and appeared to make the immigration minister much more powerful. Amendments to the Immigration and Refugee

Protection Act would give the minister greater selection powers to limit the number of new immigrant applicants. The amendments would also allow the government to fast-track applications from the types of immigrants it wants such as skilled workers, while freezing applications from others. The Tories argued that the measures were necessary to reduce a current backlog of more than 900,000 immigration applications, which had created wait times of between three and six years even for those who meet all the requirements for acceptance. However, a group of immigrant service organisations attacked the proposed changes on the grounds that the new measures would place too much power in the hands of the minister. The then Liberal deputy leader, Michael Ignatieff, said the government's change of one word in the existing legislation would give the minister the power to reject even those who met all the visa requirements. The proposed legislation laid down that a visa or document 'may' be issued to an applicant who has been ruled admissible by immigration officers, while the existing law says a visa or document 'shall' be issued. The Liberals abstained from the vote on the amendments because they were part of a budget implementation act, making it a confidence motion. Had the vote not passed, Prime Minister Stephen Harper's government would have been brought down, forcing an election.[6]

In the census of 2001, 13 per cent of Canadians identified themselves as belonging to a visible minority. But by 2017, if Statistics Canada projections hold true, that number could climb to between 19 and 23 per cent. Furthermore, by that date (Canada's 150th birthday), almost 95 per cent of the visible minorities would live in metropolitan areas, with three-quarters living in Toronto, Vancouver or Montreal. About half the people living in Toronto and Vancouver would belong to a visible minority by 2017. According to present projections, the visible minority population of Toronto will range between 2.8 million and 3.9 million within twelve years. The justification for these predictions, according to Statistics Canada, is an expectation of sustained immigration to Canada over a period of twelve years from 2005, and the fact that a high proportion of these immigrants will be non-white. Statistics Canada set up five different scenarios for future immigration rates and population growth. According to these scenarios Canada's immigrant population could reach between 7 million and 9.3 million in 2017. Part of these predictions was fulfilled in 2006, when one in five Canadian residents was born outside the country – the highest level in 75 years. That proportion had grown substantially from 18.4 per cent of the population, just five years earlier. According to the census of 2001 Chinese and South Asians were the largest visible minority groups in Canada, and the projection does not see this changing. Black people would remain Canada's third largest minority group, reaching a population of about 1 million. In Toronto, about a third of visible minorities would be South Asians while nearly half the visible minority population of Vancouver would be Chinese. In Montreal black people and Arabs would remain the largest visible minority groups, representing 27 per cent and 19 per cent of the minority population, respectively.

In February 2009 there was an important debate about immigration in the Canadian parliament. The Immigration Minister Jason Kenney said the number of new arrivals in Canada could fall if labour markets contracted and there were no jobs for them to fill. 'Obviously we will monitor the economic situation and, if it's absolutely necessary, the government can always modify the targets. But it's our intention to maintain those targets where we are today.' He said that Canada was planning to receive 245,000 to 260,000 permanent residents in 2010. That meant immigration levels would remain about the same as in 2008 when there were 247,000 permanent residents allowed into the country. The minister told MPs at a parliamentary committee that most other developed countries had made significant cuts to their intake levels for 2009 because of the economic situation.

Canada stands alone in having announced its intention to maintain the same planning levels for permanent residents because we are looking to the mid to long-term. We believe that when we have reached the recovery we have to face the labour market realities that we will need newcomers to help fuel the jobs of the future.

Meanwhile, the government would closely monitor labour market developments during 2009. This was a realistic and optimistic approach to Canada's long-term requirements, despite fears that may have arisen as a result of the recession. In addition to the permanent residents, the government allows foreigners to come to Canada on a temporary basis to fill jobs that have gone vacant. There were nearly 170,000 of those temporary immigrants in 2008. As the immigration critic Olivia Chow of the New Democrats Party (NDP) said, if the government had to cut immigration targets because of rising unemployment then this temporary class of incomers should be the first group to be trimmed. She added:

Permanent immigrants increase the economic vitality and productivity of Canada. We have an ageing population and we need more young families coming to Canada. The target of 265,000 permanent immigrants should not be lowered ... In an economic downturn, the minister should curb the temporary foreign workers programme instead. The Conservatives fast tracked 200,000 temporary foreign workers into Canada last year. Many of them are exploited and drove down wages of ordinary working families.

Liberal Senator Pierrette Ringuette of New Brunswick characterised job losses across Canada as 'statistically huge'. She said she would like the government to bring back a 'Canada First' policy with regard to jobs and to 'halt the programme of foreign workers so that Canadians will have the first opportunity to obtain these jobs and to work in Canada'.[7]

In 2003 the International Adult Literacy and Skills Survey (IALSS) collected data from samples of recent and established immigrants about their literacy levels. It published the report on the Canadian results, *Building on Our*

Competencies, in 2005. Over 23,000 individuals aged 16 and over from across the ten provinces and three territories of Canada were interviewed. The report makes a number of observations that pinpoint vital issues connected with immigration, and particularly for a society that has long based its growth upon being open to immigration. It says, 'A knowledge economy requires workers who can adapt quickly to the changing skill requirements of the labour market.' This must be a first essential for any economic migrant. The report claims that differences in the level and distribution of skill are associated with large differences in outcomes in multiple facets of life such as work, education, home and community. People were assessed at five levels. Level 1 contained respondents displaying the lowest level of ability; Level 4/5 contained those with the highest. For literacy and numeracy Level 3 performance was taken as the benchmark since performance at or above that level is generally associated with a number of positive outcomes. In Canada, individuals at Levels 1 and 2 had typically not yet mastered the minimum foundation of literacy skills needed to perform tasks generally seen as important for full participation in social and economic life.

> Immigrants aged 16 to 65 performed significantly below the average for the Canadian-born population in all four domains. The average prose literacy score for the Canadian-born population corresponded to Level 3 proficiency, while for recent immigrants the average score was at Level 2. Differences in performance between Canadian-born and recent as well as established immigrants were largest for prose literacy and smallest for numeracy.

At the top end of the proficiency scale, 12 per cent of established and 8 per cent of recent immigrants performed at Level 4/5. This compared with 22 per cent of the Canadian-born population, indicating that the differences between Canadian-born and immigrants were larger than they were between the two immigrant groups. In prose literacy younger immigrants generally performed better than older immigrants or Canadian-born individuals, possibly because these younger immigrants were likely to have pursued part of their education in Canada. At the top end of the scale 37 per cent of university-educated Canadian-born scored at Levels 4/5 compared to 21 per cent of university-educated established immigrants and 11 per cent of university-educated recent immigrants. However, the relatively poor literacy performance of recent immigrants may reflect a lack of proficiency in English or French but not in their mother tongues. Changes in proficiency in English or French have altered substantially because of the changes in source countries of immigrants. Thus, in 2003 one in ten immigrants spoke English or French as their mother tongue whereas almost one in three did so in 1980. It is, therefore, important to note that low literacy scores in the test language in IALSS do not necessarily reflect low literacy in the respondent's mother tongue. A not unexpected result of the IALSS findings showed that proficiency of Canadians aged 16 to 65 in literacy, numeracy and problem solving was clearly linked to their labour market outcomes. 'The average proficiency scores of employed individuals are higher than the scores of those who are either unemployed or not in the labour force; employment rates are also higher for those with higher proficiency levels.' A final point in the report, that immigrants tended to perform at lower proficiency than the Canadian-born population, is cause for concern. 'This is especially the case because immigration will account for all the net labour force growth in the coming years.'

THE CARIBBEAN

While Canada has always been an immigrant receiving country, the modern history of the Caribbean has been one of exodus as the poverty of most islands has forced people to seek a better life elsewhere. Apart from Cuba, Haiti, the Dominican Republic and the French overseas territories of Guadeloupe and Martinique, the majority of the islands were British colonies (a few still are) and the relationship between them and Britain has been emphasised in recent decades by substantial migration to Britain, though a significant number of migrants have also targeted Canada and the United States. There was a growth of the Afro-Caribbean population in Britain during the seventeenth and eighteenth centuries, and, in the early years of the Napoleonic Wars, up to a third of the sailors on Nelson's fleet were blacks shanghaied from the islands. When the war came to an end discharged black sailors settled in British ports such as Bristol, Cardiff or Liverpool. Following the end of slavery in the British Empire in 1833, the Afro-Caribbean people who came to Britain were mainly seamen, students or entertainers. A significant number of Afro-Caribbean people came to Britain during the First World War (1914–18) to fight or to work in war industries and the merchant navy. They often met with racist antagonism and this sometimes led to riots. During the Second World War another wave of West Indians arrived in Britain as volunteers to join the armed forces. Since 1945 Caribbean migrants have become an integral and vital part of British life.

When the *Empire Windrush* docked at Tilbury on 22 June 1948, carrying some 450 Jamaicans, it marked a turning point in both West Indian and British relations. At that time any Commonwealth or Colonial subject had the right to enter Britain without question and this first boatload of immigrants heralded a steady flow of migrants for the next 20 years. Then, in 1962, the British government passed the Commonwealth Immigration Act to restrict the entry of immigrants – and not just from the Caribbean.

Apart from a minority of indigenous Carib Amerindians, the majority of Caribbean people are immigrants. They are also a migratory people and have settled in South, Central and North America as well as Britain. The islands were settled by three categories of migrants. First came merchants, adventurers, indentured servants, East Indian labourers and, after 1834, African labourers and discharged soldiers and sailors. Then came the involuntary settlers: slaves for the sugar plantations and transported criminals. Finally, liberated slaves, refugees from the United States (Empire Loyalists), French and Spanish monarchists. In other words, the settlers of the islands came from many sources in a region that was constantly fought over by the British, Dutch, French and Spanish during the turbulent seventeenth and eighteenth centuries as the European powers fought each other to establish their empires in the New World.

The numbers of Caribbean migrants in Britain are revealed in census figures from 1891 to 1961 as follows:

1891 – 8,689
1901 – 8,680
1911 – 9,189
1921 – 9,054
1931 – 8,585
1951 – 15,301
1961 – 171,800

Until 1962 Britain's colonial subjects were also British subjects and did not need to naturalise. Under the 1948 Nationality Act, people from the self-governing Commonwealth (Canada, Australia, New Zealand) could register as citizens of the UK. The 1962 Commonwealth Immigrants Act restricted free migration to Britain from the Commonwealth and Colonies, except for students, visitors and dependants. People who did not have a passport issued in the United Kingdom were not registered as Citizens of the UK and Colonies and had first to obtain labour vouchers from the Ministry of Labour in order to be granted entry. There were three categories of voucher: for those with a definite offer of a job; for those who held certain professional qualifications or skills; and a general category of vouchers issued in order of application, with priority given to those with war service.

The restrictions imposed by the British Commonwealth Immigration Act of 1962 signalled the beginning of a new era in relation to migration generally in which migrant target countries such as Britain and others in Europe and elsewhere became increasingly wary of unrestricted migration. The year witnessed the end of the war in Algeria, which was followed by a mass exodus of both white settlers back to France but also of Algerians who had supported France during the war. Slowly, in the decades that followed, Europe began to tighten its regulations in order to restrict the number of migrants who sought entry to one of the two most attractive economic regions of the world (the other being North America).

4
South America

Although a majority of Latin American migrants head north, usually through Mexico, for the United States, there are other movements: to Argentina, Brazil and Mexico. For example, an estimated 200,000 'illegals' from Bolivia, Paraguay and Peru work in Argentina. Mexico is a secondary target for migrants whose ultimate destination is the United States. However, destinations change according to the vagaries of economics. Thus, while many Latin Americans used to migrate to Argentina, today Argentineans and Ecuadorians leave for Spain or Italy. And while in the 1980s most workers in the south of the United States came from Mexico, more recently they come from all over Latin America, although Mexicans still make up the majority. One result of this pattern of migration is to make Mexico a transit country, a country of destination and a sending country. This is also true of other Central American countries such as Guatemala. The American Friends Services Committee has warned about the negative impact of free trade agreements (NAFTA) driving down labour standards and undermining support for the basic rights of documented and undocumented migrant workers. Thus, rural workers in Mexico have been forced to migrate in search of other employment since small farm agriculture could not compete with large US corporations. In recent years Latinos have left the region in large numbers as migrants, an indication of economic and other political concerns. Yet 100 years ago millions of migrants from Europe settled there, especially in Argentina, Uruguay and Brazil. At the beginning of the present century more than 25 million Latin Americans are believed to live outside their own countries. In 2006, remittances back to Latin America from outside came to $62 billion. This was an increase of 50 per cent from the $40 billion sent back in 2004 and exceeded the combined flow into the region of both foreign direct investment and aid.[1]

ARGENTINA

With a population of 39 million in 2008 and an average per capita income of only $5,150, Argentina had clearly not achieved its potential or realised the expectations that had been attached to its development at the beginning of the twentieth century, when it was seen as the 'jewel' of Latin America with an abundance of natural resources and a highly educated population. For most of its history it has been a magnet for immigrants, mostly from Spain and Italy. From its earliest emergence as a country, Argentina's rulers intended to welcome migrants, selectively, to be productive citizens. Article 25 of the 1853 Constitution reads:

> The Federal Government will encourage European immigration, and it
> will not restrict, limit or burden with any taxes the entrance into Argentine
> territory of foreigners who come with the goal of working the land,
> improving the industries and teaching the sciences and the arts.

In its Preamble the Constitution also dictates a number of goals – justice,
peace, defence, welfare and liberty – that apply 'to all men in the world who
wish to dwell on Argentine soil'. The Constitution quotes the precept of
Juan Bautista Alberdi who said: 'to rule is to populate'. As early as 1825 the
government had established an Immigration Commission, the forerunner of
the present National Migrations Office. The first law dealing with immigration
policies was Law 817 of Immigration and Colonisation (1876). The General
Immigration Office was created in 1898 together with an Immigrants' Hotel
and an Immigrant's Hospital in Buenos Aires. In the late nineteenth century
Argentina's 'liberal' rulers saw immigration as the means of bringing people
from supposedly more civilised societies into a sparsely populated land so as
to diminish the influence of aboriginal elements and to turn Argentina into
a modern society with a dynamic economy. ('Diminishing the influence of
aboriginal elements' is a typical example of how racism has almost always
been an integral aspect of immigration policies.) Immigrants did not just bring
skills into the country; they also brought ideas. In 1902 a Law of Residence
was passed, which mandated the expulsion of foreigners who 'compromise
national security or disturb public order'. This was followed in 1910 by a Law
of Social Defence, which explicitly named ideologies deemed to have such
effects, such as unionism, anarchism or other brands of popular organisation.

The original inhabitants of Argentina had crossed into the Americas from
Asia and gradually made their way southwards until reaching the southern
extremity of the continent. Spanish colonisation began in the sixteenth century
but only after Argentina had thrown off Spanish colonial control in 1816
did immigrants from other European countries begin to arrive in Argentina.
These early settlers were essentially colonisers sponsored by the government
and sometimes offered land that had been 'freed' of the native inhabitants.
A certain number of African slaves had been introduced into the country
between the seventeenth and nineteenth centuries. From 1880 onwards
Argentina experienced a period of rapid growth, which lasted through the
first half of the twentieth century. A further wave of economic migrants from
Korea, China, from elsewhere in Latin America and from Eastern Europe
came in the last years of the twentieth and into the twenty-first century.
Most of the nineteenth-century immigrants came from Europe, including
a proportion of Jews escaping persecution. Largely due to immigration the
population of Argentina rose from 4 million in 1895 to 7.9 million in 1914,
to 15.8 million in 1947. Immigrants over these years came from Spain (1.5
million), Italy (1.4 million) and then from Poland, Russia, and France, which
each contributed 100,000 or more settlers. Immigrants from Germany and
Austria jointly accounted for a further 100,000. Other immigrants came
from Portugal, Greece, Ukraine, Yugoslavia and Czechoslovakia (after 1919),

Ireland, Scotland, Wales, England, the Netherlands, Scandinavia and some from Middle Eastern countries. The current breakdown of foreign-born residents in Argentina is as follows: Paraguay, Bolivia, Chile, Italy more than 200,000 from each; Spain, Uruguay between 100,000 and 200,000 each; Peru, Brazil, Poland, Germany between 10,000 and 100,000 each; and South Korea, France, Japan, China, Russia, Taiwan, Serbia, Syria and Lebanon between 1,000 and 10,000 each.

Under President Juan Domingo Peron (1946–55), immigration was restricted to whites except for relations of non-whites who were already in the country. At the same time people from rural areas began an exodus to the cities. Peron encouraged workers to move to Buenos Aires with the result that agriculture and animal husbandry, the basis of the country's wealth, both suffered. This exodus from the rural areas to the towns, and especially Buenos Aires, upset the economic balance and created social and economic problems whose legacy still holds back national development.

Most immigrants arriving in Argentina came through the port of Buenos Aires and either stayed in the capital or Buenos Aires Province: this remains the usual pattern. In 1895, for example, immigrants accounted for 52 per cent of the population in the capital and 31 per cent in the Province. By 1914 the overall proportion of the foreign-born population had reached 30 per cent. However, many immigrants then returned to Europe to enlist in their former country's armies. Even so, a significant proportion of immigrants settled in the interior and created agricultural colonies. For most of the twentieth century Argentina provided a home for one of the largest Jewish communities in the world, numbering 500,000, fifth after the United States, France, Israel and Russia. The distinctive Welsh settlement in Patagonia was the largest outside Wales. Other settlements include the Irish in Formosa and the Mesopotamian regions, and Ukrainians in Misiones where they accounted for 9 per cent of the population. There were also strong German settlements as well as Austrian and Swiss ones.

At the end of the twentieth century, substantial immigration into Argentina took place from its neighbours Bolivia, Brazil, Chile, Paraguay and Uruguay, at a time when numbers of Argentineans were emigrating, following the economic collapse of 2000. Even so, the number of Latinos entering Argentina has been large, as much perhaps a reflection of conditions in their own countries as of the attractions of Argentina. The 1990s witnessed the arrival of 600,000 migrants from Paraguay, 500,000 from Bolivia, 400,000 from Chile, 150,000 from Uruguay and 100,000 from Brazil. In 1992 the government granted amnesty to 300,000 illegal aliens. Foreigners, on application, may become Argentine citizens after two years. From the middle to late 1990s Argentina received significant numbers of Asian migrants from the two Koreas, China and Vietnam. There had been earlier settlements of Japanese and Chinese migrants in Buenos Aires. In 2000 Argentina was host to an estimated 2,400 refugees, hardly a significant number or burden.

Argentineans leaving the country over the last decades of the twentieth century became an increasing concern for the government. Few Argentineans had emigrated before the 1970s, but then a 'brain drain' of professionals and technicians began to develop. In reverse, however, during the mid 1980s, following the collapse of the military junta some 10,000 of the 60,000–80,000 political exiles returned to the country. The political and economic events of 2000 and 2001 led to further emigration: some were weary of government corruption, others had lost too much in the economic collapse and so turned to emigration in the hope that they would be able to improve their standard of living elsewhere. It was a familiar pattern. Over two and a half years, according to the National Migration Directorate, an estimated 255,000 Argentineans emigrated. Emigration had been rising since the beginning of the 1990s but not on this scale, which equalled that of the years of military dictatorship from 1976 to 1983, when students, intellectuals, artists and left-wing activists had fled the country. A majority of these emigrants headed back to Europe, and especially to Spain and Italy where they could claim citizenship due to ancestral ties. Moreover, they were welcomed as 'preferred' in these two countries since they had high skill levels, similar cultures and, for those who went to Spain, the same language. Other target countries were the United States and Israel for a number of Argentinean Jews. Most of those leaving blamed economic conditions for their departure.

A poll of Latin Americans conducted by MORI in 2002 ranked Argentina third after Nicaragua and Colombia for outward emigration. Argentineans were mainly motivated by economic considerations as the country faced the longest recession in its history. Over 2001–3 Argentina defaulted on $141 billion of foreign debt, unemployment rose to 21.5 per cent while an estimated 55 per cent of the country's 37 million population fell below the poverty line. The average industrial wage fell by 7.9 per cent from 2001 to 2002 and over four years the number of homeless doubled. Given these economic conditions it is unsurprising that so many Argentineans decided to emigrate.

A relatively new Argentine immigrant community of 21,000 grew up in the United States in 2003, especially in Miami, although following the terrorist attacks of 11 September 2001 the United States imposed harsher restrictions upon immigrants and removed Argentina from the US visa waiver programme, insisting instead that would-be immigrants would have to obtain a visa in Argentina. In a relatively new departure Argentineans began to look to Canada, Australia and New Zealand as possible destinations. They were attracted, for example, by the skill-based visa aspect of Canada's immigration policy. Even so, the numbers who actually emigrated to these three countries were not large. Emigration to Israel rose dramatically at this time: Argentinean Jews had no difficulty in gaining acceptance in Israel, where they were welcomed and given financial assistance.

There was a reaction to this outward movement in the new century and, between 2000 and 2008, nearly 1 million permanent residency applications were filed from a wide range of countries. Despite the financial and economic crisis that Argentina suffered at the turn of the century, people from many countries continued to arrive as immigrants. Official statistics show that between 1992 and 2003 an average of 13,187 people a year migrated legally into Argentina, although a total of 504,000 people entered the country over this period, so that approximately 345,000 were illegals. There were about 750,000 illegals in Argentina as of 2008. In April 2008, the government launched the Patria Grande plan to regularise the position of the illegals. The plan is designed to ease the bureaucratic process of obtaining documentation and residence papers and is aimed particularly at migrants from Argentina's Mercosur neighbours – Bolivia, Brazil, Chile, Colombia, Ecuador, Paraguay, Peru, Uruguay and Venezuela. The plan was introduced following a fire in a Buenos Aires sweatshop, which brought to light the widespread utilisation of undocumented Bolivian immigrants as a cheap labour force, working in inhumane conditions under a regime of virtual debt slavery.

Immigrants have made their own cultural and other impacts in Argentina. For example, immigrant communities have given Buenos Aires some of its most famous landmarks, such as the Monumento de los Españoles. Ukrainians, Armenians and Swiss have erected monuments and churches at popular spots in Buenos Aires. Immigrant's Day, on 4 September, is celebrated every year since its inauguration in 1949. The National Immigrants' Festival has been celebrated in Obera, Misiones, during the first fortnight of September since 1980 and there are many other immigrant celebrations throughout the country. Nestor Kirchner became President in May 2003 and at once tackled corruption while the economy also began to improve under his direction, with the result that the rate of emigration slowed down. As public support for the government rose and economic conditions improved so more Argentineans stayed put.

BRAZIL

This huge country of 3 million square miles, with a population of 188 million, has been designated one of the emerging economies along with Russia, India and China (the BRICs). Following its colonisation by Portugal in the sixteenth century, Brazil became an immigrant country for both Portuguese settlers (and later others) as well as African slaves brought in to work the plantations. In the early twentieth century the birth rate began to decrease, most significantly in the 1940s when there was a marked drop in the flow of immigrants. Subsequently, the fertility rate dropped from 5.8 children per woman in the 1960s to 3.2 in the 1980s leading to an overall drop in the rate of population growth. Over the decade 1980–91 there was a lower population growth rate than at any time since official surveys began. By the beginning of the twenty-first century the rate of population growth was only 1.6 per cent. Should this tendency continue, an annual growth of only 0.6 per cent has been estimated for 2000–75.

Over the period 1953–60, with positive encouragement from the government, immigrants came to Brazil from Spain, Syria and Lebanon to work in the new industrial sector. By 1970, as a consequence, there were 115,000 Spaniards and 32,000 Syrians and Lebanese living in the country. However, following the military coup of 1964, government policy changed to become strongly 'nationalist'. The government wanted the country to rely on the native population and a major feature of the latter part of the twentieth century was a high level of internal migration from the rural areas to the cities. In 1940 Brazil had 51 cities with more than 20,000 inhabitants. By 1990 the number had risen to 500 while today 75 per cent of the Brazilian population live in cities. About 30 per cent of those cities are concentrated in ten national metropolitan regions: São Paulo, Rio de Janeiro, Belo Horizonte, Porto Alegre, Recife, Salvador, Fontaleza, Curitiba, Belem and the Federal District. During the 1950s, 1960s and 1970s, some 20 million people moved from rural to urban areas, constituting one of the largest such movements in history. Thus, according to official estimates, the urban population grew at a rate of 5 per cent a year.

The 1991 census revealed a new pattern of population redistribution, which involved less inter-regional migration, with more people staying in their regions of origin or moving to large cities nearby rather than to the mega-cities. Over the last 20 years industrial decentralisation has taken place. This has been caused by an increase in industrial facilities located farther and farther away from the metropolitan area of São Paulo, which is the most important industrial centre in the country. In fact, this spread has really represented an enlargement of the São Paulo metropolis, which has also enhanced its national influence. Government efforts to stimulate settlement in the interior have met with only limited success. The government has also tried to limit the growth of the largest cities and strengthen the middle-sized cities, although most public policies, in fact, have favoured the concentration of population in the southeast by promoting industry at the expense of agriculture. As a consequence of the build-up of cities, the environmental situation in them is both dramatic and tragic, creating ecological imbalance, social misery, environmental degradation and wastage of natural and human resources.

In the 1930s most migrants came from Japan and worked in agriculture, but this flow came to an end in 1941 with Japan's entry into the Second World War. Japanese migration recommenced in the 1950s. In 1980, the government established the National Immigration Council to implement and supervise immigration. The council defined the criteria for giving foreigners legal residence and permission to work. A new immigration law went into effect in 1981. It outlined different visa categories for foreigners and established rules for visa renewals. Between 1997 and 2004 Brazil implemented a variety of normative resolutions regarding rules for foreigner workers. The intention was to ensure that visas and work permits went to foreigners who at the least had a college degree. In reality, though, work permits became more difficult to obtain: most new immigrants had fewer skills and were less educated than the government intended. The relative ease with which foreign workers came into the country led workers' organisations to exert pressure upon the government to create new obstacles for foreign workers so that Brazilian workers did not have to compete with them for jobs. However, this pressure did not lead to any change of policy.

From the mid 1980s an increasing number of Brazilians from various economic levels began to migrate to other countries in search of economic opportunities. The 1980s came to be called the 'lost decade'. It was a period of high inflation and low growth and many people emigrated in search of better opportunities. In fact, such emigration had started earlier, for although the economy was booming it did not necessarily provide jobs for many people with low skills. Thus, from the 1960s to the 1970s some 200,000 Brazilians moved to neighbouring countries, especially Paraguay and Argentina, in search of opportunities not available in Brazil. Most such migrants were peasants who settled in the border areas of Uruguay, Argentina, Paraguay and Venezuela, though such emigration diminished during the 1990s as earlier emigrants began to return home. Some of these peasant migrants became small landholders across the border in Paraguay. What became known as 'yo-yo' migration took place during the 1980s. A Brazilian would enter the United States on a tourist visa, work for a year or two, return to Brazil for another year or two, then return to the United States and repeat the process as long as he needed the extra income. When the United States tightened visa requirements for Brazilians, many then obtained tourist visas to Mexico and tried to enter the United States from there. According to a report by Reuters, 8,629 Brazilians crossed from Mexico into the United States in 2004. Other Brazilians, the descendants of earlier Japanese immigrants, have migrated to Japan, which they can enter legally and are assisted to find work. There is no formal policy to attract emigrants back to Brazil, though many do choose to return.

Economic crisis in Brazil during the 1980s combined with cheap and improved transportation services meant that a proportion of these migrants went farther afield than to neighbouring Latin American countries and reached the United States, Canada, Portugal and Japan, where they had to take menial jobs. It was during these years that Brazil became a net exporter of people for the first time in its history. Yet, even as some of its own citizens emigrated, conditions elsewhere led to a new surge of immigrants into Brazil from both neighbouring countries and Europe. However, in the new century Brazil experienced a period of robust economic growth, which led the government to hope that there would be a decrease in emigration to Europe and the United States.

With over 14,500 km of poorly secured land borders, it is relatively easy for low-skilled workers from neighbouring countries to cross illegally into Brazil. They obtain work in factories or on the land. Brazil, indeed, has become an important and attractive destination for Latin American immigrants from a range of socio-economic backgrounds. In 1991 the Asunción Agreement created a common market of the Southern Cone countries – Uruguay, Brazil, Argentina and Paraguay – collectively known as the Mercosur (Mercado Comum do Sul). The Agreement has contributed to an increase in the movement of people between these four countries. Chile, with no Brazilian border, and Argentina have become the source of highly skilled labour migrating to the São Paulo metropolitan area. A 1997 estimate suggested that 300,000 immigrants from Chile, Bolivia and Paraguay were living in the state of São Paulo. As immigrants from neighbouring South American countries were moving into

Brazil, a significant number of immigrants from Europe, Africa and Asia were also entering the country.

According to the 2000 census, South and Central American migrants constituted 46.5 per cent (43,125 people) of the total international flow into Brazil between 1990 and 2000. The next highest group – 23.4 per cent or 21,636 people – came from Europe, while 15.5 per cent (14,368 people) were from Asian countries and 9.7 per cent (9,029 people) were from North America. The southeast of Brazil, which is the most developed region, is the main destination for immigrants: it is home to 73.4 per cent of the total immigrant population (683,830). Over half these immigrants live in the state of São Paulo. Other states with high levels of international migration include Rio de Janeiro, Parana, Minas Gerais and Rio Grande do Sul. In 2000, 56.3 per cent of Brazil's total foreign population came from Europe, 21 per cent from South and Central America, and 17.8 per cent from Asia. The largest populations were from Portugal (31.2 per cent), Japan (10.4 per cent) and Italy (8 per cent). In order to attract high-skilled employees, the government provides temporary work visas for experts, managers and administrators and between 1998 and 2004, 109,824 such visas were issued, of which 17.2 per cent went to applicants from the United States, 5.9 per cent to applicants from France, 5.7 per cent from Britain and 5.6 per cent from Germany. Undocumented immigrants, not covered by the census, were estimated at 200,000 Bolivians, 20,000 Peruvians and 50,000 Koreans. So far, perhaps reflecting the extent of its borders, Brazil has not made any serious attempts to control illegal immigration.

In the early 1990s Brazil began to take in asylum seekers from West Africa, especially Angola and Sierra Leone, and by the 2000s the majority (81.5 per cent) of asylum seekers were from Africa. The National Committee for Refugees (CONARE) granted refugee status to just over 3,000 people between January 1998 and February 2005. In 1999, Brazil signed an agreement with the UNHCR to begin a formal refugee resettlement programme that was launched in 2001. The first refugees to arrive under this programme came from Afghanistan. The programme also focused on refugees from the long-lasting conflict in Colombia. The government said it would accept 275 resettled refugees in 2005 but they would have to be financed by the UNHCR.

Part II

Europe

The term Europe covers the world's most complex region in terms of migration and its impact. First comes the European Union (EU), which now comprises 27 countries that collectively have a slightly larger GDP than the United States. The EU can be divided in several ways. There are the 15 developed members of Western Europe of which 12 had come together prior to the end of the Cold War to be joined by Austria, Finland and Sweden in the mid 1990s. Then come the eight less developed countries of Eastern Europe, and the Mediterranean two (Cyprus and Malta) that joined in the Big Bang of 2004 to be followed by Bulgaria and Romania in 2007. The Big Bang was followed by a substantial internal migration in search of work from Eastern Europe to Western Europe, though many of these migrants returned home as a result of the recession that began in 2008 and the consequent collapse of job opportunities in Western Europe. The Big Four in the EU – Britain, France, Germany and Italy – had a combined GDP in 2006 of $9,319 trillion compared with $13,201 trillion for the USA, and these four effectively control EU policies. A second tier consists of Poland and Spain, the former being a source of migrant labour moving into Western Europe, the latter being one of the principal countries through which migrants make their way into the EU. Spain, Italy, Greece and Malta act as target countries for migrants crossing the Mediterranean on their way to the EU. Two of the wealthiest European countries – Norway and Switzerland – are not members of the EU, though they enjoy very close links with it and are potential target countries for migrants. Next come the Balkan countries that are hoping for EU membership – Croatia, Bosnia and Herzegovina, Serbia, Kosovo, Macedonia, Montenegro and Albania with, in addition, Georgia and Ukraine seeking membership as they sit uneasily on the southern flank of Russia. Above all, the EU faces the problems that come with Turkey's application to join.

As though these European divisions are not enough, there is the further complication of EU's relationship with Russia, half of which can claim to be European. This complex tangle of 40 countries both attracts migrants and provides them. And inherent in the migrant question are a range of problems: an ageing and static EU population in urgent need of new blood that only immigrants can provide; uneven development; the expectations of the newer, less affluent members that the older, wealthier ones will help their economies grow; religious differences raised by the prospect of 70 million plus Muslim Turks joining an EU that Poland insists should be Christian; racism; arguments about an 'open' or a 'fortress' Europe.

5
The European Union

The difficulties inherent in achieving a single policy acceptable to 27 countries have been highlighted by the problems associated with immigration into the EU. Some members are simply too small to cope with a major influx of immigrants; others feel they are in the front line as migrants from Africa try to gain access to the EU through Spain, Malta or Italy; while target countries such as France or Germany would like to close their borders or pass the migrants on to another member. Since the beginning of the new century immigration as a problem has moved to the top of the political agenda and efforts to find viable solutions to an ever changing situation form the backdrop to a steady stream of arguments, debates and legislation.

The first decade of the present century has witnessed a steady growth of migration into Europe accompanied by a great deal of debate that has done as much to obfuscate as it has to resolve the problems. Nonetheless, the outlines of an EU policy have begun to emerge, despite the many reservations or differences between individual member states. In September 2003, the EU terminated the Dublin Asylum Convention and replaced it with two regulations adopted in February and September 2003. These were the Asylum Applications (Examining State) Regulation 343/2003 and the Consequential Implementing Regulation 1560/2003. However, both regulations were criticised by interior ministers, as were the regulations limiting asylum applications by refugees who had already landed in another member state and defining which state had the exclusive right to determine refugee status. Another treaty came into force on 28 January 2004, the Protocol against the Smuggling of Migrants by Land, Air and Sea, which was supplementary to the UN Convention against Transnational Organized Crime. The Protocol was designed to criminalise the smuggling of migrants while also recognising that migrants were often victims and needed protection.

Speaking in August 2004, the new EU Justice and Home Affairs Commissioner Rocco Buttiglione, who had been Italy's European affairs minister for three years, warned that the flow of economic migrants had become a major problem and called for member states to work more closely together to stem the numbers of refugees heading for the EU: 'People seeking asylum for economic reasons is a growing problem. It's a time bomb.' He said EU states had to agree extra aid to developing nations to cut the flow of refugees, and he backed the German proposal to set up immigrant 'holding centres' in countries such as Tunisia or Libya. He dismissed fears that such camps could infringe human rights. 'We have to ask transit countries to establish the camps that would take in immigrants…to offer them humanitarian aid and information about job possibilities in Europe.' At the same time 'they would also investigate, identify and send back those who don't meet criteria or who would not be able to integrate in our society'. He also said the idea of a police force to patrol the EU's borders should be examined. After enumerating those who could reasonably claim asylum, Buttiglione said, 'We have to talk about it.'

By October 2004, when the idea of asylum-processing camps in North Africa had been debated, France and Spain came out in opposition after two days of informal talks in Florence between the interior ministers of five EU nations – Britain, France, Germany, Italy and Spain. The deadlock was a defeat for Germany and Italy and for Britain, which had supported a similar idea in 2003 only to be rebuffed. French Interior Minister Dominique de Villepin said: 'for France, it's out of the question to accept transit camps or shelters of any kind'. He added: 'It is not for Europe to take this issue forward.' Critics of refugee centres in countries such as Libya claimed they would not be able to guarantee the legal and human rights standards expected in Western Europe. German Interior Minister Otto Schily argued that such camps would mean migrants would not have to embark on a 'life-endangering trip across the Mediterranean, but would have the possibility of making such an application outside the borders of the European Union.'[1] So the EU had to fall back upon the Italian suggestion to 'help transit countries which agree [to cooperate] to control their borders and improve their capacity to repatriate illegal immigrants'. A spokesman for the then British Home Secretary, David Blunkett, said there was 'a pressing need to tackle flows of illegal immigration at sources, working with countries of origin and transit. We believe the focus should be on working with third countries to strengthen their capacity for dealing with migration'.

In late October 2004, EU ministers met in Luxembourg to consider a five-year strategy programme and discuss coordinating policies on economic immigration and asylum policy, including a proposal to set up a European public prosecutor to combat fraud and ideas for EU asylum-processing camps in North Africa. EU diplomats saw the justice and home affairs portfolio becoming the biggest growth area of policy over the next few years because of sensitivity about immigration and terrorism. In an interview for *The Independent*, the European Commissioner for Justice and Home Affairs, Antonio Vitorino, argued, 'we must have a system of coordination of economic immigration'. He said that individual governments should retain the prerogative 'to define the number and the profile of the economic immigrants admitted'. And referring to countries that periodically regularise the position of illegal immigrants (that is, offer an amnesty), he said:

When there is an amnesty in one country it has immediate consequences for the situation of all immigrants in all member states, most of all for those in countries where there are no border controls [because of the Schengen free-travel zone].

Britain made clear that it would oppose the creation of a common asylum system or any common border guard.[2]

Unsurprisingly, 2004 was a year of EU controversy. On the one hand, it witnessed a huge expansion with the admission of ten new member states; on the other hand, it raised a range of new fears about labour migration within the EU as a whole. Yet, at the same time, the European Commission began to increase its programme of opening up EU labour markets for third-country (non-EU) nationals. Several member states – Britain, Germany and Ireland, for example – moved towards new policies to attract certain categories of immigrant. In Britain, the reform of the Immigration Act 2002 included the introduction of a programme to attract highly skilled immigrants, based on a points system. Both Germany and Ireland promoted the 'green card' for IT specialists and the introduction of the work visa scheme to foster immigration in certain sectors of the economy.[3] Such measures were a recognition of skill gaps in the labour markets of the EU, and an ageing and shrinking work force that could only be replenished by foreign labour. Yet the EU did not achieve any comprehensive reform of national immigration policies. Instead, its individual members were only prepared to attempt limited reforms of their own rather than work together in producing a single EU immigration policy. EU member countries would rather handle immigration individually instead of working together on an EU basis. The result is to make the issue even more complex than it needs to be. Thus, in preparation for the Big Bang, the EU Treaty of Accession, signed in Athens on 16 April 2003, restricted access to the EU-15 labour markets for workers from the ten new member states; for a period of up to seven years (May 2011) member states could apply bilateral agreements that limit 'the right to move and reside freely' within the EU.

On 12 January 2005, the EU Justice, Freedom and Security Commissioner, Franco Frattini, recommended that the EU, rather than national governments, regulate skilled immigration. The EU suggested that the 25 member states should create an early warning system to keep each other informed of important changes in their immigration policies.[4] The EU pressed member nations to implement fully the four freedoms: freedom to move goods, capital, workers and services over national borders within the EU. Nationals of the EU-10 countries that joined the EU on 1 May 2004 could visit the EU-15 without visas, but could not work unless they obtained work permits, except in Ireland and Britain. A report by the European Commission, released in March 2005, predicted that a drastic drop in birth rates combined with an ageing population would undermine Europe's economic growth within the next 20 years unless life was made easier for parents and immigration was encouraged. The report concluded that, 'ever larger migrant flows may be needed to meet the need for labour and safeguard Europe's prosperity'.[5]

At a meeting in France during July 2005, five leading EU countries (Britain, France, Germany, Italy and Spain) agreed to organise joint charter flights to return illegal immigrants to their home countries. Formerly, Germany and Italy had cooperated in joint flights, but this was the first time that these five countries had agreed to a single repatriation programme, to share the political responsibility for repatriation and to show that the EU was capable of acting together on the issue. The Interior Minister of France, Nicolas Sarkozy, said France had increased expulsions of illegal immigrants by half in the past year and argued that the meeting should send a strong message 'that only those with valid papers have a right to enter our countries. Anyone else, who tries to stay on in contravention of our laws, will be sent home.' The EU would establish joint naval patrols in the Mediterranean and send missions to countries such as Albania and Romania to discourage people from travelling without visas or work permits. In November the EU as a whole was reminded how closely immigration and racism are connected, when urban violence erupted in the Paris suburbs and demonstrated the extent of the polarisation between France's immigrant underclass and its white middle class.

> Nowhere is that polarisation more evident than in Paris, a city divided by a palpable racial barrier. Within its inner ring road, Paris is almost universally white and middle class. The city's black and Arab population is confined to the housing projects beyond.[6]

As Paul Vallely wrote in *The Independent*:

> Burning cars on the streets of Paris. Pitched battles between Asian and black people in Birmingham. Islamic terrorists planting bombs in the London rush hour. All at once, more than a decade's mixing of race and religion on the streets of Europe has exploded, and large questions are being asked about the relationship of ethnic minorities to our pluralist democracies.[7]

Such questions will continue to be asked, as immigration changes the demography of the EU.

As migrants from Africa kept trying to gain entry into the EU, so moves to stop the flood became more urgent. During 2006 it was decided to create elite teams of EU border guards, Frontex. The move, following an experiment in the Canary Islands, involved the creation of a permanent rapid reaction force of 250–300 experts who could be despatched within ten days to deal with sudden movements of population. Four boats and two aircraft were to be assigned to the force. The European Commission also contemplated setting up a database to register all third-country nationals entering or leaving the EU so as to help member states check whether a migrant was overstaying illegally. The proposals, if anything, gave the impression of a policy of despair.

The immediate purpose was to assist the EU's southern frontiers – Malta, Greece and Italy's southern islands. By mid 2006 11,000 illegal immigrants had travelled by boat to the Canary Islands off the northwest coast of Africa – nearly double the total for 2005. Franco Frattini, the Justice and Home Affairs Commissioner, said:

> The idea is to have at the disposal of Frontex a permanent team of 250–300 people from the member states which will be able to intervene quickly at

the request of a member state – within 10 days from the request. We are talking about helping member states that are under particular, unexpected pressure. We're not talking about normal border checks.

However, the legal officer for the European Council on Refugees and Exiles, Chris Nash, said:

> We support measures which increase capacity of EU member states to identify asylum seekers and assess their claims. But we would be concerned about measures which exclusively focus on controlling borders and maintaining Fortress Europe, as these have had unfortunate consequences already.[8]

Malta and the Italian island of Lampedusa had been inundated with migrants crossing from Libya, while the Spanish Moroccan enclaves of Ceuta and Melilla were a second pair of targets. At the same time, thousands of migrants had died making the sea crossing from Mauritania to the Canary Islands. According to the UN, migrants were coming from Somalia and Yemen in ever greater numbers and heading for Turkey and Greece.

As 1 January 2007 – the date when Bulgaria and Romania were to join the EU – approached there was little sign of any coordinated EU policy, as the existing 25 members could not decide how they would react to large-scale movement westwards of migrants from the two new members in search of jobs. Most countries, in their different ways, were keeping their options open.

By the end of the year, the European Commission unveiled plans to set up job centres in Africa. Under the scheme, nations such as Mali, Senegal and Mauritania would inform the European authorities of the numbers of would-be immigrants on their books and of their qualifications. Teams of experts might also be sent to African countries to help root out human traffickers. Franco Frattini suggested a network of job centres across Africa 'somewhat similar to placement agencies'. This approach reeked of neo-colonialism and had little chance of working even if it got off the ground. Generally, throughout 2006, there was increased resistance by wealthier countries to the arrival of more immigrants. The basic policy of individual members was to tighten the inflow while ensuring their own skill needs were met. Otherwise, the aim was to reduce the total flow and discourage permanent settlement. New restrictions were imposed by the older EU countries to contain the movement west by workers from the new Big Bang countries. In both Britain and Sweden, for example, popular hostility towards new flows of immigrants grew stronger.

Despite national distinctions between members, most EU states had actively promoted labour immigration since the Second World War, although sharp changes of attitude began to emerge in the new century. When in November 2005 France suffered some of the worst riots it had seen in decades over the immigrant question, the Minister of the Interior, Nicolas Sarkozy, told the National Assembly that France did not want 'those people that nobody else in the world wants'. 'We want selective immigration,' he said. Targeting Muslims became part of an overall EU approach to immigration, though attempts were made to deny that this was so. In 2005, the International Helsinki Federation for Human Rights published a report on *Intolerance and Discrimination against Muslims in the EU*. It observed: 'As the fight against terrorism has been stepped up – pre-existing prejudice and discrimination against Muslims have been reinforced.' The numbers of Muslims in Europe were approximately as follows: France (4.5 million), Germany (over 3 million), Britain (1.5 million), Spain (about 1 million), Italy and the Netherlands (close to 1 million), Belgium (400,000–500,000), Greece (up to 400,000), Austria (more than 300,000), Sweden (more than 300,000) and Denmark (up to 180,000). In many cases they were subject to discrimination in employment, housing, and access to services.[9]

On 1 January 2007, Bulgaria and Romania joined the EU with rights to free movement across its 27 member countries but there was no open door policy as there had been in 2004. Skilled Bulgarians and Romanians could get work if they obtained a permit, were students or self-employed, while the only sectors likely to provide employment for the unskilled were food processing or agriculture. In Britain, predictions as to how many job seekers from the two countries would arrive during the year varied from 56,000 to 180,000. Slowly, meanwhile, the EU was developing a plan to launch a global job-advertising scheme to attract skilled workers. The object was to improve the EU's ability to attract and retain professionals such as doctors, nurses, engineers and IT workers from outside Europe to fill shortages by means of a fast-track 'blue card' worker visa programme. According to the European Commission President José Manuel Barroso, 'We are not good enough at attracting highly skilled people.' He wanted to offer highly skilled job seekers a simpler way to get a job within the EU and, if possible, do away with complex national procedures to obtain residence and work permits. These new measures would be designed to lure professionals from Asia, Africa and Latin America to the EU. According to the commissioner in charge of immigration, Franco Frattini, the US, Australia and Canada were all ahead of the EU at attracting skilled labour. While skilled workers from outside its borders accounted for only 0.9 per cent of all workers in the EU, the figure for Australia was 9.9 per cent, for Canada 7.3 per cent and for the US 3.5 per cent.[10]

What constantly emerges from the debates and proposals within the EU is the fact that it does not have a viable central policy on immigration, unlike the United States, Australia or Canada. The debate about immigration is always confused: concerns over cultural conflicts and growing fundamentalism, safeguarding borders and stopping migrants at source (which is all but impossible) make it impossible to come to terms with the undeniable fact that Europe needs both skilled and unskilled immigrants if its future work force is going to keep the EU competitive and provide the wealth needed to finance the social mechanisms required for an ageing population. A common EU migration policy should cover integration, economic migration and family reunification.

Agreements within the EU about a uniform approach to immigration are often belied by behaviour on the ground. African immigrants crossing the Mediterranean from Libya to Malta or Lampedusa provoke arguments between these three countries as to which must take responsibility for them. By mid 2007 there was a consensus that at least 6,000 Africans had perished attempting to cross the Mediterranean (the figure was based upon the number of bodies found, but many more would also have drowned without trace). The destination countries for these immigrants in northern Europe put pressure upon the southern frontline states to stop the flow, although no one knows how to do this. Meanwhile, global warming leading to desertification, deep poverty and the widening disparity in wealth between North and South mean that the flow of migrants will grow. The EU needs to deal positively with the movement of immigrants rather than trying to devise a Fortress Europe that keeps them out. All member states are affected by the flow of migrants and it is in their interest to manage migration flows with a coordinated approach that takes account of the economic and demographic situation within the EU. In the absence of a coordinated policy, smuggling and people trafficking networks have grown up across Europe and considerable resources have been mobilised to fight these activities.

At the October 1999 European Council meeting in Tampere, Finland, the EU began to develop a common policy towards migration. This meeting was followed up at The Hague in 2004 with the adoption of a programme that set out the objectives for strengthening freedom, security and justice in the EU for the period 2005–10. The Commission produced a Green Paper on an EU approach to managing economic migration (COM (2004) 811) which led to the adoption in December 2005 of a Policy Plan on Legal Migration (COM (2005) 669) that listed the actions and legislative initiatives that the Commission intended to take so as to pursue the consistent development of the EU legal migration policy. A Commission report of June 2006 provided an overview of migration trends in the EU. The elements required for an EU immigration policy were agreed at Tampere as follows: a comprehensive approach to the management of migratory flows so as to find a balance between humanitarian and economic admission; fair treatment for third-country nationals, aiming as far as possible to give them comparable rights and obligations to those of nationals of the member state in which they live; the development of partnerships with countries of origin, including policies of co-development. Other conditions for a common approach to migration management, which were set out by the European Commission in November 2000, required taking into account the following: the economic and demographic development of the EU; the reception capacity of each member state along with their historical and cultural links with the countries of origin; the situation in the countries of origin and the impact of migration policy on them (brain drain); the need to develop specific integration policies. Advances have been achieved in relation to family reunification, EU long-term resident status, students, and researchers. There is a plethora of EU communications, plans and programmes relating to all aspects of immigration; of huge importance is the degree to which member states take account of them when faced with political pressures against immigration that they must deal with at home. The common EU immigration policy does not apply to Denmark, which has decided to opt out of the Title IV of the Treaty establishing the European Community. Britain and Ireland decide on their involvement on a case-by-case basis (the possibility of opt-in).

Whether or not there is to be a working Fortress Europe will be debated for some time. The concept is essentially negative: that rich, developed Europe is threatened by immigrants and should seal itself off from them. In fact this will not be possible for several reasons: first, its land and sea borders are simply too lengthy to police; second, despite various degrees of xenophobia, Europe needs immigrants to re-energise its declining or static population; third, its current 27 members will never agree simultaneously to accept a common migration policy. The individual member states have the machinery to deal with immigrants while the EU does not, though it can and does pass resolutions. Individual members will break the EU rules or not, depending upon their labour and economic needs. The Schengen Agreement became operational in 1995 and under its terms there could be uncontrolled movement across the borders of the ten EU countries that had adopted it (the ten countries, of the then 15-member EU, were Benelux, France, Germany, Italy, Portugal, Spain, Greece and Austria). Asylum seekers and refugees, having entered the Schengen area, were obliged to seek asylum in the first country of entry and could not legally move on to elsewhere in the EU. Standards of admission for refugees and asylum seekers differ widely from one member country to another and it is all but inevitable that conflicts will arise between EU migration laws and national migration policies. Asylum seekers generally are not wanted.

> EU members, meanwhile, will be trying to find a way to 'share the burden' of asylum seekers. The impetus, understandably, comes largely from Germany. In 1992, alone, of roughly 700,000 applications in 14 European states, nearly half a million were lodged in Germany.[11]

The EU may be determined to reduce the number of asylum seekers entering its territory but its success in doing so has been limited.

> The rights of EU citizens and those of asylum seekers have become major preoccupations in Europe. The two exist in a state of great tension. As a result of the Treaty of Amsterdam, which came into effect in May 1999, asylum, immigration and other 'freedom of movement' issues are now subject both to tighter judicial control and to closer European Parliamentary oversight – eventually, perhaps, they may become the object of Parliamentary legislation.[12]

The complications to which immigration gives rise can lead to unintended consequences. Thus, to inhibit immigration in one way simply ensures that would-be immigrants will try another, while to deny entry altogether will simply invite a growing disregard for the law. After the post-1945 years, Europe was relaxed about immigration and received comparatively large numbers of immigrants from former colonies – West Indians to Britain, Algerians to France, Indonesians to Holland (or Turkish *gastarbeiter* to Germany). The main European countries changed their attitudes in the 1980s, ironically when Europe had become more prosperous than ever before. At the same time cheap air travel favoured the movement of migrants, some of whom claimed asylum in transit, until in 1998 Britain introduced the Direct Airline Transit Visa after a group of Kosovans claimed asylum while in transit through London. The following year the EU proposed to extend the British policy to other states by means of a standard-format transit visa.

Any decisions about asylum seekers must take account of political considerations in the receiving country. Thus, governments are less interested in devising a fair asylum policy than in whether or not they are seen by electorates as willing hosts to the 'scum of the earth'.[13]

Part of the ethos of the EU is burden sharing. In economic terms this means the richer members have to help the poorer ones catch up. In terms of immigration it means distributing unwanted migrants equally among its members, an approach that many of these members will resent and try to evade. What the EU would like to do, therefore, is create 'support' programmes inside countries that, for whatever reasons, are major sources of migrants to Europe. The object would be to 'ensure' (it is not explained how) that the endangered (for example in Afghanistan) who might otherwise become asylum seekers, are not at risk. The EU may be able to put up the money to finance such programmes but it cannot control the forces that put such would-be migrants at risk in their own countries. A number of EU countries – Britain, Italy, the Netherlands, Spain and Germany – have favoured linking aid to repatriation agreements, an approach that either would not work at all or even if it did initially would almost certainly break down. Such arguments constantly overlook the most crucial factor of all: that when individuals decide they are going to move they will do so, whatever agreements their own government may have made with the EU or any other target area.

The scale of immigration into Europe, whether legal or illegal, has led the EU to formulate a range of policies or controls while it has also revealed a wide variety of approaches to immigration among the 27 member states. The need to attract high-skilled immigrants has to be matched by the determination of the EU to reduce the flow of low-skilled or illegal immigrants. The influx of illegal immigrants who cross the Mediterranean and enter the EU through Spain, Italy, Malta or Greece presents huge problems of control. During 2008, for example, EU patrol boats stopped more than 20,000 people trying to cross the Mediterranean from Africa. The second most porous EU border is that with the former Soviet bloc countries in the East. In any case, border checks are often minimal in the now 24-nation Schengen zone, which includes the former East European countries, where passport-free travel is allowed.

In 2007 Sweden received 18,000 Iraqi asylum seekers, more than half the total entering the EU, to join an already established Iraqi community. The new EU pact to deal with immigrants is more a political statement than a binding set of rules or laws since it is admitted that the EU 'does not have the resources to decently receive all the migrants hoping to find a better life here'.[14] The pact argues that it is 'imperative that each member state take account of its partners' interests when designing and implementing its immigration integration and asylum policies.' If this condition were to be fully observed it would be impossible for individual member states to grant an amnesty, as Spain did in 2005 for some 700,000 illegal immigrants. Spain was criticised by other EU members for granting the amnesty, but none of the critics had to deal with illegal immigrants on such a large scale.

That particular episode highlights the difficulty of making a single EU policy work for all the member states. One aspect of the pact is a return directive that will apply across the EU (except for Britain and Ireland, which have not accepted this area of Community law). The British government, in any case, does not believe that the directive will make it any easier to return illegal immigrants to their countries of origin. France wanted the pact to include 'immigration contracts' that obliged migrants to pass language and culture tests in the host country, but Spain vetoed the suggestion. Interestingly, certain South American leaders condemned the pact and the Venezuelan President Hugo Chávez threatened to cut off oil exports to the EU if it was adopted, on the grounds that South American countries had taken in many European migrants in the past and now provided many workers for the EU, especially for Spain.

The immigration problems the EU faces can be classified under a number of headings: the flow of people into Europe; border controls and their effectiveness; people smuggling to circumvent the controls; overseas recruitment of certain skills; and long-term EU needs in terms of population and skills. There has been much debate about these problems over the first decade of the twenty-first century and controlling immigration has become one of the top social/political priorities both for individual member states and for the EU as a whole, and yet in-migration into the EU accounts for only 5 per cent of the world's total migration while the EU, with the United States, is one of the two richest, most advanced regions in the world and, as such, should be better able to cope with immigration than most other regions. What seems clear, however, is that the EU is still feeling its way towards a viable and acceptable policy that suits all its members.

In *Towards a Better EU Migration Policy* Hugo Brady gives a balanced survey of the position as of 2009.[15] There has been a rapid rise in both legal and illegal migration into Europe over the last ten years. Each spring and summer the European Mediterranean states have to cope with thousands of African migrants desperately trying to reach Europe in un-seaworthy boats. There are growing demands for collective EU action to manage migration better, including more effective border controls. There is the long-term problem of filling the 50 million skilled vacancies that Europe will face in 2060. There is insufficient information available about where migrants settle and this has led to suggestions that national immigration profiles be created 'to maintain a precise and detailed picture of migration and border management in each member state'. Compiling information is no doubt helpful, but it is not a policy: the biggest bar to a single EU policy remains the individual agendas of its 27 member states.

6
Britain

Following the London terror attacks of July 2005, Britain began to question its multicultural policies. The argument centred round the extent to which migrants should be obliged to 'fit in' with British society.[1] British immigration policies have always been strongly affected by racial considerations. Thus, in 1997, 0.49 per cent of US citizens requesting settlement in Britain were denied entry; the figure for the Indian subcontinent was 29 per cent. In the same year, while only 0.18 per cent of Australian visitors' applications were refused, the refusal rate for Ghanaian applications was over 30 per cent.[2]

While great publicity is given to immigrants coming into Britain, less attention is paid to emigrants from Britain. A World Bank report in 2005 showed that Britain lost more skilled workers to the 'global brain drain' than any other country. While 1.44 million graduates left Britain for better-paid jobs in the United States, Australia or Canada, 1.26 million immigrant graduates came to the country, leaving a net 'brain loss' of 200,000 people. This represented a loss of 16.7 per cent – or one in six graduates – higher than any other major industrialised country, from a country (Britain) that has a smaller percentage of graduates than many others. Official figures showed that more than 350,000 men and women were emigrating every year, a rise of 30 per cent over 10 years. Many nurses recruited to work in Britain used the country as a stepping-stone before going on to the United States. Figures from the Nursing and Midwifery Council showed that in 2005, 24,393 nurses left Britain for jobs in Australia and New Zealand – double the number that went in 1995. Pay differentials play an important role in emigration. Thus, a junior economist will earn about £25,000 in Britain while in America he will start at £50,000 or £60,000. Debate in Britain is focused relentlessly upon immigrants coming into the country while the emigration of Britons is usually ignored or overlooked although they are part of the overall picture. During 2005 about 1,500 immigrants arrived in Britain every day while 1,000 left. Danny Sriskandaraja, a migration specialist with the Institute for Public Policy Research said: 'With record numbers of people coming and going from the UK in recent years, it is clear that the UK more than any other country is becoming a global hub for the movement of people.'[3] The principal source countries for immigrants into Britain are China, India, Pakistan, Australia, New Zealand and South Africa, and from Europe Poland, Germany and Spain, while the principal destination countries for British emigrants are the United States, Australia and New Zealand. An estimate of Britons resident abroad at the end of 2007 was:

Australia – 1.3 million
Spain – 761,000
US – 678,000
Canada – 603,000
Ireland – 291,000
New Zealand – 215,000
South Africa – 212,000
France – 200,000

THE INWARD FLOW

In anticipation of EU enlargement in 2004, Britain and Ireland were the only member countries not to introduce restrictions on the movement of workers within the Union. New British measures agreed in February 2004 were, first, that people from the new accession countries would have to apply for a 'worker's registration certificate' and prove they could support themselves; and that anyone arriving without a job or other form of income would be ineligible to claim benefits for at least two years. The measures proved effective. It was reported in July 2004 that the number of new arrivals had already peaked and that 24,000 people from the new member states had registered for work. Of this 24,000, the majority had been in the country before enlargement and only about a third (8,000) were new arrivals.[4] At the same time, Northern Ireland experienced an upsurge in ethnic tension, especially involving new migrant workers, and the government announced coordinated actions to tackle racism and racial inequalities.

The 2005 report on immigration published by the Institute for Public Policy Research claimed that Britain had become a thoroughly diverse country and a magnet for immigration, while London had become a genuinely 'world' city in which 41 per cent of all immigrants settled. It also pointed out that the sources of immigration into the country had changed: there had been a sharp increase in numbers from former Yugoslavia, Sierra Leone and South America, while the number of those born in traditional 'source' regions and countries, such as the Caribbean and Ireland, had fallen. The number of people coming to Britain in 2004 had jumped by 70,000 to 582,000 while the number leaving was 360,000, a record net influx of 222,000. Immigrants from 'new' Commonwealth countries in Africa and Asia had risen by 40,000 to 143,000 for 2004. A Home Office spokesman, rebutting opposition criticisms of the government's immigration policy, said: 'New immigrants bring considerable benefit to the UK, whether contributing to our wealth, our culture or our diversity.'[5]

By early 2006, it was estimated that 300,000 workers, half from Poland, had come to Britain (one of the three countries, with Ireland and Sweden that had decided not to impose work restrictions). Yet the European Commission had noted that the three countries had 'experienced high economic growth, a drop of unemployment and a rise of employment'. The total of East Europeans who came to work in Britain over this period were as follows:

Poles – 162,870
Lithuanians – 37,275
Slovakians – 29,395
Latvians – 18,480
Czechs – 16,385
Hungarians – 8,200
Estonians – 3,855
Slovenians – 270
TOTAL – 290,695

This number was equivalent to just 0.4 per cent of the work force, as opposed to 0.7 per cent in Germany and 1.4 per cent in Austria.[6] According to the head of the Commission for Racial Equality, Trevor Phillips, these immigrants had supplied 5,700 bus, lorry and coach drivers, 11,500 care workers, 1,400 teaching staff, 550 dental practitioners and 1,750 GPs, hospital doctors, nurses and specialists. Such figures helped dispel the myth that the country would be swamped with immigrants only concerned to live off social services or – a contradiction – to take jobs from Britons. According to National Statistics, net migration into Britain over the ten-year period 1996–2005 was as follows:

1996 – 54,000
1997 – 47,000
1998 – 139,000
1999 – 163,000
2000 – 163,000
2001 – 172,000
2002 – 153,000
2003 – 151,000
2004 – 223,000
2005 – 185,000

At the end of 2006 the top ten occupations in which registered workers were employed were: process operative or other factory worker – 37 per cent; warehouse operative – 10 per cent; kitchen and catering assistants – 9 per cent; packers – 9 per cent; cleaners, domestic staff – 8 per cent; farm workers – 7 per cent; waiter, waitress – 6 per cent; maid, room attendant – 5 per cent; care assistants and home carers – 5 per cent; labourer, building – 4 per cent. Despite fears that such numbers from East Europe would prove to be a strain on the economy, this was not the case since they either filled jobs that were not being filled or created new ones.

Over the two-year period 2004–5 the following ten countries were the principal sources of immigration into Britain:

India – 99,000
Poland – 76,000
China – 59,000

South Africa – 57,000
Australia – 52,000
Pakistan – 42,000
United States – 31,000
Germany – 26,000
Spain – 24,000
New Zealand – 23,000

One encouraging aspect of immigration has been its impact upon fertility rates. At the end of 2007 these were at their highest level in over 25 years with an increase in births among both British-born and immigrant women. The annual report on population by the National Statistician, Karen Dunnell, said the total fertility rate in the UK had gone up from 1.6 children per woman in 2001 to 1.8. Immigrants were found to have a higher fertility rate of 2.5 – up from 2.3 in 2002. There was also a rise in the number of children being born to British-born parents from 1.5 to 1.7. The report appeared in the National Statistician's Annual Article and revealed that 154,000 births in 2006 were to non-British-born women and accounted for almost 21 per cent of total births.

The lesson of the immediate post-Big Bang years was that as long as the British economy was growing and there were domestic labour shortages, the country would continue to suck in workers from abroad. According to government estimates published in early 2008, the population of 60.6 million in 2006 would reach 71 million in 2031 and 69 per cent of that increase would be due to immigration. Such forecasts have to be regarded with caution. A large proportion of immigrants at this time came from Eastern Europe and many of them had no desire either to become British or to stay in Britain for long. They came to work while conditions were good and as the recession began to bite towards the end of 2008, many of them returned home. Modern migration is no longer a one-off bid to start a new life; it has become a fluid ever-moving search for best employment opportunities.

The 2001 census revealed that Britain's minority ethnic population stood at 4.6 million or 7.9 per cent of the total population as opposed to 6 per cent in 1991. Half this minority ethnic population were of Asian origin while other ethnic groups were mainly black (Caribbean or African). People of mixed race accounted for 15 per cent of the total minority population. Nearly half of all minorities lived in the London area and one in three Londoners claimed to belong to an ethnic group.

THE NEEDS OF THE ECONOMY AND BUSINESS ATTITUDES

In 2005 the British economy was growing at the rate of 2.75 per cent and that was sufficient to allow it to employ most of the people already in the country and to provide jobs for immigrants from as far afield as Australia, Poland or Nigeria. Australia's largest expatriate community of 370,000 was in Britain and 87 per cent of them were employed. From the point of view of business, migrants keep down wage pressures and inflation, so they are welcome.

Academic researchers from University College London examined migration trends since the Second World War and compared them with economic trends in a number of nations, including Britain. They argued that much large-scale immigration into Europe and between European nations was driven by labour shortages and came to the conclusion: 'An economy embedded in a competitive international market can always expand production, absorbing new workers by creating new jobs.' Although migrants could depress wages for the lower skilled, this was temporary. Interestingly, considering the claims of anti-immigration groups that Britain had too many migrants, they found that while 8.3 per cent of the British population were foreign-born, the figure for France was 10 per cent, for the Netherlands 10.1 per cent, for Germany 11.1 per cent and for the United States 12.3 per cent. They argued that European nations 'vastly over-estimate the true size of the number of immigrants and the foreign-born population'. They point out: 'It is likely that residents' perception of immigration is more important for policy than evidence that has been established by social scientists.'

In this case, however, their findings were welcomed by the government. A Home Office spokesman said: 'Tourists, students and migrant workers make an important contribution to the UK economy. We cannot simply be a "Fortress Britain" if our businesses and economy are to grow and thrive.'

Statistics bore out the need for immigrants across a range of occupations. Thus, one-third of the 212,000 doctors on the medical register qualified overseas, while of 20,000 nurses who joined the register in 2003–4 more than 15,000 were from overseas. Home Office figures showed that the annual number of work permits issued to health care staff from outside the EU had risen 27-fold since 1993, to more than 40,000 and that most of them came from the developing world, with the Philippines and South Africa the leading sources. The education system also depended upon staff from overseas. In 2003, for example, 5,560 work permits were issued to people from Commonwealth countries to work as teachers.

Britain had become a magnet for hard-working people from the new EU member states. However, there was also a dark side to the immigration saga, as scandals revealed how some foreign workers were forced to pay premiums for jobs and compelled to work long hours for appallingly low pay.

The positive impact of migrants upon the British economy led one organisation, Business for New Europe Group (BNEG), to call upon the government to keep an open door for immigrants, arguing that further migration was 'cause for celebration, not cowardice'. In the years 2005 and 2006 immigration contributed between 0.5 to 1 per cent to the country's economic growth. As Ronald Rudd, chairman of BNEG, said:

> As well as Polish plumbers and property investors, the UK economy benefits from Hungarians in hospitality, Estonian engineers, Czech caterers and Slovakian scientists. This is because of our open labour markets following the EU enlargement of 2004. We have reaped the reward of this approach. We should abandon it at our peril.

At the same time (August 2006) the National Farmers' Union said that its members were dependent upon as many as 70,000 migrant workers to bring in the harvest. Representatives of industry, health care, education, the armed forces, arts, science and sport paid tribute to the contributions in these fields made by immigrants. Government figures produced in 2007 suggested that migration was throwing a lifeline to an economy that was suffering from skills shortages. With 574,000 migrants arriving and 385,000 people leaving there was a net inflow of 189,000 to mid 2006. The migrants earned an average of £425 a week compared with British-born workers earning £395 a week. The contribution of migration to economic growth over the year came to £6 billion, with migrants contributing 10 per cent of revenue but only using 9.1 per cent of expenditure. The economy grew by 5.3 per cent over 2004 and 2005, and 0.9 per cent of that growth was attributable to immigration. Foreigners represented 12.5 per cent of the work force.

There has always been a partial readiness on the part of business to welcome immigrant labour since it helps to keep wages down and companies look to hire people from abroad rather than pay their existing staff a higher wage. Particular professions have come to depend increasingly upon immigrants as a source of new employees. Thus, in 2005 the majority of the 2,200 dentists entering the profession came from Eastern Europe, a figure that emphasised Britain's growing reliance upon workers from the EU. The National Health Service (NHS), the teaching profession or the transport system have all become deeply reliant upon immigrants to fill gaps. As Philip Hudson, chief horticultural adviser to the National Farmer's Union, says:

> The horticulture sector has always employed workers from outside these shores … A lot of businesses rely on these people to pick the harvest, and the harvest doesn't wait. It's ready, and it has to be delivered to customers. These people (immigrants) are absolutely vital. Without them, some businesses wouldn't be able to function at all.[7]

The BNEG called for a continued open-door policy for immigrants and criticised government ministers for equivocation in the face of 'scare stories' in the right-wing media about a flood of Bulgarian and Romanian migrants. 'The simple fact is that workers from other European countries come to the UK because there are jobs. It is a cause for support, not retrenchment.' The BNEG called on the government to be guided both by economic reason and by recent historical experience. The government, however, wanted managed immigration rather than an open-door policy. Roger Carr, the chairman of Centrica, said ministers could not pick and choose which elements of an open-market system they liked. 'It is essential to harvest the upside and manage the downside on the side of market freedom not protectionism.'[8] This strong business support for immigration came prior to the recession that would alter a number of perspectives as it led to increasing unemployment in Britain and the EU. Certainly, the statistics of 2006 supported those who argued for immigration and of these the most interesting figure related to the 80 per cent of new migrants who were working people between the ages of 18 and 35, who offset the tendency for the country's population to age, addressing the difficulties in providing for an ageing population.

However, through 2008 Britain appeared to be losing its allure for migrant workers, as the recession began to bite. Official figures showed that the number of new arrivals from Eastern Europe had fallen by 16 per cent in the first three months of the year and applications for National Insurance numbers from foreign workers had dropped by a quarter. During the boom of the decade to 2008, migrants helped keep the lid on inflation by filling key gaps in the labour market and preventing a surge in wages. In the face of recession, immigrants could provide a different safety valve by leaving the country rather than competing for increasingly scarce jobs. This attitude illustrates perfectly the fact that much migration is economic: migrants go where the jobs are.

One of the most controversial aspects of immigration is the deliberate poaching of much-needed professional staff – especially doctors, nurses and teachers – from developing countries that can ill afford to lose their services. However, at the beginning of September in 2004 the British government entered into an agreement with representatives of more than 20 African and Caribbean Commonwealth countries to stop recruiting their teaching staff, and in the process denuding their schools of qualified staff. In 2003, for example, Britain had recruited more than 5,500 teachers from Commonwealth countries, the largest number (1,492) from South Africa. Four other countries lost substantial numbers of teachers poached in this way: Jamaica (523), Zimbabwe (268), Ghana (126) and Kenya (116). As the general secretary of the National Union of Teachers, Steve Sinnott said: 'They have no regard to the impact of their recruitment on vulnerable education systems.' There are 110 million children around the world who do not receive any schooling, 85 million of them in the Commonwealth where most of the poaching takes place.

Despite this agreement large numbers of Commonwealth teachers continued to come to Britain, often recruited by private agencies or voluntarily coming to obtain higher salaries. One suggestion was that Britain should provide such teachers with extra training so as to improve the teaching in their own countries when they returned.

A similar story applies to the thousands of nurses recruited overseas to service the NHS. Ironically, having been recruited, overseas nurses have often been poorly treated and undervalued compared with their British colleagues so that a poll found that four in ten wanted to leave. The King's Fund and the Royal College of Nursing carried out a poll and published a report which found that London hospitals were 'exploiting' overseas nurses by placing them in poorly paid, low-grade jobs, despite their qualifications and experience. The sources of the largest groups of nurses were the Philippines, India, South Africa and Australia. Although the NHS was banned from poaching doctors and nurses from developing countries in 1999, and this ban was widened to include private agency hiring in 2001, the number of doctors from Ghana more than doubled over the period 1999 to 2005. Ghana has 2,000 doctors for 20 million people, while Britain, with three times the population, has 60 times more doctors. Ghana has been losing or exporting on a yearly basis more nurses than it can train, while between 2001 and 2004 there was a steady rise in the number of Ghanaian doctors coming to Britain. Of course, a proportion of these doctors came voluntarily, but Britain has been lax in its application of the agreements about poaching skills from developing countries.

> In Canada, New Zealand, the United Kingdom and the United States, a quarter or more of all physicians had been imported from other countries. On average one in four doctors and one nurse in 20 trained in Africa is working in OECD countries.[9]

In 2005 the British NGO Save the Children and the charity Medact estimated that Britain saved £65 million in training costs for doctors and £38 million for nurses it had taken from Ghana alone since 1999. Such poaching of professionals may be a cheap way of meeting requirements in Britain's teaching and health services, but it represents a huge loss to the developing countries from which they come.

REFUGEES AND ASYLUM SEEKERS

By 2007 Britain's immigration laws had become complex and confusing, but when the government announced its intention of replacing them with a 'single, consistent and coherent framework' it aroused fears that it might use its new bill to bring in hard-line policies by stealth. The 1971 Act, which owed its genesis to Enoch Powell's 1968 'rivers of blood' speech, had imposed strict controls on settlement in Britain. However, over the succeeding years 10 further Acts and 30 statutory instruments or minor laws had followed so that the Home Office was obliged to admit that it was not always easy to know the exact legal position over particular issues, with the result that foreigners found it difficult to know their rights. By 2007 immigration had become one of the most divisive political issues in the country.

Following the US-led invasion of Iraq in 2003 some 2 million Iraqis fled their homeland, yet up to mid 2007 only 9,000 had claimed asylum in Britain and only 1,305 Iraqi asylum seekers landed in Britain in 2006, as opposed to 8,950 who arrived in Sweden, 2,765 in the Netherlands, 2,065 in Germany and 1,415 in Greece. Britain rejected 88 per cent of asylum applications in 2006, with 12 per cent either being granted asylum or discretionary leave to remain. More Iraqis were being returned to their country than were arriving. As Donna Covey, the chief executive of the Refugee Council said:

> Along with the rest of the international community, the United Kingdom has a responsibility to refugees displaced by the conflict in Iraq and we are not living up to that responsibility. The scale of the refugee crisis is growing and is now so acute that a change in policy towards Iraqi refugees is surely now imperative.

As with so many refugee crises, the longer they last and the greater the numbers involved, the harsher becomes the response. Britain's uncompromising attitude to Iraqi refugees was followed by the Netherlands and Germany while Greece refused all applications. By contrast, Sweden allowed more than 90 per cent, with the result that it received almost half of Europe's Iraqi asylum seekers. As the European director of the UNHCR, Pirkko Kourula, said: 'Given the seriousness of the situation in Iraq, one would certainly expect a much higher recognition rate for refugees from that country.' And given Britain's role in Iraq it ought to have been the foremost country in assisting refugees.

Proposed changes to immigration laws in 2008 could lead to legitimate claims for asylum being blocked for up to a decade. The new rules would mean that anyone deported from Britain would be barred from claiming asylum in the country for the succeeding ten years. The changes had obvious implications for Zimbabwean asylum seekers living in Britain. Implementation of the changes was postponed from April to October so as to encourage people to leave voluntarily. The government's determination to refuse as many applications as possible was in direct contravention of its duty to aid those fleeing persecution. At this time its duty applied especially to the thousands of Zimbabweans who had come to Britain to escape persecution under the Robert Mugabe regime. Britain is a signatory to the Refugee Convention and as such has an obligation to protect people who are fleeing for their lives.

In mid 2009 the UNHCR decided to establish a full-time presence in Calais to help migrants, refugees and asylum seekers negotiate the French and British immigration systems. The focus would be upon helping those who want to request asylum in France. Part of the UNHCR initiative is designed to protect migrants and asylum seekers from the misinformation given them by traffickers. It was estimated that 1,600 people were camped outside Calais, one-fifth of them children. This was a very different situation from the Sangatte camp, which saw 68,000 people pass through it between 1998 and 2002, when it was closed. Nonetheless, conditions in the camps are squalid, with few basic amenities, and they have to accommodate refugees from Afghanistan, Somalia, Pakistan, Eritrea and elsewhere, many of whom believe that their chance of a better future is to be found in Britain, if they can get there. The French people of Calais – though some show great sympathy and provide help and food – believe that the presence of the refugees deters people from visiting the port and town and they blame Britain for not doing enough to discourage asylum seekers. Many of the asylum seekers believe they have a genuine claim upon Britain because, for example, Afghans and Iraqis worked for the British in those countries during the wars and would not be safe back at home. Many are well educated and would bring welcome expertise to the country in which they settle. The problem is a huge one. In 2008 nearly 20,000 illegal attempts to enter Britain were prevented by the UK Border Authority in Calais. According to Phil Woolas, Britain's then border and immigration minister:

Last year alone, UK Border Agency staff at our French and Belgian controls not only searched more than one million lorries but also stopped 28,000 attempts to cross the Channel illegally. The illegal migrants in France are not queuing to get into Britain – they have been locked out.[10]

British efforts to keep asylum seekers out are often imbued with obviously racist attitudes and these can surface only too quickly where immigration is concerned. In 2004 Britain was judged to have discriminated against Gypsies trying to escape persecution in the Czech Republic. A panel of law lords ruled that, although a group of Roma were in fear of persecution in the Czech Republic, Britain in the summer of 2001 had deliberately blocked them flying to Britain as part of a Home Office initiative to cut asylum claims by preventing people, in this case mainly Roma, from boarding flights to Britain from the Czech capital of Prague. The civil rights group Liberty said the ruling exposed 'racism at the heart of the Government's asylum policy'. This and other similar actions have convinced lawyers and civil rights groups that Britain's record had become the worst in Europe. Britain is the only EU country to have opted out of the European Convention on Human Rights in order to detain foreign terror suspects indefinitely under new powers granted in emergency legislation following the 11 September 2001 attacks in the United States.

On 7 February 2005 the then Home Secretary Charles Clarke published a five-year strategy for the comprehensive reform of immigration and political asylum policy intended to ensure that inward migration provided long-term economic and social benefits for Britain. However, his proposals were seen as an attempt to pre-empt Conservatives from benefiting from public concern at immigrant influx. Called 'Controlling Our Borders: Making Migration Work for Britain' the strategy combined proposals to simplify beneficial legal immigration with robust measures to combat illegal entry and unfounded asylum applications. A 'transparent points system' would determine who should be permitted to work in the UK and only skilled workers would be granted permanent settlement, with low-skilled migration being phased out. A House of Lords ruling laid down that asylum should be granted to a person who was suspected in his own country of having committed terrorist acts and who had consequently been subjected to extreme torture. In 2006 the government announced a scheme under which rejected asylum seekers would be offered up to £3,000 each to return home voluntarily. Tony McNulty, the immigration minister, insisted that the scheme represented good value compared with the average £11,000 that it cost to remove an asylum seeker forcibly. He predicted that the scheme could boost the number of voluntary returns of asylum seekers from 300 a month to 500. In 2006 Britain received the third highest number of asylum seekers – 9 per cent worldwide – after France and the United States. The highest number of applicants for asylum in Britain in 2005 were: Iran (3,480), Pakistan (2,260), Somalia (2,100), Eritrea (1,890), Afghanistan (1,775), China (1,760), Iraq (1,605), Zimbabwe (1,355), Democratic Republic of Congo (1,390) and Nigeria (1,155).[11] About 3,000 unaccompanied children arrive in Britain to seek asylum every year. They are the most vulnerable of all immigrants. The abuse of asylum seekers is also routine. Thus, the law forbids them from working while their claims are processed. This condemns them to poverty and a meagre existence on benefits. This is both cruel and a waste since many of them possess skills that Britain could use. At the beginning of 2008 the National Audit Office estimated that there were between 155,000 and 283,500 refused asylum seekers in the country. Many were destitute, others in detention centres pending deportation. Britain detains more asylum seekers than any other European country and for a longer time. It is also the only European country that detains children. Periodically, while pursuing illiberal policies, politicians and others refer to Britain's 'proud tradition' of offering refuge to those in fear of persecution, as if such an assertion justifies actions that cannot be justified. However, in December 2008 a landmark legal ruling paved the way for thousands of asylum seekers in the country to be allowed to work. The High Court ruled that the existing laws, which prevented an Eritrean asylum seeker from taking a job, were incompatible with the European Convention on Human Rights.

Much of the debate about which immigrants should be allowed into Britain centres upon the differential between skilled and unskilled applicants. Ministers in Britain appear determined to establish an elaborate points system for migrants under which those who can notch up the largest score are most likely to get in. Such a system ignores the market, which in general is far better suited to deciding what it needs, and this includes unskilled workers, many of whom were crucial to the booming conditions that preceded the recession. The unskilled in fact have contributed as much as the 'scientists and entrepreneurs', who are the most favoured immigrant group under the new system. Too often, government measures to limit immigration are designed to placate those who want to stop immigration altogether. Liam Byrne, the Home Office Minister, contributed to a pamphlet in which he argued that although immigration had made Britain richer, it had also 'deeply unsettled the country' and was 'damaging' some of Britain's poorest communities.[12] There is a pattern in the approach of those who would limit immigration: first, to parade their liberal credentials, they say how much immigrants have contributed to the economy and then, as in the case of Byrne above, talk about unsettling or damaging the country. Immigrants do nothing of the kind; it is the extremists with their racist and often brutal propaganda who do the damage. Immigrants make easy scapegoats and very few politicians have the courage to speak out on their behalf.

FORCES OPPOSED TO IMMIGRATION

Alistair McConochie, in an article for Migration Watch UK, advances a well-reasoned argument against migration. He begins by asking why economics alone should be the criterion for allowing immigration and says we should also consider the impact migrants have upon national resources, population levels, the environment, levels of congestion, levels of crime and violence, health, language, infrastructure, schools and housing, culture and ethnicity. All these factors, he argues, have political and social consequences. He is perfectly correct but he leaves the list hanging in the air, as it were, and does not add that immigrant impact upon these various factors can be positive as well as negative. McConochie then advances a much more interesting argument: if we admit migrants because of their energy, talent and skills, we are depriving their country of origin of these same qualities. As a result, such a loss will prolong the poverty and underdevelopment of the sending country. Therefore, he argues, it is both irresponsible and immoral to deprive countries of their most educated and skilled personnel. British policy, he suggests, should be based on helping people achieve a decent standard of living, where they live, in order that they do not have to migrate for economic purposes. He proposes that those who oppose migration should advocate cancellation of international debts, localised economic policies, national economic freedom from the IMF, World Bank and World Trade Organization (WTO), proposals that he hopes will enlist the aid lobby to his cause. At the same time the right of every people and nation to have absolute control over their borders (over any form of immigration) should be acknowledged. One is entitled to ask at this point whether he would agree that British citizens have an absolute right, if they choose, to emigrate?

On the other hand, a report of the Work Foundation think tank claims that widespread public hostility to immigration threatens to undermine efforts to attract skilled foreign workers into Britain. The Foundation warns that recruitment problems are growing for specialised computer, science and health care firms, and that a lack of skilled employees would deter multinational companies moving to Britain. Katerina Rudiger, the author of the report, said:

The UK needs to be seen ... as being among the most open and attractive places for highly skilled people to want to move. At present, despite the hype, numbers are relatively low – only 167,000 high-skilled workers came to this country on official figures from 2005. Politicians need to actively make the case for highly skilled migration.

The report concludes:

The UK is not sufficiently tapping into the global supply of labour to an extent that it would enhance its competitiveness ... A good example is the biomedical and pharmaceutical sector, an industry in which the UK was seen as having a comparative advantage, but which is now facing severe problems connected to the availability of skills.

Racism, which usually means opposition to immigrants who are not white, is a factor that cannot be ignored. At one of the most basic levels it is being defeated, as a report commissioned by the Institute for Social and Economic Research has described a Britain in which people of Caribbean, black African, Chinese, Indian and white British heritage are far more likely to fall in love, marry and have children with people of different races – while the vast majority of their mixed race children will go on to enter relationships with people of yet another ethnic background.[13] The author of the report, Lucinda Platt, says: 'There will be an increasing number of children with some Caribbean origin, but fewer who will be categorically Caribbean. That group is likely to almost disappear.' Intermarriage is a process that in the end defeats racism.

Since 1945, to go back no further, Britain has witnessed a steady influx of immigrants, many from the new states that have emerged out of the disappearing British Empire. This influx has included East African Asians, Hong Kong Chinese, Greek and Turkish Cypriots, people from the Caribbean, Africa and the Indian subcontinent – that is Indians, Pakistanis and Bangladeshis – Vietnamese, Arabs, Iranians, South Americans, Afghans, Iraqis, East Europeans.

It is possible to pinpoint major political events according to the different incomings: the 1948 *Empire Windrush* heralded the Caribbean influx, Ugandan Asians marked the nationalist exclusiveness of Idi Amin, the Iranian influx followed the 1979 revolution that turned Iran into an Islamic state, Afghans and Iraqis fled the twenty-first-century wars in their countries. Each new influx has met with racist hostility, usually disguised under a well-known list of objections: there are too many to absorb, they are taking our jobs, they are jumping the housing queue, they cannot speak English. Yet, despite such objections, they continue to come and are gradually integrated into British society.

To parallel these influxes there has been a political-legal struggle to outlaw racial discrimination. The 1965 Race Relations Act began a long process of outlawing racial discrimination though it did not cover housing or employment. In 1976 the Commission for Racial Equality was established to examine racial discrimination and promote equality of opportunity. Lord Scarman's report on the Brixton riots of the early 1980s pinpointed the iniquities of policing in London, what later came to be described as institutional racism, a practice that is not confined to the police.

Despite the persistence of racism, however, and the struggle to combat it, the 2001 census showed that Britain has one of the fastest growing mixed race populations in the world. And that does represent an achievement.

Terrorism opened another dimension in perceptions of immigrants. The London bombings of 7 July 2005 were a watershed for at least a sizeable part of the population. Part of the problem was disenchantment by Pakistanis and other Muslims with British foreign policy in the Middle East and especially Iraq. Of the 1 million plus Muslims in Britain, 45 per cent were Pakistanis and many of their young people were clearly losing faith in mainstream politics. Senior Muslims, who were appointed by the then Home Secretary Charles Clarke to investigate the causes of the attacks in which 52 people died, warned him that his anti-terror legislation could prove counter-productive and concluded: 'British foreign policy – especially in the Middle East – cannot be left unconsidered as a factor in the motivations of criminal radical extremists. We believe it is a key contributory factor.' They pointed out: 'Criticism of some British foreign policy should not be assumed to be disloyal. Peaceful disagreement is a sign of a healthy democracy. Dissent should not be conflated with "terrorism", "violence" or deemed inimical to British values.'[14] In 2006, Scotland Yard's Deputy Assistant Commissioner Peter Clarke, head of the Met's Anti-Terrorist Branch, defended Section 44 powers as an essential tool for the police. Yet in 2005 of 10,941 pedestrians who were stopped and searched only 177 were arrested.

Migrants have always been made scapegoats and their arrival in any country triggers xenophobia, no matter why they have come or what they contribute to the society. They will be regarded as a threat and maligned even when the economy is booming and they undertake jobs that no one else will touch. Migrants are not to blame when they are exploited by unscrupulous employers. In 2006, when the Confederation of British Industry was calling for a curb on immigration, the Trades Union Congress (TUC), to its credit, insisted that immigrants should be regarded as fellow employees. Popular reaction to immigration is not something politicians can or will ignore. The 2005 election revealed working-class fears of immigration and Michael Howard, then the leader of the Tory party, led a populist campaign that focused on the 'failure' of Labour's immigration policy. The British National Party doubled its share of the vote in the 112 seats it contested. However, politics being what it is, in 2006 Damian Green, the Tory spokesman on immigration, called for a more civilised debate on immigration and wrote in *The Observer* to say it was 'unfair and untrue' in the vast majority of cases to suggest that people were coming to Britain to gain from the welfare state. He said: 'We welcome immigration. It has enriched British society and widened the horizons of the whole British people to the rest of the world. It brings economic benefits and cultural diversity.'[15]

Yet from 2006 through to 2009, by which time the recession was biting, there had developed a sort of bidding war between the political parties to show which was toughest on immigration. The prospect of Bulgarians and Romanians coming in large numbers to Britain led the *Sunday Express* to warn of Romania's 'HIV Children Bringing Time-bomb to Britain', while *The Sun* claimed that British workers had already lost half their wages as a result of Eastern European migration, and the *Daily Star* warned 'Immigrants to Flood In'. By 2007 immigration had become the preoccupation of both main parties and one of the three top issues that most affected the electorate. However, as *The Observer* pointed out: 'Millions of Britons take up the freedom to live and work abroad; there are more Britons living abroad today than there are non-UK citizens living here. We should never lightly deny the freedom of movement to others that we so fully enjoy ourselves.'[16]

POPULATION

Immigrants over recent years have accounted for more than half Britain's population growth, and people entering Britain from outside Europe and the Commonwealth outstrip other migrants. Figures based on the 1991 and 2001 censuses show that immigrant communities account for 7.9 per cent of the population. Among the immigrants responsible for the increasing diversity of 'rainbow Britain', according to research by the Institute of Public Policy Research, the largest groups came from India and Pakistan, followed by Germany, the Caribbean and the United States while there were increased numbers coming from former Yugoslavia, Sierra Leone, South Africa, China and Sweden. One in four Londoners had been born abroad and many groups entering Britain produced a large proportion of people in top pay brackets, earning at least £750 a week, although others suffered high levels of unemployment. Nearly 20 per cent of people born in India were classified as high earners as were 13 per cent of people from Nigeria. The London suburb of Wembley is the first area in Britain where the majority of the population (Indians) are immigrants.

According to the UN, Britain will become one of the major destinations for migrants as the world heats up. On average more than 174,000 people will be added to the British population every year for the next four decades and by 2050 only the United States and Canada will be receiving more immigrants than Britain. Another ongoing debate concerns the strains such extra numbers would place upon housing, water supplies and transport. Moreover, demographers point out that by 2050 a third of the population will be over 60. Total world population in 2050 is predicted to reach 9.2 billion, while Britain will have increased from its current 61 million to 71 million; Germany, by comparison, will have slumped from 82 million to 71 million. Sustainability has become the new catchword and, according to Professor Aubrey Manning of Edinburgh University:

> There are far too many people living in Britain already. Once our population passed the 20 million level around 1850, it became too numerous. That is the figure at which we could no longer sustain our population from our own resources. We are now three times over the limit and heading for more. We have long passed the line of sustainability. As for the planet, its maximum sustainable population is no more than 3 billion, I would say.[17]

In fact, the debate was less concerned with sustainability than with arguing against further immigration. James Lovelock, the environmentalist, argued that by the end of the present century the world's population would be suffering a calamitous decline until its numbers were reduced to about 1 billion. 'By 2100, pestilence, war and famine will have dealt with the majority of humans.'[18] Such gloomy predictions call to mind Maynard Keynes' remark that 'In the long term, we are all dead.'

7
France and Germany

The two core countries at the heart of the European experiment, France and Germany, have long dominated EU policies. Both are highly developed and wealthy by world standards, and both face difficult economic and social problems that are made more complex by the steady movement into Europe of migrants from many parts of the world. The constant pressure of immigrants into wealthy Europe may be seen as a paradigm of the relationship of the EU to the developing world, whose poverty provides the motor force for migration. How the EU faces the challenge of migration will determine how it develops a new relationship with the countries of the South.

For France, its present attitude to immigrants begins with the aftermath of the Algerian War (1954–62) when nearly a million *colons* (white settlers) returned to France to be followed by large numbers of Algerians who had supported the French colonial government. Their children and grandchildren, second- or third-generation French citizens, were at the centre of the violence that erupted in the outer suburbs of Paris in November 2005 and forced France to reassess its policy towards immigrants.

Much of the work force that ensured the success of the German economic miracle of the 1950s and 1960s consisted of immigrants from the poorer countries of southern Europe – Italy and Spain – but also the Turkish guest workers, who numbered 1.6 million by 1992. The presence of these Turkish guest workers created problems between the two countries over split families and never ending questions about visas. The immigrants from Turkey now form the majority of the country's Muslim minority. Acceptance, assimilation or integration of these minorities has a long way to go before either country can be comfortable with its new citizens.

FRANCE

In September 2004 France put into effect a law banning Islamic headscarves and other religious symbols from state schools. In part, the move was an assertion of the secular nature of the French state, but it was also an expression of its unease at the presence on French soil of several million immigrants from Muslim countries. At the end of October and through the first half of November 2005, France faced a violent outbreak of rioting in the greater Paris area – the suburbs where the immigrants or their descendants live, where there is little available work nor any promise of the situation changing – to be copied in many cities across the country. The violence – involving gangs of youths burning cars and buildings – spread like a bush fire to other poor suburbs. The motives of the rioters appeared to be a mix of anger against the police and the perceived racism against Arabs and black people on the part of French society. The riots began in Clichy-sous-Bois in the northeast of Paris after two teenage boys were electrocuted in a power station into which they had climbed in an attempt to escape a police identity check. It was never clear exactly what had happened between the boys and the police but friends of the boys insisted that the police knew that the boys were in mortal danger but did nothing to help them. Local anger was increased by a government statement, later withdrawn, that the boys had been involved in a burglary. As the subsequent rioting spread, tempers were further inflamed by the Interior Minister, Nicolas Sarkozy, describing all young people in poor suburbs as 'scum'. After eight days of rioting, with no end in sight, hundreds of cars had been burnt. The riots were not specifically racist-inspired but rather about the huge gap between France's 'haves' and 'have-nots', the latter comprising a high proportion of immigrants or their descendants. As Ziad, the ringleader of a group of young men, said: 'It's hard to just sit here and watch the rich people driving past in their swanky vehicles. They have everything and we have absolutely nothing.'

Beyond the Paris ring-road (the Périphérique) to the north, east and south, there is a different world of 'tower blocks, sink schools, 20 per cent unemployment, violent youth gangs, police brutality and – it should be said – many people trying their best to make a living and keep their children out of trouble'.[1] By the end of the first week of rioting some 2,000 vehicles had been destroyed. As John Lichfield went on to ask, 'Why such violence? Why such blind destruction of the painfully acquired property of equally poor neighbours?' Those taking part in the riots represented the ethnic mix of the *banlieues* – 50 per cent were of Arab or African origin, 30 per cent black, and the remainder either poor French or European immigrants – but the riots themselves were not about race but exclusion. Of five youths put on trial for rioting, two were of Arab origin, while three were white and of these one was Italian. Only one of the five had not been born in France. A majority of the different gang members were educational drop-outs, unemployed or from fatherless homes. The government insisted it would stand firm against the violence, which was described as the worst civil unrest since 1968. By the end of the first week similar rioting was reported from cities all over France, many normally known for their calm. Cities as far apart as Nantes, Lille, Rennes, Saint-Dizier, Strasbourg and Toulouse were infected by the unrest. While the Prime Minister Dominique de Villepin was presiding over a crisis meeting of his cabinet, hundreds of people joined marches in Paris to protest against the violence carrying banners, which read 'No to violence' and 'Yes to dialogue'.

The question of integration lay at the heart of this confrontation.

French integration policies have been based around the republican tenet of secularism. On the basis that France should be indivisible and able to assimilate all its components by officially erasing their particularities, the government does not allow official statistics to be broken down by ethnicity and religion.[2]

The policy had clearly not worked. Thus, in an age of Islamic militancy, France found it had a large minority of Muslims whose religious particularity was not to be assimilated. Moreover, adding to the crisis, a high proportion of these Muslims were found to be ill-educated, jobless, and ignored by both government and 'wealthy' French citizens who either did not want to know about the immigrants in the *banlieues* or looked upon them as undesirable enemies.

A French immigration specialist, Christophe Bertossian, wanted a rethink of policy towards immigrants: 'Part of the problem is the French approach to integration, based on the concept that everyone is equal. The idea that we are equal is fiction. Ethnic minorities keep being told they do not exist.'[3] In the Seine-Saint-Denis quarter of Paris, with a population of 1.3 million, a third of the population are Muslim, more than half the population receive some sort of family benefit, more than 30 per cent live below the poverty threshold (€590 a month), 63 per cent of residents live in state accommodation/council flats, 28 per cent of the population are under 20, unemployment is 4 per cent above the national average of 10.1 per cent and the number of job seekers not from the EU is three times the national average. This represents a formidable list of handicaps and this deprived, resentful society of supposedly equal French citizens has grown up in the heart of France's capital under the blind eyes of successive governments that have simply not wanted to know.

Mary Dejevsky, like other commentators, refers to these deprived communities of the *banlieues* as 'the France that is marooned between town and country, shut away behind ugly concrete walls, confined inside rotting tower blocks: the France of the *cités*, the *banlieues* and the *quartiers sensibles* or *difficiles*. The France that has failed.'[4] She continues:

The truth is that these vast estates that surround most of France's cities and towns have been the obverse of France's agreeable reputation for quality of life for two decades or more. They have been convenient repositories for all those who could not, or would not, join the French mainstream: the poor, certainly – but mostly first-, second- and now third-generation immigrants.

The *quartiers sensibles* or *difficiles* for mainstream France refer only to places populated largely by immigrants and their offspring. Clearly, the French model for integration has failed and France has yet to decide what to do about it. France rejected the American model of the 'melting pot' and the British one of tolerance for the customs of ethnic minorities, instead acting as though race, creed or colour would destroy the France of Liberty, Equality and Fraternity. In fact, these three revolutionary principles have never been applied to the immigrants.

Sarkozy, demonstrating a ruthless streak that made him many enemies but also appealed to the hard political right, ordered the expulsion from France of all foreigners convicted over two weeks of rioting. He told French deputies that he had asked prefects to expel the 120 foreigners convicted of rioting, including those whose papers were in order. Human rights organisations denounced the measures as applying a double penalty against rioters. Of the 2,800 youths who had been arrested only 120 were not born in France. However, taking the opportunity to apportion responsibility in a speech to the National Assembly, Sarkozy implicitly blamed President Chirac and the whole French political system for allowing economic and social problems to accumulate over 30 years. Chirac's response to weeks of crisis was to suggest that the violence and unrest could be connected to France's generous laws on 'family' immigration. No political leader came out of the crisis well. When, after 20 successive nights of rioting, calm was restored, the damage was assessed: 9,000 vehicles had been burnt, 80 schools destroyed as well as many business premises, while 126 policemen had been injured. The bulk of the rioters had been young men whose parents or grandparents had come from Algeria, Morocco and black territories further south, virtually all from the former French Empire. They had at least succeeded in making themselves heard, though tragically only by violence. On the other side, the government had said and done nothing throughout the crisis that had any impact or effect. Perhaps the time had come for France to copy the United Sates and resort to affirmative action on behalf of these deprived members of their society. By the end of November the Prime Minister de Villepin was announcing plans to restrict the reunification of immigrant families and to impose tighter selection rules upon foreign students from outside the EU. Such harsh and retributive measures were not calculated to heal the breach. Opponents of the measures said the riots had not been caused by the current level of immigration but by the failure of the French state and society to absorb the second and third generations of the immigrant influx of the 1960s and 1970s.

In Calais, just prior to Christmas 2005, the contrast between British day visitors who had crossed the Channel to stock up with drink and the 'shadows' (the name given to the illegal immigrants waiting for their chance to cross to Britain) could hardly have been more stark. The latter, 250 young men and four young women, form an orderly queue to obtain their one warm meal of the day, a stew served by four elderly women volunteers. It is a night when the police have held a periodic purge of the *sans papiers*, while others are absent from the queue for food as they have gone to attempt to board one of the Dover-bound trucks.[5] The Calais scene provides a window onto part of the huge international saga of immigration. There are the immigrants, hoping to get across the Channel to Britain, who come from many countries – Afghanistan, Pakistan, Eritrea, Iran, Sudan and elsewhere – all far from France or Britain. There are the French volunteers who, in simple humanity, provide clothes and a daily meal for these desperate asylum seekers. There are the police and border guards: the French want to get them out, the British don't want to let them in. Many appear to have a simple belief that if they can only get to England that will solve their problems. And behind the public scene are the criminal gangs that help, mislead or rob the immigrants, a growth industry that preys upon desperation. The roles of the various players can be replicated in many other places round Europe which, against its collective will, is targeted by asylum seekers and immigrants from Asia and Africa.

Perhaps the year 2005 will act as a watershed in French perceptions of its immigrant problem. President Chirac acknowledged the 'lack of dialogue' between the government and the authorities and the largely immigrant populations who lived in France's sink estates, and thereby recognised how the riots had revealed a 'deep malaise' in French society. One immediate result of the riots was the announcement by the government of a 'social cohesion' programme to include more housing, more apprenticeships and scholarships, and the creation of development zones in the affected areas. Such a programme, however, will take years to materialise. On the other hand, pressure from right-wingers led Prime Minister de Villepin to announce new restrictions upon immigrants that would take immediate effect. The government would also make it more difficult to win the right to come to France, or become French by marrying a French citizen. Such marriages had risen to 34,000 a year during the preceding decade to become the biggest single source of immigration. The prime minister also called for tougher enforcement of French laws against polygamy. Left-wing politicians and humanitarian workers challenged these measures, pointing out that only 120 of the people arrested during the riots were born outside France. At least the riots had shaken the accepted wisdom about how France incorporated immigrants into its society. The prevailing expectation that immigrants would integrate into French society on their own and accept traditional republican values had clearly not been borne out. On the contrary, the immigrant communities had experienced discrimination and dismissal. In addition, they had cultures that were resistant to assimilation.

By 2005 France had an estimated 5 million mainly Muslim immigrants or second- or third-generation descendants who presented the country with a major problem since, having arrived, immigrants were expected to be French even if no further interest had been shown in their welfare in terms of education, housing and employment. Unfortunately, the reaction to the events of 2005 was almost entirely restrictive or negative. Nicolas Sarkozy, in his role as Minister of the Interior took a generally harsh line towards immigrants and further immigration. He introduced a policy of 'selective immigration' that discriminated in favour of workers with skills identified as important to France while making it more difficult for family members to join these selected immigrants and requiring them to sign an 'integration contract' that committed them to respect 'the French way of life'. Moreover, they would not automatically be eligible for permanent residence after living in France for ten years. During 2006 Sarkozy oversaw the expulsion of 25,000 undocumented immigrants. Opposition to these expulsions by teachers, parents, and humanitarian organisations forced him to agree that most families with children in school would be spared. In 2006, the anniversary of the November 2005 disturbances passed peacefully with only a few limited disturbances, but in December the National Assembly adopted a bill, supported by Sarkozy, which brought in tougher punishments for young offenders. No measures offering more positive solutions to the problems of the immigrant minority were advanced in the National Assembly.

New legislation in 2007 was designed to tighten controls so that fewer immigrants would enter the country legally. It included a controversial provision for voluntary DNA testing for immigrants. Many protesters from different backgrounds demonstrated outside the National Assembly in September 2007 when the bill was being debated. One demonstrator, Majid Messoudene, was a Socialist Party official from the Seine-Saint-Denis region of Paris, whose parents had emigrated to France from Algeria in the 1960s. He said France had a tradition of immigration and he called this part of the country's wealth. Whether the government liked it or not, he said, France would remain a country of immigration.[6] Other African immigrants from former French colonies said they should be allowed to come to France to work. The government clampdown infuriated immigration rights activists. Mouloud Aounit, the head of the Movement Against Racism and for Friendship between Peoples, described the government as xenophobic. He said immigrants' rights should be respected and that France could not have immigration legislation that threatened fundamental liberties. But according to a poll published in Le Figaro, a majority of French people supported immigration quotas and favoured French language requirements for immigrants. While this 'debate' was in progress, the EU Justice Commissioner, Franco Frattini, made the point that the EU only drew about 5 per cent of the skilled foreign labour force compared with 55 per cent that went to the United States. Immigration specialists, however, argue that as more and more Europeans head towards retirement, the region will need all kinds of immigrants to fill labour shortages – including unskilled ones.[7] This was clearly not the view of the Sarkozy government after he won the 2007 presidential election. Thus, at the beginning of 2009, the immigration minister, Brice Hortefeux, applauded the fact that nearly 30,000 illegal immigrants had been deported in 2008.

France, with a long tradition of liberalism dating back to the revolution of 1789, was exhibiting narrow nationalist anti-immigration tendencies, ironically under a president who himself was the son of immigrants. The mood was in tune with possibly a majority of EU countries that were more in favour of a Fortress Europe policy than an open door one.

GERMANY

Following the end of the Second World War, a massive resettlement took place in Germany as Germans from Russia and East European countries moved back into the German heartland. By 1950, as a result of this movement, 15.7 per cent of West Germans and 19.6 per cent of East Germans were immigrants. A total of 11.5 million people entered what is now the Federal Republic of Germany. Even so, as a result of war losses and other disruptions, West Germany faced a shortage of labour needed for its reconstruction. Between 1955 and 1968 West Germany signed labour agreements with the southern

European Mediterranean and North African countries: Italy, Spain, Greece, Turkey, Morocco, Portugal, Tunisia and Yugoslavia. During this period the foreign population grew from half a million (0.9 per cent of the population) to 4 million (6.4 per cent). These 'guest workers' (*gastarbeiter*) were generally employed in low-skilled and labour-intensive jobs. The guest worker policy was scrapped in 1973 in the wake of the economic (Organization of Petroleum Exporting Countries – OPEC) crisis. Germany had come to see these guest workers as temporary and assumed that they would leave when there were no longer jobs for them to do. However, many of them decided to stay in Germany. The government subsequently made little effort to integrate them and did not recognise them as permanent members of German society. The result of this neglect (as in France) was that the former guest workers lived in poor neighbourhoods where they were forced to create their own subcultures. In most cases their education was limited, access to skilled work was difficult and any prospect of naturalisation was severely restricted. Thus, Germany saw the rise of parallel societies and, although overseas recruitment had stopped in 1973, migrants continued to arrive. They consisted of family members of the guest workers, a growing number of asylum seekers from Asia and ethnic Germans from Poland and Romania. In relative terms their numbers were not great: between 1973 and 1988 the number of immigrants rose from 4 million to 4.8 million. Again, as in France, Germany had difficulty in integrating the second generation of immigrants, mainly the Turks. In its determination to protect its job market, high standard of living and much admired social welfare system, Germany became one of the most reluctant countries in Europe to accept immigrants.

The end of the Cold War saw a new surge of immigration into Germany from East Europe; 1992 was the peak year, with 1.2 million arrivals of whom 438,000 were asylum seekers while others were fleeing conflicts in Africa, disintegrating Yugoslavia and the Turkish/Kurdish war. After 1991 there came an influx of Jews from Russia who wished to reconstruct Germany's former Jewish community. All these incomers qualified for housing and basic incomes, and these demands exerted huge pressures upon local or state governments in Germany's federal system. Reforms in 1993 reduced the number of asylum seekers by excluding any from other EU countries, attracted by social benefits rather than suffering oppression, and no asylum was extended to people coming from countries deemed to be 'safe'. At the same time, immigration was leading to a growth of racism from right-wing parties and other organisations. By 2006 the numbers seeking asylum had dropped to 21,000, the lowest figure since 1983.[8]

Following the collapse of the Berlin Wall, Germany became a magnet for Germans from the East as 2 million Germans from Russia and the former USSR moved to the West. Deeply committed to reunification, Germany took in many refugees or immigrants in the early 1990s. However, by the middle of the decade a reaction set in.

Germany had also responded to the collapse of Yugoslavia by receiving 350,000 Bosnians, on the understanding that they would return home when the war was over, as most of them had done by late 1998, though some had to be forcibly repatriated.[9] Even ethnic Germans from Eastern Europe faced restrictions when, in 1996, a language test and the requirement to prove that anti-German discrimination was applied to them in their country of origin. Between 1999 and 2002 the German Federal Parliament passed nationality and immigration acts, without reference to EU institutions, as sovereign laws.

By the beginning of the new century European attitudes towards immigration were becoming much more restrictive and, despite the general acceptance of expanding globalisation in terms of economic links, trade, investment and banking, few countries, it seemed, favoured the globalisation of people. In Germany many people were opposed to further immigration. Between 1950 and 2000 the proportion of foreigners in the population had risen from 1.1 per cent to 10 per cent, many of them (especially the large Turkish minority) dating back to the 'guest worker' period. Illogically, perhaps, tensions over immigration had increased as an extremely low national birth rate made immigration all the more necessary to maintain economic growth. According to the German Institute for Economic Research (DIW) an annual influx of 140,000 people would be required to offset the annual decrease in potential workers. Attitudes towards immigration were still affected by the old nationalist belief in blood ties as the prerequisite for citizenship so that a child of foreign descent born and raised in Germany is not automatically entitled to apply for citizenship. In regional elections politicians raised fears of job losses and advanced racial arguments against incomers. As the conservative vice-leader in the German parliament, Wolfgang Bosbach, argued: 'Concerning immigration the government goes too far, concerning integration not far enough. We don't want a multicultural society; we don't want more immigration.'[10] As Turkish community representatives and sympathetic politicians have long argued, the humiliating status of a 'foreigner' prevents minorities from identifying with German society and politics. 'Their marginalized status they hold breeds cynicism and isolated communities that are no longer connected by any kind of social consensus.'[11]

Despite many doubts and efforts to restrict immigration, Germany has become a country of immigration. Between 1954 and 2004, some 31 million people have moved into Germany and 22 million have left. Labour or economic migration has been officially banned since 1973 when Germany ended its guest worker programme. The result is a contradictory policy, for although the government officially denies third-country nationals entrance to the labour market, it allows for loopholes in the system. Thus in 2002, the Federal Agency for Employment reported that roughly 320,000 new work permits were issued to citizens from the Central and Eastern European Countries (before the Big Bang) under different temporary employment schemes. Part of the problem arises from the fact that, like other EU members, Germany has no coherent immigration policy; rather, over the years, it has reacted to specific problems and today a number of different ministries or government agencies have certain responsibilities while there is no central or overall control.

During 2005, two events demonstrated the negative aspects of German policy: the first concerned the illegal issue of visas, the second the racist treatment of the Roma. On 20 January 2005 a parliamentary inquiry was launched into allegations that German embassy personnel in Central and East European countries had approved large numbers of visa applications without proper checks. The inquiry was to examine whether officials 'made it possible or easier' for people engaged in 'the black economy, prostitution, women-trafficking, terrorism, and organised crime' to enter Germany. Figures published by the Interior Ministry on 23 January showed that applications for political asylum totalled 35,607 in 2004, a reduction of 29.6 per cent compared with 2003. The main countries of origin were Turkey, Serbia and Montenegro, Russia, Vietnam, Iran, Azerbaijan and Iraq. Meanwhile, the visa scandal continued, with entry to Germany being exploited by criminal gangs. In May it became clear that Germany was deporting thousands of Roma refugees to Kosovo, despite warnings from human rights groups that they would face massive discrimination on arrival. The first planeloads of deportees flew to Kosovo in mid May. All together 50,000 people were going to be sent back. The German government had decided to deport the Roma and other minority refugee groups in November 2004, when, at a meeting of state legislators, officials told the central government that the Roma were unwanted and should be deported as soon as possible, starting with those who were receiving welfare payments. Claude Cahn of the European Roma Rights Centre said the main motive for the mass deportation was anti-Gypsy racism. 'They don't want Gypsies, it's as simple as that. These people face massive discrimination, limits on their freedom of movement and residence rights.' The Roma had fled to Germany in 1999 when long-term antagonism between Serbs and ethnic Albanians developed into open warfare. In subsequent years members of other minorities, such as Albanians and Egyptians, had been able to return, but not the Roma.

Germany does not appear to have accepted the many predictions of the UN, the World Bank, the Organisation for Economic Co-operation and Development (OECD) and others that with a declining birth rate it needs immigrants to add to its work force if it is to maintain its economic growth and development. Although it ended the practice of seeking guest workers in 1973 and has subsequently been a reluctant recipient of immigrants, Germany cannot afford to lose people and yet that is what is happening. Figures released by the Federal Statistics Office in 2007 showed that in 2006 155,290 Germans emigrated. This was the highest number to do so since reunification in 1990 and equalled the levels achieved in the late 1940s in the aftermath of the Second World War. The statistics further revealed that the number of immigrants had declined steadily since 2001. Some leading economists and employers have warned that the trend is alarming. According to OECD figures, Germany is near the top of a league of industrial nations that is experiencing a brain drain and, for the first time since the 1950s, more people are leaving Germany than immigrants coming in. More than 18,000 Germans moved to Switzerland in 2006, 13,245 to the United States and

9,309 to Austria. The German minority in Switzerland is 170,000 strong and is viewed with mixed feelings, with Swiss nationals describing the Germans as 'arrogant and rude'. Many immigrants, however, say the benefits of lower taxes and much higher pay outweigh local xenophobia. One German, Claus Boche, living in Zurich, said: 'Nearly everything is less bureaucratic and more go-ahead than in Germany. I also pay about 40 per cent less tax. I have no plans to go back.'[12]

An OECD report of 2008 said bluntly that Germany needed to fix its immigration policy to match its future work force needs. In 2006 just 216,000 foreigners settled permanently in Germany, 11 per cent fewer than in 2005. This was in stark contrast to the number of permanent immigrants moving into the 30-country OECD region, which had risen by 5 per cent. In 2006 only Japan, Portugal, Finland and France had lower rates of permanent foreign immigration. The OECD estimated that if this trend continues, the number of employable people in Germany would shrink by 2.5 per cent by 2020. The work force is expected to grow in most other industrialised countries. The OECD urged Germany to update its immigration policy, target both skilled and unskilled immigrants and avoid short-term solutions. Demographic changes could result in a lack of workers in many sectors that cannot be covered by seasonal workers. It suggested that an immigration policy based on the concept of short-term stays by immigrants was neither efficient nor practical. In 2006, for example, Germany hosted 380,000 seasonal and temporary workers, nearly double the OECD average. Germany also lagged behind other states in recognising foreign diplomas and qualifications. Workers most frequently affected came from Eastern Europe. German authorities failed to translate both higher education and technical diplomas. The OECD suggested that practical examinations could stand for diplomas. Poles were the largest group of long-term immigrants in Germany, accounting for 27 per cent. They were followed by Turks (8 per cent), Romanians (4 per cent), and then Hungarians and Italians. At the same time, increasing numbers of Germans had emigrated to other OECD countries and formed some of the strongest migrant groups in Denmark, Luxemburg, the Netherlands, Austria, Poland and Switzerland.[13] The report suggests a country floundering uncertainly with regard to how it should tackle immigration and its long-term problem of a declining work force.

The Germans find the concept of being a country of immigration difficult to accept. Nonetheless, the citizenship reforms of 2000 standardised naturalisation and nationality was no longer to be based on blood ties. Children born with at least one parent living in Germany for a minimum of four years with a permanent residence permit automatically became German citizens. They would keep both German nationality and that of their parents until they were 18 to 23, during which time they had to choose one of the two nationalities. In 2006 124,566 people, mainly Turks, took German citizenship. In 2008 an obligatory citizenship test of language and knowledge of German culture and the constitution was introduced. By 2004, finally, a new Immigration Law recognised the need for foreign labour in order to address its demographic problems. Crucially, Germany had to recognise that immigration should not be treated as a temporary phenomenon and that immigrants had to be fully integrated into German society. It had taken a long time to reach this point.

In 2007, 6.74 million foreign nationals lived in Germany, mainly in former West Germany and the big cities, and they represented 8.9 per cent of the total population. There had grown up the discriminatory phrase 'persons of immigrant background' and in 2006 it was estimated that 15.1 million people or 18.4 per cent of the German population fell into this category. The biggest immigrant groups without citizenship were: Turks (1.7 million), Italians (541,000), Poles (327,000), Greeks (310,000) and Serbs (297,000). One in five foreigners (i.e. non-naturalised immigrants) were German-born, 70 per cent had been resident for at least eight years, two-thirds had a permanent residency permit.[14] In 2006, Germany, of all EU members, received the second largest share of foreigners after Spain, and came third in the number of naturalisations.

8
Spain, Italy, Malta and Greece

Spain, Italy, Malta and Greece form the southern tier of the European Union. They project far into the Mediterranean and act either as the entry points or the border guards to control the flow of desperate African migrants into the EU. The first decade of the twenty-first century has witnessed a constant movement of Africans crossing the Sahara through Libya or Morocco, or travelling on flimsy boats to the Canary Islands and thence to Spain. The reaction of the EU countries is a mixture of anger at numbers that represent a political burden and compassion for the migrants, who often arrive in a desperate state after perilous journeys that may have lasted for two years. The interface between the migrants and the Europeans is part of a wider interface between the developed North and the developing South.

SPAIN

Large-scale immigration, both legal and illegal from Latin America and Morocco, led to a rise in Spain's officially registered population as of 1 January 2003 by 879,170 to 42.7 million. The greater part of this increase, the largest in 30 years, was due to immigration since the natural population increase was just short of 50,000. Spain, with the lowest fertility rate in the EU of only 1.25 children for every women of childbearing age, found that the immigrant influx reversed the country's population decline. At the end of 2003 the number of immigrants living legally in Spain with residency permits was officially 1.6 million, three times higher than in 1996. Of considerable historical interest was the 're-conquest' of Spain by Muslims in July 2003, when they opened their first mosque in Granada, near the Alhambra. A year later, in July 2004, the foreign population in Spain was estimated at 3.1 million, equivalent to 7 per cent of the total population. This represented a huge rise from the figure of 165,000 in 1976 and was due, in the main, to the arrival of non-EU immigrants. Nearly half a million immigrants arrived in Spain during the first seven months of 2004 and Spain was then receiving one in every three migrants arriving in the EU. At the end of 2004 a new law allowed illegal immigrants who had been registered with their local town hall before 7 August for more than six months and who had a pre-contract job for at least six months (three for agricultural workers) to request residency permits as of 7 February 2005. The large influx of Moroccan immigrants and the involvement of Moroccan-Algerian radicals in the 11 March 2004 terror attacks led the government to examine ways of supervising mosques and imams in an effort to ensure that they were in moderate hands. Islam is Spain's second largest religion.

The Association for Human Rights in Andalusia claimed in January 2005 that 289 would-be immigrants had died in Spain or off Spain's coast in 2004, an increase over 2003 of 53 people. The government, however, had put the death toll lower at 141. The Association claimed that a new anti-immigration 'early warning' system was to blame, since it led immigrants to take longer and more dangerous sea routes in order to escape detection. Official figures released on 30 January revealed that the government was chartering aeroplanes to take immigrants without documents from the Canary Islands to mainland Spain where they were left in major cities to fend for themselves. According to international laws immigrants without documents who came from countries with which Spain did not have repatriation agreements could not be deported. By this time estimates suggested that between 800,000 and 1 million undocumented immigrants entered Spain each year. An amnesty for illegal immigrants was expected to legalise over 1 million during 2005 and they would then be liable to pay taxes and be eligible to benefit from workers' rights, but while the government claimed that the measures would meet Spain's demands for unskilled labour, opponents of the policy said the amnesty would encourage further immigration; and both France and Germany complained that because of freedom of movement across EU borders many of these immigrants would move out of Spain to their countries. By this time Fuerteventura in the Canary Islands, 56 miles from El Aioun on the African coast, had become the most important entry point for illegal immigrants into Europe. During 2004 the interior minister had chartered 227 flights to transport 7,920 *indocumentados* from the Canary Islands to mainland Spain. Each of these chartered flights cost €10,000. In most cases the immigrants arriving in the Canary Islands could not be expelled because they came from countries without a repatriation agreement with Spain (or they said they did) and without papers. Since they had committed no crime in Spain they must be freed after 40 days according to the law. They then seek work, sleep in the parks or under bridges, subsist on charity and risk 'marginalisation, prostitution and labour exploitation'. The government estimated that between 800,000 and 1 million *indocumentados*, mainly from Latin America and Morocco, arrived in Spain during 2004, while permits for immigrant workers were pegged at 30,000. The government tried to regularise the position of the 'illegals' by granting residence to those who had worked in the country for three years but this led to criticism from Germany and the Netherlands. They argued, 'If some countries are regularising "illegals", they cannot look just at their own situation because this decision could affect other countries.' The Dutch Immigration Minister, Rita Verdonk, said: 'We must discuss the consequences of such measures for other EU countries.'[1]

Ceuta and Melilla, Spain's two enclaves on Morocco's Mediterranean coast, have become target destinations for African migrants. Once inside them, they are on Spanish soil and can claim asylum. In September 2005, 500 desperate Africans tried to scale the wall of barbed wire entanglements that guarded

Melilla. It was the biggest attempt to that date to force entrance to the enclave. An estimated 270 ladders made from tree branches were employed and about a fifth of the immigrants did gain entry to the enclave before being detained by the police. About 19 people were slightly injured in the incident. These 500 represented an especially dramatic attempt by desperate immigrants to breach the walls of Fortress Europe. The attack on Melilla's defences came immediately after two Spanish secretaries of state had visited the 'walled' enclave. One of them, Consuelo Rumi, said Morocco was doing its best to stem the flow of illegal immigrants to Spain but that it faced problems of its own. 'Morocco today ... is a country which not only sends out immigrants but also receives immigration from sub-Saharan Africa.'

Another similar attempt was mounted a week later: the migrants clearly took the Spanish security forces – police reinforced with soldiers – by surprise. An attempt at Ceuta, the other enclave, resulted in five deaths. The government had thought the anti-immigrant fences were strong enough but, after scaling a three metre fence topped with razor wire the immigrants clambered up a second fence, twice as high, and ripped through the mesh while the massed weight of the immigrants brought down at least two 20 metre sections of the fence.[2] The outcome of these attempts to break into Melilla was an announcement by the Spanish government that immigrants who crashed the barriers would immediately be deported. A sixth mass attack on the barriers by 1,000 immigrants was repulsed by a massive security operation on both sides of the barrier, with Morocco cooperating with Spain. Precautions taken by the government at Melilla were now reminiscent of a war situation. Spanish and Moroccan military jeeps patrolled Melilla's four mile barrier through the night, headlights sweeping the rugged countryside, while helicopters with heat-seeking cameras and spotlights hovered overhead.

On 6 October 2005, Spain's Deputy Prime Minister, Maria Teresa Fernandez de la Vega, said on a visit to Ceuta, 'Under exceptional measures, in coming hours, probably today or tomorrow, illegal immigrants will be returned to Morocco ... Citizens of Ceuta and Melilla, and Spain in general, must be assured that this government guarantees the security of our borders.' However, José Alonso, the secretary of Melilla's Human Rights Association, said, 'We completely disagree with mass expulsions. They amount to a death sentence. If immigrants are returned to Morocco, Moroccan police will dump them on the Algerian border, which is wild desert country, where they will surely die.' This view was echoed by migrants, one of whom, a 20-year-old farmer from Mali, said, 'It's terrible news. We are very afraid of being sent back. I've suffered so much to get here, I prefer death to expulsion.' It had taken him two years to reach Melilla.[3]

The EU finally released a long-promised €40 million to help Morocco combat illegal immigration, the money seen as a payment conditional upon Morocco's active cooperation in controlling the immigrant flood. Meanwhile, the government in Rabat was pushing for a 'Marshall Plan' for sub-Saharan Africa to combat the poverty that drove people to migrate. Spain's Prime Minister, Jose Luis Rodriguez Zapatero, said the crisis was a matter for all

Europeans. 'We must work rapidly to reduce the gap in prosperity between Spain and Morocco and countries to the south of Morocco. The prosperity gap between Spain and Morocco is the largest in the world between bordering countries.' The main source countries for this flood of migrants were Gabon, Nigeria, Ivory Coast, Burkina Faso, Mali, Niger, with Gabon the farthest south.[4] Fiercely criticised for abandoning immigrants on the Algerian border, Morocco changed its policy and rounded up those it had abandoned to deport them to their countries of origin. Amnesty International and other humanitarian groups denounced mass expulsions as illegal and Amnesty's director in Spain, Esteban Beltrán, said:

> No immigrant can be deported unless he has been identified, with a lawyer present, and his case heard. Collective expulsions are contrary to international law and, if carried out with violence and the prospect of death, could be considered a crime against humanity.

Publicity helped the cause of the immigrants as TV coverage and newspaper pictures of desperate Africans horrified the Spanish people, as did the brutal way in which those who had gained entry to one of the enclaves were treated. Similarly, Morocco, which had abandoned hundreds of these would-be migrants in remote desert areas without food or water, was forced by international outcry to rescue them and ship them out of the country in buses. An agreement between Spain and Morocco of 1992 on the immediate repatriation of illegal immigrants, which had been dormant, was reactivated. The breaching of the enclaves followed the Spanish government's grant of amnesty to 700,000 illegal immigrants. Those 'illegals' in Spain who could produce some form of employment contract and prove they had lived in the country for six months were able to regularise their situation over the period 7 February to 7 March 2005. The object of the exercise was to end the exploitation of migrant labour and increase income tax and social security revenue. Spain's foreign-born (immigrant) population had grown rapidly in the first years of the twenty-first century and, by 2005, accounted for 9 per cent of the total population of 44.1 million, double the figure for 2000. During 2005, 1.9 million immigrants arrived in the EU: of these, one-third came to Spain.

By 2006 the flood of people from the poorest parts of Africa desperately seeking entry into Europe and risking everything to get there had become the biggest humanitarian and political problem facing the EU. Speaking from Fuerteventura, the Canary Island that has become a kind of reception centre for the boat people from Africa, the president of the Red Cross, Gerardo Mesa, said:

> These people don't come to Fuerteventura, they come to Europe. They see on the television the opportunities that exist and they put all their efforts and all their money into coming here. But they don't ask for anything. All they want is the chance to work. They don't mind putting in 12 hours a

day or working on Saturdays and Sundays. They don't mind being paid a pittance, doing menial jobs and never getting a holiday. They will put up with bad working conditions that you or I would never tolerate. People fear they bring disease, but it's only the young and the very strong that can make this journey. All they want is to stay. Why are we so against them?[5]

It is difficult to fault Mesa's statement as he goes to the heart of the immigration dilemma: 'Why are we so against them?' However, by 2006 Italy as well as Spain was raising ever-higher security barriers and in both countries the flow had been slowed as Europe became more of an anti-immigrant fortress.

The first three months of 2006 witnessed continuing tragedies in the Atlantic between the African jumping off points – Aayoun, Dakar and Banjul – and Fuerteventura. The Red Crescent estimated that 1,300 people died trying to make the crossing, while in the Mauritanian port of Nouadhibou an estimated 12,000 people were waiting to make the crossing. So Spain negotiated with Mauritania to close this new route to Europe and provided patrol vessels and crew training. Critics of such negative and defensive attitudes argue about the root of the problem, which is deep poverty in Africa and how to combat it. The UN says the private sector (of developed countries) should engage more seriously in Africa and focus on providing jobs for young workers, while African governments should make their democracies solid and stamp out corruption. Even if these two aspirations could be achieved it would take many years and meanwhile the emigrants will continue to leave their countries and head for Europe. Spain asked the EU for help in dealing with the immigrant problem, including migration experts to advise its border guards on how to deal with migrants arriving in the Canary Islands. The UNHCR opened a two-day 'rescue at sea' conference with the International Maritime Organisation in Madrid to work out possible cooperation between Mediterranean states. The majority of the boat people are economic migrants but some are genuine refugees and a spokesman for the UNHCR, William Spindler, said, 'refugees are being turned back. There are fears that Europe is failing in its international obligations',[6] while Amnesty's Esteban Beltrán said, 'You can't confuse not having documents with not having human rights.'

Over the decade to 2006 the Spanish economy grew by 2.6 per cent a year but without the contribution of immigrants the GDP would have fallen by 0.6 per cent, according to the Caixa Catalunya, a leading Spanish bank. Over the same period the number of immigrants in Spain grew by 8.4 per cent, compared with a growth figure of only 3.7 per cent in the EU as a whole. According to Caixa Catalunya's economist, Raquel Vazquez:

Immigration is responsible for more than 50 per cent of employment growth in Spain, and the influence of immigrants has been decisive in raising private consumption and demand for housing, which, as is known, are the twin pillars of GDP growth in our country.

Carlos Martin, an economist with the Trade Union Confederation of Workers' Commissions (CCOO) said, 'There is no doubt that the impact has been decisive, but we must keep in mind that a large proportion of the 3 million immigrant workers in the country – between 30 and 50 per cent – are here illegally and have no labour rights.'

The steady flood from Africa continued through 2006. In December 2005 the Spanish police estimated that between 1,200 and 1,700 lives were lost annually in these hazardous crossings and possibly many more. A government spokesman for the Autonomous Community of the Canary Islands, Miguel Becerra, said that the archipelago 'is under heavy migration pressure' and that it feels 'unprotected' against the large numbers of undocumented immigrants. There was growing consensus in Spain that a solution to the immigrant influx could not be solved by one country but required the cooperation of all members of the EU and others such as Morocco.

Starting in 2006, Spain patrolled the Atlantic Ocean off the shores of Morocco, Western Sahara, Senegal and Mauritania by air and sea. According to government sources the boat operations had changed: 'It's no longer a question of a makeshift craft trying to reach our shores as best it can, but a complex operation involving synchronised movements of vessels.' On 11 May 2007, for example, eleven boats arrived within nine hours, eight of them simultaneously at different points along the shorelines of the islands. The vessels had come northwards from places close to Cabo Bojador in Western Sahara. They covered 225 km in 25–30 hours and, shortly before approaching within twelve miles of the coast and in order not to be detected by radar, they dispersed and made separate landfalls so as to avoid the patrol boats. The police stopped some of the boats but the others reached the shore. In any case, once within the twelve mile limit the immigrants were in Spanish waters and could not be expelled unless they came from countries that had signed deportation agreements with Spain. Successful immigrants – those who land in Spain – admit they are fully aware of the risks involved in making the journey but that these are worth taking to avoid a miserable life of abject poverty or violence in their own countries. Those who secure a place on the frail craft that make the crossing have to pay between $1,000 and $1,500 and to find such money means the whole family has to help.

Despite Spain's need for immigrants to fill job vacancies, the socialist government of Zapatero decided to tighten measures to keep out immigrants without visas. The new measures included reinforcing surveillance systems and increasing efforts to negotiate bilateral agreements with African countries to persuade them to accept the repatriation of their nationals caught trying to enter Spain. Although the drama attending the boat people makes news headlines, they only represent 5 per cent of illegal entrants to Spain. Two-thirds of the undocumented immigrants in Spain arrived on tourist visas: those from Latin America and the Caribbean come by air, and those from Eastern Europe overland.

A former culture minister from Mali, Aminata Traore, said that it is only 'white people and their products that can circulate freely, and they are the only ones who can come to Africa with their trade agreements which impose sanctions on African countries that refuse to let foreign companies in'. This happened, she said:

> while the doors to immigration are closed, and people are even being selected, like raw materials are selected. This is the great paradox. Europe takes everything it wants from Africa, but then it creates a barricade to keep out people from Africa.

Despite measures to tighten border or entry requirements, Spain with Italy, Greece and Portugal – the southern European frontline – have repeatedly carried out regularisation of their unauthorised populations. There have been 15 such programmes over 20 years. In 1986, 1991, 1996 and 2000–1, Spain carried out regularisation programmes to control the illegal migration flows but with only partial success. However, only since the new century has Spain seen significant inflows of illegal immigrants who have been attracted to Spain by its robust demand for low-skilled labour while the country has one of the largest informal economies in the EU. Spain has created a new national employment catalogue covering jobs that Spaniards do not want to do. These include domestic workers, cooks, truck drivers, waiters and waitresses. Despite the attention that African migrants have attracted, of the top ten countries of origin for the 2005 applications for regularisation only one was African: Ecuador (21 per cent), Romania (17 per cent), Morocco (13 per cent), Colombia (8 per cent), Bolivia (7 per cent), Bulgaria (4 per cent), Argentina (3 per cent), Ukraine (3 per cent), Pakistan (2 per cent) and China (2 per cent).

A new initiative in 2007 came from Spanish businessmen who travelled to Senegal to hire workers directly, thereby offering them an alternative to a dangerous journey in an un-seaworthy boat. In 2006, 35,000 Africans reached the shores of the Canary Islands, but countless others drowned. Many of the young Senegalese who take risky journeys to reach Europe are among their own country's brightest people. Their relatives see them as a form of future support. Spain has made a special effort to aid Senegal to regularise the outward flow of immigrants. About 40,000 Senegalese already worked legally in Spain and they have been praised by industrialists and politicians as hard-working and law-abiding. More than 500 Senegalese moved to Spain under a pilot scheme that gave them a contract, a work permit and a residence permit that would help get them jobs in the construction, retail, tourist and agricultural industries. At the same time, Spain planned to open five vocational training schools in Dakar to provide recruits for Spanish companies while Spanish executives were encouraged to look for investment opportunities in Senegal. These measures, however, only touch the tip of the iceberg and do little to alter the development problems of Senegal in particular or sub-Saharan Africa more generally. The exodus of migrants will continue until African economies can provide a reasonable livelihood for the majority of their people.

In 2009, when the recession was biting, Spain launched a new programme that would allow legal immigrants from South America to take their unemployment payments in a lump sum if they agreed to leave and not return for three years. Only about 3,000 immigrants took advantage of the plan, although others were leaving of their own accord. Until recent times Spain (and Italy) were emigrant countries but this was reversed in the late 1990s as Spain enjoyed explosive growth so that the foreign population rose to 5.2 million in 2008 out of a total population of 45 million as opposed to 750,000 foreigners in 1999.

ITALY

In the 1980s, Italy, which in the late nineteenth and early twentieth centuries had provided more immigrants for the United States than any other European country, now became a net recipient of immigrants, a condition that was to develop alarmingly at the end of the twentieth century and into the twenty-first century. The country now faces a number of immigration challenges. Its geographical projection far into the Mediterranean and its long coastline make it an easy target country for illegal migrants from Africa and elsewhere. In 2000, Italy's official statistics reported 272,000 legal admissions, mainly from Albania, Morocco, Romania, China and the Philippines, which together accounted for 38 per cent of total residence permits granted. The number represented a significant increase over the 1998 total of legal admissions, which were 111,000. Some of the 2000 increase was due to the regularisation of previously illegal immigrants.[7] The change from emigrant sending to immigrant receiving country, which began in the 1980s, was affected in a major way by the conflicts in disintegrating Yugoslavia during the 1990s. Other sources of immigrants at this time were Albania and Turkey. Italy was both a final destination for immigrants but also an obvious route northwards into other EU countries. In 2000, most of the 24,500 applications for asylum came from Turkish or Iraqi Kurds, Iraq or Iran – the flood from Africa had not yet got under way. However, the problem of illegal immigrants had built up so that in 1986, 1990, 1995 and 1998 Italy had regularisation programmes for them. The increase of foreign-born people in Italy holding a residence permit was about 423,000 in 1985, 896,000 in 1991 and 1.3 million in 2000, and by the latter year Morocco and Albania accounted for 20 per cent of the foreign population while there was also an increase in the number of immigrants coming from South America and China.[8] A majority of Italy's immigrants work and reside in central (34 per cent) and northern Italy (54 per cent). Like other immigrant-attracting countries, Italy faced the dilemma of needing labour that only the immigrants could supply and wanting to control an influx that it regarded as a political and social threat as an increasing number of immigrants entered the country over its exposed shores. As the number of immigrants grew, so much political debate linked them with increased crime and poverty. The 1998 Immigration Act had separated for the first time humanitarian and refugee issues from immigration policy matters and tougher action was proposed to deal with 'illegals'. A second law, No. 189 of 2002 (Bossi-Fini Law) amended that of 1998 and included the following provisions: immigrant quotas, mandatory employer–immigrant contracts, stricter illegal immigrant deportation practices. Some of these provisions were opposed by trade unions and employers' organisations since they needed the labour. EU governments, always afraid that immigrants into Italy might find their way north, welcomed these tougher laws.

In June 2003, Tunisian navy rescue vessels were searching for possible survivors when 200 people went missing, believed drowned, as they made the journey across the Mediterranean from Africa in an overloaded boat to Europe: they were heading for the Italian island of Lampedusa. There were 41 survivors. Already 3,000 immigrants had arrived in Italy that month. The Lampedusa makeshift 'welcome centre', surrounded by high fences and barbed wire, held triple the numbers it was designed to receive. The mayor of Lampedusa called for support from Rome and the numbers of immigrants he had to deal with led to a debate that blamed Libya for failing to stem the flow. According to reports by Italian intelligence, 2 million people were waiting on the coast of Libya to catch boats to Italy. Enzo Bianco, head of a parliamentary committee on information and security said, 'Libya can't buy the planes it needs to patrol its own territory', while Loris de Filippi, Italy's head of mission for *Médécins Sans Frontières*, said 'Libya has no special interest in stopping the flow of immigrants. They are using this to put pressure on Italy to lift the embargo.' A Lampedusa restaurant owner, Angela Maraventano, said: 'Someone's got to decide who camps here – us or them. There isn't room for both. They should put two battle ships out to sea to guard the island and make the *extracomunitari* [illegal immigrants] go somewhere else.'

Despite some of the drama surrounding the immigrant question, Italy, with 7,600 kilometres of coastline, has earned a reputation among immigrants as one of the easiest doorways into Europe. Most immigrants do not stay in Italy but move north into other European countries to obtain work or claim political asylum. In 2003, the UNHCR estimated that while Italy had only 10,000 political refugees, Germany had 900,000.

Ferruccio Pastore[9] examined Italy's historical role in relation to migration. The Italian peninsula, like a long pier jutting into the Mediterranean, has been a 'border region' for centuries. In the twentieth century it was central to the global divide between the east and west, with Europe's largest Communist Party and one of the highest concentrations of US troops in Europe. Since 1989, Italy has experienced a new 'border identity' crisis. It is the crossroads between North Africa, the Balkans and continental Europe. It is on a fault line – one of the most unstable economic, political and demographic fault lines in the world. Thus, he argues, 'during the 1990s, people fleeing war-torn Yugoslavia, breaking out of collapsing Albania or escaping from a repressive/ stagnant Maghreb regime migrated into Italy'. And so, from being the largest migrant sending country in the world, Italy has become an attractive destination for irregular labour immigration into Europe. This position was highlighted at the end of 2003 when 700,000 illegal immigrants were given legal recognition. Prosperity during the 1970s and 1980s led Italy to welcome migrants to undertake jobs that many Italians no longer wished to do. An estimate for 2004 showed that 2.5 million non-EU citizens were residing in the country. The great majority of Italians tend to be schizophrenic about these incomers. 'Thus, while immigrant labour is utilised daily, usually to everyone's advantage and satisfaction yet any visible sign of an immigrant presence – beyond the impact of their work – is seen as a disturbing interference in the country's domestic affairs.' Between 1996 and 2001 Italian governments made consistent attempts to regain strategic control over immigration and, from the late 1990s, devised a national integration policy based on increased finances available to assist migrants and streamline integration measures. No matter what measures, either to integrate immigrants or restrict their entry into the country, 'By 2002 it had become plain that Italy was a major target country for migrants – legal and illegal.' Like an equally targeted Spain, Italy sometimes calls for a common EU policy towards immigrants but, with 27 member countries each facing their own particular immigration problems, such an effective policy has yet to emerge.

Many thousands of sub-Saharan Africans pass through Libya on their way, they hope, to Europe: Italy has tried to reach agreement with Libya's Gaddafi for the two countries to work together by combined navy patrols to clamp down on the boat people. Measures to control immigration are constantly thwarted by economic facts. Thus, the agricultural sector in Italy relies upon immigrants for the annual harvest and Giuseppe Pisanu, the Interior Minister in 2004, demanded a modification of the anti-immigration law. He proposed an increase in the quotas for legal immigrants and pointed out that low-paid immigrants from beyond the EU had become an essential part of the Italian economy: 'If it wasn't for immigrants we couldn't pick apples in Trentino, tomatoes in Campania, or bring in the grape harvest. Neither could we milk a single fanatical Northern League cow.' About 900,000 immigrants work in Italy's agricultural sector.[10]

Joint efforts by the main EU countries to control the immigrant influx have not proved very successful. In 2003, Britain's then Prime Minister, Tony Blair, advanced the idea of setting up asylum camps outside Europe where would-be immigrants could first be screened. Countries suggested for such camps included Tunisia, Egypt and Ukraine. Italy and Germany pushed the idea in 2004 and obtained support for it from Spain and the Netherlands, but it was opposed by France and Sweden on the grounds that it breached international law, while Amnesty International worried that asylum seekers could be left at the mercy of nations with poor human rights records. Despite this mixed reception, Italy's Pisanu, after meeting with Libyan officials, told *Il Messagero* newspaper: 'The camps will go ahead. There was never a problem with the proposal; there were only polemics that ended up in newspapers.'[11] The German-Italian scheme was apparently designed to prevent would-be immigrants from leaving Libya before their cases had been examined.

Another area of conflict concerned the internal movement of migrants from Eastern to Western Europe. Many people in Italy and across the EU would like to see their governments take more draconian action against immigrants, especially when they are associated with crimes, which is often the case. The free movement of people across the continent is a cornerstone of the union of 27 member states, so that once an immigrant is inside the EU he can move where he likes. Italy, which is often blamed for accepting immigrants who later move north into other EU countries, favoured the idea of camps in Libya through which so many migrants pass on their way to Europe, but any effective measure would require the support of most EU countries and the cooperation of Libya, which was anything but certain. The civil war in Libya during 2011 will curtail Sub-Saharan African migration through Libya but will create Libyan refugees seeking asylum in Europe. Racist accusations against migrants surface whenever they are linked to violent (or other) crimes. The murder of Giovanna Ruggiani, the wife of a naval captain, allegedly by a member of the Roma community living on the outskirts of Rome, led to public outrage and induced the government to bring in emergency legislation that would allow EU citizens who pose a threat to public security to be summarily expelled. It led to the immediate expulsion of 38 Romanian Roma. The expulsions caused Romania's Prime Minister, Cali Tariceanu, to announce that his government would give legal support to those expelled and require solid arguments in support of their expulsions.[12]

Earlier in the year seven Tunisian fishermen were jailed in Sicily for the crime of rescuing 44 immigrants from certain death at sea. They were accused of aiding and abetting illegal immigration and, if found guilty, faced between 1 and 15 years in prison. They were arrested on 8 August 2007 after bringing the migrants – found at sea in an overcrowded sinking rubber boat – ashore at Lampedusa. They were kept in custody until 10 September, when five were released on bail and the two officers put under house arrest. The incident put ordinary human compassion on a collision course with laws designed to deter immigration at almost any cost. By December 2008 more than 30,000 people had landed in Italy during the year, double the figure for 2007 and the highest since the traffic from Africa had begun. In July 2009, the Italian parliament gave final approval to a controversial law, which criminalized illegal immigration and legalised unarmed vigilante patrols by citizens. Some of Italy's most famous writers signed an open letter condemning the legislation as the 'reintroduction of race laws', and compared the measure to the infamous Race Laws introduced by Mussolini in 1938, which banned Jews from work and education. The letter claimed that 'irregular' immigrants could be barred from marrying Italians and from registering the birth of their children, 'so the children ... shall for their entire lives be the children of unknown parents ... Not even Fascists went that far.'[13]

The Italian government, spurred by public anger, has over-reacted to the immigrant influx with draconian legislation and rapid expulsions. On the other hand, as a 'frontline' Mediterranean country it has been offered little help by the EU over an issue that concerns all of Europe. Italy's focus upon border controls and security has led to the neglect of the much more important task of integration since the immigrant population now amounts to 7 per cent of the country's total population. According to Sergio Carrera of the Brussels Centre for European Policy Studies:

> Italy is becoming a caricature. It's becoming the example of a very extreme political discourse framing migration as a security issue, and justifying the implementation of very restrictive policies, having huge implications for human rights, fundamental rights, and social inclusion.

What was painfully clear by 2009 was that immigration had become a highly emotive, front-page issue in Italy.

MALTA

Lying on the sea route from Libya to Italy, Malta became a target country for migrants from Africa, even if they only saw it as a stepping-stone to other richer countries to the north, where job opportunities would compensate for the rigours of their long journey. In any case, with the Big Bang of 2004, Malta had become a member of the EU and, once on its territory, immigrants could travel to other parts of Europe. The problems connected with the immigrants multiplied in 2005 as Malta tried to cope with a greatly increased influx of migrants and refugees who had become stranded, were adrift at sea or shipwrecked on their way to mainland Europe, which in most cases meant Italy. There was considerable foreign criticism of the way Malta handled the migrants in its detention centres. At the same time there were demands that it should take back migrants who had succeeded in reaching Italy from Malta. Reacting to these criticisms, Malta called upon the EU to treat the problem as a European one (not just confined to one country) and provide help to patrol the sea routes used by the migrants and also to absorb some of the refugees. Malta then appealed to Libya, whence most of the migrants were coming. The Libyan response to Malta's appeal was to claim that it was unable to patrol its 2,000 km coastline. In June 2005, however, a meeting was held in Malta of the foreign ministers of the 'Five plus Five' group consisting of the five southern European and five North African countries on the Mediterranean, and they agreed to hold an international conference in Libya in 2006 to consider the problem. Malta's main concern in terms of foreign affairs was the continuous flow of cross-Mediterranean migrants and the cost of handling those who landed in Malta. Further talks with the EU did not lead to the establishment of a Euro-North Africa cooperative mechanism. However, in August 2006, the EU external border security agency, Frontex, extended its operations to the Mediterranean to assist Malta, Italy and Spain to intercept and send back the boatloads of immigrants. The EU and Libya agreed that Frontex could operate near the Libyan coast on condition that these activities were conducted by Italy and Malta with Libyan collaboration.

Trans-Mediterranean migration was to remain a major issue between Malta and the EU. A familiar pattern had emerged, with boatloads of African immigrants landing in Malta, either directly or after rescue at sea, as soon as the summer weather arrived. By 2007 the earlier EU criticisms of Malta were replaced by a more understanding view of its predicament as Frontex increased its operations in the Mediterranean and began to understand the size of the problem. The pattern hardly changed except for tighter controls and the possibility that the recession in Europe would persuade at least some would-be immigrants to stay away.

GREECE

Greece's immigration policies since the beginning of the century have been chaotic as a result of too much bureaucracy and incompetence. In 2001, Greece launched the second of its amnesty programmes yet, when the final deadline was reached, many immigrants had been unable to submit applications or renew residence permits as a result of government incompetence. Migrants formed an estimated 10 per cent of the population and a critical proportion of them would return to illegality and be socially marginalised. As in other immigrant receiving countries, racism plays its part in Greece. In 2003 it took the spiteful form of banning non-Greek children from carrying the Greek flag in national holiday parades. As the prefect of Thessaloniki said: 'Greeks are born, not made.'[14]

The border between Greece and European Turkey is heavily mined, and claims a steady toll of casualties as desperate immigrants try to cross them. Two immigrants lost their lives in April 2005 when crossing a minefield to bring the total number of deaths to 72 since Greece signed the Mine Ban Treaty in 1997, while others have been severely mutilated in attempts to enter the EU through the Turkish 'back door'. The Greek government has been repeatedly accused of dragging its feet over de-mining the border after taking seven years to ratify the treaty. These minefields are a leftover of decades of tension between Greece and Turkey, despite their both being members of the North Atlantic Treaty Organization (NATO), while by this time Turkey had applied to join the EU. With thousands of miles of shore and remote, mountainous land borders, Greece is a major transit point for immigrants. Tens of thousands of people cross illegally every year. Greece has mined the Evros River on its frontier with Turkey since the 1970s and an estimate of 2004 revealed that 24,751 mines remained to be cleared, making it one of the least friendly EU frontiers.[15]

The immigrant population in Greece passed 1 million people in 2005, including Pontic and Albanian Greeks, and was equivalent to 9 per cent of the population. Twenty years earlier Greece had been a migrant exporting country rather than an immigrant receiving one. As a result of this change Greece began to develop an immigration policy that covered the regularisation of undocumented aliens, the integration of the immigrant population across all sectors of the economy and country, as well as stricter border controls. As of 2005 three-quarters of the total immigrant population had legal status with work and residence permits. Originally, the majority of immigrants entered the country illegally and were able to survive without papers. In the last century the Greek media tended to be hostile or negative about migrants but this attitude changed in the early years of the present century to a more positive approach that played down xenophobia. This change was partly due to EU initiatives that promoted tolerance and cultural pluralism while also extolling the economic advantages that came with an immigrant influx. Like other immigrant receiving countries in the EU, Greece needs to achieve a balance between hostile public opinion and the impact the immigrants have upon the economy and the need to counterbalance the country's ageing population. The end of the Cold War (1989–92) marked the turnaround as Greece became a net importer of migrants. These were encouraged to come from the ex-USSR and the former Third World (now South) to take advantage of Greece's rising prosperity, but the recession of the late 2000s led to a catastrophic economic decline. Also, the strain that large numbers of immigrants placed upon the administration made even more inadequate the performance of an already less than perfect bureaucracy and this in its turn produced anti-immigrant sentiments and growing xenophobia. In 1991 Greece enacted Law 1975 (of that year). Its title: Entry, Exit, Sojourn, Employment, Removal of Aliens, Procedure for the Recognition of Refugees and other Measures. The principal aim of the law was to curb migration and facilitate the removal of undocumented migrants. In theory, it made it impracticable for economic migrants to enter the country. In fact, over the succeeding years hundreds and thousands of immigrants found their way into Greece: they came over the mountains from Albania and Bulgaria, or by sea, landing from small boats on the Greek islands. Such migrants were often assisted by the growing trade in people smuggling. It became clear that the immigrants meant to stay and that Greece had neither the mechanisms nor the capacity to stop the flow or deport the 'illegals'. In 1998, therefore, Greece carried out its first immigrant regularisation programme under which 371,641 immigrants applied for white cards (limited duration permits). In 2001 the government issued a three-year programme: the Action Plan for the Social Integration of Immigrants (for the period 2002–5). The plan covered labour market access, health, cultural dialogue and combating xenophobia. In January 2004, the government decided to issue permits of a two-year duration to ease the task of administration and application by immigrants. In August 2005, in an effort to rationalise policy, the Greek parliament adopted a new immigration bill on entry, stay and integration of third-country nationals in Greece, which was to become effective in January 2006. The bill was criticised for ignoring the majority of the illegal migrant population and preventing 70 per cent of the immigrants from obtaining residence permits.

Census figures for 2001 revealed that more than half of all foreigners registered were Albanian citizens (438,000 – 57 per cent): of these, 240,000 (54 per cent) came to Greece to seek work, 70,000 (15 per cent) came for family reunion. Roughly a third worked in the construction industry and 20 per cent in agriculture. The second largest group of foreigners were Bulgarians. Of the Pontic Greeks from the former USSR who came into Greece during the late 1980s or early 1990s, most sought work. Of these, 80,000 came from Georgia, 31,000 from Kazakhstan, 23,000 from Russia and 9,000 from Armenia. About 50 per cent of these immigrants had secondary education, including technical school skills, and 10 per cent had higher education. The Albanians had the lowest level of education and former Soviet citizens the highest; more women had higher education. Law 2130 of 1993 lays down that immigrants who wish to become Greek citizens have to be resident in the country for more than ten of the preceding twelve years, which is one of the longest requirements for residence: the authorities are not required to justify the rejection of an application. The Greek constitution reserves a number of rights, such as taking part in rallies or associations, for Greek citizens only. Despite reservations, various restrictive practices and periodic outbreaks of xenophobia, immigrants are also coming to be seen as making positive contributions to the economy.

The Greek Minister of the Interior, Prokopis Pavlopoulos, speaking in December 2007, raised the issue of Turkey's accession to the EU.[16] He said the problem of illegal immigration was a European one and that Europe should protect EU borders, especially countries of the south, such as Cyprus and Greece, The EU, he said, should not make concessions to ease Turkey's accession.

> There cannot be concessions because if Europe acts along these lines, then the whole thing will degenerate. The issue is not for Europe to shift in order to meet Turkey or other states, but for Turkey to go forward to meet Europe.

In July 2009, Greece introduced strict policies to combat irregular immigration and passed legislation that could downgrade the effective protection of people applying for asylum for the first time or on appeal. The new measures were queried by the UNHCR. Among 'illegals' are many people in need of protection whom the state is obliged to protect; harsher policy at the border must be coupled with the creation of reception facilities. Asylum seekers and unaccompanied children should be referred to special accommodation facilities. Many who have a right to such treatment are homeless. However, the EU is avoiding laying down binding mechanisms and practices for sharing responsibility more fairly among member states. The asylum processing and decision-making is unreliable: there is a lack of shelter and social care, informal push-backs or returns to Turkey across the Evros River in northeast Greece and ill-treatment.[17]

Greece has been consistently criticised by the UN, the EU and human rights organisations for its handling of immigrants. On 12 June 2009, the Greek authorities flattened a squatter camp of illegal immigrants from Afghanistan in the port city of Patras. The Afghans were waiting to take boats to Italy. The government claimed that Greece was overwhelmed by illegal immigration. New legislation, rushed through parliament at the end of June, increased the time 'illegals' could be held from three to six months and in certain circumstances for a year. Human rights organisations argue that incarceration is not the way to deal with the immigrant crisis. Moreover, existing detention centres have repeatedly been condemned by the UN and by EU courts for failing to ensure basic human rights. A Council of Europe report, based on visits to detention sites in 2008, found that conditions remained unacceptable. The new tough line adopted by Greece in mid 2009 was in accord with a Europe-wide trend to resort to long-term detention to address illegal immigration. Philip Amaral of the Jesuit Refugee Service, which opposes the detention of refugees and illegal migrants, said: 'Most definitely in the case of illegally staying migrants, countries are detaining more frequently and some are even starting to deport more frequently.' In 2008, the European parliament passed legislation to allow member states to detain illegal migrants for up to 18 months under certain conditions. The law also sets out the conditions under which illegal immigrants can be deported from the EU. In 2009, most illegal migrants are detained at Greece's borders and held for three months before being released with an order to leave the country within one month. Few leave and so they become illegal and subject to periodic arrest and release.[18]

9
Europe's Small Developed States

Although major states such as Spain, Italy or Britain are the principal targets for migrants, no European country escapes involvement in the movement of people that is currently taking place. Thus, Portugal joins with Spain in calling for the establishment of a 'common policy' on immigration across the EU: 'This common policy should include integration policies for the 25 million immigrants who currently live in Europe legally,' according to Alberto Navarro, Spain's Secretary of State for European affairs. He added that an additional 7 million to 10 million foreigners currently reside in Europe without the required residence papers. The combined figure of 35 million is equivalent to the population of a sizeable country and that is the extent of the problem. His Portuguese counterpart, Manuel Lobo Antunes, said his country would offer help to Spain in its struggle to deal with an unprecedented wave of immigrants coming through the Canary Islands. Portugal has deployed a ship to the Cape Verde Islands as part of a new European initiative to prevent people risking a dangerous crossing to Europe from West Africa. The European Commission has urged member states to drop their veto on matters concerning terrorism and immigration, and to accept a majority decision, which could smooth the way towards adopting a common policy. By 2009 the EU had been groping for several years to find a common policy on immigration but found instead that while its 27 member states expected the EU to assist them when they faced particular problems, few were prepared to surrender their control of immigration to Brussels so as to achieve a uniform policy for Europe as a whole. On the eve of a meeting of EU justice and interior ministers in Finland, the Commission spokesman, Johannes Laitenberger, said the time had come to show the political will to be more efficient on these issues. While recognising that the idea would meet 'resistance', Laitenberger stressed that 'the practical needs' (for controls) should overcome any ideological objections.

AUSTRIA

Austria, strategically placed at the eastern extremity of rich developed Europe and to the north of the Balkans, which have become both an immigrant route into Europe as well as a source of immigrants from their own poor countries, found that asylum and immigration had become a major issue in 2004. In the previous year the government had introduced a number of strict asylum laws in an attempt to reverse Austria's position as a major destination for asylum seekers. These laws were strongly criticised by the UNHCR during the course of 2004 and were also judged to be illegal in parts by the Austrian courts. Immigration, with all its complexities, naturally attracts a range of individuals and organisations that hope to profit from it. In 2007 a company specialising in removing failed asylum seekers decided to approach the British government with plans to use specially adapted aircraft to deport hundreds of 'disruptive' refugees. This was Asylum Airways, run by an Austrian aviation consultant with ties to British security firms. It was ready to operate aircraft for European countries which did not wish to use established airlines for the forced removal of asylum seekers (since to do so results in unfavourable publicity for draconian government measures). 'Hundreds of asylum-seeker removals have had to be aborted in the past two years because of what the Home Office [in Britain] describes as "disruptive behaviour".'[1] Heinz Berger, who set up Asylum Airlines, identified Britain as a key market for his service. He also said there was 'ongoing interest all over Europe' for an airline that would organise flights around Europe, picking up failed asylum seekers from various countries and flying them back to their home nations in Africa, the Middle East and Asia. 'A special feature will be bespoke aircraft with padded rooms and restraining equipment.' It is a measure of growing European brutality in relation to immigrants that it should invent a flying prison service.

BELGIUM

With a population of 10.5 million and an average per capita income in excess of $40,000, Belgium is one of the richest small countries in the world. It is also a target country for immigrants, including those from its former colony, the Democratic Republic of the Congo (DRC) and Morocco. In addition, it is a transit country for immigrants on their way to Britain. In 2003, an Albanian gangster was sentenced to eight years for smuggling an estimated 12,000 illegal immigrants into Britain – one of the largest such operations to be uncovered. The policy of forcibly deporting failed asylum seekers had to be suspended in December after four police officers were convicted of 'involuntarily' causing the death of a Nigerian woman.[2] Challenges presented by immigration, racism and security tend to erupt side by side as the Belgian government was discovering.

A social problem that came with Moroccan immigrants concerned marriage and Islam. A study published by Antwerp University, *Aspects of Moroccan Marriage – Immigration and Moroccan Family Law*, examined the Moroccan community in Belgium, which consisted mainly of young men, whose choice was either to marry a Belgian woman or go back home to seek a bride. The study revealed that a Moroccan brought up in Belgium, who returned home to seek a bride, thought he would find someone from the same community when in fact:

> people who grew up in a Western country and people who grew up in Morocco have a very different view of life. Among boys there was a wish to marry a more traditional woman, seeing the Moroccan-Belgian girls as too 'free'. Among girls there was a quite contrasting wish – it seems

Moroccan boys have a bad reputation inside their own community. The girls are looking for somebody who has an education and a job.

Such social complications are all part of the immigrant puzzle.

The girls expect to move to a country where they will be ensured freedom. Freedom to advance a career, freedom to learn. Reality doesn't always live up to that. The boys expect to come to a 'promised land' as well, but instead they face high bills and pressure to get immediately to work.

Many European Moroccans spend their summers in Morocco. Many of the worker-immigrants saved everything they had in order to build expensive homes in Morocco. Expectations form a major part of all immigrant dreams; often they are not realised. If marriage migrants (women) divorce their spouse before receiving a permanent residence permit, they have to go back; but, of women interviewed, none wanted to, since back in Morocco they would never be able to marry again – so they remain in Belgium as 'illegals'. Finally, the study brought up an interesting point: 'on the one hand the Belgian government declares that illegals will be expelled and works toward that end. On the other, it financially supports organizations which help out illegals'.[3]

In July 2009, the Belgian government announced an agreement over new rules on dealing with immigrants. The issue had sharply divided the ruling coalition over the previous two years. The agreement set out the conditions under which residency permits could be given. Illegals who had lived in Belgium for at least five years would be able to apply to regularise their situation between 15 September and 15 December 2009. The Prime Minister, Herman Van Rompuy, said he was satisfied with the new regulations. There was to be no more mass amnesties for those living in Belgium without residency permits, but applications would be treated on a case-by-case basis and among those who could expect a favourable outcome would be: long-term residents, parents of Belgian children, parents of children at school, those with work permits and those whose applications had taken an excessive amount of time. To obtain approval, applicants would have to prove that they were already integrated into Belgian society. Then, if successful, they would be granted papers allowing them legally to stay and work in the country. Other factors favouring applicants include language skills and attendance at literacy classes. Thus, while launching a new wave of admissions for illegal immigrants, the government insisted its decision did not herald 'mass regularisation', as many EU countries, including neighbouring France, are strongly opposed to such practices. During the French EU presidency in the second half of 2008, Paris proposed an EU-wide ban on mass regularisation, but this was dropped during negotiations on a European asylum and immigration pact in order to win the necessary support of the Spanish government.

Political parties generally welcomed the agreement but raised a number of particular questions, one of which was that the asylum and immigration secretary had been given too much power. On the other hand, the nationalist and anti-immigration New Flemish Alliance N-VA slammed the agreement. Its leader, Bant de Wever, said the French-speaking community had got what it wanted, while Flemish concerns had not been addressed. Other N-VA representatives warned that the federal government had opened the door for a second round of regularisations in the near future.[4]

SCANDINAVIA – DENMARK

By 2003 immigration had become a major political issue in Scandinavia. In Denmark on 24 April the unicameral legislature voted to tighten the laws relating to refugees. Under the new laws, asylum seekers whose claims had been rejected could be forced by the police to sign the documents required for repatriation. The Immigration Minister, Berttel Haarder, also advocated measures against young criminals and those committing anti-social acts. Further, the government claimed that immigrants from non-Western countries were receiving too great a proportion of welfare benefits. The chairman of the populist Danish Peoples' Party (DF), Pier Kjaersgaard, presented more far-reaching proposals. He wanted Denmark to end its obligations under various international conventions on human rights: the UN Covenant on Civil and Political Rights (ICCPR), the UN International Convention on All Forms of Racial Discrimination (ICERD), and the European Convention on Human Rights (ECHR). Although his proposals were rejected, they were not untypical of some of the more extreme views surfacing at the time.

In 2005, the Danish cartoon controversy made headline news in many parts of the world. The daily *Iyllands-Posten* published twelve cartoons of the Prophet Muhammed which outraged Muslims in Denmark and elsewhere. The editor of the paper later claimed they just wanted to treat Muslims equally. 'By publishing these cartoons, we are saying to the Muslim Community in Denmark "we treat you as we treat everybody else".' But the paper had refused to publish cartoons about Jesus Christ because, the editor thought, the cartoons were 'offensive' and 'not funny'. In fact, Christianity is protected by blasphemy laws in many EU countries. Traditionally, with a relatively homogeneous population of 5.6 million, Denmark has not seen itself as a country of immigration and the cartoon episode could be taken as a sign of a lack of awareness of the problems that come with new immigrant communities. Moreover, most immigrants in Denmark, until recently, have come from other Nordic or Western countries and the number of Danish migrants has exceeded that of immigrants. After the guest worker programme of the early 1970s came to an end, a growing number of immigrants, mainly refugees, family dependants of refugees and former 'guest workers' have altered the country's ethnic balance. Thus, over the 35 years to 2006 more than half the growth of the Danish population (250,000) has been accounted for by immigrants and their descendants, while non-naturalised Asian and African immigrants and their descendants constitute 6 per cent of the population. Figures for migrant communities at the end of 2005 were: Europe – 233,924; Africa – 43,182; North America – 8,441; South/Central America – 7,968; Asia – 153,561;

Oceania – 1,656; Stateless – 3,363. They totalled 452,095 people representing 8.4 per cent of the population. The figures exclude asylum seekers.[5]

A ruling by the European Court of Justice of 25 July 2008 could sound the death knell for Denmark's restrictive immigration policy by forcing it to ease family reunification rules. The European Court of Justice stipulated that under a 2004 EU directive on free circulation of people in the EU, members may not refuse entry or right of residence to non-EU spouses and family. The ruling sparked a fierce debate in Denmark, where strict laws blocked family reunification for non-EU citizens residing in the country illegally and in cases where one spouse is under the age of 24. The Danish Prime Minister, Fogh Rasmussen, said: 'The Danish government strongly disagrees with this ruling ... Denmark determines its own immigration policy and it remains unchanged. The government will not tolerate having its family reunification rules hijacked.' He called the ruling 'unreasonable' and formally objected to the EU Commission. Rasmussen tried to obtain support from other EU states to have the ruling changed; Britain, Germany and Italy were sympathetic. Denmark's immigration legislation, broadly supported by the Danish people, is one of the most restrictive in Europe, with the result that there was a sharp drop in immigrant arrivals for family reunification between 2001, when 13,000 were admitted, and 2007, when the figure had fallen to 4,500. The Danish Integration Minister Birthe Roenn Hornbech said the European Court of Justice ruling 'opens the way for wide scale approval of illegal immigration' through marriages of convenience. 'I wonder if the European court has been given too much power – and if the EU is not determining a bit too much of Denmark's immigration policy.' There was clearly a conflict between EU law and Danish immigration policy but the prime minister, who had signed the 2004 directive on free movement, said he would comply with the directive. Six out of ten Danes support the country's immigration policy and the ruling had made Danes increasingly sceptical of EU policy, which has come to be seen as an infringement of the country's sovereignty.

Denmark, which joined the EU in 1973 at the same time as Britain, insisted upon four opt-outs to make the Maastricht Treaty more palatable, after Denmark had first rejected the treaty. These allow Denmark to remain outside the eurozone, the EU joint defence policy, EU citizenship and judicial cooperation. The Prime Minister, Rasmussen, has urged that Denmark should scrap these four exceptions as 'incompatible with Danish interests' since they prevent the country fully participating in European cooperation.[6] The EU has constantly to overcome individual member objections to various all-embracing policies and none more so than those on immigration. Following EU enlargement, Sweden, Denmark and Finland announced that they would impose 'transition rules' in an attempt to regulate the immigration of citizens of these new members. At the same time, Norway, which is not a member of the EU, announced similar measures (it is a member of the European Economic Area – EEA). In the event, however, the effects of enlargement turned out to be much less consequential than had been feared. Nonetheless, there was disagreement between the Scandinavian countries. In August 2004, the Swedish justice minister angered the Danish government with his criticism of Denmark's strict immigration laws and in particular the law on family reunification. Denmark insisted on maintaining the law and was further criticised in a Council of Europe report.

SWEDEN

The most liberal of the Scandinavian countries in its attitudes towards immigration, Sweden has endeavoured, through its foreign policy, and security, trade and development assistance policies, to work towards the removal of the underlying reasons that compelled people to leave their countries of origin, hoping to make it easier for them to return home. The idea is not confined to Sweden, although in terms of world imbalances this approach can only be seen as an aspiration, rather than an attainable goal. Migration in its various forms is a cross-border issue of people constantly moving from one country to another, whether to escape persecution or for economic and social reasons, and in the long run can have as big an impact upon the country of origin as on the country of destination. Sweden has ratified the UN Convention Relating to the Status of Refugees (the Geneva Convention) so that it is obliged to examine each asylum application and grant asylum to those people who qualify as refugees under the Convention. On 31 March 2006, a new Aliens Act entered into force to replace the 1989 Aliens Act. The new act emphasises that the examination of an asylum seeker's case must focus on the need for protection. The refugee concept has been expanded to include people who are persecuted because of their gender or sexual orientation. Sweden works closely with the UNHCR, while cooperation with the EU is a central aspect of its policy.

Up to 2008 the right to stay in Sweden as a refugee was straightforward and, for example, the Swedish town of Sodertalje alone had accepted more Iraqi refugees than Britain and the US combined. However, Sweden then embarked upon a national debate over its asylum policy in a changing political climate. A new court process for screening refugees has meant that while 72 per cent of Iraqi asylum seekers (the largest group entering Sweden) were accepted in 2007, the percentage had fallen to 27 per cent in 2008. Two years in which record numbers of Iraqi asylum seekers were accepted – 18,599 in 2007 – led to a fresh examination of the country's policy. First, could a country with one of the most open policies towards refugees continue to be so generous? Second, should new requirements for integration be devised so that incomers would be required to be more Swedish and be dispersed from core communities where most of them have settled? The rethink followed a political change in 2006 that brought a centre-right government to power and also saw the re-emergence of the far right in the form of the Sweden Democrats.

In March 2008, despite severe criticism from the UNHCR, the Swedish government drew up a memorandum of understanding with the government of Iraq to return 3,000 failed asylum seekers after the Migration Board had ruled that there was 'no armed internal conflict' in Iraq. The ruling came as a shock to Madeleine Seidlitz, the Swedish Amnesty International refugee coordinator, who said the situation for refugees in Sweden was now more difficult than any time she could remember.

> We rarely see the courts giving the benefit of the doubt. We see judgements that are simply incorrect under international law. And there seems to be no interest in the courts in understanding the nature of the situation in the countries of the refugees they are dealing with.[7]

By stating that there was 'no armed internal conflict' in Iraq, the Swedish government was eliminating the reason for people to leave that country and come to Sweden as refugees. Such statements are devices that allow a government to evict asylum seekers with a 'clear' conscience. As with other countries that try to restrict the flow of immigrants, Sweden increasingly requires high levels of immigration in all sectors of its economy as it faces the challenges of an ageing population. In 2007, for example, one-third of all new jobs went to people born outside the country.

IRELAND

For most of its history Ireland was a prime source of migrants going elsewhere, especially to the United States as permanent settlers, and to Britain for work. It joined the European Community in 1973 and, as a result, achieved an unprecedented level of prosperity by the 1990s, when Irish emigrants returned home to enjoy the wealth of an expanding economy and, simultaneously, it became a magnet for immigrants from Europe and elsewhere for the first time in its history. Many of these immigrants were themselves Irish, who had left Ireland in search of work during the years when the country was economically in the doldrums. These immigrants represented a wholly new set of problems for Ireland to absorb and, as one Dubliner said: 'I'm not a racist, but people from outside are abusing the system.' By 2004 80 per cent of the electorate were in favour of changing the constitution to limit the rights of 'non-nationals'. Although Ireland had been described as the country of '100,000 welcomes', there were many who remembered what had happened to them in Britain in the 1960s: 'No dogs, no blacks, no Irish.' Ireland had been generous with its passports – anyone born on Irish soil was an Irish citizen – but there now developed a reaction against 'citizenship tourists', who came to give birth in Ireland and then used their babies as a backdoor into the EU. Voters approved a referendum that sought to ensure that children of non-national parents were no longer Irish unless one of their parents had been resident for three years. The migrant problem was something new for Ireland. It arose out of the prosperity of the 1990s when Ireland came to enjoy a standard of living that would have been unthinkable a decade or so earlier. The country had been transformed into one with a small population whose people had a high per capita income. While it attracted migrants, there was no coherent policy as to how they should be treated. Thus, asylum seekers were dispersed from Dublin and sent to small rural towns that had had no previous contact with foreigners and were ill-prepared to receive them. Prosperity was accompanied by emerging xenophobia and racism as the country moved to the right politically, although politicians had promised to pass legislation to make Ireland the most 'immigrant friendly' country in Europe. As a people who, proportionately, have one of the largest diasporas in the world, the Irish now found that they had to face the new experience of welcoming immigrants instead of being immigrants themselves.

As the 'Celtic Tiger' Ireland became a magnet for East Europeans both before and after the Big Bang of 2004. But the recession that got under way in 2008 brought about significant changes.

> With a drop of close to 25 per cent in Ireland's once booming construction industry, fears are also rising that concerns over job losses, the credit crunch and the still high cost of living will produce an unprecedented wave of racism and xenophobia. The Polish community in Ireland, which is estimated at around 230,000, is experiencing the largest exodus of workers back either to their homeland or other parts of the EU in search of work.[8]

As is usual in such situations of economic collapse, foreign workers are the first to suffer redundancy and discrimination. As one Pole remarked: 'We are perceived as cheap, disposable labour.' Irish employers began to ban the use of Polish workers. Such attitudes are not surprising. Ireland had experienced one of the fastest rates of immigration in history. Over a decade its non-indigenous population had increased from under 1 per cent to 12 per cent or half a million non-Irish in a state of 4.5 million people.

In response to growing fears about immigrants, the Irish government appointed Conor Lenihan as Minister for Integration with a mandate to plan for the absorption of those immigrants who chose to stay in Ireland, regardless of the deepening recession. Lenihan insisted that, given their history both as a former colony and a net exporter of people round the world, the Irish were better inoculated against racism and xenophobia than other EU nations, but he warned that a further increase in illegal immigration would upset the social balance. He said:

> Unless you manage the flow of people, you do a disservice to the indigenous community. You undermine Irish public support for integration. By allowing illegality you radically reduce backing for immigration, which Ireland needs. Ireland is still an under-populated country.[9]

In the year ending in April 2007, the total number of immigrants that entered Ireland was 109,500 – up almost 2,000 over 2006 and substantially higher than for any other year since 1987, when specific immigration figures were collected. At the same time, however, there was an increase in emigration with 42,200 people leaving the country. The natural increase in the population was 38,800 for the year ending in April 2007. Immigration was responsible for nearly two-thirds of the population increase while 48 per cent of immigrants were nationals of the twelve new EU members that joined in 2004 and 2007.[10]

THE NETHERLANDS

In 2002, Pim Fortuyn, a populist politician whose career had been built on anti-Muslim and anti-immigrant slogans, was murdered, his death drawing attention to the explosive issues of race and religion that went with immigration. In 2003 it became clear that the immigrant issue had risen to the top of the political agenda. In August, seven members of a gang responsible for smuggling thousands of people into Britain were sentenced to from 18 months to six years in prison. Two of them were responsible for the lorry in which 58 Chinese immigrants were suffocated. In December, Rotterdam, with nearly half its population of non-Dutch origin, announced proposals to 'restore long-term balance' by deporting illegal immigrants and preventing unemployed low earners from moving into the city. Ethnic tensions rose in 2004 following the assassination of the controversial film maker Theo van Gogh: scores of Muslim schools and mosques were burnt, stoking bitterness on both sides of the 'Dutch'–Muslim divide. As police cracked down on 'Islamism', people complained, 'We are paying for being so tolerant and open.'[11] The move mirrored policies that had been advocated by Pim Fortuyn.

In 2005, the Netherlands decided to require new immigrants to undertake an examination to test their knowledge of Dutch history and language before taking up residence. There was growing concern at the failure to integrate ethnic minorities. A poll of January 2005 found that only 19 per cent of Dutch people did not regard the presence of 1 million Muslims in the country as a threat. Tensions increased in July during the trial of Mohammed Bouyeri (of Moroccan origin) for the murder of Theo van Gogh, the previous year. Bouyeri, unrepentant, was sentenced to life imprisonment. A campaign was launched to encourage women from ethnic minorities to become more socially involved. A number of mosques produced a code of conduct to combat extremism in their congregations. The government adopted a more rigorous approach towards resident aliens who broke the law. It also endorsed a university training scheme for imams. In December 2005, the Dutch parliament voted 80 to 30 to ban the *burka* in public places; the ban was implemented in 2007.

Immigration issues provided a permanent political backdrop in 2006, while immigration debates always involved racism and religion. Extremism in various guises was never far from the surface. In January the Immigration and Integration Minister, Rita Verdonk, caused uproar by suggesting that Dutch should be the only language spoken in the streets. Then in May she threatened to remove the citizenship of the Somali-born MP, Ayaan Hirsi Ali, of the People's Party for Freedom and Democracy, who had been under police protection after criticising Islam for its treatment of women. It then transpired that Hirsi had lied to obtain asylum: she resigned her seat and emigrated to the United States. The larger political parties favoured a tougher line on immigration. A specific issue related to 26,000 asylum seekers who had been refused refuge but had continued to remain in the country for five years: should they be expelled or amnestied and given residence permits?

The year 2007 witnessed markedly virulent hostility to immigrants, especially Muslims. Geert Wilders, leader of the Freedom Party, warned against Islam taking over Europe and again called for a ban on the *burka* in public places, which was implemented that year. Rita Verdonk, the former justice minister, who had been expelled in September from the Party of Freedom and Democracy for her extreme views, formed a Proud of the Netherlands (TN) party. Even the Queen was drawn into the debate, in her Christmas message criticising growing intolerance and suggesting there was a danger of losing sight of what bound people together as a society. Wilders took umbrage and demanded that the Queen be confined to a purely ceremonial role. In a more moderate vein, the government agreed an amnesty for long-term asylum seekers. In January 2008 a gathering of far-right politicians called for a charter against the 'Islamisation of European cities' and Geert Wilders, the parliamentary leader of the anti-immigration Dutch Freedom Party (PVV), released a strongly anti-Islamic film, *Fitna*, which continues to attract controversy.

SWITZERLAND

In September 2004, Swiss voters rejected a law that would have made it easier for young foreigners (many of them born in Switzerland) to gain Swiss nationality. Voters rejected two proposals: to grant automatic citizenship to third-generation immigrants and to make naturalisation easier for second-generation immigrants. Switzerland's foreign-born population in 2004 stood at 1.5 million or 20 per cent of the total. The Swiss People's Party (SVP) mounted a racist campaign of advertisements, such as one of black hands grabbing at Swiss passports or a Swiss identity card in the name of Osama bin Laden. Other parties condemned such tactics. Since 1970, the Swiss authorities had found it increasingly difficult to control the flow of immigrants while many newcomers were not covered by the quotas allotted to different groups. With the twenty-first century came a new era of greater mobility within the EU and between the EU and the European Free Trade Association (EFTA). The national debate in Switzerland on immigration was marked by fundamental differences between left and right and did not adequately take account of European integration. Laws to bar immigrants of any kind are by definition discriminatory. A new law proposed in 2006 aimed to limit immigration from countries outside the EU and EFTA, although highly skilled workers from elsewhere would be exempted. As the historian Thomas Gees argued, 'Ideology and prejudice is part of the discussion ... there are good reasons to limit the free movement of people to protect the domestic labour market, and this has next to nothing to do with xenophobia.'[12] In Europe, Switzerland has one of the highest rates of foreign-born residents. Gees also pointed out that 'Switzerland has signed an accord on the free movement of people within the EU, so the immigration law does not apply to these citizens.' It was suggested at this time that Swiss law was targeting people from the Balkans, who made up the biggest group of immigrants from non-EU states, and this raised the question of how restrictive the rules for non-European immigrants should be.

By 2007 it was apparent that there was growing racism and xenophobia in Switzerland. This was highlighted by a poster of the Swiss People's Party (SVP), which showed three white sheep and one black sheep. The three white sheep are standing on the Swiss flag and one of them is kicking the black sheep off the flag. The UN saw this as a sinister symbol of the rise of a new racism 'in the heart of one of the world's oldest independent democracies'. The caption was 'For More Security'. The SVP at that time had the largest number of seats in the Swiss parliament and was a member of the country's coalition government. The party had launched a campaign to raise 100,000 signatures to force a referendum to reintroduce into the penal code a measure that would allow judges to deport foreigners who committed serious crimes once they have served their jail sentence. It also wanted parliament to pass a law that would allow the entire family of a criminal under the age of 18 to be deported as soon as sentence was passed. (It would be the first such law in Europe since the Nazis had introduced the practice of kin liability.)

Despite such draconian suggestions, the Swiss People's Party was politically ambivalent on the whole issue of immigration. A quarter of the country's workers are foreign immigrants who have contributed hugely to Swiss economic stability and its high GDP. On the other hand, Dr Ulrich Schluer of the SVP wants to ban the building of Muslim minarets. Some 4.3 per cent of the country's 7.5 million population are Muslims. On the other side of the debate Mario Fehr, a Social Democrat MP, argues:

> Deporting people who have committed no crime is not just unjust and inhumane, it's stupid. Three quarters of the Swiss people think that foreigners who work here are helping the economy. We have a lot of qualified workers – IT specialists, doctors, dentists. [To get rid of foreigners would lead to] economic disaster.[13]

The antagonism towards Muslims, however, is part of a wider debate in both Europe and the United States about national identity: how many foreigners with demonstrably different customs and religions can these countries absorb? It is a question that goes to the heart of many debates about immigration. Direct democracy, including the system that allows regular referenda on important topics, makes Switzerland the most democratic country in Europe. Its opposition to joining the EU has been greatly influenced by the undemocratic decision-making process in Brussels to which it would have to surrender powers that at present can be voted upon by the Swiss people. Switzerland has the toughest naturalisation laws in Europe: candidates for naturalisation must spend a minimum of twelve years residence and gain fluency in one of the national languages. At the present time, 20 per cent of the Swiss population and 25 per cent of the work force are non-naturalised. Such figures suggest that, as time passes, naturalisation will become less important for immigrants than it is seen to be at present.

10
East Europe, Turkey

The complications and contradictions inherent in understanding migration are always more difficult to deal with than the prejudices. The opening of Europe to the unfettered movement within the EU of its people that followed the Big Bang represents one of the most advanced social and civil developments of modern times. There were always going to be objections to such uncontrolled movement yet acceptance of the principle led to a grudging acceptance of the fact, while fears on the part of the rich Western members of the EU that they would be flooded with job-seekers were to be tempered by the impact of the recession.

Three EU members that gave unrestricted access to Central and Eastern Europeans after enlargement in 2004 filled vital skill shortages thanks to these immigrants. Britain, Sweden and Ireland benefited from recruits who, according to the lobby group European Citizen Action Service, took 'hard-to-fill' jobs in the health care, farming and tourist sectors. During 2004–5 about 175,000 workers from the former East European communist countries arrived in Britain, which then had one of the lowest unemployment rates in the EU, while a further 85,000 came to Ireland and another 22,000 to Sweden. France, which feared being overrun by a wave of Polish workers, issued only 1,600 work permits to Poles in the first eleven months following enlargement, though many more were believed to have entered France to work there illegally. French fears of the influx of 'Polish plumbers' taking jobs when employment ran at 10 per cent contributed to the French 'no' vote in the May 2005 referendum on the proposed European constitution. The other twelve EU countries (apart from Britain, Ireland and Sweden) imposed various last-minute restrictions upon the entry of new workers before the May 2004 enlargement. They did so, in part, because of concerns that some immigrants from East Europe would try to obtain social benefits unfairly and also because they feared that low-wage recruits would flood their labour markets. The bulk of the post-Big Bang new immigrant workers came from Poland, while Slovenes and Czechs, whose economies were doing better, were least likely to move. Poles accounted for more than half the migration from East to West Europe at this time. Apart from Britain, many went to Germany, Italy, the Netherlands and Ireland. The numbers of Poles in Britain were sufficiently large that the Polish political parties campaigned there for votes for the 2005 Polish elections.

Immediately after the Big Bang, Eastern European workers were most likely to choose to immigrate into one of the three countries – Britain, Ireland and Sweden – that had opened their borders to immigration from the ten new member states. The European Citizen Action Service (ECAS) claimed that most of these incomers were generally young (between 18 and 34 years of age) and male. ECAS, however, was unable to confirm whether the immigrants represented a brain drain or not: that is, whether the immigrants – or a proportion of them – were highly qualified, although the figures did include between 3 and 5 per cent of young adults who had completed a university course.[1]

West European reluctance to accept immigrants from former Communist Eastern Europe was not universal. Ireland, booming as the Celtic Tiger, had been actively recruiting non-European nationals since 1999 and so welcomed low-cost workers from East Europe as did Sweden. In Britain, London clearly welcomed Eastern European workers because of shortages in certain sectors, such as waiters and manual workers, although there were doubts as to how long public opinion would accept such an influx willingly. The better-educated Eastern Europeans wanted experience and training to take home rather than seeking to settle permanently outside their own countries. A Slovakian couple, Jozef and Silvia, working in Dublin – he had a degree in architecture and she in marketing – explained: 'We each have a job that matches the level of our education, something which our country could never have given us. But we would like to return to Slovakia.' Job experience for the better educated rather than permanent settlement seemed to be the norm. The ECAS report concluded: 'The British, Irish and Swedish can remain calm. Immigration from the East seems to be a temporary thing.'

Movement from the East may prove to be temporary in the long run, but by April 2006 more than 3.5 million Eastern and Central Europeans had visited Britain since enlargement. Such a movement in so short a time spelt a real change in both the flexibility and fluidity of European people, even though most of the visitors were holiday-makers. The British budget airline Ryanair was flying regularly to eight Polish cities. The strengthening of economic links between East and West Europe also meant a growth in business trips both ways. Figures from the British Office of National Statistics showed that 3.2 million visitors from Poland, Hungary, the Czech Republic, Slovakia, Slovenia, Lithuania, Latvia and Estonia visited Britain between May 2004 and the end of 2005, and another 370,000 visited Britain in the first two months of 2006. Over half of these visitors were Poles (1.7 million), followed by 420,000 Czechs, 344,000 Hungarians, 283,000 Slovakians, 194,000 Lithuanians, 119,000 Latvians, 84,000 Slovenians and 66,000 Estonians.[2] This East European influx set off the usual scare stories about overstretching British social services and led the Immigration Advisory Service (IAS) to condemn 'ill-informed comment' and 'hysteria'. The British Labour Party called for a pause while the UK economy absorbed the estimated 600,000 migrant workers from the ten countries that joined the EU in 2004. Popular views on immigration tend to harden in direct proportion to any increase in unemployment, but, speaking for business, Sir Digby Jones, the former director-general of the Confederation of British Industry, said:

You cannot blame migrants if they are prepared to ... work for wages, which though they may seem low to us, are a lot higher than in their own country. They come here with the skills and the education that we no longer seem to be able to provide our own workforce.[3]

By 2007, however, the rate of European workers registering in Britain was dropping, with 66 per cent of all applications from Poles. While there were other concerns, it was the influx of East Europeans that persuaded Britain to tighten its immigration system. The Home Office Minister Tony McNulty announced:

We have said we will double resources for immigration policing and last year we delivered record removals of those still in Britain illegally – with one being deported every eight minutes. In the next 12 months we are introducing a single border force, fingerprint checks for all visa applicants, ID cards for foreign nationals, electronic passenger screening and an Australian style points system.

Like Europe's other main immigrant destination countries – France, Germany, Italy and Spain – Britain was tightening, or trying to tighten, its system of controls.

By 2009, however, there had occurred a substantial reversal of traffic from East to West as the recession bit in all the major European economies. Ireland's capital Dublin, nicknamed Dublinski, had taken in 180,000 Poles, Czechs and other East Europeans in the years following enlargement in 2004, but a dramatic rise in unemployment to 11 per cent of the work force prompted many of these East European immigrants to reconsider: between April 2008 and the end of April 2009, as many as 50,000 workers probably returned to Eastern Europe. In recession, as many immigrants concluded, it is easier to be unemployed at home with your family than unemployed in a foreign country.

The Czech Republic had its own problem with immigrant workers and in February 2009 offered to pay €500 and provide a one-way plane ticket to all foreigners who had lost their jobs and wanted to go home. The reverse exodus from the more prosperous countries in Western Europe added in turn to the pressures buffeting Central and Eastern Europe, where migrants from developing countries were being encouraged to leave.[4]

POLAND

Situated between the two great powers of Germany and Russia, fought over and overrun in numerous wars, partitioned and occupied, Poland has been one of Europe's most battered states and its fierce nationalism has increased in proportion to the pressures exerted upon it by more powerful neighbours. One consequence of this history has been to make Poland a country of migration, while its location on the eastern extremity of Europe has turned it into a major transit route both east and west. In the years following the break-up of the Soviet empire, Poland has privatised and liberalised its economy just as the IMF, the EU and the British government had advised it to do. It has also had the benefit of very substantial foreign investment, to the extent that the 'commanding heights' of its economy are now mainly Western- rather than Polish-owned. Seen as a success in the West and a determined would-be member of the EU, which it joined in 2004, Poland found itself facing a rapid fall in population due to a high rate of emigration and a declining birth rate. Ironically, the recession has reversed this trend, at least in part, as the collapse of the construction and other sectors in the Western economies persuaded immigrant Poles to return home. Even so, Poland had been one of the largest sources of migrants between 2000 and 2005, providing a reservoir of labour for countries in Western Europe and North America. Now, depending upon the overall impact of the recession, Poland could find its role as a source of emigrant labour being reversed, as its modernised industries and rising prosperity attract immigrants, while it will continue as a major transit country for migrants coming into Europe from points farther east.

From 1945 to 1989, Poland's migration policy reflected that of the Soviet bloc as a whole. Tight visa and passport controls meant that few Poles could leave. Those Poles who did manage to emigrate, mainly to Germany, were not able to return home, so any decision to leave Poland was a difficult one. Germany was the main destination for communist-era Poles, who entered the country illegally through East Germany. Once there, they were allowed to stay provided they had a document which was accepted as confirming their German ancestry. This German readiness to accept Poles lasted until 1991, when a more stringent procedure for obtaining German ancestry status was put in place. The United States was the second most popular destination after Germany and from 1945 to 1989 accepted between 120,000 and 150,000 Poles, granting them refugee status from communist Europe. The collapse of the USSR in 1989 transformed Poland's political and economic structure. At the same time Poles were free to emigrate and, for a number of years, there was higher emigration than immigration into the country. In 1989 26,000 people left Poland while only 2,200 entered it. In 1991 the figure was 21,000 leaving and 5,000 entering and, thereafter, about 20,000 people left Poland every year with a peak of 26,900 leaving in 2000. When it became clear in 2003 that Poland would be admitted to the EU the following year, there was an influx of migrants seeking work permits, no doubt hoping they could then move to other parts of Europe. Incomers seeking temporary work permits in 2003 numbered 28,767 while 1,805 sought permanent permits. These were granted mainly to people from states that were members of the former USSR: Ukrainians 8,456, Belarussians 2,507, Russians 2,081, Armenians 1,018, while 1,316 went to Vietnamese.[5] During the period from 1989 to 2003, Poland received a growing number of asylum applications, especially from Russians escaping from war-torn Chechnya. Under pressure from external forces, Poland also had to work out a political structure to deal with immigrants. There was massive mobility of citizens from the former Soviet Union, permanent migration into Poland, mainly from Eastern European countries, the growth of new immigrant communities from such countries as China, Vietnam and Armenia, and the return of Polish citizens who had been living abroad. Between 1992 and 1997 Poland devised a new Aliens Act, which allowed the free movement of persons and outlined conditions for entry, stay and transit through Poland, while also gearing Polish practice to the possibility of EU accession and human rights practices. When Poland did join the EU in 2004, this helped it formulate appropriate visa policies and border protection, since it had to take account of EU legislation relating to immigration and the laws known as the *acquis* that constituted membership obligations. Meanwhile, in 2001 Poland had passed a separate Repatriation Act to resettle people of 'Polish ethnicity or descent' from the Asian part of the former USSR.

As a requirement of EU membership, Poland was obligated to implement the Schengen agreement, which, among other things, made visas for Poland's eastern neighbours mandatory. This applied to Belarus, Russia and Ukraine, but Poland believed, correctly as it turned out, that such visas would immediately weaken cross-border trade with those countries and hurt the border populations who benefited from such trade. When the new visa system was applied, cross-border mobility decreased by 30 per cent, but this proved to be a temporary consequence, for by March 2005 cross-border movement had returned to its previous level. In 2003 the Polish Office of Repatriation and Foreigners estimated that in 2003 there were 30,000 illegal Vietnamese in the country and a total undocumented population of between 45,000 and 50,000.[6]

For the best part of four years from 2004 Britain's construction and hospitality industries had flourished courtesy of an influx of up to 1 million Poles, but by April 2008 Poland wanted them back. According to Jerome Taylor: 'The Warsaw government is so worried about a national labour shortage in the industries that it plans to advertise in Britain to encourage expatriate Poles to return to the country.'[7] The new government under Prime Minister Donald Tusk, which won the Polish elections at the end of 2007, had pledged to encourage Polish migrants to return home. He was pushing a policy that was supported by many Polish immigrants in Britain, where deteriorating economic conditions had so weakened the currency that they were getting fewer zlotys for their pounds. Poland, meanwhile, had been suffering labour shortages in the building and hospitality industries, precisely those in which Polish immigrants had been employed in Britain. By 2008, more Poles were leaving Britain to return home than were arriving in the country. The role of the Poles in relation to Britain where, in the popular imagination they were swamping the country, is worth examining because it demonstrates very clearly how economics dominates immigration and how, when the jobs dry up, the migrants leave.

BULGARIA AND ROMANIA

The democratic changes in Bulgaria and the economic opportunities that globalisation presented to it meant, among other new developments, that after 1989, migration became a positive choice for its citizens. Prior to 1989–92, Bulgaria, like the other Soviet bloc countries of Eastern Europe, had limited, strictly controlled migration. Now, however, Bulgaria became part of the European and world migration system, with a substantial number of its citizens exercising their new freedom to emigrate. A new government priority was to regulate and control the processes of migration, to increase the security of Bulgarian citizens and combat trafficking and illegal migration. Government policy aimed at achieving an optimal balance between the freedom of movement of people and the control of illegal immigration, while respecting the fundamental human rights and freedoms guaranteed by international treaties and the standards of the EU, which Bulgaria aspired to join. By 2004, Bulgaria had completed its membership negotiations and was set to join the EU in January 2007, while the national assembly adopted new laws and regulations to bring Bulgaria into compliance with EU standards.[8]

Enthusiasm for the expansion of Europe was constantly tempered by sudden doubts and this was the case in relation to Bulgaria and Romania. While the EU expansion of 2004 was regarded as a triumph for the European idea, the prospect of Bulgaria and Romania joining raised a number of fears that the two countries would present the EU with problems. The President of Bulgaria, Georgi Purvanov, might describe accession as a 'heavenly moment' but sceptics in countries like Britain pointed to the fact that the two countries had a combined population of nearly 30 million, that their average per capita GDP of roughly $4,400 was the lowest in Europe, equivalent to only 33 per cent of the EU average, that both still had a long way to go in achieving compliance with EU standards in terms of the judiciary, the rule of law, and controlling corruption and organized crime. In other words, they presented more of a challenge than a positive addition, with the added fear that large numbers of them would seek work in Western Europe, prompting the then British Secretary of State for Trade, Alistair Darling, to say that there would be no 'open door' policy. Bulgaria and Romania faced an uphill task in gaining full EU acceptance. As always, the British believed that their country would be the primary target of such immigrants and, through much of 2006, debated how to control or curb them. In a dramatic policy U-turn, clearly designed as a sop to the anti-immigration lobby, the British Home Secretary John Reid unveiled plans to prevent thousands of people from Rumania and Bulgaria coming to Britain – and this despite the positive impact of the Polish contribution to the economy.

As a consequence of the global recession most Bulgarian immigrants who had worked abroad were returning home in 2009. Of 55,000 Bulgarians registered in Spain 9,800 were in receipt of social security payments after losing their jobs. A new Bulgarian Citizenship Act specifies the procedures and conditions for acquisition, loss and reinstatement of Bulgarian citizenship. Any citizen of other states will only be considered a Bulgarian citizen in accordance with Bulgarian legislation and, for example, adoption will not change the citizenship of an individual. The Bulgarian Foreigners Act was changed in May 2005 to cover both foreigners and also family members of

Bulgarian nationals not considered as European Economic Area or EU citizens. Under the country's new immigration programme high net worth individuals and their families are allowed to obtain permanent residence status provided they invest a sum of $500,000 before taking up residence in Bulgaria. The deposit will be returned after five years. The Bulgarian business immigrant must prove he has a minimum amount of money obtained legally and is not under criminal investigation.

Following the break-up of the USSR, Romania introduced new, lenient citizenship rules. In the run-up to 1 January 2007, many thousands of potential candidates for Romanian citizenship applied for it so as to qualify for EU membership and the right to move from Romania into other parts of the EU. According to the new Romanian citizenship law, large populations with ethnic Romanian roots are eligible to obtain Romanian citizenship.

When Romania was founded as a modern state in 1878, it had strict citizenship rules and, while it allowed citizens of adjacent countries to obtain citizenship, it forced them to relinquish their existing citizenship: this policy applied during the period of Soviet 'control' of Romania, when citizenship laws were used as a tool for political control. In theory, therefore, former Romanian citizens were free to return to the country, although in practice only a small number did and then only if they met acceptable political criteria. New citizenship rules were introduced following the fall of the Ceaucescu regime, and Romania's disengagement from Russia. In 1991 a new citizenship law sought to reunite parts of Romania that had been taken over by the Soviet Union at the end of the Second World War, and especially Moldavia, which had been part of Romania before the war (although historically it had long been a subject of dispute, first between Russia and the Ottoman Empire, and then by Communist Russia). The new law determined that a person could acquire Romanian citizenship in one of four ways: by naturalisation – living in Romania for between five and eight years; by birth in Romanian territory or by virtue of being a second or third generation descendant of a Romanian citizen; by adoption – by a parent who was a Romanian citizen; and by repatriation. Further, Romanians who had had their citizenship revoked prior to 1989 could re-acquire citizenship by request, even though they possessed other citizenship and even if they did not intend to settle in Romania. This lenient legislation and the decision to admit Romania to EU membership in 2007 significantly increased the numbers of those eligible for Romanian citizenship and the highest number of new applications came from Moldova. Between 1990 and 2005 about 100,000 Moldavans obtained Romanian citizenship. Then, in the first half of 2006, over 300,000 Moldavans applied for Romanian citizenship. It is estimated that more than 75 per cent of Moldova's population of 4 million are entitled to Romanian citizenship.[9]

DISINTEGRATION AND RECONSTRUCTION

The disintegration of the USSR was paralleled by the collapse of Yugoslavia. The consequence of these two upheavals was to create a region of more than a score of countries stretching from the three Baltic states of Estonia, Latvia and Lithuania in the north to Albania and Bulgaria in the south, an area which was deeply disturbed and subject to major dislocations and civil wars, causing massive dislocations of people – as refugees, IDPs, asylum seekers and finally economic migrants desperate to escape the poverty and violence of their own countries – and for the first time since the end of the Cold War, they were able to do so.

Without attempting to diagnose the eruption of ethnic hatreds and violence that tore 'Tito's' Yugoslavia apart between 1990 and the Dayton Accord of 1995, it is enough to show that in 1997, two years after the precarious peace and two years before the Kosovo war, the statistics of death and movement were as follows. According to the World Bank the war in disintegrating Yugoslavia had cost an estimated 250,000 dead and 200,000 wounded. The UNHCR statistics revealed 1.4 million Bosnian refugees. There were approximately 343,000 refugees in the other countries of former Yugoslavia, mainly Croatia and the Federal Republic of Yugoslavia, a further 266,000 Bosnian refugees in West and Central Europe, mainly in Germany, and 825,000 IDPs in Bosnia and Herzegovina. In addition, between 1996 and December 1997 200,000 Bosnians had been repatriated and over 200,000 IDPs returned to their home areas.

As of August 1997, the most significant number of UNHCR-assisted returns were from Slovenia, Switzerland and Turkey, accounting for 3,332 persons. Germany had helped 35,223 refugees to return to Bosnia and Herzegovina. The UNHCR estimated that about 220,000 Bosnian refugees might return in 1998, while there were then still over 330,000 Croatian refugees who had not been repatriated.[10] The collapse of Yugoslavia led to the emergence of seven small, mainly poor independent states – Slovenia (joined the EU in 2004), Croatia (negotiating to join), Bosnia and Herzegovina, Serbia, Montenegro (broke from Serbia in 2006), Macedonia and Kosovo (a UN-monitored independent state since 2007). Albania, which became involved in the Kosovo war, had been independent since the beginning of the twentieth century.

Of the European Soviet Socialist Republics – Estonia, Latvia, Lithuania, Belarus, Moldova and Ukraine, and the three Caucasian states of Armenia, Azerbaijan and Georgia – none had escaped conflict of one kind or another as they re-oriented their politics westwards, while at the same time coming to terms with their continuing semi-dependence upon Russia. They looked enviously at the more advanced economies of the EU, which most of them hoped to join, while many of their citizens in search of a better economic future became migrants to the EU, either in the hope of obtaining permanent residence leading eventually to citizenship or, more realistically, seeking temporary work permits or illegal status. The disturbed condition of Eastern Europe and the territories of former Yugoslavia between 1989 and 2009 prompted mixed EU reactions. On the one hand, the EU expanded to take into its membership a total of ten Eastern European countries between 2004 and 2007, while other states such as Croatia lined up to qualify for membership.

As so often in world affairs, there are unintended consequences that have to be taken into account. Just as poor Europe saw rich Europe lifting it out of economic poverty, the credit crunch and recession that got under way at the end of 2007 did more to restrain the flood of immigrants than any of the control measures that were hastily pushed through the parliaments of Western Europe. However, once (if) the recession passes, the economic disparities between rich Europe and poor Europe will remain to be resolved.

TURKEY

Turkey's population in 2007 was 73.8 million (by 2009 it passed 75 million) and its per capita income, at just over $8,000, is double that of Bulgaria and Romania while its population, although it is officially a secular society, is 99 per cent Muslim. Turkey wants to join the EU and first applied in the 1960s. There is an ongoing debate as to whether Turkey qualifies as a European country at all, since the bulk of its geographical area and four-fifths of the population are in Asia. But a fifth of the population, approximately 15 million, as well as the ancient capital Istanbul, now one of the largest cities in the world, are in Europe. After years of applying for consideration, membership talks were formally launched in October 2005, though Turkey was warned that the negotiations would last ten years. Europe is sharply divided over the Turkish issue: France has made plain its opposition to full Turkish membership, though President Sarkozy has suggested he would accept associate membership for Turkey. Poland also opposes Turkish admission on the grounds that it wants a 'Christian' Europe. Germany, though a long-standing ally, has also expressed doubts about Turkish EU membership. A number of arguments have been advanced in opposition to Turkey joining the EU: that it is poor and bringing more than 70 million people up to the economic standards of the EU would cost too much; that it has a poor human rights record; that it resorts to torture (denied); that it does not have a fully free press or media. These objections could all be overcome if both sides really wanted a positive solution. The core objection, usually unstated, is that Turkey would bring more than 70 million Muslims into Europe and change forever its religious and cultural composition. Whether Turkey joins the EU or not is highly relevant to the migration issue. As a full member of the EU, Turkey would enjoy the right of free movement within the Union and present members fear an influx of low-skilled Turkish job-seekers. If, on the other hand, it is excluded, Turkey could still become the conduit for an illegal influx of immigrants, both its own people and those from farther east, a situation that already exists but could become something much worse.

During 2009, the EU tried to persuade Turkey to assist in rounding up people-smuggling rings so as to stem the movement of illegal immigrants into the EU. Turkey has become a major transit country for illegal immigrants from Asia. They cross Turkey to its Mediterranean coast on the Aegean Sea and then make their way through the Greek islands into the EU. According to France's Immigration Minister, Eric Besson, the battle to stop illegal immigrants 'can only be fought by resolving two issues: ties with Turkey and Libya'. He continued: 'When it comes to Turkey, their willingness to cooperate with the EU needs to be tested. The first comments by Turkey's interior minister have been encouraging. But now we have to see the concrete details.' There is a whiff of blackmail in this arrogant and accusatory statement. The EU Justice Commissioner Jacques Barrot was likewise determined to curb the influx of illegal immigrants, which threatens to destabilise some countries in Europe, such as Greece, and hampers EU efforts to handle legitimate asylum requests. As he has said: 'If we don't link migration to development and diplomacy we won't succeed.' However, a number of obstacles have to be overcome before Turkey is likely to cooperate with the EU. Thus, although Turkey is prepared to sign readmission agreements to take back immigrants who left its shores, it argues that it is only a transit country and therefore must have similar agreements signed with Pakistan and Afghanistan (two of the principal sources of illegal immigrants) so that Ankara can send immigrants back to those countries.

The argument escalated in July 2009 when Barrot described illegal immigration through Turkey into Greece as a threat to Greek democracy, and called on Turkey to do more to combat people traffickers. Following a visit to Athens, Barrot told a news briefing that he had promised the Greek government financial help to deal with the problem of illegal immigrants; he also argued that the EU should hold more active talks with Turkey to persuade it to establish better supervision of illegal migration. He said: 'Because we can indeed imagine a major risk of destabilising Greek democracy through migrations that are absolutely uncontrolled and uncontrollable.' The executive European Commission would work more actively towards an agreement on readmission to Turkey of illegal immigrants and on better monitoring of illegal departures from the Turkish coast. 'Turkey has to help us to fight against facilitators and traffickers', Barrot said. 'We cannot do nothing and we need to obtain, with Turkey, much firmer and stricter negotiations ... we will, for our part, help Turkey through readmission agreements we hope to sign with Pakistan and maybe other Asian countries.' Greece claimed (July 2009) that it had arrested about 47,000 illegal migrants coming from Turkey during the course of 2008. It insisted that Turkey should take back illegal migrants who had crossed its territory.[11] One of the principal drug trafficking transit routes has long been through Turkey from Pakistan, across Afghanistan and Iran into eastern Turkey, then to Istanbul and thence through the Balkans into the main drugs markets of the EU. It is unlikely to change.

MUSLIMS IN EUROPE

One of the main objections to Turkish accession to the EU is that it would add more than 70 million Muslims to the present EU population of about 475 million, most of whom, in the widest meaning of the term, are Christian. There are already about 20 million Muslims in Europe, although exact figures are hard to come by since some countries do not compile such statistics and allowance must be made for illegal immigrants who do not willingly declare themselves. Although the majority of these European Muslims are recent immigrants or their descendants, a significant proportion of them have been present in Europe for centuries. Historically, Muslims have been present in the two extremities of Europe – the Iberian Peninsula in the West and the Balkans in the East. The Moors invaded Spain through Gibraltar in 711 and dominated much of Spain and Portugal for seven centuries until their final expulsion from Granada in 1492. The Balkans were part of the Ottoman Empire for 500 years and the oldest Muslim settlements in Europe are found in Albania, Bosnia, Macedonia, Kosovo, Serbia and Montenegro; these small countries account for 6.5 million of Europe's 20 million Muslims. There are 2.2 million Albanian Muslims, accounting for 70 per cent of the population, 1.5 million in Bosnia and Herzegovina, accounting for 40 per cent of the population, 630,000 in Macedonia, accounting for 30 per cent of the population and 1.8 million in Kosovo, accounting for 90 per cent of the population. Other countries in the region, such as Bulgaria and Romania, had close links with Islam through their incorporation in the Ottoman Empire, while the Austrian Habsburg Empire annexed Bosnia and Herzegovina in 1908. Today, Islam is recognised as an official religion in Austria.

However, the majority of Europe's Muslims are either recent immigrants or the descendants of immigrants who have arrived in Europe since 1945. The leading ten countries in terms of the size of their Muslim minorities are shown in Table 10.1:

Table 10.1   Countries with the largest Muslim minorities

Country	Population	Muslim population	Percentage of total
France	62.3m	5–6m	8–9%
Germany	82.5m	3m	3.6%
Britain	58.8m	1.6m	2.8%
Spain	43.1m	1.0m	2.3%
Netherlands	16.3m	945,000	5.8%
Italy	58.4m	825,000	1.4%
Belgium	10.3m	400,000	4.0%
Switzerland	7.4m	310,800	4.2%
Sweden	9.0m	300,000	3.0%
Denmark	5.4m	270,000	5.0%

France has the largest Muslim population in Europe, a majority of whom came from former French territories in Africa, most notably Algeria, Morocco and Tunisia. In the case of Germany, a majority are Turkish and came originally as 'guest workers'. Germany also took in a large number of Bosnian refugees during the collapse of Yugoslavia in the 1990s. Muslim communities were established in Britain during the nineteenth century. In the post-1945 period they came from East Africa and then South Asia (former British India) and, more recently, as refugees from Afghanistan, Iraq and Pakistan. At least 50 per cent of the present population were born in Britain and, according to the 2001 census, a third of the Muslim population was under 16. Spain's present Muslim population began to enter the country in the 1970s, many as job-seekers from Morocco. The state recognises Islam as one of the country's religions. The first Muslim immigrants in the post-1945 years to come to the Netherlands were from Indonesia and Suriname, its former colonies. Later, its tolerant immigration policy attracted other Muslims from Somalia, Turkey and Morocco. Substantial numbers of Muslim immigrants began to arrive in Italy during the 1980s from North Africa, South Asia, Albania and the Middle East. Islam is one of seven recognised religions in Belgium and the majority of its Muslims come from Morocco, Turkey and Albania. The Muslim population in Switzerland came as workers in the 1960s, mainly from Turkey, former Yugoslavia and Albania. Muslims in Sweden come from a number of countries, though in the twenty-first century it has welcomed a relatively high number of refugees or asylum seekers from Iraq. Denmark has Muslims from a range of countries, though in recent years strong nationalist feelings have led to anti-Islam demonstrations and some violence.[12]

Muslim immigrants, though accounting for less than 5 per cent of the total EU population, are making a profound impact upon their new host countries in terms of culture, religion and, increasingly, politics, and will affect perceptions of multiculturalism while also influencing EU relations with an increasingly assertive Islamic world.

11
Russia

In 1990, just before the break-up of the USSR, its population at 280 million was somewhat greater than that of the United States, which then stood at 250 million. After the 15 Soviet Socialist Republics had declared their independence and withdrawn from the Union, Russia alone was left with a population of 148 million; from 1993 this steadily declined until it stood at 141,636,000 in 2008. Of the 1990 population of 280 million, approximately 130 million, almost half of the total, had been lost to Russia. Taking the population figures for 2008, six former Soviet republics – Belarus (9.7 million), Ukraine (46.3 million), Moldova (3.7 million), Armenia (3.0 million), Georgia (4.3 million) and Azerbaijan (8.5 million) between them had a population of 73.8 million. The five former Soviets in Central Asia – Kazakhstan (15.4 million), Turkmenistan (4.9 million), Uzbekistan (26.8 million), Kyrgyzstan (5.2 million) and Tajikistan (6.7 million) – had a combined population of 49.4 million, while the three Baltic states – Estonia (1.3 million), Latvia (2.2 million) and Lithuania (3.3 million) – brought the second total to 56.2 million. Thus, Russia, in control of the Soviet Union of 280 million people at the beginning of the 1990s had been reduced to a Russia of 141 million in 2008. In demographic, land and resource terms, that added up to a formidable reduction in Russian power and influence. Given Russia's huge size of 17 million square km, even after the departure of its imperial satellites, there is no country in the world in greater need of an expanding population than Russia, whether this comes from encouraging an increased birth rate (a policy now being pursued), attracting members of the worldwide Russian diaspora back or pursuing a positive policy of attracting immigrants, whether ethnic Russians or others. Both to sustain control of its vast area and to develop its huge resource base to the full, Russia needs more people. This is bound to be an important factor in Moscow's migration policies in the decades to come.

The British Empire was dismantled over a period of more than 40 years, beginning with independence for India in 1947, and in many respects the loss of power involved proved a traumatic experience for the British people. The Russian Empire was dismantled over three years, from 1989 to 1992. Its loss must be even harder for the Russians to accept. As a result, Moscow faces huge problems, one of which is how to deal with the remaining, often substantial Russian minorities left behind in its former Soviet republics. They cannot be ignored. There are two choices: try, with inducements, to persuade them to return to Russia to boost its population; or leave them in place and use them as political levers to exercise influence in the former Soviet republics. The latter option may seem the more attractive to those who pursue Realpolitik policies but could lead to unintended and dangerous consequences. The first option makes more sense, especially in the light of Russia's declining population.

For most of the post-Second World War period Russia exercised tight control over immigration into the USSR and emigration from it. Even so, there was large-scale movement within the Soviet Union as people changed their jobs and places of residence and, despite the controls, substantial numbers of certain ethnic groups, mainly Jews, Germans and Armenians, managed to emigrate – over 2 million Jews left the Soviet Union between 1945 and 1991. Even so, such emigration did not have any major impact upon the population as a whole. However, once Mikail Gorbachev had come to power in 1985 and introduced his policies of *glasnost* and *perestroika*, migration policy began to change. Thus, in 1985 only 2,943 people received official permission to emigrate, a figure that had leapt to 100,000 by 1991. Once the USSR had broken up, new migration policies were introduced. The internal passport that gave people permission to work and live in a particular area was abolished, allowing freedom of movement within Russia. Then, the general right to emigrate was written into law in the 1993 constitution. One of Russia's major problems is the vast size of its eastern and northern regions – as well as the severe climate – which makes it hard to persuade people to settle there. Despite pay and other benefits to attract people to these regions, the turnover is high and this hampers steady development. Since few refugees or economic migrants had been attracted to the Soviet Union prior to its break-up, the government had not created any efficient system of control. Such a system is now urgently needed to cope with possibly large immigration into Russia in the changed circumstances of the new century. As early as 1992 the ILO recorded that 9 million ethnic Russians were in the process of moving into Russia from the former Soviets, their numbers swelled by illegal foreign workers.

In 1995, migrants from ex-Soviet states and the Third World were continuing to enter Russia. Since 1994, according to the Russian Migration Federal Service, about 2.5 million people had moved to Russia from the former Soviet states. Russia's Centre for Economic Affairs estimated that by 2000 there would have been a net migration of 2.8 million people from the former Soviet republics into Russia. Most of these migrants were expected to come from Tajikistan, Azerbaijan and Uzbekistan, as well as Kazakhstan. Meanwhile, the bitter conflict with Chechnya had produced 300,000 internal refugees. Although figures for immigrants into Russia at this time may have looked encouraging from the point of view of boosting the Russian population, many of them were in transit to the West, with some 500,000 from Afghanistan, Iraq, Somalia, Sri Lanka, Ethiopia, Iran, Sudan, Angola, Pakistan and Nigeria – a huge ethnic mix – waiting for the chance to leave Moscow and head West. Meanwhile, Russia had launched 'Operation Foreigner', a programme to rid the country of illegal Chinese immigrants that the government claimed to be successful. The programme required more border guards on the Russian frontier with China and closer screening of documents. In some border towns, Chinese workers had both Russian and Chinese documents and to enter Russia a Chinese citizen only needed a certificate or special passport.[1]

Both during the Soviet era and post 1991, racism often in virulent forms has been a destructive aspect of Russian social life. Anti-Semitism long pre-dated the communist era. The Soviet policy of offering a large number of scholarships to students from the Third World, particularly Africa, gave such students a valuable training, but they were often the targets of brutal racist attacks. In 2006, Amnesty International produced a damning report on racist violence spinning out of control and accused the government of deferring to far-right groups who appeared able to attack and murder non-white foreigners at will. 'Racist attacks and killings of foreigners and ethnic minorities are reported with shocking regularity in Russia and, disturbingly, their frequency seems to be increasing', the report said.

> Anyone who does not look typically ethnic Russian ... is at risk. The attacks are unexpected and almost always unprompted. The attackers usually attack in large groups, are often armed, for example with baseball bats and knives, and often choose targets who will not be able to defend themselves.

Most of the attacks took place in three cities – Moscow, St Petersburg and Voronezh (a university city) – while the victims were students, asylum seekers, people of Jewish origin, and refugees from Africa and Asia. Other victims came from the Middle East, Latin America and the former Soviet Central Asian republics. Russian human rights activists opposing such attacks were also targets.[2] Lack of government action to prevent such racist attacks encouraged the growth of extreme xenophobia by nationalist organisations such as the Movement Against Illegal Migration, which advocates the deportation of non-white migrants, or the Slavic Union, which is another white supremacist group.

In 2005, 95 per cent of documented migrants came from other Commonwealth of Independent States (CIS) countries and were mainly Russian or at least Russian-speaking, repatriating from Kazakhstan (29.3 per cent), Ukraine (17.4 per cent), Uzbekistan (17.2 per cent) and Kyrgyzstan (8.8 per cent). As citizens of CIS countries these migrants could enter Russia without a visa. However, in 2006 the government began to tighten controls so as to limit the inflow of workers from other CIS countries. Non-Russians were banned from working in large parts of the retail sector so as to boost employment opportunities for ethnic Russians while also defusing racial tensions. Although President Vladimir Putin promised to protect 'the native population', by 2007 there were an estimated 12 million illegal immigrants in the country, although this figure was contested by official data. By this time it was appreciated that Russia's population was in dramatic decline and legislation introduced at the beginning of 2007 was designed to compensate for this by attracting immigrants to meet labour shortages and maintain the country's economic growth. Russia has the second largest number of immigrants after the United States: according to official figures, 180,000 official immigrants enter Russia every year while the number of unregistered immigrants is estimated to be between 3 and 4 million. Striking a balance is far from easy. It was generally recognised that controlled migration could compensate for the country's population decline, which had reached a shrinkage figure of 700,000 a year, due to high mortality and low birth rates. Since 1992 the Russian birth rate has stood at 10.4 per 1,000 people, while the death rate was 16.2 per 1,000. Should these trends continue, Russia's population could fall below 100 million by 2050. On the other hand, the high level of unregistered labour migration to Russia means that migrants do not enjoy citizen rights and, as a consequence, are vulnerable to underground employers; also, popular fears are created about the changing nature of the country's ethnic make-up.

A new immigration law, effective from January 2007, was expected to provide 6.5 million migrants with a registration and working permit. The law defines quotas for migrant sending countries and imposes stiff penalties for employers who illegally employ migrants. From 2008 migration was to be linked to the demands of the Russian economy. Provisions of the law protect certain economic sectors. As of June 2007, a six-year government programme encourages 'compatriots' living abroad to return to Russia where they will receive money, social benefits and support to regain Russian citizenship. Immediately, the programme attracted 20,000 people. Despite racism and narrow nationalist arguments about ethnicity, it had become clear that the Russian economy needed migrants, both as workers and to boost the population. In particular, immigrants filled labour shortages in construction, the wholesale trade, communal and personal services and public transport. As 80 per cent of migrants are not required to have a qualification, they only compete with unqualified Russian workers. Migrants will work for significantly lower wages than Russians but it is still to their advantage to do so, since the income level of Russians is 13 times higher than the income of a typical immigrant from Tajikistan, for example. Unemployment in most sending countries is high and many migrants send more than half their earnings home to support their families. Remittances from Russia to other CIS countries in 2005 came to $3 billion and these form vital inputs for the recipient economies. According to a UN study, between 2000 and 2050 Russia will require a net immigration of 24.9 million people to maintain the size of its population and a net immigration of 35.8 million to maintain its working age population.[3]

In a perceptive article, 'Domestic Factors Driving Russia's Foreign Policy',[4] the author suggests that behind the façade of an energy empire on the rise, the government is in fact incapable of dealing with some of Russia's 'critical demographic, social, economic, and political vulnerabilities', and that these flaws could upset the country's sense of stability. Russia's many weaknesses limit its ability to act as one: 'Continuing state weakness combined with an increasingly bold foreign policy is a recipe for imperial overreach and systemic breakdown.' Unsurprisingly, Russia, indeed, is suffering a period of nostalgia for its past 'superpower' status just as Britain suffered nostalgia for its lost empire in the 1960s and 1970s. The question is: how soon can it begin dealing effectively with a totally different power scenario? The most important problem to tackle for the future is that of demography. Since the

1980s, 'Russia has experienced dramatic declines in population, fertility, and life expectancy combined with increases in mortality and disease rates, including a rise in the rates of HIV/AIDS and tuberculosis infection.'[5] On current projections, although at present the Russian population is the world's ninth largest, it could fall to 128.5 million by 2025 and 109.4 million by 2050. Only a substantial and sustained level of immigration can prevent this decline, and only by encouraging immigrants in much the same way as the United States can Russia hope to maintain and improve its economic growth and increase its standard of living. One measure that has been adopted is to stimulate births by paying $4,000 per baby. Another essential requirement is for Russia to improve its health services to cope effectively with deadly epidemics. The HIV infection rate is growing faster in Russia than in any other country outside Sub-Saharan Africa, while the country has also had to cope with a tuberculosis epidemic: these diseases thrive on poverty. Despite the new aggressive face of Russia that was Putin's principal achievement as president, poverty, lack of proper sanitation and inadequate health services affect a large proportion of the total population.

Like the EU, Russia has a growing Muslim population, many of whom were part of the USSR before its break-up. Since 1989, Russia's Muslim population has increased by 40 per cent to between 20 and 25 million. Moscow alone has a Muslim population of 2.5 million, which is larger than that of any other European city. As in the EU, many Russians are fearful of the way a growing Muslim community will alter the nation's ethnic balance.

RUSSIA AND CHINA

The Russian fear that China, with its huge population, would one day move to fill some of the empty lands to the north goes back a long way, as does the possibility of a military clash between the two. Following the ideological break between the Soviet Union and Maoist China at the beginning of the 1960s, the USSR stationed 175 divisions of troops along the 4,000-mile border between the two communist powers, more than all the forces it had facing NATO in the West. By the end of the twentieth century, both the Russian press and its officials were becoming alarmed at the prospect of growing migration from China into the Far Eastern territories of Russia. The fear was that China would embark upon a positive policy of migration into the Far East of Russia and Siberia. Estimates of the Chinese migrant population in Russia varied widely, with some putting the figure as high as 5 million,[6] although official estimates in 1998, when the Chinese influx was at its height, suggested a total of about half a million. However, official numbers double-counted 'shuttle traders', who entered and re-entered Russia several times a year. As the report already referred to claims:

Those afraid of the demographic expansion of China often maintain that most Chinese do not return home and, instead, come to Russia with the intention of staying. However, the share of tourists leaving on time was

64% in 1994, 68% in 1995, and 97% in 1996. From 1997–98, it exceeded 99%, and for the first five months of 1999 amounted to 99.2%.[7]

Such figures contradict popular beliefs that, once in Russia, Chinese visitors stayed there. Moreover, Russian law enforcement agencies in the border areas are very active and the Chinese, in any case, are easily distinguished from the local population. In 1999, when these investigations were carried out, there was only one sizeable Chinese community in Russia and that was in Moscow where between 20,000 and 25,000 Chinese had formed a stable community. Between 1989, when the census registered 11,000 Chinese in the USSR and 1999 when the numbers had increased to half a million, it might have appeared that Chinese migration was becoming uncontrollable, yet by the end of 1998 the flow had fallen dramatically, largely due to the deterioration in the Russian economy.

Russian fears focus on the huge disparity in the size and density of populations on either side of the Russo-Chinese border. The population of the Russian southern districts of the Far East is about 5 million, whereas the population of the three Chinese provinces across the border is in the region of 100 million. The population density of Chinese frontier territories is 15 to 30 times higher than on the Russian side. Given the decline in Russia's population and the difficulty in persuading young Russians to settle in these Far Eastern regions, there is a real concern that China might view these sparsely settled lands as an area into which its surplus population could migrate. Illegal immigrants have become a worldwide phenomenon and they almost necessarily bring with them criminal activities: forged papers, law-breaking, trafficking and exploitation by Russian entrepreneurs. Another problem is the potential danger to Russia's health situation, since infectious and parasitic diseases are widespread in China. Bubonic plague has been found in 11 Chinese provinces out of 22. Draconian measures to keep immigrants out can be as counter-productive as they are successful; what Russia needs is a migration policy that accepts the need for migrants, and uses them to the mutual advantage of both sides.

> Experts believe that it would be wiser to look for acceptable forms for legalizing the Chinese migrants and their activities in Russia, to vest the diaspora leaders with responsibility, to develop cooperation between diaspora leaders and local authorities, and to establish mutually beneficial partnerships with the government and businesses of the People's Republic of China.[8]

Chinese migration into the Far East of Russia is bound to continue and grow and Russia should develop a strategy to deal with it effectively.

Russia and China drew closer together in the new century and formed a relatively strong alliance as joint members of the Shanghai Cooperation Organisation. In mid 2009 they held a major joint military exercise in China's Shenyang province, involving tanks, fighter jets and 3,000 soldiers. The two countries were about to celebrate 60 years of diplomatic relations, not all of them warm. One aim of the exercise – Peace Operation 2009 – was to send an unambiguous message to their internal Muslim minorities that dissent would not be tolerated. China faces stubborn revolt by the Uighurs of its western province of Xinjiang, while Russia faces insurgency in the Caucasus republics of Ingushetia, Chechnya and Dagestan. The two countries have a good deal in common, especially their opposition to US penetration of Central Asia, which the war in Afghanistan made possible, but their present alliance is fragile; a programme on Russian TV, for example, claimed that Beijing had drawn up a secret plan to take back Russia's vast but remote eastern region by persuading migrants to settle in Russia and marry locally.

However, fears by Russian nationalists of a Chinese takeover are almost certainly without basis. Moreover, since the turn of the century, Russian immigration officers have been far stricter in controlling Chinese immigrants. In June 2009, the authorities closed down the huge Cherkizovsky market in Moscow, throwing thousands of Chinese, who dominated the market, out of work while deporting 150 workers and seizing stock worth $800 million. China does not want a military confrontation with Russia. Its aim is economic power and eventual superpower status to rival the US. Good relations suit both countries though illegal migrants are always a factor to be reckoned with.[9]

In 2008, migrants from the Central Asian countries of Tajikistan, Kyrgyzstan and Uzbekistan were badly affected by the recession in Russia and elsewhere, which caused the collapse of the construction industry. The migrant labour force from these countries was unofficially estimated at 800,000 Kyrgyz, 2 million Tajiks and 3 million Uzbeks who had been working in Russia or Kazakhstan, while some had been in the Gulf. Their remittances to their families were worth billions of dollars annually: in the case of Tajikistan they were equivalent to 50 per cent of GDP and 40 per cent for Kyrgyzstan. The return of migrant workers placed a double burden upon their countries, which lost a major source of income in their remittances and had to absorb an influx of jobless labourers.

THE RUSSIAN DIASPORA

The Russian global diaspora is approximately 20 million strong, ranging from more than 8 million in Ukraine to a mere 200 in Egypt. The largest number of diaspora Russians are to be found in the former Soviet republics, followed by the United States, the EU and Israel. According to Russian government figures there are 10 million in the three Central Asian countries (over half in Kazakhstan) and up to 11 million in Ukraine, though this figure is disputed. There are about 1 million in the independent Caucasus republics of Armenia, Azerbaijan and Georgia, 1.3 million in Belarus and 500,000 in Moldova. In the Baltic countries, there are about 800,000 in Latvia, 330,000 in Estonia and 340,000 in Lithuania. In Western Europe there are an estimated 500,000 Russian speakers in the EU (including 200,000 in Britain), while in North America there are 850,000 and a further 158,850 in Canada. In Latin America there are 70,000 in Brazil, 70,000 in Chile and 50,000 in Argentina. A further 20,000 have settled in Australia and New Zealand. Russians form one of the 56 recognised ethnic minorities in China.

Various historical upheavals in Russia have created migrant movements such as that of the Doukhobors (a religious sect) in the nineteenth and twentieth centuries to Canada. There were also periodic waves of Jewish emigration following anti-semitic pogroms in Tsarist Russia; a flood of emigrants to Europe after the 1917 October Revolution; and, in the immediate post-Second World War period, substantial numbers of Russian migrants into Germany, Canada, the US, Britain and Australia. In the 1920s, as many as 200,000 Russians fled the revolution into China and, by the 1930s, Shanghai's Russian community had grown to 25,000. During the 1970s, Russian-speaking Soviet citizens, mainly Jews, left for Israel or the US, while the KGB forced certain dissidents to leave Russia. Another major wave of migrants left Russia in the aftermath of the Soviet break-up in 1991, with the largest number heading for Israel and Germany. Russia in the 1990s witnessed a good deal of internal migration. In some cases, such as the three Baltic states with huge minorities of Russians, it is believed that the Russians were planted there to colonise and Russify the populations and their presence is deeply resented.

In 2006, President Putin announced a plan to introduce a national policy aimed at encouraging overseas ethnic Russians to return to Russia. In China an estimated 15,600 Russians are to be found in north Xinjiang, Inner Mongolia and Heilongjiang. In recent years a significant proportion of Russian migrants have been businessmen and in 2008, for example, there were 1,000 Russians in Singapore, mainly in business. The Russian diaspora is not as large as those of either China or India but it is significant and is likely to grow substantially in the coming years.

Part III

Africa

Africa cannot escape the European connection and, more than either side might realise, the affairs of the two continents are inextricably intertwined. At the present time Africa is the world's poorest, least developed continent, though one that is rich in resources. Global warming, poverty, aid dependence, civil wars, lack of development and corruption, as well as ruling elites whose only concerns are their own wealth and power, have all created widespread unemployment. Lack of opportunity with no prospect of change persuades many Africans to migrate in search of a better life, either somewhere within the continent itself – to Nigeria or South Africa, for example – or outwards to join the growing worldwide African diaspora. Europe, or more precisely the European Union, is the principal target of African emigrants. With the United States, the EU is one of the two most attractive target destinations for migrants seeking a better life. Moreover, for many would-be emigrants the former colonial links of language and culture assist their choice of destination. French-speaking Africans from the Maghreb, Francophone West and Equatorial Africa head for France, as do emigrants from the devastated Democratic Republic of Congo (DRC), though they will also aim for Belgium. English-speaking Africans try for Britain first. If they have the skills that are needed they will be accepted.

The EU pursues three contradictory policies. The first is to limit all immigration, to pander to the growing xenophobia of the political right that fights in vain for a racial purity that has never existed and tries to create a Fortress Europe. The second policy is to attract skilled migrants who will make an immediate contribution to the economy while also depriving their own homelands of much-needed skills. The third policy is to open the door wider and admit that the unskilled are also required in a continent with an ageing population whose growth is broadly static.

In addition to economic migrants, civil wars and repressive regimes have created large numbers of refugees, many of whom head for Europe and apply for asylum. In recent years a majority of these have come as a result of civil wars in West Africa from Côte d'Ivoire to Sierra Leone, in the Horn and in the DRC. In the case of deeply troubled Zimbabwe, an estimated 3 million of its people have fled to South Africa.

12
Africa and Europe

INTRODUCTION

In recent years the Canary Islands, an attractive European tourist resort, have gained notoriety as a primary destination for desperate African boat migrants. During the first seven months of 2006, for example, more than 11,000 Africans arrived at the Islands by boat in the hope that once on European (Spanish) territory they have passed through the doorway to Europe. As one commentator put it, 'The Brits and the Spaniards and the Germans on these beaches are here because they have money and spare time to burn. The Africans are here because they have nothing left but hope.'[1] The Africans have used their money, often the pooled resources of their extended families, on the long journeys across the Sahara. They have neither passports nor identifying papers so the authorities cannot send them back anywhere. Europe has little idea of how to handle this problem effectively. Can the most economically and politically advanced group of countries in the world really create a Fortress Europe to keep them out? The boats keep coming, airplanes lift the migrants to Spain where they disappear into an anonymous but growing population of illegal migrants. Spanish humanitarianism in granting amnesties to illegal immigrants is assailed by other EU countries who fear that the influx into Spain will spread northwards. It is possible to measure the desperation of many of these immigrants by the fact that if they succeed in entering the EU, by whatever means, they will become members of the underclass of illegal immigrants that live on the margins of European society.[2] What both sides are learning is that if you block one route from Africa to Europe, the migrants will open another: controls may make the passage more difficult, they do not stop the flow. Jumping-off places for the boats change: migrants from Mali, Mauritania, the Gambia and Guinea may take to the Atlantic in boats from the Casamance region of Senegal, but if that route is closed they will head for Nouakchott in Mauritania or somewhere else. This steady movement of people has created its own service sector of people smugglers, suppliers of equipment and services, wheeler-dealers who corrupt border police and customs or border guards – always at a price.

Although these boat people made the news headlines, they represent only a fraction of the total African migration that is taking place. Temporary labour migration, the brain drain of skills, refugees from civil wars or unwanted but persevering illegals are increasing in numbers with a significant proportion of the total heading for the EU, although less than half first-generation migrants go to Europe. Those who do head for Europe, boat people or others, take little if anything with them. Yet all hope to earn enough to be able to send money back to their families. In the east of Africa the town of Bosaso in Puntland in northern Somalia has become the centre of the Horn of Africa's people trafficking industry. Hundreds of Somalis, Eritreans and Ethiopians arrive in Bosaso every day, determined to escape the poverty, drought and wars that engulf the region: Somalia itself has not had a properly functioning government since the beginning of the 1990s and has become a base for piracy in the Indian Ocean. 'But as long as poverty and conflict continues to blight the African continent people will continue to find a way out. And as long as Europe needs unskilled labour this will continue to be their destination.'[3] There have been unseemly arguments between Italy, Libya and Malta as to who should take responsibility for boatloads of migrants foundering at sea and being bypassed by fishing vessels that did not want to take any responsibility. In 2007 the UNHCR reckoned that 7,000 migrants had drowned in the sea between Libya, Malta and Italy. Laura Boldrini, speaking for the UNHCR, said:

> Governments must encourage fishermen to save lives. Now they fear that if they help, they can be stuck for days and weeks. But international maritime law says that governments have a duty to allow the speedy disembarkation of people rescued at sea. We say, let's save human lives first. This must be the priority for all the parties involved.[4]

According to UN estimates, 27,000 African professionals left to work abroad in the 15 years from 1960 to 1975; 60,000 from 1985 to 1990; and 200,000 in the period 1990–99. By the new century, an estimated one in three African university graduates was working outside Africa. African wealth is depleted by skilled labour migration, though the loss is partially mitigated by the return flow of remittances. About 20,000 skilled workers leave Africa every year and, according to the World Bank, the share of Africa's skilled workers with a tertiary education who emigrate is more than 15 per cent, higher than in any other region. The globalisation of people presupposes the end to border patrols and immigrant restrictions. However, the Blair Commission for Africa argued that even for temporary migration full liberalisation of borders 'is unlikely to happen, and may be politically unfeasible even though there are substantial gains to "temporary movement". Most OECD governments, their public and media, are extremely sensitive to security concerns.'[5]

Migration has been integral to African development throughout its history and movement in search of work, goods and land was not stopped by the borders colonialism created, nor when those borders became national boundaries in the postcolonial era. Borders are regarded as areas of opportunity rather than barriers and do not exist for those who know how to use or circumvent them. Today, Africans travel far and wide in pursuit of economic opportunities or to escape oppressive economic or political policies.[6]

The European media coverage would suggest that almost all African migration is aimed at Europe, but this is far from the case. Migration to Europe, the United States or the Gulf is only part of the story, for intra-African movement is more important and becomes easier to understand when the geographic and geopolitical make-up of the continent is understood. Africa covers 11.5 million square miles and consists of 53 countries comprising mini-states like Cape Verde, whose economy depends upon remittances from its citizens in the United States, to oil-rich states such as Angola and Libya, where there are many openings for economic migrants, to South Africa, which is seen as the most developed and therefore most attractive of all target countries inside Africa for economic migrants. On the geopolitical side the first decade of the twenty-first century has seen wars, civil unrest and repression in Côte d'Ivoire, Liberia, Sierra Leone, Sudan, Eritrea, Ethiopia, Somalia, the DRC and Zimbabwe, to name only the most obvious cases that have led to an emigrant population seeking a new life in other African countries or farther afield. These migrants are likely to be dynamic additions in the economies to which they migrate since the decision to move in itself requires a special kind of initiative, while the removal of migrants goes against a core African tradition that is based upon trade and the movement of people.

Anti-immigration policies in Europe make it increasingly difficult for Africans to move in search of better economic conditions, with the result that migration is driven underground, rather than halted, and migrants have to use precious resources to 'buy' illegal entry into Europe or fall back upon desperate measures such as the boat trade across the Mediterranean. The EU's negative approach to immigrants fuels the informal and illegal economy, and reinforces the informalisation of Africa's political economy. If Africans cannot migrate openly they become more dependent upon underground, informal and often criminal networks.[7] Already, there is a large resident diaspora of Africans in Europe, and this includes communities in Scandinavia or Eastern Europe that have no historical links to Africa. Other factors are changing the nature of migration; in Africa these include the mobile phone and the internet – cyber cafes throughout Africa provide fast communications which facilitate diaspora economic activities. Migrants become ever more sophisticated in the means they employ to reach their target countries even as these impose ever tighter controls. Another aspect of present-day immigration is the changing role of women. Formerly, women emigrated to join their husbands but now, increasingly, they migrate independently to improve their economic conditions.

AFRICA AND THE EU

Since the early 1990s, thousands of North Africans and Sub-Saharan Africans have attempted to cross the Mediterranean to reach Spain and Italy. By 2005 and 2006 immigrant pressures upon the Canary Islands and the Spanish enclaves of Ceuta and Melilla in Morocco led to violence as more and more migrants from Sub-Saharan Africa arrived at these jumping-off points for Europe. When they were turned back, a substantial number decided to remain in North Africa instead. They were coming from an ever widening number of countries, including Senegal, The Gambia, Sierra Leone, Liberia, Mali, Côte d'Ivoire, Ghana and Nigeria in West Africa, the DRC and Cameroon in

Central Africa, Sudan, Ethiopia, Eritrea and Somalia in the Horn of Africa and there was also an increasing number of Asians who entered Africa through Egypt. Various estimates suggest that between 65,000 and 120,000 people from Sub-Saharan Africa enter the five Maghreb countries (Mauritania, Morocco, Algeria, Tunisia and Libya) every year, with a majority (70–80 per cent) migrating through Libya, until the uprisings of 2011, and the remainder through Algeria and Morocco. A significant proportion of these migrants hope to cross the Mediterranean and enter the EU.[8] The author of this report goes on to say: 'Although commonly portrayed as "destitute" or "desperate" migrants are often relatively well educated and from moderate socio-economic backgrounds. They move because of a general lack of opportunities, fear of persecution and violence, or a combination of both.' Apart from the boat people, many migrants use tourist visas or false documents, hide in vehicles or ferries, or swim round the fences that guard the Spanish enclaves of Ceuta and Melilla in Morocco. For many of these migrants North Africa is their final destination, or it becomes so when they fail to make Europe. Estimates for 2006 suggested that there were at least 100,000 Sub-Saharan migrants then living in Mauritania and Algeria, 1 to 1.5 million in Libya and between 2.2 and 4 million, mainly Sudanese, in Egypt.

Migration both links and divides Africa and the EU. The EU is trying to persuade African countries to take responsibility for halting the flow of migrants to the EU but African countries will do this only reluctantly and at a price – more aid.[9] North African countries are not prepared to act as policemen over an immigrant flow which they have only limited capacity to control. They have to consider the reactions of their own people, who, like Europeans, are becoming increasingly xenophobic, and they would prefer to see the migrants move on to Europe so that the North African countries do not become major destination targets. Although it has been erratic in maintaining policies it agrees to implement, Libya has allowed large numbers of illegal migrants to be returned to Libya from Europe.

The EU has proposed that migrant processing centres be established in Africa and that EU naval vessels should patrol the African coastline. These suggestions have met with little enthusiasm and are seen as threats to African national sovereignty. In any case, Africa has its own human rights problems and policing migrants on behalf of the EU will add to those problems. Furthermore, North Africa needs to maintain good relations with its southerly neighbours who are the source of the migrations, and draconian moves designed to assist the EU carry out mass expulsions would harm those relations. The EU wants West African states such as Senegal to crack down on illegal migrants, but to do so would bring these countries into conflict with the principle of 'freedom of movement' which, among other principles, is enshrined in the 1975 ECOWAS (Economic Community of West African States) Treaty. If ECOWAS citizens (like those of the EU) are free to move within ECOWAS, they should also be free to move out. In fact, the countries of North Africa and Sub-Saharan Africa have no incentive to stop the outflow of migrants since these relieve pressures upon labour markets and become the source of remittances from Europe that have become a regular and important addition to national income. And while the EU attempts to put the onus upon North Africa to contain the immigrant flow, at the same time it seeks migrants with particular skills that most African countries cannot afford to lose.

Nonetheless, from 2003 onwards Spain, Italy, Morocco and Libya began to collaborate over border controls and in 2006 Spain received support from FOREX (a newly created EU border control agency) to patrol routes between Senegal, Mauritania and Cape Verde to the Canary Islands, using aeroplanes, helicopters and patrol boats. FOREX also undertook to coordinate patrols between Italy, Greece and Malta to monitor the sea between Malta and Lampedusa and the Libyan and Tunisian coasts. Over 2003–4 both Morocco and Tunisia passed new immigration laws that included severe penalties for illegal immigration and people smuggling; the two countries appeared to be giving way to pressures from the EU to police their own migrants. In 2004, Italy's Prime Minister Silvio Berlusconi and Libya's Muammar al-Gaddafi agreed to stop illegal migration to Italy and Libya seemingly undertook to deport unauthorised migrants from Sub-Saharan Africa back to their own countries and subsequently to seal the Libyan borders. It was clearly a special political bargain: two months after the agreement, the EU lifted its 18-year arms embargo on Libya because Libya had abandoned its weapons of mass destruction (WMD) programme. This allowed Italy to sell Libya equipment for border surveillance. From August 2003 to December 2004 Italy contributed to 50 charter flights from Libya that returned 5,688 people to their alleged countries of origin – Bangladesh, Egypt, Eritrea, Ghana, Mali, Niger, Nigeria, Pakistan, Sudan and Syria.

NORTH AFRICA

North Africa forms a distinct region of the African continent and comprises six countries (Mauritania, Morocco, Algeria, Tunisia, Libya and Egypt) that share a number of characteristics in common: Arab ancestry, the Muslim religion, a state of economic development that is somewhat more advanced than that of most Sub-Saharan states, close ties with the rest of the Arab-Islamic world in the Middle East and a long history of intercourse with Europe across the Mediterranean. In terms of African northwards migration towards Europe, North Africa finds itself on a sort of devil's anvil. Many migrants cross the Sahara in search of jobs and a better economic life that they believe they can find in Morocco or Libya. If they do, they stay. Others see North Africa as a stepping-stone to Europe and wait in these North African countries until they can cross the Mediterranean. They forget or overlook the fact that the EU has a different agenda. The countries of North Africa have major trade links with the EU and do not wish to become involved in a confrontation over immigration that would endanger these links. The EU, for its part, uses this connection, which is more important to North Africa than it is to Europe, as a lever to persuade North Africa to control the migrants and take responsibility for preventing them reaching Europe. As in all attempts to curb migration, there is a level of dishonesty at work. The European countries want some migrants to get through – and not just those with skills – for the Italian summer harvest depends upon hundreds of thousands of part-time or illegal immigrant workers.

While the EU wishes to make North Africa responsible for curbing the migrant flow, North Africa has its own agenda. It is not in its interest to stop migrants on their way to Europe and any control measures are likely to be half-hearted at most. The nub of the problem is whether the countries of North Africa agree to take back illegal migrants who have made their way into Europe and then been apprehended. EU pressures on North African countries to tighten their controls over migrants have produced unintended consequences in the form of human rights abuses. Immigrants, including asylum seekers, are subject to arbitrary arrest, detention and deportation after they have been stripped of their assets. Deportation often means no more than being taken to land borders, which they may well re-cross at a later stage. On the other hand, migrants who are allowed to stay in North Africa but without legal status may be subject to various forms of exploitation, including working for a pittance at the mercy of unscrupulous employers and living in appalling conditions without recourse to legal assistance. There are periodic outbursts of violence when migrants erupt in anger at such conditions: 20 migrants were killed in Cairo in 2005 when the police attacked Sudanese refugees and migrants demonstrating about the conditions in a Cairo camp.

There is another twist in the migrant story. Both North Africa and the EU refer to immigrants as 'economic migrants', a designation that allows them to avoid acknowledging that at least a proportion of them are genuine refugees or asylum seekers. Although the UNHCR has expanded its operations in North Africa – or tried to do so – state authorities often refuse to cooperate because they do not want migrants to be re-categorised as refugees or asylum seekers that they would be obliged to treat as such and care for. Both Amnesty International and Human Rights Watch have accused Spain and Italy of swiftly deporting migrants without first discovering whether they had any asylum or refugee rights and those returned to North Africa would face similar treatment. Unhappily, there is complicity in the ill treatment of migrants on both sides of the Mediterranean.

CROSSING THE SAHARA

Trans-Saharan migration increased dramatically during the 1990s, driven by civil wars and economic decline. Most of these migrants came from West Africa, the Horn, Sudan and the DRC. Early in the new century an anti-immigrant backlash in Libya persuaded an increasing number of Sub-Saharan Africans to relocate to other Maghreb countries or the EU and these became the largest group to be intercepted by EU border guards. Although they make exceptions, in broad terms the Maghreb countries do not wish to be seen as destination countries, since they have their own problems of poverty and unemployment and see migrants as exacerbating them. In any case, the EU assumed that

Morocco, Tunisia and Algeria were major migrant sending countries – but of their own people. The increase in migration across the Sahara has progressively involved a growing number of countries and greatly increased tensions between the EU and North Africa. What is happening is not a new phenomenon. Trans-Saharan migration has existed for centuries: despite its forbidding terrain, the region has long been a vast transition zone. This point can be better understood by studying the diverse ethnic populations of its oases.

During the 1970s and 1980s, wars and drought in the Sahel countries forced many of the nomads to migrate in search of work, which they found on construction sites and oilfields in Algeria and Libya, while many refugees settled in the towns and cities of Algeria, Libya, Mauritania and Egypt. Following the 1973 OPEC-induced oil crisis and fourfold increase in the price of oil, there was a surge in the movement of migrants seeking work that local people avoided and Libya became North Africa's major attraction for migrants. The movement of migrants across the Sahara provided nomads with new occupations, providing essential goods and food, and acting as people smugglers across borders. By the beginning of the twenty-first century a number of routes had been established. Migrants who came to southern Libya would move north to its coastal cities and towns, while some would enter Tunisia. These would cross the Mediterranean to Malta or Lampedusa by boat. From Tamanrasset in southern Algeria, migrants would head for its northern cities or cross into Morocco where they had three choices: to move into Western Sahara in order to travel by sea to the Canary Islands; to move north and try to gain entry into the two Spanish enclaves of Ceuta and Melilla; or to see Morocco as their final destination and seek work in its cities. When the Libyan leader, Muammar al-Gaddafi, adopted a pan-African policy at the end of the 1990s, he also affected the pattern of trans-Sahara migration; migrants from Sudan and the Horn of Africa, who had formerly settled in Cairo, now moved on to Libya. A further development saw Asian migrants from China, India, Pakistan and Bangladesh moving to Cairo or travelling by air to cities such as Bamako and thence north to Morocco and on to Europe. For some, the cities of North Africa were their choice of destination; those who had tried and failed to get into Europe stayed in North Africa, reluctant to return to their countries of origin in the south. A number of North African cities now have sizeable migrant communities.

THE EURO-AFRICAN LINK

The presence of migrant communities in the cities of North Africa and the large numbers of migrants in southern Europe who have succeeded in crossing the Mediterranean between them create a symbiosis that links the two continents. In Europe many illegal immigrants manage to stay, while only a minority of those apprehended by border guards in Spain, Italy or Malta are sent back. Another factor helps to consolidate the Euro-African link and that is the reluctance of the countries in Sub-Saharan Africa from which the migrants originate to cooperate in any policy of forced return. This possibility in any case is difficult to enforce since many migrants destroy their papers so as to avoid expulsion, while asylum seekers, children and pregnant women have the right to stay, at least temporarily, on humanitarian grounds while their status is verified. In the case of illegal immigrants in Europe, they often serve the maximum detention period, are released and served with formal expulsion orders, which they ignore, disappearing into the underground world of migrants or moving to another EU country and finding work in the informal sector.

Although the Western media have depicted the 'boat people' as the victims of unscrupulous traffickers or merciless smuggling networks, this is only a part of the story, since a majority migrate on their own initiative and pay for a leg of the journey at a time. People smugglers are not part of international organised crime so much as former nomads or immigrants operating small networks of their own. They may cooperate with corrupt local police or border officials and sometimes will also connect migrants to possible employers in Europe. In the long journey across the Sahara, whichever route is followed, migrants have to spend hundreds of dollars on bribes, smugglers, transportation and daily necessities. At the end of the journey the migrant would be involved in further expense in crossing the Mediterranean. A 2003 estimate, for example, showed that a boat from Morocco to Spain cost $200 for minors, $500–$800 for Moroccans and $800–$1200 for migrants from Francophone or Anglophone Sub-Saharan Africa. Many migrants obtained the money to pay for these expenses from their extended families before they set off. It is almost a law of migration that barriers erected to stop migrants in fact encourage them to find ways round them. The increased surveillance from the Straits of Gibraltar to the Libyan coast and Malta to Lampedusa forced migrants to develop new and often more dangerous routes to their chosen destinations.

In 2006 there was a sharp increase in attempted crossings of the Mediterranean. Between January and September of that year, 24,000 migrants arrived in the Canary Islands, compared with 4,722 in 2005 and 9,900 in 2002. In 2006, 10,400 migrants were apprehended on the Italian island of Lampedusa, compared to 6,900 in 2005. Yet the boat people represent only a fraction of the total entering the EU. Figures for entrants to the 15 EU countries (less Greece) for 2004, according to the OECD, came to 2.6 million. The majority of these migrated legally and then overstayed their visas.

LIBYA

According to the Migration Information Service:

> The air and arms embargo imposed on Libya by the UN Security Council between 1992 and 2000 played an unintended but decisive role in an unprecedented increase in trans-Saharan migration and the consolidation of migration routes and networks. Disappointed by the perceived lack of support from fellow Arab countries during the embargo, Libyan leader Muammar al-Gaddafi embarked upon a radical reorientation of Libyan foreign policy, in which he positioned himself as an African leader.[10]

In his new role, Gaddafi welcomed Sub-Saharan Africans to work in Libya in the spirit of pan-African solidarity that he was espousing. Already a destination for Arab migrants from other North African countries, attracted by its oil wealth, Libya now became a major destination for migrants from both West Africa and the Horn of Africa. After the slump years of low oil prices in the 1980s, and of the UN embargo in the 1990s, accompanied by demands that the work force should be indigenised, few Libyans were prepared to take up unattractive low-paid jobs and the country came to rely increasingly upon migrants from Sub-Saharan Africa who were usually employed in the construction and agriculture sectors. The troubled years at the end of the twentieth century in Sub-Saharan Africa produced new waves of migrants. The DRC lapsed into chaos following the death of Mobutu in 1997 and suffered what came to be called Africa's Great War from 1998 to 2003, leading to a refugee crisis including a migrant movement to the north. Other refugees came from West Africa, where Sierra Leone suffered ten years of civil war (1991–2001), while Liberia underwent a second civil war (1999–2003). In the east, Sudan, Eritrea, Ethiopia and Somalia each became sources of migrants and refugees, many of whom eventually arrived in Libya.

Gaddafi might have decided to be a pan-Africanist but in 2000 there was an anti-immigrant backlash in Libya when the indigenous people clashed with African workers from elsewhere. Dozens of immigrants were killed and the disturbances persuaded the government to pass a number of repressive measures. These included greater restrictions on immigrants entering Libya, lengthy and arbitrary detention of illegal immigrants in poor conditions, physical abuse and the repatriation of tens of thousands of migrants. Between 2003 and 2005 the government deported about 145,000 illegal migrants, mainly to countries of Sub-Saharan Africa.

The Libyan authorities employed harsh and often brutal methods against the migrants. They levelled blanket accusations of crimes against them, launched physical attacks, employed harassment tactics and extortion, and in some cases were accused of using torture. Libya has not signed the 1951 Geneva Convention but is a party to the African Refugee Convention, yet it expelled unwanted refugees to their alleged countries of origin, regardless of whether they faced torture or other persecution in countries such as Eritrea or Sudan. However welcome migrants thought they would be as a result of Gaddafi's 'African policy', many of them discovered that they were pawns as the Libyan leader re-positioned himself in relation to Italy and the EU so as to re-open his country to Western trade and investment, following his 'maverick' years of isolation.

MOROCCO

Unlike Libya, Morocco is a major source country of migrants. By 2005 there was a Moroccan diaspora in Europe of more than 2.25 million. Writing in 2005, Hein de Haas said: 'Over the second half of the 20th century Morocco has evolved into one of the world's leading emigration countries. Moroccans form one of the largest and most dispersed non-Western migrant communities in Western Europe.'[11] In addition, an increasing number of Moroccan migrants have settled in Canada and the US. In receipt of $3.6 billion in official remittances in 2003, Morocco was then the fourth largest remittance recipient in the developing world. The first major wave of emigration out of Morocco took place between 1948 (when the state of Israel was created) and the Six Day War of 1967, when thousands of Moroccan Jews emigrated to Israel, Canada (Quebec Province) and France, reducing the Jewish population of Morocco from 250,000 to its present figure of about 5,000. Between 1965 and 1972 the number of Moroccans living in Europe rose from 30,000 to 300,000, and then to 400,000 by 1975. By 2005, Moroccan migrant communities in six European countries were as follows: France – 1.02 million; Netherlands – 316,000; Belgium – 214,000; Germany – 73,000; Spain – 397,000; Italy – 253,000 to make a total of 2.27 million. A majority of Moroccan migrants, once they have obtained work in Europe, will stay there if it is possible to do so. Although between 1985 and 1995 some 314,000 migrants returned to Morocco from West European countries – the number of returnees peaking in 1991 when 40,000 returned home – thereafter return migration fell to an average of 20,000 a year, one of the lowest rates of return in Europe. By 1998 there were 1.6 million Moroccans in Europe and between 1992 and 2001, 430,000 Moroccans were granted nationality by one of the EU states. An increasing number of Moroccan migrants to Europe are women who work as domestics, nannies and cleaners, or in agriculture and small businesses.

By 2005, however, Morocco found itself the recipient of an increasing flow of African migrants who had crossed the Sahara and aimed for the Moroccan Mediterranean coast where they sought a passage to Europe or tried to gain access to the Spanish enclaves of Ceuta and Melilla. Others stayed in Morocco and joined the sizeable migrant communities in the big cities, especially Casablanca, Rabat and Tangier. The build-up of African migrants in Morocco since 2000 includes a growing number from Sub-Saharan countries such as Nigeria, Senegal, the Gambia, Liberia, Mali, Ghana, Burkina-Faso, Niger, Sudan, Central African Republic and Cameroon. These African migrants are facing increasing xenophobia and economic exploitation.

From the 1960s onwards, Morocco encouraged emigration since this proved an outlet for some of the unemployed whose remittances home helped the economy. Over the years, remittances became a significant addition to the economy, rising from $23 million in 1968 to $2.1 billion in 1992. Remittances remained static in the 1990s but rose again at the end of the century, reaching a figure of $3.6 billion a year: by 2002 they accounted for 6.4 per cent of GDP and 22 per cent of the total value of all imports, becoming more important than foreign direct investment. Estimates suggest that a further $1 billion of remittances are not declared.

Morocco finds itself in the paradoxical position of encouraging migration of its own citizens to Europe, where they represent an overseas asset, while at the same time being a target country for migrants from other parts of Africa whose primary aim is to obtain access to Europe, though a significant proportion of them are prepared to settle in Morocco. The dilemma of being both an emigrant country and a target country for immigrants illustrates the complexity of migration issues. Thus, although the EU calls upon the Maghreb countries to control immigrant movements it still wants some migrants and feels it has the right to pick and choose for skills. Libya, with its oil wealth, needs immigrants to do jobs that its own people shun, while many migrants regard North Africa as a final destination, offering economic opportunities that are not available in their own countries. Given the current problems of poverty, civil disturbances and under-development in Sub-Saharan Africa there is every reason to believe that the flow northwards of migrants across the Sahara will continue into the foreseeable future.

13
Sudan and the Horn of Africa

This huge region, covering 4.3 million square km, has witnessed more permanent conflict since independence half a century ago than any other part of Africa. Sudan, with a population of 38.5 million and an area of 2.5 million square km (967,000 square miles), is the largest state in Africa (this was written prior to the division of Sudan into two countries on 9 July 2011) and for most of the period since independence in 1956 has been divided by a brutal civil war between North and South; as that war was brought to an end in the twenty-first century with a precarious settlement, attention switched to a new conflict in Darfur. Both conflicts resulted in huge numbers of refugees or IDPs, the majority of whom remained in the region. The Horn consists of four countries: Ethiopia, Eritrea, Somalia and Djibouti. Ethiopia covers an area of 1.1 million square km and has a population of 79 million, the second largest in Africa after Nigeria. Eritrea covers an area of 117,600 square km but has a population of only 4.8 million. Somalia, covering an area of 637,660 square km, attracts far greater attention than its population of 8.6 million might warrant. Finally, the tiny enclave territory of Djibouti, with less than a million people, is wedged between Eritrea, Ethiopia and Somalia and is host to two military bases, one for the French Foreign Legion, the other for US special forces.

The area and population of these countries must be seen in relation to the numbers of people who have been displaced. Forced migration appears to be a permanent feature of the region. In 2004, for example, Sudan had a million newly displaced people, mainly in Darfur. Since the late 1950s, Sudan has endured two civil wars: the first between North and South; the second in Darfur, an area that comprises roughly a fifth of the country. Ethiopia was at war from 1962 to 1991: there was a civil war between government and the Tigrayan people and the Eritreans, who finally achieved independence in 1991, and the Ogaden War with Somalia (1977–8). It fought a further border war with independent Eritrea in 1998–2000 and, with US support, sent an army into Somalia at the end of 2006 to ensure the overthrow of an Islamist regime that was not to Washington's taste. Apart from the Ogaden War, Somalia has been in a permanent state of civil conflict since the overthrow of President Siad Barre at the beginning of 1991. These endless conflicts over half a century have created millions of refugees or IDPs who cross and recross borders, according to circumstances, or are forced to move within their countries as conflicts spread. During the first decade of the twenty-first century over Africa as a whole, at any one time, there have been an estimated 3.25 million refugees and asylum seekers, the great majority of whom have moved to neighbouring African countries rather than outside the continent.

Protracted refugee communities (people in camps or settlements for more than five years) have been a particular feature of the region.

SUDAN

From 1956 to 1972, the country suffered from a civil war between the North (Arabicised and Islamic) and the South (partially Christian and composed of distinct ethnic groups that saw themselves as widely different from the people of the North). President Jaafar Nimeiri, who came to power in 1969 following a coup, managed to reconcile the two sides in 1972 to give the country twelve years of peace. However, civil war resumed in 1983–4 and continued until a precarious peace was achieved in 2003. The long years of warfare had displaced or turned into refugees millions of Sudanese, many of whom went north into Egypt where they became illegal migrants or refugees. This long civil war defied any attempts by outsiders to end it, although Sudan's neighbours – Ethiopia and Uganda – became involved on the fringes. Between the resumption of the fighting in 1983 and 1989 an estimated 500,000 people were killed or died of war-related diseases and famine. By 1992 7 million people were suffering from food shortages. In May 1993 the UN identified 1.5 million people in southern Sudan who required food aid and of these 600,000 were wholly dependent upon UN supplies. In February 1994 the UN was urgently seeking humanitarian aid for another 100,000 IDPs. This long civil war created refugees and migrants on a major scale.

A new conflict emerged in 2003 in Darfur, the huge western region of Sudan that is roughly equivalent to one-fifth of the country's land space. The situation in Darfur deteriorated through 2003 to create a large number of refugees. Amnesty International claimed that 500,000 people had been displaced by the conflict and by mid 2004 an estimated 1.2 million people had fled the region, 300,000 of them crossing the border into neighbouring Chad. They presented the international community with a massive problem of chronic food shortage. On 6 February 2006, the *Guardian* reported that Darfur, which had shown some signs of stabilising, was slipping back into major violence and that up to 70,000 people had fled the displacement camps. At the end of 2006 the UN estimated that at least 200,000 people had been killed in the Darfur region and that more than 2 million had been displaced. Moreover, the crisis touched new depths during the year as ethnic violence continued and spread into neighbouring Chad. There were fears that refugees from Sudan would destabilise both Chad and the Central African Republic. In November 2006 the UNHCR reported the presence of 218,000 refugees from Darfur in twelve camps in eastern Chad, up from 200,000 in eleven camps in 2004. Further, the UNHCR reported that 90,000 people had been internally displaced in eastern Chad itself. Sudanese militias attacked Chadians living near the border and forced some of them to flee into Darfur. To complicate the situation still further, Chadian Arabs were reported attacking non-Arab Chadians as far as 60 miles from the border. The Sudanese government was accused of arming local militias (Janjaweed) to attack villages belonging primarily to the Fur, Zaghawa, and Massalit tribes that the government suspected of supporting rebel groups. According to Human Rights Watch the government ordered its planes to bomb civilians in northwestern Darfur and Chad, killing and injuring hundreds. Grudgingly, the Sudan government had agreed to an African Union peace-keeping force to separate combatants, but the 7,000 peace-keeping troops could do very little without cooperation from the Sudanese government. Initially, the government refused to allow UN peacekeepers into the country, despite a UN Security Council Resolution calling for such a deployment. However, in November 2006, President Omar al-Bashir agreed to admit a mixed UN-African Union force of up to 20,000 troops, though Khartoum stipulated that UN troops would only be allowed to assist the African force. By 2007 there were estimated to be 400,000 Sudanese refugees in Kenya, 400,000 in Chad and 100,000 in Egypt.

The Sudanese conflict produced unexpected outcomes. Thus, for example, a small number of Sudanese migrants found life so awful for them in Egypt that they crossed the Sinai desert into Israel. As one of the first to get to Israel explained: 'In Israel Sudanese can earn $4 per hour. In Egypt such a wage is unheard of. Moreover, medical care and educational opportunities are far better in Israel than in Egypt.' On the other hand, many of the Sudanese who managed to reach Israel were jailed and, as Muslims, suspected of being allies of the Palestinians. A few were allowed to live in kibbutzim. Israel wanted to return the majority of the Sudanese migrants but required assurances from Egypt that they would not then be deported to Sudan, where they would face the death penalty for entering Israel. Of the estimated 4,000 Sudanese in Israel, 24.5 per cent were from Darfur (and were Muslims) and 61 per cent from southern Sudan; according to the UNHCR 86 per cent of them had refugee status.

A major offensive in February 2008 by Sudanese government forces against rebels in western Darfur caused the displacement of 12,000 civilians who fled into eastern Chad. By this time 3 million people required food aid. In April it was estimated that 300,000 people had died of malnutrition and in such circumstances more people moved to become refugees or IDPs. Meanwhile, there had been a build-up of Sudanese refugees in Egypt, but their refugee status was disputed by the Egyptian authorities and they were subjected to racial discrimination and police violence. The size of the Sudanese population in Egypt has been estimated at more than 2 million (estimates range from 750,000 to 4 million), many of them economic migrants. However, according to the US Committee for Refugees and Immigrants, a significant proportion of them may qualify as refugees, but see no benefit in applying for recognition.

Many refugees currently residing in Egypt escaped from the Second Sudanese Civil War, where was 'pitted black African separatists' and 'Christians' against a 'Sudanese government run by Muslim, Arabic speaking northerners who had tried to impose Islamic law on the country'.[1]

In January 2004 Egyptian politicians formulated legislation for a 'Four Freedoms Agreement', which would grant Sudanese and Egyptians the freedom of movement, residence, ownership and work in either country. It would allow Sudanese nationals to live indefinitely in Egypt without having to seek refugee status, although it would not enable them to receive educational, medical or social benefits. This legislation has yet to be ratified. In fact, refugees in Egypt experience discrimination by both government and civil services, while new laws have prevented refugees of all nationalities from achieving legal or financial gains. The deeply restrictive attitude of Egypt towards refugees has met with little or no international criticism. Legal employment for the Sudanese in Egypt is virtually impossible since the laws of 2003 and 2004 force all foreigners (including refugees) to have a permit to work in 'gainful' employment but to obtain such employment the individual faces stringent requirements covering legal status, employer sponsorship, and non-competition with Egyptian nationals. Since 2006 employers have been required to submit a certificate verifying that Sudanese nationals are not carrying AIDS. Such requirements ensure that only a fraction of Sudanese immigrants have been able to obtain work permits. Numerous protests by Sudanese migrants have been met by police brutality. In the December 2005 protests and subsequent police reprisals there were between 28 and 100 Sudanese fatalities, while many more were injured. A refugee camp was forcibly dismantled and 2,174 protesters were arrested and detained. The treatment of these refugees belied the concept of an 'Arab Nation' once personified by Abdul Nasser. Meanwhile, clashes between the Sudan People's Liberation Army (SPLA) and the national Sudanese army in Sudan itself in March 2008 led to 50 deaths,[2] but the displacement of 50,000 and the difference proportionately between deaths and displaced gives a realistic indication of the sheer numbers of people regularly displaced in Sudan's wars.

Sudan is also the recipient of refugees from neighbouring Ethiopia and in July 2009 the Sudanese police began a series of crackdowns on Ethiopian and Eritrean refugee communities in Khartoum. Truckloads of police accompanied by government security forces raided homes and refugee-owned business centres and confiscated properties. According to refugees, women and children were beaten and raped. There were about 30,000 refugees in Khartoum and about 100,000 in eastern Sudan bordering on Eritrea. Many of these refugees go to Khartoum in search of a better life. Similar crackdowns were carried out in the ten southern Sudanese states, targeting illegal immigrants who are linked to the worsening insecurity in the region. Kenyan refugees have been blamed for growing insecurity in the South, where they are involved in armed gangs that terrorise residents in Juba City.[3] In August, the Sudanese interior minister said his ministry was committed to assisting the migration of Ethiopian workers. Sudan and Ethiopia have signed a series of agreements covering the migration of manpower between the two countries. There are many Ethiopian nationals working illegally in Sudan. In a meeting between the Ethiopian Ambassador to Sudan, Ali Abdo, and the Interior Minister Ibrahim Mahmoud Hamid on 30 July 2009 the two agreed to ensure the success of the Social Affairs Joint Ministerial Commission between their two countries. Despite the world financial crisis, Sudan continued to enjoy an oil-fuelled economic boom that was maintained because of ongoing Chinese and Gulf investment in the country. As a consequence of this, the government was considering signing bilateral agreements on manpower importation with different countries. Meanwhile, the Central Bank of Sudan decided to exempt Egyptians working in Sudan from the requirement of residence and work permits when they transfer money to their own country.[4]

There are constant ironies in almost all migration situations. On the one hand, maybe 2 million Sudanese have fled their own country to Egypt, where they are harshly treated and have little chance of obtaining reasonable employment. On the other hand, Sudan encourages worker migrants from Ethiopia and makes it easy for Egyptians to send money back home from Khartoum.

ETHIOPIA AND ERITREA

Forced migration in Ethiopia falls under three categories: IDPs, refugees in Ethiopia, and trafficking. The border war between Ethiopia and Eritrea that erupted in May 1998 accounted for the largest number of displaced people since the present government came to power in 1991. Some 350,000 people were displaced at the start of the war from areas along the common border of the Tigray and Afar regions, while an additional 95,000 Ethiopians were deported from Eritrea. As the conflict escalated people living close to the disputed border had to be evacuated.

Drought- or famine-induced displacements are also chronic aspects of life in Ethiopia. Issues concerning IDPs include the presence of landmines, HIV/AIDS as well as the poverty of families of deceased soldiers. Most refugees in Ethiopia come from Somalia, Sudan and Eritrea and have migrated as a result of ongoing political and civil unrest in the region as well as in response to a natural disaster – normally another drought. Another form of forced migration in Ethiopia is the trafficking of women and young girls.

Warfare and migration are built into the psyche of Eritrea, which in any case is a desperately poor country. It waged a war of independence against Ethiopia from 1962 to 1991, one of the longest continuing conflicts in Africa. When the war came to an end, the Eritrean People's Liberation Front (EPLF) held a referendum on 23–5 April 1993 over independence and, of the 1.01 million people registered to vote, 800,000 were in Eritrea, 150,000 in Sudan, 40,000 in Ethiopia and 28,000 in the United States: this spread is indicative of the way in which warfare had dispersed Eritreans throughout the region and beyond.[5] The peace between Eritrea and Ethiopia was never easy, partly, because Eritrea had been incorporated within Ethiopia, which was humiliated by its loss, and partly because the independent state of Eritrea, which now controlled the ports on the Red Sea that were vital to Ethiopia's trade, had reduced the larger country to becoming the fifteenth landlocked state in Africa. It was hardly surprising, therefore, that the two countries clashed over their joint border and went to war with each other at the end of the century. Two-way expulsions took place and by December 1999 Ethiopia had deported an estimated 65,000 Eritreans while about 22,000 Ethiopians had been expelled the other way. In addition to these expulsions, an estimated 300,000 people on each side had been displaced by the fighting.

Ethiopia remains committed to offering asylum to refugees arriving on its territory from neighbouring countries and, over the decade to 2008, the country has hosted about 1 million refugees, although most of them have been able to return to their own countries over the years. In 2008, Ethiopia was home to approximately 80,000 refugees, mainly from Eritrea, Somalia, Sudan and Kenya. More than a quarter, 23,000, were from Eritrea: over 1,700 Eritrean refugees had registered in the first quarter of the year. Years of insurrection and drought in the Ogaden region of Ethiopa left 8 million people in need of food assistance. In June 2008, Human Rights Watch issued a report, sub-titled *War Crimes and Crimes against Humanity in the Ogaden Area*, which detailed mass rape, the torturing of children, and the displacement of tens of thousands of people in a 'scorched earth' campaign.[6]

A sort of peace prevailed in the tiny state of Djibouti, where the presence of US troops was blamed in 2003 for thousands of illegal immigrants. These were 'invited' to return to their home countries since Djibouti had passed its 'tolerance threshold'. Over 100,000 illegal immigrants subsequently left the country.

SOMALIA

Independent Somalia was created in 1960 by the union of British Somaliland in the north and former Italian Somaliland (then a UN Trusteeship Territory) in the south. It was to prove an uneasy union. The five-pointed star in the centre of the Somali flag gave warning of conflicts to come: two points of the star stood for the two Somalilands that had been united, but the other three stood respectively for the Territory of the Afars and Issas (subsequently Djibouti), the Ogaden triangle of Ethiopia and a stretch of northeast Kenya that bordered on Somalia. The Somalis claimed these three territories on the grounds that their nomadic people had grazed their herds over them since time immemorial. In the case of Kenya, there was a border war, known as the Shifta War, between the two countries from 1964 to 1967, but Kenya made plain it would not yield an inch of territory and in the end Somalia accepted this. In 1960 the Territory of the Afars and Issas was a French colony with French troops stationed there. When it became independent in 1977, France, by agreement, kept 3,000 troops of the French Foreign Legion in the country, 'at the disposal of the government'. Somalia avoided a conflict with Djibouti. In any case its real concern was with the Ogaden triangle. In 1977, when huge changes were under way in Ethiopia, following the deposition and death of the Emperor Haile Selassie, Somalia launched its war to take control of the Ogaden and brutal fighting followed between its forces and those of Ethiopia. Although the Ogaden War was fought between two states there were elements of a civil war about it, since the Somalis had traditionally moved back and forth across the whole region and many of the people then living there had close ties with Somalia. By the time the war came to an end in 1978, 1 million Somalis had become refugees in their own country.

Following Somalia's defeat in the Ogaden War, there was a steady growth of opposition to President Siad Barre, partly because he had lost the war and partly because his centralising tendencies were increasingly resented in what was – overwhelmingly – a clan-based society. By the mid 1980s there had developed growing strains between the north (former British Somaliland) and the south (former Italian Somaliland), and by 1988 a rebellion against Barre in the north had turned into a full-scale civil war. In June of that year it was estimated that 10,000 people had been killed in the fighting and 100,000 had fled into Ethiopia as refugees. The following month President Barre launched a major offensive to regain control of northern Somalia, driving another 120,000 refugees into Ethiopia. In January 1990, the American human rights group Africa Watch claimed that government forces had killed between 50,000 and 60,000 civilians in the north and driven 500,000 into exile. On 18 May 1991 the northern Somali National Movement (SNM) proclaimed an independent Somaliland Republic, thus separating itself from the rest of Somalia. The collapse of the Barre government during 1990 and his flight to Nigeria in January 1991 left the country in a state of chaos from which it has never recovered.

For 20 years since 1990, Somali refugees and asylum seekers have moved into neighbouring countries and crossed the Red Sea to Yemen, whence they travel to the Gulf or Europe. By 2005 Somali asylum seekers in Britain were regarded as a growing problem: the government forced around 100 Somali asylum seekers to leave Britain in the first half of the year, sending them back to their war-torn country despite warnings from the Somali government and the UN that such action would endanger lives. Emma Ginn, of the National Coalition of Anti-Deportation Campaigns, said: 'There have been numerous reports highlighting how unsafe the situation is in parts of Somalia. The government cannot have been unaware of the grave situation that confronts asylum seekers once they arrive back in the country.'[7] Somalis in 2005 constituted the largest source of asylum seekers in Britain; there had been 4,600 applications for asylum in 2004 and the government had reacted by 'fast-tracking' their applications. Meanwhile, the human trafficking trade out of Somalia had become one of the busiest, most lucrative and lethal in the world. 'The ferocious violence and anarchy in the region has kept the scale of profits and misery hidden from outside eyes.'[8] According to the UN, people smuggling in the region rivalled traditional routes from Africa across the Mediterranean, in which mass drowning had become a common feature. The body count on the route from Somalia to Yemen (to lead to the Middle East and Europe) had become higher and more shocking since many of the corpses found on the Arabian Sea every month had gunshot wounds or hands tied behind backs as the traffickers jettisoned their cargo rather than deliver the migrants to Yemen's shores.

Bosaso, on the tip of the Horn of Africa had become the centre of the trafficking trade to Yemen. Both Somalis and Ethiopians came to the town in the hope of escaping poverty and war. The UNHCR claimed that 30 boats a month were arriving in Yemen from Bosaso. The numbers of deaths were said to be in the hundreds but could easily have been higher. 'Boosaaso in Puntland, a self-declared autonomous area in northeast Somalia, is the world's busiest smuggling hub. The port city, with a population of 200,000, is hosting another 12,000 from the rest of Somalia and Ethiopia seeking a passage out.'[9] Desperation keeps people trying to migrate from the region and the remittances that successful migrants send back to their families are the biggest source of foreign revenue for Somaliland. At this time (2006) there were 80,000 registered refugees in Yemen, of whom 75,000 were Somalis. However, unofficial estimates put the real figure at several hundred thousand. Most of these migrants hope to obtain jobs in Saudi Arabia or the Gulf states, though a proportion of them aim for the EU. The ruthlessness of the traffickers is balanced by the desperation of the migrants, who entrust such people with their lives. As Dennis McNamara, the UN's special adviser on displaced people, said:

What is happening here is horrific. As bad as the worst cases involving migration. In fact, we have never seen photos like the ones we are seeing here, of men, women and children drowned with their hands tied behind their backs.

Mr McNamara went on to say that it was in the self-interest of Western nations who do not want a migrant influx from the south to help the region so that people no longer had to make such perilous journeys. The idea of large injections of aid into poor countries to alleviate the conditions that lead to migration is not new, but the attempt to assist refugees and deal with famine in Somalia in the first half of the 1990s, with a massive UN humanitarian relief programme and the American intervention with 28,000 marines – Operation Restore Hope – ended in abysmal failure.

Trafficking is now big business and wherever there is an anarchic situation, such as that in the Horn, desperate people will take desperate risks. Between September 2006 and March 2007, according to the UNHCR, 100 people a day attempted to cross from Somalia to Yemen and, for example, over six days in January 2007, the UNHCR counted 22 smuggling boats arriving in Yemen. In general these smuggling boats are always overcrowded and if a storm develops during the 30-hour crossing the traffickers will force passengers at gun point to jump into the sea to lighten the load. Even when boats reach the coast of Yemen, passengers, including children, are forced to swim to shore so the boat is not detected by the Yemen authorities. Most passengers cannot swim and drown. Despite such hazards, between 200 and 300 Ethiopians were arriving in Bosaso every day in the hope of crossing to Yemen. Meanwhile, they live in appalling conditions in the town.

South, in Mogadishu, due to the Ethiopian intervention to oust the Islamist government, bitter fighting through 2007 created yet another IDP problem. According to the UN, 170,000 people were displaced by the clashes in Mogadishu, in addition to 330,000 already driven out of the city and, by November 2007, the UNHCR reckoned that the total number of displaced people in the country was over 1 million. During the year about 20,000 refugees tried to make the dangerous crossing to Yemen, with over 400 known to have drowned. The UN Special Representative to Somalia, Ahmedou Ould-Abdullah, described the situation as the worst humanitarian crisis in Africa, exacerbated by floods, locust swarms, malnutrition and preventable epidemics.[10] The situation had not changed in 2009. In August Somalia was said to be facing the worst humanitarian crisis of the past 18 years, with an estimated 3.76 million people – half the population – needing aid, as the security situation deteriorated. The position was made worse by drought, which drove people from the rural areas to the towns. There was no amelioration of the situation in sight.

14
The Congo, Rwanda, Burundi

The Democratic Republic of the Congo (DRC), a huge sprawling country occupying the centre of the African continent, is difficult to control at the best of times, while its vast mineral wealth has attracted predators ever since King Leopold II of the Belgians turned it into his private fief during the scramble for Africa. Later, as a Belgian colony it was run from Brussels solely as a source of wealth. Following independence in 1960 it became a point of confrontation between the two superpowers at the height of the Cold War. Mobutu Sese Seko was to rule the Congo, which he renamed Zaire, for 32 years and, like Leopold before him, regarded it as a personal fief whose wealth was extracted for his benefit. His mode of government came to be described as 'state kleptocracy'. The horrific genocide in the tiny neighbouring state of Rwanda during 1994 was to link the two countries in a brutal military embrace that would last through the first decade of the twenty-first century. By the late 1990s, as Mobutu's time ran out, the Congo became the centre of Africa's 'Great War', and predators in the form of its African neighbours and transnational corporations once more closed in to extract resources and profit from the benighted country. During 1995, as a result of the genocide in Rwanda and the near genocidal civil war in Burundi, huge numbers of refugees from those two countries crossed the border into eastern Zaire and, by the middle of the year, up to 1 million refugees from Rwanda and a further 130,000 from Burundi had been settled in camps in Zaire. This marked the beginning of years of refugee movement across the region. Camps for the Hutu refugees from Rwanda included many of the hardcore extremists who had masterminded the holocaust in Rwanda and now talked openly of how they would carry on 'killing all Tutsi who prevent us from returning'.[1]

In August 1995, the Zaire authorities embarked upon the forcible repatriation of refugees but on 24 August gave up using force when the UNHCR advanced a plan for voluntary repatriation. Agreement was reached on 6 September between the government and the UNHCR to set 31 December as the deadline by which time all refugees would be repatriated. Then, following a meeting on 25 September between Rwanda and the UNHCR, Zaire promised to stop the activities of the Hutu extremists in the camps and at least some of these extremists were detained in December. In 1996, meanwhile, Laurent Kabila and his Alliance of Democratic Forces for the Liberation of Congo-Zaire (AFDL) launched a civil war to oust Mobutu. On 16 May 1997 President Mobutu Sese Seko abandoned Kinshasa and left the country to seek asylum, first in Togo and then Morocco. He died of cancer on 7 September. On 17 May the rebel AFDL entered Kinshasa to a warm welcome. Kabila proclaimed himself president and renamed the country the Democratic Republic of the Congo. The international community, meanwhile, was concerned about the conditions of the refugees from Rwanda. Of the 1.1 million who had fled from Rwanda to Zaire in 1994, at least 600,000 had returned. This left many unaccounted for and ugly stories surfaced of refugees with the Armed Forces of Zaire (FAZ) who were first abandoned and then massacred. Though the international community expressed its concern, its representatives had little control on the ground. Often, where huge movements of people are concerned, a significant proportion quickly return home when they believe the violent disruption that caused them to flee has passed. Home, even if threatened, is seen as preferable to the bleak misery of refugee camps. Almost from the beginning of his rule, relations between Kabila and the country's major donors were strained because of uncertainty about the fate of Rwandan refugees. Some massacres had certainly taken place, but attempts by the UN to establish a commission to investigate met with Congolese obstruction. In October 1997, Human Rights Watch/Africa published a report *What Kabila is Hiding*. The report began:

> The Rwandan Patriotic Army and the AFDL carried out massive killings of civilian refugees and other violations of basic principles of international humanitarian law during attacks on refugee camps in the former Zaire that began in late 1996 and in the ensuing seven months as war spread across the country.

Human Rights Watch had uncovered plenty of evidence of wanton killing. There were clear indications that the Congolese government was trying to remove all physical traces of any massacres and was also intimidating eye-witnesses into silence.

The Kabila government faced formidable problems and was not strongly based. Kabila himself had no solid political base and his victory had depended largely upon the support of the Banyamulenge (Tutsis) of South Kivu in the east of the country and the Rwandan and Ugandan armies. Kabila, obsessed with power and his own place in history, feared a coup by the Banyamulenge and Rwandans, who had helped him to power, and so in July 1998 he removed Tutsis and Rwandans from posts in his administration. By so doing he turned doubtful allies into immediate enemies: they returned to the east of the country and launched a second civil war to topple him. Uganda and Rwanda came out in support of the rebels, Kabila appealed to other African countries for help, and Angola, Namibia and Zimbabwe sent troops to aid him. With five neighbouring countries coming to the assistance of one or other side in the Congo's civil war, this was turned into Africa's Great War, which would last until 2003. By late 1998, the *Economist* wrote: 'The main players in Congo are seen by many as greedy warlords with ready-made armies at their disposal and a clear interest in enriching themselves. Continued war would be their best way of doing this.'[2]

Despite UN, African and other international efforts to broker a peace, the war continued. Ceasefires were never sustained for long, casualty rates were high and atrocities were committed on both sides. Thus all the conditions conducive to the creation of large numbers of refugees and the constant movement of displaced persons from the civilian populations were in place. The year 2001 began with the assassination of Kabila on 16 January. He was 'succeeded' by his son Joseph, who established a better rapport with the international community and sought actively to achieve a peace. The fighting continued into 2002. When Uganda and Rwanda finally withdrew their forces from eastern Congo in October 2002, the situation on the ground became increasingly uncertain; fighting in the northeast led to another flight of refugees. Nonetheless, by the end of the year, agreement had been reached between the government and various opposition groups upon a power-sharing transitional period until elections could be held. In 2003, however, following the withdrawal of Ugandan forces, fierce fighting broke out between the local militias of the Hema and Lendu ethnic groups and killing in Ituri district reached near genocidal proportions. Human Rights Watch calculated that 50,000 people had been killed in Ituri and another 500,000 refugees had been created as a consequence of the fighting. Meanwhile, the US aid agency, the International Rescue Committee (IRC), estimated that the whole conflict, sparked in 1998 by the Rwandan invasion, had caused the death of between 3.1 and 4.7 million people and, of these, 90 per cent died as the result of lack of medical care, food insecurity leading to famine and generalised violence. War-induced hunger and disease were the biggest killers. South Africa's President Thabo Mbeki worked tirelessly to broker a peace and on 30 June 2003 Joseph Kabila declared the war to be over. The transitional government then came into being. If the war was over, the peace was precarious. Up to 40,000 Hutu militiamen responsible for the 1994 genocide in Rwanda, continued to reside in the eastern Congo, launching periodic raids across the border into Tutsi-dominated Rwanda, which gave Rwanda the excuse to retaliate against the Congo.

The peace remained a fragile affair through 2004. There was open fighting in May when soldiers loyal to the pro-Rwanda Rassemblement congolais pour la démocratie (RCD-Goma) seized the eastern town of Bukavu. President Kabila declared a state of emergency and 'general mobilisation' and once more, refugees began to flee from the border area. It was also, as usual, a question of who controlled or had access to resources: coltan and cassiterite in the east, cobalt and copper in Katanga. Despite the presence in the east of 10,000 UN troops, little respect for human rights or the rule of law was evident. Full-scale war again appeared to be a possibility when President Kabila announced that he would send 10,000 troops to the east. Rwanda promptly threatened to invade the Congo once more in support of its proxies, while Angola and Tanzania offered to send troops to support Kabila. The UN warned foreign countries to stay out of the conflict. In August tensions escalated after news of the massacre of 160 Banyamulenge refugees and a further 100 injured in the Gatumba refugee camp west of Bujumbura in

Burundi. At this point both Rwanda and Burundi threatened to invade the Congo unless it hunted down the Hutu extremists who threatened the Tutsi communities in the region. The UN Secretary-General Kofi Annan asked for an additional 13,500 troops and 37 helicopter gunships for the United Nations Mission in the Congo (MONUC) force in the Congo. In November, Kabila again threatened to send 10,000 troops to the east and President Kagame of Rwanda again threatened to invade. He claimed the right to oust armed Hutu groups such as the Interahamwe that the UN had failed to bring under control. In December, anticipating the arrival of 10,000 Congo army troops – who were feared by Congolese citizens as much as the invaders – people started to move out of the eastern provinces to become refugees once more. It was an unhappy end to a year in which nothing appeared to have been resolved.

The crisis in eastern Congo continued through 2005. UN and government troops faced rebellious militia groups and the situation was complicated by the interventions of Uganda and Rwanda. In January there was renewed fighting between the Hema and Lendu factions that led to the displacement of yet more people. Further relief operations to support them were mounted by the UN and NGOs. Nonetheless, during the year some of the 4.5 million Congolese who had been displaced by the violence began to return and, as the fighting subsided, more refugees from Tanzania, the Republic of Congo and the Central African Republic also returned, many of them travelling by boat along the Congo and Obangi rivers and across Lake Tanganyika. As with so many apparent improvements in the Congo, the suspicion always remained that more violence and further displacements of people were likely to follow.

Real advances were achieved in 2006. Presidential and legislative elections were held on 30 July 2006, with 33 presidential candidates and 10,000 contenders for 500 seats in the National Assembly. In a run-off on 29 October between Kabila and his main presidential rival Jean-Pierre Bemba, Kabila received 58 per cent of the votes. International observers said the elections had been free and fair despite irregularities. However, these political advances were achieved against a background of continuing outbursts of violence. In January 100,000 people fled the government campaign against the Mayi Mayi militias in Katanga and by May the number of displaced people had risen to between 165,000 and 200,000, although in June people began to return to their homes as the fighting died down. In December the UNHCR calculated that there were 1.2 million displaced persons inside the Congo and 410,000 refugees in neighbouring countries. The UN estimated it required an immediate $67 million to deal with the post-conflict aftermath, while thousands of IDPs were receiving no support of any kind. By this time MONUC had 20,000 troops in the country.

The IDPs in the war zones suffered badly. In South Kivu 42,000 women received treatment in local clinics for rape. Figures for rape on a national scale were estimated in the hundreds of thousands. Although the 2006 elections were generally accepted, there was further violence in 2007 when those loyal to Bemba, the defeated presidential candidate, clashed with government forces. In North Kivu, the National Congress for the Defence of the People (CNDP), led by Laurent Nkunda (Nkundabatware), forced villagers to flee. There were then an estimated 370,000 IDPs in the east of the country as a whole. The Democratic Forces for the Liberation of Rwanda became active in South Kivu, leading to the displacement of some 8,000 people, while government forces were involved in North Kivu. Although groups of people became refugees or IDPs as a result of violence in particular areas and were then able to return to their homes, 1.2 million people were permanently displaced. They suffered health problems and malnutrition. At this time about 60 per cent of government expenditure came from donors. During July 2007 there was a political row in Britain about government deportation of Congolese refugees or asylum seekers, with demonstrations across the country demanding that all deportations to the Congo should be suspended: thousands of asylum seekers feared they would face torture or possibly murder on their return. Nonetheless, planeloads were returned to the Congo, with the British embassy in Kinshasa insisting there was no evidence that they faced mistreatment. The attitude of the British Home Office was criticised by, among others, the Bishop of Winchester who said it 'always makes Kinshasa sound like Dorking' and that everyone with experience in the Congo found the 'mantra-like assurances of the department simply incredible'.[3] John McDonnell, the Labour MP for Hayes and Harlington, whose constituency included two immigration detention centres, warned that many people had simply disappeared when they arrived back in the DRC. As one asylum seeker said: 'I am not here for economic reasons. I'm here to seek protection until the situation changes in my country. When it changes, I would be happy to go back.'[4]

Problems in eastern Congo showed no sign of abating through 2008. Though a peace agreement between the government and the rebels was signed in January, it quickly unravelled and conflict escalated. By October 1 million people had been displaced and were sheltered in unsanitary camps where cholera was rife (by the end of the year there were an estimated 5 million cases of cholera across the country). The CNDP leader, Nkunda, was now making the running and was the principal cause of the renewed violence. In April the government finalised an agreement with China that allowed a Chinese consortium to finance a $6 billion mining project that would include roads, railways and social infrastructure in return for China being given access to cobalt and copper resources. The arrival in the country of the Chinese was seen as a boost for economic recovery. A report by Refugees International summarised the situation in 2008:

The long-running conflict in the Democratic Republic of the Congo (DRC) has been one of the deadliest in the last half century. More than 5 million people have died from causes associated with the conflict. About 1.4 million people remain internally displaced and there are approximately 340,000 Congolese refugees in neighbouring countries. Civilians in eastern DRC continue to endure targeted attacks by all armed groups. Before conditions can improve for displaced Congolese, the ongoing violence and insecurity in eastern DRC must be addressed.

By the end of the year there were more than 250,000 new displacements in North Kivu as a result of operations carried out by the Congolese and Rwandan national armies against the Democratic Forces for the Liberation of Rwanda (FDLR). After the Rwandan army had been withdrawn, the Congolese army expanded its military campaign against the FDLR into South Kivu, leading to further displacements and human rights abuses. As the insecurity continued and people remained displaced for longer periods, both they and their host communities in eastern DRC required assistance beyond basic services and in particular livelihood and education programmes. Although a decrease in violence in parts of the Congo allowed hundreds of thousands of people to return to their homes, poor infrastructure, particularly roads, meant that returnees were often cut off from services and access to economic opportunities.

Early in 2009, General Laurent Nkunda, whose rebel group though apparently independent had been backed by the Rwanda government, was arrested. It was then hoped that his forces would lay down their weapons and join the national army. His group split; fighters loyal to Nkunda's former chief of staff, Bosco Ntaganda, were already working with the Congolese army. A UN report accused Rwanda and the Congo of fighting a proxy war in eastern Congo, with Rwanda using Nkunda and the Congo backing Rwandan Hutu rebels based on its territory. Nkunda was a Tutsi, like Rwanda's leaders, and they were determined to wipe out the Hutu FDLR, some of whose leaders took part in the 1994 genocide in Rwanda. After Nkunda's arrest, a Rwandan force of 4,000 troops crossed into eastern Congo as part of a new deal with the Congolese government. Under its terms the Congo government would allow Rwanda to take action against the FDLR provided it first arrested Nkunda. The Congo government wanted to extradite Nkunda to face charges of treason and war crimes, or at the very least to neutralise him. Cooperation between the Congo and Rwanda against the FDLR could change the situation in eastern Congo although the FDLR had until then successfully resisted all attempts by Rwanda and the Congo to disarm them. With 20,000 peace-keeping troops in eastern Congo, the UN, despite operating under a Chapter Seven mandate that allows it to protect the civilian population and themselves, had proved singularly inept at providing any protection.

Although the war in the Congo was originally sparked by the genocide in Rwanda and the mass movement of refugees into the country, including the hard-line Hutus seen as the perpetrators of the genocide, it subsequently became more complicated. A rift between Kabila and his former allies sparked a new rebellion, backed by Rwanda and Uganda. Angola, Namibia and Zimbabwe then came to Kabila's assistance and, with five neighbouring countries involved, the original conflict escalated to become Africa's Great War, with the five countries taking payment for their services by exploiting the Congo's vast resources, so that it was as much about plundering the resources of the Congo as about a political settlement. In 2009, many of the country's 65 million population had yet to experience the benefits of peace. President Joseph Kabila, who won the election in 2006, has the support of

Western governments, particularly the United States and France, as well as regional allies such as South Africa and mining transnationals, all eager to exploit the Congo's resources.

RWANDA

Recurring communal violence has been a factor in Rwanda from before independence in 1962, and before and after the overthrow of the monarchy, which led many of the Tutsi minority to flee into Uganda, Burundi and the Congo. Then came the genocide of 1994. In February 1993 the ceasefire arranged between the Rwanda (Hutu) government and the Rwanda Patriotic Front (RPF) that had invaded from its bases in Uganda broke down. The RPF rebels launched a four-day offensive that doubled the amount of territory under their control and set off the flight of 600,000 people. The RPF justified the new offensive because of an anti-Tutsi outbreak in January 1993 in which 300 Tutsis were killed. The human rights agency, Africa Watch, reported that President Juvenal Habyarimana's party, the National Republican Movement for Democracy and Development (MRND) was involved in the killings. France then sent 600 troops in support of the Habyarimana government which otherwise might have collapsed. The RPF made no further advances. The spark that ignited the genocide came on 6 April 1994 when the plane carrying the two presidents – Habyarimana of Rwanda and Cyprien Ntaryamina of Burundi, who had been in peace talks together – was shot down as it approached Kigali airport. Their deaths set off the massacres of Tutsis and moderate Hutus that had long been planned and which continued until September, causing many people to flee their homes and become refugees in neighbouring countries.

In the aftermath of the 1994 genocide in which some 800,000 Tutsi and moderate Hutus were massacred, camps for over 2 million Rwandan refugees were established in the eastern Congo. Over 1994–6 leaders of the just defeated Rwandan government, commanders of the Forces Armées Rwandaises (FAR) and leaders of the Interahamwe militia, who had just coordinated the mass murder of up to a million people, worked together in the camps with the Zairean government and armed forces. Militarisation in the Bukavu and Goma refugee camps followed.[5] The current security threats posed by the militarised remnants of the exodus resident in the eastern Congo provided the Rwandan government with a justification for cross-border interventions. In its turn, Rwanda hosted Congolese refugees after 1996 and again in 2004, following the ethnic cleansing by the Congolese armed forces directed at the Banyamulenge (Congolese Tutsis from South Kivu) as well as residents of Bukavu and Uvira. Precision in assessing the numbers of refugees involved at any given time is exceptionally difficult. The UNHCR, for example, estimated that in the aftermath of the 1994 genocide 850,000 Rwandan refugees moved into the Goma area of eastern Congo, but when figures are on that scale they are bound to be imprecise. Where else did refugees go at that time and how many remained uncounted?

The Rwandan Hutu flight to eastern Congo led to the wars of 1996, 1998 and later. One observer described the UN response to 'a series of political and humanitarian crises in the Great Lakes region since 1994 with a "long litany of non-decisions and non-interventions"' as inexcusable.[6] Had the West intervened in Rwanda decisively in 1994, much that followed, including the Congo's Great African War, might have been avoided. But, according to the former Secretary-General of the UN, Boutros Boutros Ghali, the Somalia syndrome persuaded the US to oppose UN intervention, while the French continued to back the Hutu regime even after the death of Habyarimana. The Clinton administration refused to recognise that genocide was taking place since Rwanda was not strategically relevant to US interests so, instead, it was called a civil war.[7] In 1997, Paul Kagame, then President of Rwanda, blamed the international community for failing to intervene in 1994 to halt the genocide. He also criticised the failure to separate ex-FAR soldiers and the Interahamwe militiamen from ordinary citizens in the refugee camps, a move that would have prevented the Hutu diehards launching attacks into Rwanda. From this he argued that there was no alternative but to dismantle the refugee camps, which led to the overthrow of Mobutu, the chief supporter of the Hutus. But the Tutsi victory in Rwanda was not absolute because, among the 600,000 refugees who returned to Rwanda in 1996, were many Hutu militants. A further consequence of the 1994 genocide was the huge number of detainees, up to 120,000, who were to be tried as perpetrators of the genocide. Most developments in Rwanda from 1994 onwards could be seen as continuing consequences of the genocide. Thus, the army became involved in the civil war in the Congo to end the perceived threat of the Hutus based there although, over the years, this was a justification that allowed Rwanda to do other things, most notably to strip the eastern Congo of mineral resources. Elements of the Rwandan army in eastern Congo were responsible for looting. Kagame was dependent upon his army and had to walk a tightrope between maintaining a strong government and attempting reconciliation and national integration.

As late as 2004, Rwanda still claimed to fear an invasion of Hutu refugees from the Congo. Kagame, meanwhile, had achieved an electoral triumph as president but, although he had brought a degree of stability to Rwanda, this was at the expense of creating a police state. In Arusha, trials of *génocidaires* proceeded slowly under the UN International Criminal Tribunal for Rwanda (ICTR), while former Rwandan militias still remained in eastern Congo. During 2005 refugees were slowly returning home from Uganda, some 500 under the auspices of the UNHCR in February and a further batch in October. In its turn Rwanda was host to 50,000 refugees from the Congo and Burundi. During 2006, trials of genocide suspects in the traditional courts led to outbreaks of violence, while the government reacted angrily to criticisms from the World Bank, the African Union and Transparency International at the lack of political freedom and transparency in Rwanda. By 2007 Rwanda had fallen out with its old ally France (which had supported the Hutu government) and was pursuing its application to join the Commonwealth. In February 2008 US

President George W. Bush visited Rwanda and effectively endorsed Kagame's position as legitimate head of state. In December the government decided to phase out French as a language of instruction in the schools by 2011. Also that month a UN report accused Rwanda and Uganda of providing direct support to the Tutsi rebellion led by General Nkunda in the eastern Congo. By this time Kagame and the Tutsis had established a stable government in Kigali, though brooking no effective political opposition and keeping tight control of the media.

BURUNDI

Although overshadowed by the genocide in Rwanda, its neighbour Burundi, with an equal preponderance of Hutus over Tutsis, suffered from what was described as a low-intensity civil war for most of the decade. In 1995 active combatants in the ranks of the Tutsi militias and in various guerrilla groups organised by the Hutu extremists, some in touch with those in Rwanda, ensured a steady death toll of approximately 200 civilians a week and three or four soldiers a day. The war continued through to 1997: it was often fierce and included civilian massacres. Between 1993 and 1999 an estimated 250,000 people had died. The Burundi policy of 'regroupement' camps into which the government decided to move 300,000 peasants was especially unpopular. Living conditions in the camps were appalling. They were a form of refugee camp designed to hold those presumed to be opponents of the regime. During these years about 6 per cent of the population was displaced. By early 2001, some 320,000 Burundian Hutu refugees were in camps in western Tanzania. President Pierre Buyoya, himself a Tutsi, nonetheless determined to stand up to Tutsi extremists and was supported in this by other African countries. In July 2001, following some of the worst Hutu–Tutsi violence since 1993, the government and opposition put together a power-sharing agreement. Under its terms a transitional government would be led by Buyoya as president, while the Hutu Domitien Ndayizeye would act as vice-president. The agreement was implemented in November 2001.

In August 2004 160 Banyamulenge, who had fled the fighting round Bukavu in the Congo, were massacred in the Gatumba refugee camp 20 km from Bujumbura. This massacre illustrated just how fragile any peace process in the region could be. While the transition to democracy was proceeding, the government faced massive poverty, continued ethnic rivalry and persistent fighting in the west of the country. These problems were exacerbated by the return of large numbers of refugees, while a further 400,000 still awaited repatriation in October 2005. When he visited Burundi in 2006, the UN Secretary-General Kofi Annan considered the situation to be fragile: food security was dire, heavy rains and floods had rendered thousands homeless during the year and the government was appealing to the international community for food aid. The next year was no better: torrential rainfall and flooding left another 23,000 people homeless. Early in 2008, according to the UNHCR, there were still 338,000 Burundians in exile, mainly in

Tanzania but also the Congo and Rwanda, as well as 150,000 IDPs in 160 camps in Burundi.

There was another factor that pre-dated the crisis years of the 1990s: there had always been internal migration in Burundi from its poor, overcrowded agricultural areas to the towns; such migration continued, despite the ongoing violence. This movement is explained as follows:

> Farming is a prison to most Burundians. In the countryside, especially in the north and centre, people desperately want to reduce their dependence on the land. The three big ways for young people to escape poverty are education, migration, and hard work.[8]

Less devastated, and with fewer killed or forced to become refugees or IDPs than its two neighbours, the Congo and Rwanda, Burundi had also suffered physical and psychological damage over these years. If we consider casualty figures in wars elsewhere in the world, Burundi, with between 250,000 and 300,000 dead, must rank high on any table of fatalities.

CONCLUSION

None of the three countries has yet been able to put all the violence and ethnic mistrust behind it. Perhaps one sign of returning confidence was the agreement of the Economic Community of the Great Lakes Countries (CEPGL) in June 2009 that the border posts of the member countries should operate around the clock, with effect from 1 September. The resolution was reached at a meeting of the Directors of Migration Services and General Commissioners at Belvedere Hotel in Rubavu District. The meeting was also attended by the EU delegation in Rwanda, representatives of the International Conference on the Great Lakes Region, and the CEPGL permanent executive staff. The meeting, chaired by Rwanda's Director of Immigration, Anaclet Kalibata, also resolved that the three member states would enhance cooperation by striving for peace, sustainable security and economic integration while seeking to improve the well-being of citizens through poverty eradication plans.[9] Yet, as encouraging as such small advances may be, the situation in the Congo remained dire. From the beginning of 2009 to September, according to the UN Organising Committee of Humanitarian Aid (OCHA), 800,000 people, 350,000 in North Kivu and 450,000 in South Kivu, had been forced to leave their homes and villages because of ongoing operations by the Armed Forces of Congo (FARDC) against the FDLR.

According to Peace for Congo, to end the cycle of violence, the Hutu people in general and Rwandan refugees in the Congo (including the FDLR) should no longer be labelled perpetrators of genocide. 'It is necessary to make a clear distinction between civilians and armed gangs, Hutu refugees in general, and the small band of men wanted by Rwandan and international justice for implication in the Rwandan genocide of 1994.'[10] Such an approach is easier for missionaries to propose than for the embattled people on the ground –

whether soldiers, refugees or civilians – to accept. The performance of the UN, which ought to have been the key to peace-making, was generally abysmal, with slow reactions, constant stalling and manipulation by the big powers.[11]

The problems of the DRC, Rwanda and Burundi over the years from 1994 to 2009, apart from more than 5 million deaths, led to an endless movement of refugees and internally displaced people within and between these three countries. While substantial numbers of refugees left the region and sought asylum in Europe or elsewhere, they were a minority. Even assuming that a permanent peace can be achieved for the region, it will take years before all the displaced people, many of whom will be deeply traumatised, can be resettled and begin to live a normal life again.

15
West Africa

This huge area, covering 7.4 million square km, comprises 17 countries: Benin, Burkina Faso, Cape Verde, Chad, Côte d'Ivoire, The Gambia, Ghana, Guinea, Guinea-Bissau, Liberia, Mali, Mauritania, Niger, Nigeria, Senegal, Sierra Leone and Togo. All of them, except Chad, are members of ECOWAS. During the 1990s and into the twenty-first century conflicts and civil wars affected Guinea, Liberia, Sierra Leone and Côte d'Ivoire, resulting in a major regional movement of refugees. The treaty establishing ECOWAS was signed by the 15 founding members in Lagos in May 1975 (the sixteenth, Cape Verde, joined in 1977); the principal aim of ECOWAS was to create a full customs union over 15 years and bring about the economic integration of the region; many of its provisions were similar to those of the European Community. It was the largest economic grouping in Africa. A major difficulty facing the group when it was founded was the fact that inter-regional trade amounted to only 6 per cent of the total trade of the members. Even so, ECOWAS provided a framework for greater economic interdependence. All the members of ECOWAS signed the 1979 Protocol on Free Movement of Persons, the Right of Residence and Establishment. The Protocol covered the movement of people within the region and allowed citizens of member states to enter other member states for a period of 90 days without a visa, although working during that time was technically not permitted. Many of those who took advantage of this provision did find jobs (the principal reason for their move) and overstayed the 90-day limit. In any case, there was a long tradition of movement within the region that pre-dated the establishment of national borders by the colonial powers.

CÔTE D'IVOIRE AND BURKINA FASO

Economic and social upheavals, civil wars and the desire to escape the poverty of the region to achieve a better life elsewhere have led to major movements of people from West Africa, both to other parts of Africa and out of the continent altogether, mainly to Europe and North America. Formerly known as the 'West African Miracle' because of its peaceful role in the region and its prosperity, Côte d'Ivoire was profoundly destabilised in December 1999, when a military coup toppled President Henri Konan. General Robert Guei, the subsequent military dictator, was himself overthrown ten months later by Laurent Gbagbo and Côte d'Ivoire descended into a crisis that continued through the first decade of the twenty-first century, with UN and French troops maintaining the status quo in a divided country.

The domestic upheaval had enormous repercussions for the migrant labour in the north of the country upon which the agricultural sector depended. Côte d'Ivoire is the leading world producer of cocoa beans but, since 1999, harvests have been threatened by a labour shortage, since a significant proportion of the harvesters come into the country as migrants every year from Burkina Faso and from Mali. Both these countries are landlocked and have southern borders with Côte d'Ivoire, and both are among the poorest countries in Africa, with large numbers of unemployed. There had been escalating anti-foreign resentment and violence in Côte d'Ivoire during the 1990s and this peaked at the time of the coups and divisions that broke the peace of the country from 1999 onwards. About 40 per cent of Côte d'Ivoire's population of 16 million in 2000 were incomers, mainly from Burkina Faso. By 2001 the crisis had led to an exodus of 200,000 Burkinabes from the cocoa and coffee plantations. In 2004 France arranged for the evacuation of 10,000 of its citizens then living and working in Côte d'Ivoire. By 2009, there had been no resolution to the crisis as, year by year, Gbagbo postponed the promised elections.

With a population of 14.7 million in 2008 and an average per capita income of only $430, Burkina Faso is one of the poorest countries in Africa. In colonial times (when it was named Upper Volta) a high proportion of its men became temporary economic migrants, particularly to Côte d'Ivoire, to earn the money they needed to pay taxes. They have continued as economic migrants in the postcolonial era, seeking seasonal work in Côte d'Ivoire to provide annual incomes that are not available in Burkina Faso. An estimated 2 million Burkinabes are abroad at any given time, half of them in Côte d'Ivoire, the remainder scattered throughout West Africa. Burkina Faso also acts as host to political refugees from Mali. In 2000, there were 700 registered refugees in the country and 355 asylum seekers. Net migration out of the country is reckoned as -5.5 migrants per 1,000 of the population, a level that is regarded as satisfactory by the government.[1]

NIGERIA

With a population now touching the 150 million mark, Nigeria is the giant of the region. Nigerians of the diaspora are to be found in most countries of Africa, spreading throughout West Africa, across the continent through Chad to Somalia and southwards through Equatorial Guinea (seasonal work on the cocoa plantations), as judges in Botswana and with a sizeable community in South Africa, especially Johannesburg, in a range of occupations. The worldwide Nigerian diaspora is variously estimated at between 17 and 20 million, which makes it one of the largest in the world. A majority of overseas Nigerians are to be found in Europe, especially Britain, and in North America, both Canada and the United States. In 2008, remittances from overseas Nigerians came to $7 billion, equivalent to approximately 5 per cent of the country's GDP, although the figure may be as high as $10 billion, as many of the remittances are conveyed privately.

In recent years Nigerians have migrated from their country in large numbers and are to be found all over the world. In their host countries they contribute a range of skills, which, unfortunately, are lost to Nigeria. One guide to the rate of emigration is the fact that over 90,000 visa applications are received by the US embassy in Nigeria every year.[2] So far, the harnessing and channelling of the diaspora's potential contribution to Nigeria's development has been largely neglected: 'By understanding more about its diaspora, Nigeria can present to them opportunities that allow them to contribute their resources effectively to its development. This must be done now before the ties the diaspora has to Nigeria start to wane.'[3] In 2005, 6,125 Nigerians qualified for the US Diversity Visa Lottery programme – the highest number of DV Lottery immigrants from any African country. The success of its migrants abroad emphasises Nigeria's loss at home, since a significant proportion of them are the brightest and most able professionals or entrepreneurs. Considerable numbers of Nigerians left the country during the 1970s and 1980s, but the rate of emigration accelerated during the 1990s (the Abacha years of military rule) to make the 'brain drain' a negative factor in Nigerian development. As professionals leave Nigeria, so the country has to replace them by importing expatriate staff from elsewhere. Apart from remittances, there are other ways in which members of the diaspora contribute to their own country's development. For example, the Association of Nigerian Physicians in the Americas (ANPA) regularly visits Nigeria to offer assistance to patients and doctors. However, remittances are the most important contribution to Nigeria's development. They help stabilise foreign exchange demand, provide opportunities for employment and assist the education of relatives. A high proportion of all remittances are used by the family recipients for immediate consumption, consisting of food, clothing, education, health care and other household needs and this money makes its way directly into the economy through the market place. The total figure for remittances – between $6 and $8 billion, compared with Nigeria's estimated GDP of $72.1 billion in 2004 and foreign reserves of $19.59 billion – is a significant contribution to the Nigerian economy as a whole.[4]

MALI

In recent years Mali has become an important staging post for the flow of Africans seeking access to the EU by sea or across the Sahara. Many Malians also wish to escape the poverty in which they live and migrate to Europe. On 6 November 2008, the EU Development Commissioner, Louis Michel, opened a Centre for Migration in Mali's capital Bamako. The centre offers Malians information about how to migrate to Europe legally. In addition, the EU financed centre will offer language courses and carry out research on migration. The EU hopes the centre will serve the dual purpose of managing acceptable migration and reducing illegal migration. Refugees from other countries travel into Mali on their way to Senegal or Guinea-Bissau, and from there they try to reach the Canary Islands. This is always a risky undertaking, which may end in disaster, and the new Centre for Migration, with a staff of 30

EU personnel, will warn visitors against taking such a route to Europe. Instead, it will explain how people can travel to Europe legally. According to Badra Alou Macalou, the Malian Minister for African Integration, 'Illegal migration is flourishing here [Mali] and that's partly because potential migrants are not given enough opportunities to emigrate legally.'[5] Karl Kopp, a Europe specialist at the German refugee group ProAsyl, said the centre is not intended to be a job centre for work in Europe and that is one of its biggest failures.

> They won't change anything in the suffering of the people who want to leave or have to flee. We are concerned that the centre will turn into just a token solution and that it will merely paper over the real situation.

In Mali, the new Centre for Migration obviously saw its task as one of recruiting skilled personnel. The EU Commission spokesman Amadeu Altafaj-Tardio rejected accusations that the centre was only for the benefit of the EU, insisting that it was intended to help Mali develop its own migration policy. 'This is by no means a European institution on African soil,' he said. 'The centre answers to the government of Mali, and it is merely supported by staff and material from the European Commission.' This blithe statement did not carry much conviction since the EU was pumping €10 million into the centre over a four-year period. That, inevitably, meant that the EU would expect to influence what happened at the centre. John Clancy, the EU spokesman, said it was a pilot centre and that other EU member states would create bilateral arrangements with the Malian authorities to open opportunities for migrants. He said: 'We hope through this centre to create a structure for the legal migration possibilities for people not only in Mali but other nationals passing through Mali, with better information on the legal possibility of finding work in Europe.' Clancy went on to say:

> Let us be realistic, there will not be a thousand jobs on offer as of today, but there is an opportunity as Europe seeks more migrants for its seasonal work, like fruit picking in certain countries. These are the types of job opportunities that may become available as long as member states of the EU enter into an agreement with the Malian authorities.

It is the first time the EU has provided this kind of support in Sub-Saharan Africa to prevent illegal migration and create a centre outside its borders to dissuade people from taking dangerous and illegal routes and risking their lives in trying to get to Europe. However, despite this EU initiative, economic instability and the lack of basic services look likely to go on forcing many Africans into opting for the often lethal path of illegal migration.[6]

Two of the more prosperous countries of West Africa, Ghana and Senegal, each have long histories of migration that both pre-date and follow the colonial era; they are worth examining in some depth to provide an insight into present-day African attitudes towards migration.

GHANA

Ghana's history is of migration and immigration mixed in equal proportions. The 2000 census shows that the country's population of 19 million is composed of many ethnic groups, almost all of which claim to have migrated into Ghana from elsewhere in Africa. As the Gold Coast, the country was a principal conduit for slaves from the interior on their way to the Americas, although today the Ghanaian government hopes to persuade some of the American and Caribbean descendants of these slaves to return to live in Ghana. Yet, at the same time, Ghanaians continue to emigrate to North America, Europe and other parts of Africa. During the last decades of the twentieth century the country suffered a range of economic, political and social problems that led to the creation of a sizeable diaspora as Ghanaians sought better opportunities for themselves outside their own country. Long before the colonial era Ghanaians travelled to many regions of Africa as traders or seasonal workers, and it was common for them to settle outside their original homeland. The arrival of the European slave trade along the coast disrupted many aspects of life both in Ghana and farther inland. Between 1450 and 1850 an estimated 12 million Africans were transported across the Atlantic and some 5,000 a year were shipped from the Gold Coast, the region encompassing modern Ghana, Togo and Benin. Only in 1874 did Britain formally make the Gold Coast a colony and the subsequent development of gold mines and cocoa farms there attracted mainly male migrants from countries of the West Coast, including The Gambia, Sierra Leone and Nigeria as well as Upper Volta (Burkina Faso), Togo, Côte d'Ivoire, Mali and Benin.[7]

Immigrants from Ghana's poorer neighbours, Burkina Faso and Togo, have come to Ghana to seek work for generations, while immigrant traders from Nigeria have conducted much petty trade alongside Lebanese and Syrian traders.[8] Ghana's 1913 census recorded a total of 4,142 foreigners working in the colony. Between 1910 and 1957 the number of migrants grew, often as a result of organised government recruitment. By the 1931 census a total of 289,217 foreigners, mainly from the French West African colonies, were recorded as living in the Gold Coast. Nigerians accounted for 95 per cent of the migrants from other British colonies. The census also revealed that between 1921 and 1931, 287,000 people from Burkina Faso entered the Gold Coast, although fewer than 190,000 were residing in the colony in 1931. A breakdown of the 1931 foreign-born population in Ghana shows that 70,536 (24.40 per cent) came from other British West African colonies; 196,282 (67.90 per cent) came from French West African colonies; 6,812 (2.30 per cent) came from Liberia; and 15,587 (5.40 per cent) came from unclassified areas.[9] When the Gold Coast became independent as Ghana in 1957, an immediate influx of migrants to the first black African nation far exceeded the numbers leaving, and by 1960 there were 827,481 foreigners living in Ghana, equivalent to 12 per cent of the population, of whom 98 per cent came from other parts of Africa (though less than 1 per cent from beyond West Africa). Togo, Burkina Faso, Nigeria and Côte d'Ivoire accounted for 88.9

per cent of this influx. Ghana enjoyed close links with these neighbours as a consequence of historical and cultural ties. However – a familiar migration story – an economic downturn in the mid 1960s led to a reversal of the migrant flow. Suddenly, moreover, there was work for Ghana's professionals – teachers, doctors, administrators and lawyers – as far afield in Africa as Uganda, Botswana, Nigeria and Zambia. The decline of the economy led the government to expel a large number of immigrants in 1969, when the migrant community had reached 2 million out of a total population of 8.4 million. The government passed the Aliens Compliance Order, under whose terms all immigrants without proper documents had to leave within two weeks. This mainly affected workers in the cocoa industry and 155,000 of 213,000 immigrants were forced to leave. As a result of these expulsions the percentage of foreigners in the total population fell to 6.6 per cent in 1970.

Ghanaians themselves have long been migrants as traders, students, professionals or fishermen along the West African coast. Many Ghanaians were attracted to Nigeria during the oil boom years of the 1970s but in 1983, when the oil boom had faded and Nigeria experienced an economic slump, the Nigerian government expelled 2 million migrant workers of whom 700,000 were Ghanaians, although many of the deportees later returned. In May 1985, Nigeria again expelled foreign workers though on a smaller scale: this time 100,000 Ghanaians were deported.

The 1970s were an unhappy decade for Ghana; it was ruled by an increasingly corrupt military regime, which presided over a declining economy. As a consequence of this military misrule an estimated 2 million Ghanaians emigrated, primarily to Nigeria and Côte d'Ivoire. By mid decade 42,000 Ghanaians had migrated to Côte d'Ivoire while others were leaving for Nigeria, which was enjoying its first oil boom, at the rate of 300 a day. These emigrants included the unskilled, the semi-skilled and a significant number of professional people as well.

The 1990s were the decade in which the Ghanaian diaspora began to play a major role in the Ghanaian economy. By the mid 1990s estimates of the size of the diaspora ranged between 2 million and 4 million (10 to 20 per cent of the country's 20 million population), spread across Africa, Europe and North America. Emigrants during the 1970s had mainly been skilled workers and professionals but from the 1980s onwards more and more unskilled or semi-skilled people had emigrated. The main countries of residence for these migrants in 2001 were as follows: the USA – 17 per cent; Germany – 14 per cent; Nigeria – 10 per cent; Italy – 9 per cent; UK – 9 per cent; other EU – 10 per cent; and other non-EU – 31 per cent.[10] Britain exercised a particular appeal for some Ghanaian migrants, who constituted the largest and longest-standing African migrant group in the country. The British census of 2001 registered 55,537 people who had been born in Ghana, an increase of 72 per cent over the 32,277 people registered in 1991. Part of the increase in Ghanaian immigrants in Britain was a direct result of the recruitment by the British National Health Service (NHS) of Ghanaian doctors and nurses. By 2003 there were 2,468 Ghanaian nurses and 300 doctors working in Britain.

The British policy of overseas recruitment was highly controversial since it deprived Ghana of crucial health workers needed in its own system and was also contrary to the growing policy of tightening controls over immigration. In addition, it highlighted one of the great dilemmas about emigration from poor to rich countries: should skilled people stay in their own countries, where their services were urgently needed, or had such people the right to exercise their freedom of choice and move to a country that offered greater economic and other opportunities? Elsewhere in Europe there had also been a surge in Ghanaian immigration. At the end of 2004, official German statistics showed that 20,000 Ghanaian passport holders then resided in the country. They were the third largest African group after Moroccans and Tunisians. In the Netherlands at this time there were 18,000 Ghanaian residents.

Although the brain drain impacts negatively on the country's development, depriving Ghana of many of its most able people, this is compensated for in part by regular remittances from overseas, which make a substantial addition to the balance of payments. In 2004 the Central Bank estimated that $1.2 billion in remittances came back to Ghana, although this figure probably represented no more than half the total, as a great deal is sent back using informal channels. Remittances are the second largest source of foreign exchange after exports and, as in other countries, a great proportion of them go to poor rural areas and are distributed by women. Government policy is to encourage those abroad to maintain regular contact with their country and in support of this policy it passed the Ghana Dual Citizenship Act (2002) so that migrants could keep their Ghanaian citizenship as well as adopting that of their host country. In a further effort to promote good relations with its citizens abroad, the government organised a Homecoming Summit in 2001, inviting members of the diaspora to Accra to promote their efforts in assisting national development. A substantial proportion of the country's migrants eventually return home to become self-employed or to establish businesses, which provide work for other Ghanaians. Even so, the drain of well-trained professionals is depleting the country of its human capital and the loss to Ghana is greater than any gain through remittances.

The loss to Ghana is most obvious in terms of the medical profession. Ghana has a high reputation for its medical training, whether for doctors or nurses, and that, ironically, is part of the problem, for they are sought after by Britain and the United States. They leave Ghana because of the low remuneration offered for their services, poor career prospects, the low value placed upon health workers generally, poor management of the medical system and fewer chances under these circumstances of saving for their retirement. So they emigrate to take advantage of prospects in a country such as Britain, which does not produce enough trained personnel of its own. Britain has become responsible for 75 per cent of Ghana's verification requests (checks on the training of migrants not trained in the country where they seek work). In most cases Ghanaians pass the checks. Vacancy levels in Ghana Ministry of Health in 1998 and 2002 were as follows: doctors 42.6 per cent (1998) and 47.3 per cent (2002); nurses 25.5 per cent (1998) and 57.0% per cent(2002).[11]

In an attempt to keep more doctors at home, the government has initiated various schemes such as overtime pay, the provision of cars for doctors who have joined the Ghana Medical Association (GMA) or insistence that those trained in Ghana must work at home for at least two years before emigrating, but these have had little impact since compliance both in Ghana and abroad has been nominal.

From 1980 onwards a significant number of Ghanaians have headed for North America. In Canada the early arrivals with high skills had little difficulty in being accepted. According to the Canadian census of 2001, there were 16,985 Ghanaians registered as living in Canada while between 1995 and 2004 approximately 960 Ghanaians gained permanent residence every year. Between 1990 and 2000 the Ghanaian population in the United States increased from 20,889 to 65,576 or by 210 per cent. However, non-official estimates suggest that as many as 300,000 Ghanaians are now resident in the United States.

During the civil wars in Sierra Leone and Liberia in the 1990s, a steady flow of refugees left those two countries and a proportion of them arrived in Ghana. In 1999 Ghana was host to 14,600 refugees from three main sources – Liberia, Togo and Sierra Leone. The UNHCR launched a plan to repatriate the Liberians, most of whom wished to go home, though some asked to remain in Ghana. In 2000 there were 614,000 migrants living in Ghana. The net rate of migration out of Ghana was then 1.2 migrants per thousand of the population, which was seen as an acceptable figure. Situated in a volatile region, Ghana remains deeply concerned at unrest in neighbouring countries that might lead to a flow of refugees who would become a burden on the economy and possibly a security risk. In 2005, for example, Ghana received refugees from as far away as Darfur and Côte d'Ivoire, which remained deeply unsettled, and from Togo, following the April elections. These Ghanaian anxieties reflected growing global concern about both migration and security issues.

SENEGAL

Until recent years migration to or from Senegal has involved its West African neighbours, but since the 1990s it has been increasingly about target countries farther afield, usually in Europe. By the middle of the first decade of the new century, Europe was becoming openly hostile to the growing influx of African immigrants, many of them illegal (without documents), and was erecting barriers or controls to keep them out. At the same time, Senegal, with a declining economy – between 1990 and 1999 the GDP per head sank by 28.1 per cent – and a rapidly growing population, half under the age of 18, was unable to create jobs for many of its young people as they came onto the labour market. As a result, an increasing number of Senegalese chose to emigrate and to target the EU as their 'promised land'. All too often, those who do migrate into Europe find that it does not live up to their expectations and many with professional qualifications have to take jobs that are well below their capacities. Many migrants, whose journey to Europe has been financed by their families, are subject to pressures to succeed that far outweigh the chances of doing so and they may disappear into the world of the 'illegals', afraid to admit their failure back at home. This is one of the many social problems connected with migration.

At the time of independence in 1960, Senegal, which had acted as the administrative centre of French West Africa, attracted migrants from neighbouring countries. Many came from Guinea to escape the repression of Sékou Touré (1958–84) and others from Guinea-Bissau, during the bitter independence struggle against the Portuguese from 1963 to 1974. Other migrants came from Mali.

Emigration out of Senegal was mainly to Mauritania, Mali, Guinea and Guinea-Bissau, but from the end of the 1960s and throughout the 1970s, Côte d'Ivoire and Gabon became major destinations for Senegalese migrants because of their high demand for labour. Subsequently migrants went as far as Congo (Brazzaville), Zaire and Cameroon. Deepening economic problems for these countries through the 1980s and 1990s led to a collapse in migration to them: the whole pattern of migration within Africa was affected by deepening economic problems at the time.

Both French and Lebanese migrants had been attracted to Senegal during colonial times and the Lebanese filled many commercial and middle-man roles – jobs that should have been filled by Senegalese traders, whose protests eventually caused the government to ban further Lebanese immigration in 1970.

France was the most important destination for Senegalese emigrants, both during and after the colonial period, but in the 1990s, Italy became an important destination after passing laws in 1990 and 1994 legalising 'illegal' migrants. Spain became another target destination at the beginning of the new century. The USA also attracted a growing number of immigrants, especially from the young middle class who were interested in trading activities. Like Ghana, Senegal began to investigate ways in which it could persuade its migrants to make a contribution to development and to this end it established the Ministry of Senegalese Abroad and tried to convince its migrants to invest some of their wealth in Senegal. France was interested in assisting Senegal to attract migrants to return and, in 1987, France and Senegal established a Bureau of Reception, Orientation and Follow-up of Actions for the Reinsertion of Emigrants, arguably one of the first moves in the recent history of Europe to reverse the influx of African migrants into the EU.

Efforts to attract migrants to return, however well thought out, depend in the end upon economic circumstances: as long as poverty in Senegal and the apparent 'promise' of a greater future in Europe ran side by side, the likelihood of many migrants returning home would be limited. By the mid 2000s large numbers of migrants were passing through Senegal on their way to the Canary Islands and this resulted in a Franco-Senegalese agreement of October 2006 to speed up the process of deporting irregular migrants from Europe, while also making it easier for professionals, students and artists to enter France. As with other such deals (see Mali above), the benefits accrued to Europe rather than Senegal: France could get rid of irregulars more quickly while making it easier for those with skills to migrate. Similar agreements were concluded with Spain. Destination countries for Senegalese migrants in 2004 were as follows: Europe 46 per cent; USA/Canada 7.5 per cent; Côte d'Ivoire 6.6 per cent; Guinea-Bissau 3.2 per cent; Mali 2.4 per cent; other African countries 31.7 per cent; and other no data 2.8 per cent.[12]

According to the World Bank, about 463,000 Senegalese (4 per cent of the population) were living abroad in 2005, while 76 per cent of urban households and 70 per cent of households nationwide had at least one family member abroad, with by far the largest number in Europe. There is a special relationship with The Gambia, which is all but surrounded by Senegal: 300,000 Senegalese live there. Most of the Senegalese who once lived in Côte d'Ivoire (125,000) returned home after that country descended into civil war in 2002. Although a significant number of Senegalese migrants stay in the host country they have chosen for long periods, others see their migration as a short-term economic expedient. As with Ghana, remittances represent an important addition to the national economy and were estimated as providing 7.6 per cent of the GDP in 2005. They had risen sharply between 1998 and 2004 from $91 million in the former year to $563.2 million in the latter.

The numbers of Senegalese living in Europe without legal status cannot easily be determined but, as with other African countries, they probably exceed the number of migrants who have permanent residence. In an effort to stem the illegal influx, Spain and Senegal agreed (October 2006) to promote legal migration. The Spanish Foreign Minister, Miguel Angel Moratinos, visited the Senegalese capital Dakar, where he argued the deal would discourage illegal migration and give Spain the opportunity to recruit a significant number of workers. Spain's readiness to enter into such an agreement reflected the fact that in 2006 more than half the 26,000 migrants who reached the Canary Islands came from Senegal. Spain also signed a cooperation deal that would provide Senegal with €15 million of Spanish aid a year for five years. As Moratinos said: 'Immigration must be legal and matched by development aid, technical assistance and the fight against clandestine immigration.'[13] Spain would open a recruitment office for workers in Senegal. He added, 'We are going to establish a new mechanism, a kind of window in order to contract directly and legally Senegalese who want to work in Spain.' Cheikh Tidiane Gadio, the Senegalese foreign minister, said he hoped the two countries would establish a satisfactory mechanism of cooperation. The agreement was similar to that between France and Senegal of the same year.

The fact that Europe is tightening its border controls and entering agreements with African countries to control immigrant flows is not going to stop these flows. Poverty in Senegal and the closure of work opportunities in neighbouring countries such as Côte d'Ivoire put a premium upon migration to Europe. Only when the economy of Senegal is able to provide sustainable employment opportunities for its people will the flow to Europe ease, and there seems little likelihood of this being achieved in the foreseeable future. Senegal needs work opportunities, while Europe needs skilled migrants of various kinds: that will be the basis of any agreement in the years ahead. Unfortunately, it leaves out of account the large number of unskilled or semi-skilled migrants who seek employment, and who will continue to breach EU controls wherever they can, to become part of the illegal African work force in Europe.

CONCLUSION

Abdou Salam Fall, a sociologist at Senegal's Institut Fondamental d'Afrique Noire (IFAN) advocated a policy of sustainable development as a solution for all sides, which applied to all West Africa rather than just Senegal. He argued that European migration policies are still in the formative stage and can be described as extremely restrictive, even draconian, though it was also necessary to distinguish between individual European countries. European migration policies, however, were mainly based upon control mechanisms. Criticising the elite immigration policy favoured by France, Salam Fall said:

> This kind of policy can never be a means for resolving the problem. Young immigrants should in general be given free choice in their actions. With migration approaches like the French policy of *migration choisie* (selective immigration) European politicians want to encourage qualified young people to leave Africa without having to first invest in their education – it's a case of: 'I take only what I want.' We are not keen to see this important potential being lured away from Africa.

He argued that developing countries have fallen into the dependency trap:

> Migration policy should aim primarily at development policy for fighting poverty, with the goal of further advancing the principles of humanity. Regulations on an international scale should first of all take into consideration all these factors. How can structural imbalances be abolished, disparities between the various countries evened out, and conditions for productivity and prosperity be created in the countries that are threatened from the start by emigration? There can be no immigration policy without meaningful development policy.[14]

16
Southern Africa

From 1960 onwards, this vast region of Africa suffered nearly half a century of wars and violence, which were accompanied by the endless movement of refugees. In Angola the liberation war against the Portuguese (1961–75) was succeeded by civil wars that only came to an end with the death of Jonas Savimbi, the leader of UNITA, in 2002. Similarly, Mozambique fought against the Portuguese from 1963 to 1974, but independence was followed by a civil war fuelled by its white-dominated neighbours, first Rhodesia and then South Africa, which only came to an end in 1992. The leader of the white minority in Rhodesia, Ian Smith, made his bid to perpetuate white rule with his Unilateral Declaration of Independence (UDI) in 1965, ushering in 15 years of warfare until 1980, followed by the so-called Dissidents War of 1983–7 whereby Robert Mugabe broke the power of the Ndebele. During the 1970s and 1980s South Africa pursued its policy of destabilisation against the frontline states to the north, with cross-border raids, while within the country tensions steadily mounted from the Sharpeville Massacre of 1960 to the Soweto uprising of 1976. Perhaps surprisingly, South Africa then achieved a moderately peaceful hand-over of power from whites to blacks over the years 1990–94. Other countries in the region – Botswana, Lesotho, Malawi, Swaziland and Zambia – were on the sidelines of these conflicts, always fearful of being drawn in and much affected by them.

Portuguese colonialism in Africa created states that were either dependent upon white migration for economic progress or provided an alternative life for poor Portuguese migrants. When Portugal finally gave up its increasingly costly effort to hold on to Angola, nearly half a million Portuguese settlers quit the country, while 250,000 left Mozambique; together these settlers represented the second largest mass withdrawal of whites from Africa after the 1 million *colons* who left Algeria early in the 1960s, following that country's independence from France. Despite its opposition to apartheid, Mozambique in the 1970s and 1980s did not want to jeopardise its relations with South Africa to the point that its migrant workers – in the mines and on white farms – would no longer be admitted and therefore would cease to send remittances back to boost the economy. A pattern of migration had developed in Mozambique through the colonial period with thousands of Mozambican labourers going to work in the Rand mines of South Africa. The mines were allowed to recruit this labour directly in Mozambique south of the Sabi River. In addition, however, clandestine migrants from northern Mozambique made their way south through Nyasaland (Malawi) and Rhodesia to South

Africa. All Mozambique's border neighbours had substantial numbers of Mozambican communities.[1]

By 1990, after 15 years of civil war, following the 15 years of struggle against the Portuguese, Angola had been devastated: towns and infrastructure had been destroyed and revenues were reduced to a trickle, while almost no economic development had taken place. In 1986 it was estimated that 600,000 Angolans had been displaced out of a population of 8.5 million, and three years later a further 400,000 had become refugees outside Angola. In fact, the civil war only finally came to an end with the death of Savimbi in 2002, by which time 4 million people had been displaced. Although it faced huge internal problems of reconstruction after 2002, Angola also had to deal with tens of thousands of refugees who returned from the Congo, Namibia and Zambia. In the aftermath of the war, Angola was enjoying an oil boom and coming to terms with a new international partner in the form of China, which offered aid with no strings attached and sought long-term contracts for oil and other resources. By the end of 2006, an estimated 50,000 Chinese had entered the country: some of them were oil or contract workers, but many more were shopkeepers or entrepreneurs determined to set up business.

RENAMO (the National Resistance Movement) had been the tool of Rhodesia and then South Africa in destabilising independent Mozambique, following the withdrawal of the Portuguese in 1975. The statistics of this brutal war were horrifying: by 1988 RENAMO campaigns had forced a minimum of 867,000 people to flee the country, had displaced a further 1 million inside the country, and reduced another 2.5 million to the point of starvation, while approximately 100,000 civilians had been killed and many more wounded or permanently maimed. By the end of the 1980s, famine threatened up to 4.5 million people throughout the country. There are variations on these figures but they each tell the same story. For example, in 1988 the World Food Programme (WFP) reported that there were 420,000 refugees in Malawi, 350,000 in South Africa, 22,500 in Swaziland, 30,000 in Zambia, 64,500 in Zimbabwe, and 15,000 in Tanzania to make a total of 902,000. Other estimates gave a total of 650,000 refugees in Malawi. By 1995 almost all the 1.7 million Mozambicans who had been refugees in neighbouring states had returned to their homes with the assistance of the UNHCR. At the turn of the century Mozambique faced a different problem when, in 2000, torrential rains led to huge floods, killing 700 people and rendering 500,000 homeless. In May 2008, Mozambique faced yet another disruption when there was an explosion of xenophobia against migrants in neighbouring South Africa and 23 Mozambicans were killed by township mobs. The government evacuated 600 Mozambican citizens from South Africa by bus. It was initially believed that 10,000 or more had made their way home to Mozambique unaided, but later it was confirmed that 36,000 Mozambicans had fled back to their country.

With the death of Savimbi in 2002 and peace in Angola, Zambia was relieved that thousands of refugees from that country could return home. However, it immediately faced another problem due to the deplorable conditions in the

Congo, and by the end of 2003, 500 refugees from that country were entering Zambia every day. In 2005 the last 17,000 Angolan refugees, who had been living in Zambia for many years, returned home.

When Bechuanaland became independent as Botswana in 1966 it found it had an inescapable role as a route of flight and as a sanctuary for anti-apartheid refugees from South Africa, a role that would continue until the beginning of the 1990s. In the new century, when the policies of Robert Mugabe brought Zimbabwe to the point of collapse, Botswana was the only country in the region that denounced his policies in no uncertain terms. Tensions with Zimbabwe mounted through 2005 as the political and economic situation in Zimbabwe continued to deteriorate. Border controls were increased by Botswana, fearful of an influx of Zimbabweans, and it accelerated the construction of a 500 km electric border fence that was intended to control both illegal migrants and cattle, since foot and mouth disease was spreading among cattle in Zimbabwe. Also in 2005, following an agreement with Namibia and the UNHCR, 2,000 refugees who had fled Namibia in 1998, after secessionist fighting on the Angolan border, returned home.

Desperately poor and lacking in resources, Lesotho is entirely surrounded by South African territory. Historically, a high proportion of its men migrate to South Africa to work in the mines or on the land. They did so throughout the apartheid era, their employment tolerated by the white government in Pretoria to ensure that a significant proportion of mine workers were non-South African, thus controlling labour in the vital mining industry. Should such migrants take part in strike action, for example, they could at once be deported. It was a control measure and resulted in many black South Africans being without jobs in the vital mining industry where they might otherwise have mounted challenges to the government. In 1994 there were 30,000 Basotho members of the South African National Union of Mineworkers, including its president James Motlasi. With the end of apartheid and the arrival of majority rule under Nelson Mandela, the old idea of Lesotho becoming a province of South Africa was mooted in both countries. The main reason for the resurrection of this idea in Lesotho was the fear of reduced employment for Basothos as mine workers in South Africa. But the idea was dropped. Unemployment in Lesotho in 1991, as changes were taking place in South Africa, ran at 40 per cent and any reduction in the number of Basothos working in South Africa was seen as potentially catastrophic. In 1994 there were 120,000 Basotho mine workers in South Africa and almost half Lesotho's gross national product (GNP) was derived from remittances by its citizens working in the Republic. By 1996, Lesotho was beginning to feel the pinch since the demand for workers in South Africa was declining as Pretoria sought to find jobs for its own unemployed. Remittances from mine workers – that year there were 88,000 in South Africa – also declined. The South African government faced growing internal pressure to restrict migrant labour. By 2000 South Africa had substantially reduced its dependence upon imported labour and whereas in 1989 its mines had employed 129,000 Basotho miners, by 2000 the figure had fallen to 64,000.

Apart from these wars and consequent disruptions, Southern Africa has long been an area where cross-border movements have been more or less constant. South Africa before, during and after apartheid was formally introduced as a policy, was a magnet for migrants from neighbouring countries because of the size of its economy and the job opportunities to be found in its mines and on the land. Today, in an era when more and more countries are erecting ever stiffer barriers to control migration, South Africa finds that it is still a largely involuntary magnet for economic migrants from many parts of Africa when it is trying to cope with huge unemployment of its own. It is one of the ironies of globalisation that, as economic barriers are reduced or dissolved, and arguments are advanced to suggest that the world will become a single market, so opposition to the free movement of people is increasing and takes the form of sometimes virulent xenophobia.

ZIMBABWE

The story of Zimbabwe's fall from grace under the stewardship of Robert Mugabe and the collapse of what was one of the most balanced economies in Africa has been headline news for years. The consequence has been a huge movement of people out of Zimbabwe, mainly into South Africa but to other countries as well. The relationship of the people of Zimbabwe with South Africa is of long standing. Almost a quarter of adult Zimbabweans have parents and grandparents who have worked in South Africa. Zimbabwe, until the present upheavals, has been the recipient of labour migrants from Zambia, Malawi and Mozambique, although in recent years Zimbabwe has become a major exporter of migrant labour, especially from the mid 1990s onwards, as both economic and political conditions in the country deteriorated. At the present time, a majority of Zimbabwean migrants to South Africa are undocumented, which means they are illegal. While this migration southwards has been under way, the flow of inward migrant labour has largely ceased. The old colonial pattern of white migration into Rhodesia began to fall away during the 15 years of UDI, while after 1980, when Rhodesia became Zimbabwe, whites emigrated from the country in increasing numbers. Although the number of whites emigrating was small in relative terms, their exodus also represented a serious brain drain. The Southern African Migration Project (SAMP) survey reported that 76 per cent of its respondents admitted that they had considered leaving Zimbabwe.

By 2000, when the Zimbabwe government was increasingly unpopular, it pushed an anti-white agenda against the 4,500 white farmers who owned 11 million hectares of land while 1 million black farmers shared 16 million hectares of land. It was an explosive situation. The ruling party, which should have tackled the problem of land redistribution after it came into power in 1980, had neglected to do so; now it incited mass invasions of white farms by landless squatters, many of whom claimed to be veterans of the 1970s war of liberation. On 8 September 2002, the remaining 2,900 white farmers were ordered off their land without compensation. Meanwhile, the economy had declined disastrously and by the end of the year an estimated 2 million Zimbabweans had migrated illegally into neighbouring countries, some prepared to face imprisonment in South Africa in return for regular meals. By the end of 2004 the number of Zimbabweans who had left the country had risen to 3.4 million, a quarter of the population. Ironically, their remittances to their families helped maintain the Mugabe regime, from which they had fled, in power. Inside the country, as a result of the government's policy of destroying the shanty towns, which were seen as centres of opposition, some 700,000 people had been made homeless.

By 2005 emigration had become a way of life in Zimbabwe, according to the International Organisation for Migration (IOM), which had started a campaign to assist those considering migration and claimed that it had the tacit cooperation of the Zimbabwe government. According to the IOM the largest group of legal emigrants – 36.8 per cent of the total – went to the United Kingdom, while only 4.8 per cent went to South Africa. These figures represent the numbers of people who have emigrated from Zimbabwe using official channels since 1990. In total, about 500,000 had left, using legal channels, in the 15 years from 1990 to 2005. The figures for illegal migrants were far higher. According to the Zimbabwe Central Bank, 1.2 million Zimbabweans had gone to South Africa since 1990. However, a South African government minister said there were then 2 million Zimbabweans living in South Africa, although Joyce Dube of the South African Women's Institute for Migration Affairs estimated that the figure was around 3 million. Other observers questioned the figures, while conceding that they were high. In any case, Zimbabweans migrating to South Africa do not appear in official statistics, do not seek work permits and will try to slip across the border again and again after being caught by the South African authorities.

SAMP, carrying out a study of health professionals leaving Zimbabwe in 2002, found that economic factors accounted for the greatest number (54 per cent of interviewees). Others pointed to inadequate working conditions or political conditions. The launch by the government of its Operation Murambatsvina, or urban clean-up, left 500,000 people homeless according to the UN, while 80 per cent of Zimbabweans migrating to South Africa were doing so for political reasons. A majority of migrants to South Africa and Botswana were unskilled and lacked the professional qualifications that would have gained them a ticket and visa to go to Europe. The crisis in Zimbabwe and the numbers of its people migrating to South Africa created a dilemma for that country. The ease of access across the border from Zimbabwe meant that many migrants could not be prevented from entering the country and so made South Africa wary of granting asylum. In any case, to do so would have undermined President Thabo Mbeki's policy of 'quiet diplomacy' aimed at persuading Mugabe to change his policies. A majority of Zimbabweans who fled from Zimbabwe at this time wanted to return as soon as circumstances there improved.[2]

The flood of Zimbabweans fleeing to Britain or South Africa increased during 2006. In Britain failed asylum seekers faced enforced removal after the government had won a landmark court ruling that cleared the way for deportations. Refugee groups warned that Zimbabweans who had sought asylum in Britain and were deported back to their country would face persecution but the British Home Office insisted that it must have the power to deport so as to deter other unwarranted asylum seekers. It was reckoned that between 7,000 and 9,000 people could be affected by the ruling by the Asylum and Immigration Tribunal (AIT) that failed asylum seekers sent back to Zimbabwe did not automatically run the risk of ill-treatment. Tim Finch, spokesperson for the Refugee Council, said the government may have won a legal victory, but it had lost the moral argument. 'We still think it's not safe to remove anybody to Zimbabwe in the present circumstances. Ministers should exercise the principle of safety first.' During the first three months of 2006, 750 Zimbabweans claimed asylum in Britain, more than any other nationality, and of these 55 were given permission to stay while 540 applications were rejected (the remainder were not accounted for). Over the preceding five years 15,000 Zimbabweans had sought asylum in Britain.[3]

If asylum seekers faced these restraints in Britain, they faced even tougher opposition to finding asylum in South Africa, where illegal immigrants often faced extortion and assault at the hands of the police. Zimbabweans awaiting deportation were held in uncovered cells, fed irregularly and detained beyond the legal 30-day limit, according to Human Rights Watch, whose report suggested: 'It's not possible to say it's just a few bad apples [in the South Africa police]. There really is a systemic problem. The primary aim is the [poor] enforcement of perfectly acceptable laws.' The South African province of Limpopo had become the key transit route for Zimbabweans fleeing their own country. As Norma Kruger, responsible for the Human Rights Watch report, said: 'It's common practice for the police to ask for money or items, and if you can provide them with what they want, you won't be arrested.'[4] The Limpopo had become Africa's Rio Grande, as thousands of impoverished Zimbabweans fled the meltdown in their country and sought illegal entry into South Africa. On the South African side of the river there were three walls of fencing, relics of the apartheid era when they had been erected to act as a barrier against African National Congress (ANC) guerrillas. By 2006 the same defences were needed, ironically, by the ANC government to stem the tide of people from the north whose numbers were fuelling discontent among South Africans who had yet to see the benefits of black rule and, in many cases, had no job. South Africa's President, Thabo Mbeki, was under increasing pressure to close the border to illegals. Thousands of border police were fighting a daily battle to drive back the Zimbabweans while those who managed to reach Johannesburg faced often brutal confinement in the notorious Lindela holding camp. There are no accurate figures for the numbers of Zimbabweans who have successfully crossed into South Africa: estimates ranged between 3 million and 5 million.[5]

A major stumbling block facing Zimbabweans crossing into South Africa was the fact that its government had not officially recognised the human rights abuses taking place under Mugabe's regime, a fact that complicated the process of seeking refugee status. Many Zimbabweans who crossed into South Africa fell prey to robbers along the border zone. Night crossings were arranged by trafficking gangs, known as 'Magumaguma', who frequently clashed violently with the police. On many occasions the Magumaguma turned on the illegals they were helping across the border, sometimes raping, robbing or killing them. According to the IOM, more than 165,000 Zimbabweans were picked up and deported during the year to July 2007, while those involved in refugee activities suggested that the migration into South Africa was an unprecedented exodus from a country not at war. By mid 2007, South Africa was sending back more than 4,000 Zimbabweans every week, a 40 per cent higher rate than in 2006. South Africa was delivering deportees to the IOM office on the Zimbabwean side of the Limpopo in Beitbridge, where they were offered a hot meal, counselling (one must wonder to what effect) and transport home. Only 55 per cent accepted, while the rest turned round and tried again. In May 2007 Thabo Mbeki conceded that the huge human influx 'is something we have to live with', but he did not comment upon the conditions in Zimbabwe that were its cause. As the number of exiles in South Africa escalated, so did resentment of them. Thus, Nepo Nkhahle said: 'They are taking our jobs. They are stealing. We should send them all back. – I know it is not their fault. They don't know where their next meal is. But many South Africans are getting fed up with this.'⁶ According to officials in the South African military and police, 4,000 migrants were crossing into South Africa every night (July 2007), which represented 100,000 a month, five times the official estimate of 20,000. Prior to the Zimbabwe elections of 2000, the census estimated Zimbabwe's population at 11 million, but by 2007, due to migration and other causes, it could have dropped as low as 7 million.

SOUTH AFRICA

Although South Africa's history in the twentieth century was dominated by racial policies that necessarily precluded normal African immigration, in the nineteenth century it had witnessed several dramatic movements of people. Early in the century there occurred the *mfecane*, 'crushing' or 'time of emptiness', when an explosion of tribal violence in the region of the former northern Natal affected tribes as much as 1,000 miles away and led subsequently to the formation of the Basotho, Swazi and Zulu states. From the Cape, the British moved up the eastern coast, fighting with the Zulus for over 40 years before finally defeating them. In the 1830s, the Boers or Afrikaners famously trekked away from the Cape and British control to establish two states of their own – the Orange Free State and Transvaal. In the 1860s and 1870s, the discovery of huge deposits of diamonds and gold brought a stream of adventurers and miners into the country from Britain and Europe. This led to cross-border labour migration to seek work in the mines as South Africa began to build a modern industrial economy. When in 1910 Britain created the Union of South Africa as a Dominion of the British Empire it ceded to the white minority control over the black majority and thereby ensured that racial division would be enshrined in the country's political system until the collapse of apartheid in the early 1990s.

One of the greatest evils under the apartheid system was the government's policy of eliminating 'black spots': that is, land owned or occupied by Africans in [what had been designated as] white areas. The number involved is uncertain but the Surplus People Project, which studied the removals, estimated that 3,548,900 people were removed between 1960 and 1983; 1,702,400 from the towns, 1,129,000 from farms, 614,000 from black spots, and 103,500 from strategic development areas.[7]

Prior to the end of the apartheid era migrants to South Africa came from neighbouring states – Lesotho, Swaziland, Botswana, Malawi, Zimbabwe and Mozambique – but not as settling migrants. They came – and were recruited as such – as temporary labour to work in the mines or on the white farms. They could be sent back home at any time and so were seen as a mechanism to control South African indigenous labour. Under the system, contract workers supplied 40 per cent or more of the mine work force, about 400,000 in the early 1970s. They were contracted for a fixed term and then went back home, though they could reapply for another term. White commercial farmers, who also used temporary labour, also often employed illegal migrants from the neighbouring countries.

South Africa was the object of worldwide censure during the apartheid era, but it was also often criticised for the way it dealt with migrants in the years after 1994. Between that date and 2003 it deported over 1 million undocumented immigrants to Mozambique, Zimbabwe and Lesotho, and was taken to task by human rights groups, including the South African Human Rights Commission, for its methods of arrest and control, which were the same as those employed under apartheid. A new moderate Immigration Act was passed in 2002 but met opposition because of widespread and growing popular panic at the mounting numbers of illegal immigrants coming into the country. The South African Human Rights Commission and the South African Migration Project both revealed in their research high levels of intolerance in the country and growing xenophobia. These attitudes, they claimed, affected official reactions towards immigrants, so that policy largely became one of control and exclusion rather than management and opportunity – hard-line officialdom versus liberal tolerance. However, there remained many migrants from Mozambique whose fathers and grandfathers had come into South Africa, either as contract labourers or illegally. After 1994, the new South Africa issued many visitors' permits for purposes of visiting family, tourism or business. There were 9.9 million such visitors in 1999, of whom 50 per cent were on 'holiday'. In any case, once South Africa had come in from the cold, it became open to a great deal of business activity in the continent to the north, while people from the north came to do business in the Republic. Between 1996 and 2000 there was a fall off in the number of temporary work permits issued from 52,704 in 1996 to 15,834 in 2000. People's fears of the impact of immigrants were enhanced because restructuring of the economy led to many job losses as well as a loss of skilled people. Between 1989 and 1997, according to official figures, approximately 82,000 South Africans, mainly white, emigrated to countries such as Britain, the US, Australia, Canada and New Zealand, although other sources suggested as many as 230,000 had left the country. At the same time, economic migrants from neighbouring countries, especially Mozambique, continued to work in the South African mines and, by 2000, a quarter of all mine workers were Mozambicans. The search for a new post-apartheid immigration policy is still in progress. South African fears of being swamped by immigrants must be taken into account, for the country has become a magnet for illegal migrants: the size of its economy is such that it appears to offer endless job opportunities to migrant labour, but these in fact do not exist.

The flow of people into and out of South Africa increased markedly in the 1990s, when the country was once more accepted by the international community. This flow posed a number of questions for the government: 'Should it seek to control the flow – in and out of the country? If so how? What should be its attitude towards illegal immigration? How would the movement of people affect relations with neighbouring states? Was there the danger of a brain drain? Were human rights issues involved?'[8] Many of the people who visited South Africa at this time were people who had shunned it because of apartheid. In 1993 20 airlines were flying into South Africa; by 1997, 120. These new incomers included many tourists, half of them from Europe, followed by Americans. In 1998 6 million people visited South Africa as tourists, creating an estimated 737,000 jobs and generating an income of 53 billion Rand, equivalent to 8.3 per cent of GDP. At the same time, many South Africans were leaving the country. There were then about 350,000 British passport holders resident in the country, which suggested that between 700,000 and 800,000 had the right to resettle in Britain. The government was concerned with the 'chicken run' as it came to be called: whites, including many skilled people, leaving the country because they were unwilling to live under a black government or fearful of the policies it might pursue. The government asked developed countries of Europe and North America not to recruit nurses and doctors. It was a contradictory situation, for South Africa had always been a migrant-attracting country. During the 1990s the number of workers, principally mine workers, from surrounding countries fell, while the number of illegal immigrants greatly increased. In 1995, for example, it was estimated that 750,000 people who had entered the country on temporary permits had stayed on. Many more entered without meeting any formal entry requirements. They sought to escape from wars, ethnic conflict, grinding poverty, natural disasters or state oppression. The end of apartheid had removed obstacles to migrants entering the country with the result that, by the late 1990s, estimates of the number of illegal immigrants in South Africa ranged between 2 million and 8 million (5–20 per cent of the population). The country, with its relative prosperity, attracted immigrants from the poorer, less stable parts of the continent. A 1999 White Paper on

'International Migration' proposed making entry easier for skilled workers and allowing market forces to determine the skills South Africa needed: 'Only industry knows what it needs, why and for how long.' An Immigration Review Board was created which set out a priority for incomers: first, the Southern Africa region, second, the rest of Africa, third, the rest of the world. In May 1996 Mandela had said that South Africa should not be 'very tough' with illegal immigrants, especially those from countries that had supported the ANC in the years of struggle. However, despite Mandela's liberalism, as the number of illegal immigrants steadily rose during the latter 1990s, an increasing number were rounded up and deported. In 1997 South Africa and Mozambique entered into an agreement that allowed troops from either country to cross the border in hot pursuit of illegal immigrants. 'It was like trying to stop an incoming tide with the walls of a sand castle.'[9]

The 'inward' and 'outward' pattern had become clear by the middle of the 1990s. Those coming into South Africa were almost entirely from other parts of the continent, both skilled and unskilled, in search of a better economic life or to escape violence or oppression in their own countries. Those leaving were predominantly whites, fearful of escalating rates of crime, the lowering of educational standards, a weak currency and high taxes. Between November 1993 and October 1995 1,000 doctors, nurses, veterinarians and paramedics left the country. From the 1990s onwards, an increasing number of writers and commentators examined the problems of migration. Vishnu Padayachee, for example, argues:

In general, migration, like HIV, is driven and exacerbated by poverty and underdevelopment and specifically by a paucity of local employment and other money-making opportunities. Thus, regular and often large-scale mobility by the poor and aspiring in search of jobs and income is characteristic of developing countries and expanding nations, and has been for many decades (indeed, centuries).[10]

A large proportion of African continental migrants favour South Africa as a destination rather than Europe, while its long borders (approximately 4,000 miles) are difficult to control. Apart from Zimbabwe, large numbers of migrants have also come from Nigeria and the Democratic Republic of the Congo, and a significant proportion of these have become involved in the drug trade that is centred upon Johannesburg.[11] Labour migration into South Africa, with more than 100 years history, is mainly a consequence of mining expansion and colonial and commercial agricultural production, and the chief source countries of this labour – Mozambique, Lesotho, Botswana and Zimbabwe – will be loathe to see it phased out since their migrants generate capital flows back to the source countries. In 1996 a new law was introduced, according to which immigrants who had lived more than five years in the country were entitled to apply for South African citizenship. By 2000, as it sought to restructure industry to employ more black people, South Africa suffered a shortage of highly skilled personnel, not least because the old

Bantu education system had not turned out people with the requisite skills. As a consequence, a new immigration bill, aimed at redressing the shortage, was introduced. However, it imposed a levy on companies for every foreign worker they employed. By 2003, South Africa faced 750,000 new job seekers coming onto the market every year and so was anxious not to provide work for migrants. Even so, they came, since South Africa was still seen as the best job market on the continent.

As with other countries where migration has become a major economic and political factor, South Africa has to achieve a balance between its need for certain categories of immigrant, the large number of illegal immigrants, refugees and asylum seekers that are uninvited but come anyway, and the reactions of their own people. The country limits the number of immigrants every year so as to protect work opportunities for the vast reserve of unskilled and semi-skilled workers. In line with international trends, potential immigrants who fall into the unskilled or semi-skilled categories will normally not be accepted as an immigrant worker in the country. The consequence of this policy is the large number of illegal immigrants who do not possess requisite skills. Even so, thousands of applicants are granted immigrant status each year and there have been wide fluctuations in the numbers of documented immigrants admitted on an annual basis. In 2002, according to Human Rights Watch, legitimate immigrants came from a range of countries, including Britain, India, Nigeria, Zimbabwe, Pakistan, China, Germany, the United States and Taiwan, as well as from other countries in Africa and Europe. In 2005 South Africa had over 140,000 asylum seekers from Zimbabwe, Côte d'Ivoire and the Great Lakes region but, although South Africa has adequate refugee laws on paper, the asylum seekers do not enjoy any protection in practice. By 2006 the signs of a coming backlash against immigrants were becoming increasingly apparent. Poor South Africans claimed they were competing for resources with illegal immigrants. In Diepsloot, a sprawling township of 120,000 people north of Johannesburg, Somali immigrants became targets for violence. Somali-owned businesses were torched and looted on several occasions through the year and Somali shopkeepers were warned by the Business Forum of Diepsloot to leave at once or face the consequences. As one Somali said: 'I left the fighting in Somalia but now I am facing the same thing here in South Africa. What do I do? I have nowhere to go.'[12]

In May 2008 xenophobic riots erupted in numerous parts of the country, leading to 62 deaths. The riots, with Africans killing Africans, sent shockwaves through the continent. The Institute for Race Relations blamed the ANC government and President Thabo Mbeki for the violence, which was the worst South Africa had seen since the dying days of apartheid; its chief executive, Frans Cronje, said corruption, failing law and order, economic mismanagement and lack of proper border controls 'contributed to create a perfect storm of lawlessness, poverty and unfulfilled expectations which has now erupted into violence'. Members of the government blamed a 'third force' for the violence without specifying what it was, while refugees from Zimbabwe, Mozambique and Malawi were shot at, burnt, raped, beaten and driven from their homes. The authorities estimated that some 10,000 had fled their homes in the townships, squatter camps and poor suburbs of Johannesburg. The Institute for Race Relations said:

> The failure to protect communities from criminal elements and to remove those elements had allowed criminals to take full advantage of chaos and disorder to rob, rape and loot. The collapse of proper border control mechanisms saw literally millions of people gaining entry to South Africa illegally ... Without adequate legal standing in the community these people became easy or soft targets for mob violence.[13]

Official (government) denial of xenophobia exacerbated the situation. Mbeki's response to the crisis was slow and inadequate: he said he would set up a committee to investigate the causes of the attacks even as the death toll was rising. What impressed the rest of Africa adversely was the fact that South Africa had recently overcome colonialism and racial segregation and South Africans had been perceived to be more tolerant. Part of the trouble was that both black and white South Africans still appeared to view their country as a subcontinent outside of or apart from the rest of Africa, an attitude that would foster racism rather than reduce its incidence. Nor had the post-apartheid government developed an effective policy to deal with the large mass immigration that had taken place. The ANC government was unable to decide whether to adopt a 'fortress' policy like that being put in place by the EU, or to open its borders to desperate refugees fleeing instability in Zimbabwe and elsewhere on the continent. The xenophobic attacks clearly had much to do with the failure of government to deliver services to the poor. As William Gumede argued:

> Making South Africa's infant democracy, institutions and leaders more responsive and accountable must be part of the solution to the problem of xenophobia ... sadly, in the eyes of outsiders, the latest incidents will probably only confirm their view of South Africa as prejudiced towards people from the rest of the continent.[14]

For eleven days, refugees from Zimbabwe, Mozambique, Malawi and other African countries were targeted by marauding gangs of armed men demanding they return home. All the usual anti-immigrant arguments were advanced to justify the violence: they were taking their jobs, getting preferential housing, forcing down wages and committing crimes. The crisis presented many of South Africa's estimated 5 million immigrants with some appalling dilemmas. President Mbeki admitted that South Africa had been 'disgraced' by the wave of anti-foreigner violence, which had convulsed the nation. Facing intense criticism over his ineffectual handling of the crisis, Mbeki said in a televised address that South Africa's heads were 'bowed' and reminded his countrymen that their economy rested on the work of migrants from across Africa. The police, meanwhile, raised the official death toll from 43 to 50 and said that

35,000 people had been left homeless as a result of the violence. Although much of the violence had taken place in Johannesburg, seven of the country's nine provinces had reported attacks upon immigrants and 10,000 people had been displaced in Cape Town. In the aftermath of the crisis, South Africa had to re-examine its immigration policy and consider the damage that it had done to the country's image, both in Africa and in the world at large.

THE FUTURE

In many ways South Africa remains a captive of its apartheid history. Countries to the north of the Limpopo were seen as both hostile and potential enemies and their people were not welcomed as immigrants. Immigration concerned contract workers for the South African mines from Mozambique, Lesotho, Malawi, Botswana or Zimbabwe and they became part of the apartheid apparatus to control labour. The only immigrants to be welcomed prior to 1994 were whites who would bolster the ruling minority and help prolong its power. In the post-1994 period South Africans who intended to visit countries to the north would say – half-jokingly – that they were going to visit Africa. Africans from the rest of the continent are often resentful that both white and black South Africans tend to regard them with disdain, despite the support they provided for the ANC in its long struggle against the apartheid regime. Although it has now been 'accepted' by the rest of Africa, South Africa still has a great deal to learn about its brother Africans before it achieves real acceptance. Any post-apartheid migration policy must take account of South Africa's changing role in Africa, the complicated relationship between migration and development, and the problem of xenophobia.[15] It has a long way to go.

Between 1994 and 2008 South Africa deported 1.7 million undocumented migrants to Mozambique, Zimbabwe and Lesotho. Human rights groups criticise the deportation system for the method of arrest and removal, which they see as being no different from the behaviour during the apartheid era,

Immediately after 1994, during the post-apartheid euphoria period, there was a great increase in the number of people entering South Africa from the rest of the continent, whether legally or illegally. Economic expansion meant many small and medium traders came to South Africa on visitors' permits to source goods to sell in their own countries, although between 1990 and 2000 the number of people granted permanent residence fell from 14,000 to 3,053. By 2003–4, Africans made up nearly half of all official immigrants into South Africa. Despite this increase in African immigrants, however, there was no marked brain drain into South Africa, partly because of the latter's restrictionist policies. On the other hand, South Africa did see a substantial brain drain of white professionals. By 2004, the South African government had come to see the need to attract skills and to this end introduced the Joint Initiative for Priority Skills Acquisition (JIPSA), which also emphasised the accelerated training of South Africans in priority areas and recognised the need to recruit certain skills from outside the country. At the same time, in some sectors only limited change had taken place, and in 2006 there was a total of 164,989 migrant labourers from Botswana, Lesotho, Mozambique and Swaziland in the South African gold mines.[16] The mining companies had fought hard to retain the right to recruit migrant labour with minimum control by government.

On the issue of refugees, South Africa only recognised refugees in 1993 and only after the transition to democracy did it sign the UN and Organization of African Unity Conventions on refugees. Only in 2000–1 did the South African government legalise the status of the Mozambican refugees from the 1980s and give them permanent residence. In 2007 there were 45,673 new applications for refugee status and, while asylum seekers from Somalia, the DRC and Angola had high rates of acceptance, most others were turned down. The processing of refugees is slow and asylum seekers, especially from Zimbabwe, are constantly at risk of deportation, despite the fact that sending people back to face persecution is against international law. Finally, the South African government claims that there are between 4 and 8 million undocumented migrants in the country, though other organisations suggest that between 500,000 and 1 million would be a more realistic figure.

Despite its generally tough approach to immigrants, South Africa entered into a bilateral agreement with Lesotho in 2007 to downgrade border controls and facilitate cross-border movement. It also agreed visa-free movement with Mozambique. Both agreements are moves towards an integrated region though there is a long way still to go. South Africa has endorsed both the AU Strategic Framework on Migration and the AU Common Position on Migration and Development. Despite such positive steps, the South African public remains extremely hostile to immigration in general and illegal migrants in particular.

Part IV

Asia

The vast extent of Asia and the huge numbers of its populations make it difficult to treat as a single entity. It includes the two countries with the largest populations in the world, China and India, whose diasporas of approximately 40 million and 25 million respectively are each equivalent to the total populations of sizeable states. A vast movement of people is taking place in Southeast Asia – comprising Myanmar, Cambodia, Laos, Malaysia, Singapore, Thailand and Vietnam – almost all of it for economic reasons. Indonesia, now with the fourth largest population in the world of 225 million, has become a major exporter of people in the region while the Philippines has developed a migration policy that positively rewards citizens who emigrate. Japan, which until recent years was closed to almost any form of immigration, is now beginning to open up, not least because of its ageing population. The wars in Afghanistan and Iraq have created large numbers of refugees, many of whom have headed for Europe to seek asylum. On the other hand, the oil-rich states of the Gulf have attracted large numbers of migrant workers from poor countries such as Bangladesh, who go there for fixed periods to work in the construction and other industries that have boomed as a result of the region's oil wealth. The countries of Central Asia, that were formerly part of the Soviet Union, suffer from high levels of poverty and unemployment and many of their people seek employment in Russia. Certain countries in the region – Malaysia is a notable example – have become target destinations for migrants because of their expanding economies and labour shortages.

Finally, Australia is included here. It is part of Oceania, not Asia, with a distinct immigrant history of its own. In recent years, however, it has come to realise that it is tied to the fortunes of the huge Asian countries to its north and must adjust its policies accordingly.

The urge to migrate is affected by a number of factors that influence both permanent migration and circular migration (where migrants move within their own countries to find gainful employment but eventually return to their original homes), including regional inequality, under-employment in rural areas, the development of labour-intensive industries, as well as civil upheavals and wars. In reverse, migrants return home when they find there is no long-term security for them in their destination countries. There are high levels of internal migration from rural to urban areas in India and Indonesia. 'It is very likely that migration, especially circular migration, will continue until the gap between different regions narrows or conditions in the sending area become so unsustainable that populations have to move out altogether.'[1] However, movements from rural to urban areas may also be curtailed or controlled by governments to prevent huge influxes of rural people into towns where there is no prospect of employment or need for their services. Demographic factors are also important in causing migration flows. Where there are large numbers of young adults, migration becomes the most obvious path to a better life and greater prosperity. Rural migrants to towns often find they are discriminated against because they do not qualify for social benefits that are available to the settled urban populations, but availability of such services will change depending upon the level of need for a larger work force. All the evidence would suggest that labour migration in large parts of Asia is set to increase in the coming years, the result of poverty and population growth. The evidence of various surveys also suggests that migration can reduce poverty and assist development as a result of a steady reverse flow of remittances.

The rapidly expanding Asian economies have led to an increase in internal migration because of declining job opportunities in rural areas and increased opportunities in urban areas. However, the full benefits to be derived from internal migration may not be realised because of government policy barriers to movement, or social exclusion on the basis of ethnicity, caste, tribe or gender. Nonetheless, in Asia there has been a marked increase in the movement of women job-seekers from rural to urban areas. India has introduced the National Rural Employment Guarantee Programme, which promises 100 days of wage labour to one adult member in every rural household who volunteers for unskilled work. If the scheme operates successfully, it will both check permanent migration from the rural areas and bring a degree of prosperity to those areas.

Traditionally, however, while migrants have always been subject to a variety of social barriers and political and economic restrictions, still they move to the centres of industry and growth where they can earn higher wages than in their home regions even if they are excluded from such social benefits as health, housing, education and sanitation. In many cases they will be subject to various forms of exploitation. Many internal migrants who move before acquiring a house or a job are regarded as illegal and this poses a further raft of problems for them. Schools are not accessible to their children and they must take the jobs that many others will not touch and often are more prone to infections, including tuberculosis and HIV/AIDS. They represent a source of cheap labour, since they are usually paid less than non-migrants, do not belong to unions and can be dispensed with without compensation by their employers.

At the ILO Asian Regional Meeting in Busan, South Korea from 29 August to 1 September 2006, the subject of migration was analysed. The meeting found that while growing mobility benefited both sending and receiving countries, as well as the migrant workers themselves, migration also posed enormous challenges to the states of the region, many of which have yet to develop policies and programmes to regulate cross-border movements. They must also protect the basic rights of migrants, including the illegal migrants who are often a majority, while adjusting to the impact of globalisation that tends to encourage the movement of people. According to the ILO, approximately 3 million people in the region leave their homes every year in search of work, while over the two decades to 2006, gross emigration of labour rose at an annual rate of 6 per cent in the Asia-Pacific region as a whole. Further, the region is recording an increase in the movement of professionals. Japan has sought more software engineers and nurses while Singapore has offered permanent residence for academics, managers and biotechnologists.[2]

The countries in Asia that attract the largest number of immigrants are Japan, South Korea, Taiwan, Malaysia, Thailand, India and the Arab countries of the Middle East. In this latter group of countries up to 80 per cent of the labour force will consist of migrants coming principally from the Philippines, Indonesia, Sri Lanka, Nepal and Bangladesh. At the same time, from the beginning of the new century there was a steady haemorrhaging of talent from Asia, especially to the United States where the 'stay' rates for students after completing their training were greatest in engineering and the sciences. Indeed, the brain drain to the United States from Asia between 1990 and 1999 reached alarming proportions: the number of foreign PhD graduates in science and engineering who chose to stay in the United States after their studies was 87 per cent for China, 82 per cent for India and 39 per cent for the Republic of Korea. Remittances from migrants have become a staple source of income in some sending countries, and have enabled the families of migrant workers to have higher standards of living and better education and health for their children. Migrants who return to their home countries may represent a technology transfer that can be wasted if they cannot find work. Remittances in the region have outstripped official development assistance and represent an important input into development. In 2003, for example, remittance income came to more than $40 billion. In 2004 the Philippines received $8 billion in remittances while India received $23 billion.

There has been a dramatic increase in the number of women migrants within and from Asia. In 1996 the ILO estimated there were 1.5 million female workers from Asia employed outside their country of citizenship, mainly as domestic servants. There were 700,000 illegal female migrants. An estimated 320,000 Asian women leave their country each year in search of jobs; they go mainly to the Middle East, Singapore and Hong Kong and they come from Sri Lanka, the Philippines, Indonesia, Thailand and India. About 69 per cent of Sri Lanka's migrants, 65 per cent of Indonesia's, 55 per cent of the Philippines', including 500,000 maids, are women. There are at least 150,000 maids in Hong Kong of whom 100,000 Filipinas are employed legally. The protection of migrant workers remains a matter of concern: only a handful of countries have signed the International Convention on the Protection of the Rights of Migrant Workers and their Families that was unanimously approved in 1990 by the UN General Assembly. Many countries specifically exclude domestic work from their labour laws. On 13 May 1996, the Philippines announced new guidelines for Filipina maids in Singapore, including a minimum monthly salary of at least $300 and a workday of 16 hours or less. The going salary for maids in Singapore was then $210 a month. In addition, Singapore employers had to pay a government tax of $231 a month for each foreign maid employed. The Philippine Migrant Workers and Overseas Filipinos Act of 1995 led to a 60 per cent drop in illegal recruitment in the Philippines. The increase in female labour migration is highest in Asia, where female migrants from the Philippines, Indonesia and Sri Lanka account for between 60 and 80 per cent of all migrants.

There are differences of approach between China and India. In the case of China, which is working towards a modern urban nation, circular migration is seen as an impediment. India, however, sees its villages and agriculture as the engine of rural growth and poverty reduction and pursues a small farmer model of development. In both countries, however, there is a need to develop social security systems that cover internal migrants so as to reduce the extent to which they are exploited by their employers.

> With the world's two largest populations, China and India have both benefited from a considerable demographic dividend and a two-edged migratory phenomenon: although emigration at first deprived these countries of part of their workforce, the Chinese and Indian diasporas have since contributed to the development of their motherland by investing in it and returning both better trained and with a wealth of business contacts so that there has been a shift from 'brain drain' to 'brain gain'.[3]

A Regional Conference on Migration and Development in Asia was held in Lanzhou, China, over 14–16 March 2005. The focus of the conference was upon the contribution that migration can make to development and poverty reduction. It was accepted that most migration in Asia occurred within rather than between countries, and the emphasis was on ways to enhance the developmental impact of internal migration. The conference focused on the experiences of six Asian countries: Bangladesh, Cambodia, China, India, Pakistan and Indonesia. The five principal topics discussed were: the role of internal migration in poverty reduction; gender-specific features of internal migration; health challenges related to internal migration; the articulation between internal and international migration; and the expansion of an evidence base for internal migration. The subject of migration, whether internal or international, has moved up the agenda to become one of the most important themes in Asia at the present time.

17
China

Shortly after the triumph of the communists in the civil war of 1946–9, internal migration became a feature of the Chinese Revolution. First to be dealt with was the question of China's ethnic minorities.

> As already in Inner Mongolia, so in Tibet and Xinjiang (formerly Sinkiang) as well, they may soon find themselves doubly minorities: in China as a whole and in their own areas where the influx of Chinese settlers and industrial workers may turn the newcomers into a majority within a few years.[1]

During the first Five Year Plan, 26 new cities had been built, 20 others were extensively reconstructed, and another 74 were remodelled. They were fast growing into large industrial conglomerates. Their new populations came mainly from the coastal provinces and this transfer of people became a mass movement. After 1956, this internal migration was organised more systematically and certain provinces helped to people selected inland regions.

> How far migration is voluntary it is difficult to tell. The press carries exhortations calling on the young to go to the 'border regions'. Their patriotism, their 'socialist consciousness', as well as their sense of adventure are appealed to. In all probability the familiar mixture of enthusiasm, persuasion and force is being applied.[2]

As the movement of people became better organised, migrants were enabled to join communities of their own kind into which they could fit more easily. Moreover, higher wages and better-stocked state stores awaited them and even 'comfort missions' were organised. These were composed of propagandists, entertainers and welfare teams ready to smooth the integration of the newcomers. In March 1959, the population of the autonomous region of Xinjiang was over 6 million – it had been 4 million in 1949. Most of the increase was due to migrants from elsewhere in China. What had become clear ten years after the Communist victory was the development of internal migration as an aspect of policy for the new China. At least 80,000 people a year were moving into Xinjiang in the period 1949–59. Huge, sparsely populated areas inhabited by non-Chinese peoples contained many of the natural resources being discovered. Inner Mongolia, Tibet, Xinjiang and smaller areas in the southwest were the most important. 'Less than 5 per cent of the people in China occupy more than half our territory', said Mao Zedong in 1957. 'They are National Minorities, tribesmen once regarded as not part of the Chinese races. We must convert them and convince them they are Chinese.'[3]

INTERNAL MIGRATION

Jumping forward to the 1990s, as China's industrial revolution took off, the large-scale movement of peasants from the rural to the urban areas presented a range of social and political problems.

> While peasant subsistence needs have been secured, rural migration has been tightly controlled through a household residence registration (*hukou*) system. This has ensured that as market reforms have deepened, China has largely kept at bay the dangers of an emerging destitute landless class feeding into an underclass of urban poor with the growth of urban slums on a huge scale.[4]

There is, for example, urban bias in the distribution and availability of health and education provision. On the other hand, as urban cash incomes average more than three times rural ones, migrants from the countryside have flooded into the cities, while the government has gradually lifted barriers to migration in order to ease the rural surplus problem. Over the ten years to 2009, China's cities and towns have absorbed about 150 million rural migrants, who have tended to form a marginal, unstable 'floating population'. Lacking official residency status, they enjoy fewer rights and social security entitlements than urban residents, and their children are often denied access to urban schools. As virtually second-class citizens, they are more vulnerable to exploitation, often working under dismal conditions below the minimum wage and without restrictions on overtime.

> In promoting a gradual reform of the *hukuo* system, the government has sought a dispersed pattern of urbanisation through the expansion of not only big and small cities, but also towns, around the development of local enterprise and rural service sectors.[5]

By 2005 China faced the need to create 24 million new jobs a year to absorb the migrants leaving the countryside, for students leaving schools and colleges, and for people left newly unemployed by the rationalisation of state-owned enterprises. China has an estimated 150 million migrant workers living in its cities (the official figure is 112 million), and at least another 200 million more are ready to leave its vast agricultural hinterland.[6]

Most of the 100 million rural migrants attracted to China's cities in the 1990s were short-term labourers rather than long-term settlers. A major reason for this rural–urban migration was the de-collectivisation of agriculture, which allowed households to choose between the countryside and the towns for labour opportunities, and the transition to a market economy, which created major wage disparities between town and country. Migrants with land in their area of origin are more likely to contribute to rural development by transferring resources in the form of remittances and investments back to their home base. On the other hand, there is considerable risk that rural migrants will become a permanent underclass in the towns. In order to achieve a balance between town and country, migrants should be given the right to permanent residency in the towns, including accompanying social benefits, but should also be able to retain residency rights in their place of origin so as to ensure a continuing commitment to the development of their home area. For some years to come, internal migration is likely to increase proportionately with the increase in population. This stood at 1.3 billion in 2005, will have reached 1.4 billion in 2020 and 1.45 billion in 2030 when it will even out and begin to fall.

In general, migrants tend to be people between the ages of 21 and 35 (70 per cent) who have average or above-average incomes as compared with others in their home towns. They view migrating as a life stage between leaving middle school and returning to marry and have children. These internal migrants respond to demand-pull, supply-push as well as other factors. Poverty, stagnating rural incomes and job scarcity lead to a rural exodus and most young people migrate to coastal cities, where they perform menial tasks. The integration of China into the world economy, following its accession to the WTO in 2001, increased both the likelihood of an accelerated exodus of labour from rural areas and the attractions of leaving, while the growth of labour-intensive sectors required more unskilled labour to meet immediate development requirements. There would remain an imbalance in terms of earnings between the 800 million Chinese living in rural villages and the 500 million people in the cities and urban areas. Male migrants tend to be employed in construction while female migrants find jobs in factories. At the beginning of the new century migrants in coastal areas earned between $2 and $3 a day, which was far more than they could earn by farming. Although household regulation was relaxed in 1994, conditions for internal migrants remained difficult if not harsh. Despite their contributions to the economy into which they had moved, these migrants often found that their rights were rarely enforced, that they were often cheated of their pay and that many were subjected to police harassment while those without correct registration papers could be sentenced to three to six months work in prison factories. City work permits cost more than most migrants could afford. Migrants would keep up links with their villages for fear that they might be forced back to the countryside. Cities, in any case, want to keep growth rates of both permanent residents and migrants in check.

In theory, internal migration is temporary; in practice many rural migrants to the towns will not return to the rural areas. Numbers have increased dramatically from about 26 million in 1988 to 126 million in 2004, while between 12 and 13 million rural labourers are projected to move to urban areas each year over the 20 years from 2006.[7] Temporary migrants could become permanent if restrictions upon settling in urban areas are relaxed. Meanwhile, the volume of internal remittances is vast, According to Chinese estimates, each migrant labourer sent home an average of 4,522 yuan (US $545) in 2000.

Internal migration in China dwarfs migration that occurs between most countries. China is continental in size and its internal migration is almost entirely confined to the rural poor moving to the towns and industrial centres. However, by 2008 two factors began to limit internal migration. The recession and consequent fall in international demand for manufactured goods with which it had flooded overseas markets forced China to switch its attention to internal development instead of exports. Second, to remain competitive, China was beginning to develop more intensive production techniques, using fewer workers. Even so, official statistics revealed that internal migrants at 130 million represented 10 per cent of the total population, which amounted to the largest single migration in the world.

These migrants meet with official discrimination as a result of China's household registration system, which limits migrant access to public services that are guaranteed for urban residents. There is some excuse for this restriction since many of these migrants, known as a 'floating population' are not expected to remain in the urban areas for any length of time. When China de-collectivised agriculture it created a large surplus labour force. The government then relaxed its restrictive migration policy, allowing the surplus labour to migrate to the towns in search of work. The result was a huge movement of rural peasants to the towns as the economic boom developed in the 1980s. There were an estimated 30 million internal migrants by 1989, rising to a phenomenal 140 million by 2008.[8] This movement led to a high level of urban unemployment so that many cities restricted the jobs available for rural migrants and most of these could only find employment in dirty or dangerous jobs that no one wanted to do. However, in 2006 the State Council passed a directive that required local governments to ensure equal rights and opportunities to migrant workers.

According to an official survey of 2004, 45 per cent of the migrants were aged 16 to 25 and 16 per cent were over 40, while nearly two-thirds of all migrants were male and 83 per cent had nine years of education or less. As rural migrants became a permanent part of urban populations, so they slowly won rights that the household registration system, established in the 1950s, denied them. These rights included health, unemployment insurance, pensions, access to education for their children and subsidised housing. Many cities now allow peasants to apply for temporary residence permits although they remain barred from access to many social benefits. The system of household registration has been kept in place because of the cost to government if the social services that are available in the towns are opened to the huge numbers of rural migrants. According to the China Labour Bulletin (CLB), a Hong Kong-based NGO: 'Migrant workers in general, and female migrants in particular, who generally work in low-paid, labour-intensive sectors, are often subjected to long overtime hours, poor or unsafe working conditions and frequently are owed back wages by employers.' Both discrimination and harassment by employers are frequent but legal redress is often unobtainable. Then came the recession, which had a particular impact upon rural migrants as demand for China's cheap exports dropped. In February 2009 the government announced that more than one in seven – 20 million migrant workers – could not find work; that 14 million migrants who had gone home for the New Year holiday remained there when it came to an end and that 11 million who had returned to the cities had not found work. During the new decade there were increasing incidents and growing unrest among migrants who protested at working conditions or because they had not been paid. In reaction to these problems the government has undertaken to retrain low-skilled workers so as to increase employment opportunities for them while at the same time shifting industry towards more advanced, high-tech sectors so as to maintain China's international competitiveness.

The exploitation of rural people who come to the towns to work is a major feature of internal migration and in many cases goes on without interference from the government. However, when 400 fathers signed an Internet petition that asked the public to rescue their children, who were working in illegal brick kilns as slaves, the e-media publication led to national outrage, so much so that the central government had to intervene to rectify the slave labour situation in China.[9]

There are unintended consequences of this huge migration. According to the Chinese official media, there was a 5.8 per cent reduction in grain production in 2003 compared with 2002, and 99 million rural residents left their homes as migrant workers in 2003, a 5 million increase compared with 2002 (Xinhua News 2004).[10] For the urban elite 'rural migrants are either quietly ignored or are seen as deserving of their situation because they are lower quality human beings and are born to be beasts of burden for the benefit of high-quality people'. Nonetheless:

> As there is no hope of earning a living by farming, millions … have to leave their homes to be migrant workers. A migrant worker from rural China has to work in appalling conditions for twelve hours a day or longer, very often for seven days a week, to earn about US$80 a month.[11]

They are often paid well below the legal minimum wage. And, apart from the appalling conditions, millions of rural Chinese have to leave their families: an estimated 20 million children have been left behind in this way.

Chinese seeking to improve their economic opportunities have been encouraged by the government to migrate into the Xinjiang Autonomous Region and the influx of Han Chinese has transformed Xinjiang: the proportion of Han in the population has grown from 6 per cent in 1949 to 40 per cent in 2000. Uighur resentment at the incomers erupted in violence in July 2009 when 184 people were brutally killed in fierce riots, the majority of them Han Chinese. As the father of one of the victims explained: 'We wanted to do business. There was a calling by the government to develop the west.

This place would be nothing without the Han.' The story was a familiar one. Migration into the region fuelled ethnic tensions, while the Uighurs complained about the loss of jobs, the proliferation of Han-owned businesses and the disintegration of their own culture. The violence followed a protest march of over 1,000 Uighurs, who battled with security forces and attacked Han civilians in Urumqi. Though the government did not release the ethnicity of the dead, the vast majority were Han Chinese.[12] In both Xinjiang and the Tibet Autonomous Region, the influx of Chinese migrants has changed the ethnic balance fundamentally and in both regions, before long, the incomers will form a majority of the population.

The world recession of 2008–9 upset the relatively smooth operation of internal migration. China's astonishing growth has been fuelled in large part by the more than 230 million people, mainly in their twenties, who have left their farms and migrated to jobs in the country's expanding urban areas. The government had calculated that in combination, its cities would need to create 24 million jobs a year to sustain the pace of rural–urban migration. Then, in the last half of 2008, as the recession began to bite and the demand for cheap exports from China collapsed, tens of thousands of the migrants found their jobs disappearing and were obliged to return home. As one disillusioned Chinese worker explained:

> Today the same corner of Dong-keng is a ghost town, its streets strewn with the raw plastic pellets that once fed the presses. Entire rows of shops are shuttered: those that remain open blare invitations to close-down sales. The staff of local barber shops, pool bars and mobile phone showrooms stand forlorn and without customers. In the centre of town, the biggest crowds swarm the walls of work-placement offices in a desperate scramble for jobs.[13]

There was much more of this gloomy picture as booming China was hit by a major setback. It will have to change course and concentrate much more of its development upon internal growth, which in the long run will be a source of strength, but as it does so, the pattern of internal migration is liable to change. Meanwhile, many of the millions who have moved to the towns, confident that they would find employment, will be obliged to move back to the rural areas.

Although there is a considerable outward migration from China, the major thrust of migration at the present time is internal and this movement of people within China has been described as the greatest mass movement in history. It was caused by the rapid industrialisation of China that got under way in the 1990s. Despite government restrictions and penalties, large numbers of rural Chinese continued to migrate to the towns and coastal provinces. China's accession to the WTO in 2001 accelerated industrialisation that provided many more openings to attract rural migrants to the towns to search for work. Entry into the WTO also helped transform China into a magnet for foreign investors since China offered low wages and a disciplined work force.

Membership of the WTO will encourage and hasten the restructuring of the economy, leading to lower import barriers, reduced subsidies to farmers, privatisation and the streamlining of large state enterprises. However, such changes could give rise to increased unemployment, as they did in 2008. Yet by October 2009 China was recovering faster than most other countries, while the IMF predicted a growth rate of 9.8 per cent in 2010 and the same for 2011.

THE CHINESE DIASPORA

There are officially 40 million overseas Chinese (though some estimates suggest as many as 55–60 million, many of them illegal and not recorded) and these, unsurprisingly, are to be found mainly in Southeast Asia. They form a majority in Singapore and make up significant minorities in Indonesia, Malaysia, Thailand, the Philippines and Vietnam. Many came from China to settle from the sixteenth to the nineteenth centuries and identify with the countries in which they have settled. There are 30.9 million overseas Chinese in Asia, representing 78.7 per cent of all overseas Chinese. Singapore, with 3.5 million Chinese, is a majority Chinese population territory. In other countries of Southeast Asia, although the Chinese population may be larger, it is nonetheless a minority. There are 8.5 million Thai Chinese, 7.3 million Indonesian Chinese, 7 million Malay Chinese, 2.3 million Vietnamese Chinese, 1.5 million Filipino Chinese and 1.3 million Burmese Chinese. There are 6 million (in 2008) Chinese in the Americas and of these 3.8 million, including local-born Chinese, are in the United States, 1.3 million in Canada and the remainder in Latin America. Europe, including Russia, is host to 1.7 million Chinese, with 680,000 in Russia, 300,000 in France, 500,000 in Britain (mainly England) and 128,000 in Spain. Periodically strife between overseas Chinese and the indigenous people of a host country (Indonesia and Myanmar for example) has forced numbers of Chinese to return to China. Other countries with significant Chinese minorities include Peru, Australia, Japan, South Korea and South Africa. The People's Republic of China and the Republic of China (Taiwan) maintain complex relationships with their overseas Chinese citizens. They have cabinet ministers to deal with the affairs of the overseas Chinese while local governments in China also maintain overseas bureaux. Some seats in the National People's Congress of China are set aside for returned overseas Chinese. Following the reforms carried out by Deng Xiaoping, the attitude of the government to its overseas citizens changed dramatically. Thus, in the period 1978 to 2003, some 700,000 Chinese were educated abroad. Currently, 130,000 Chinese students are studying abroad at any one time.[14] Overseas Chinese were no longer regarded as capitalist traitors but as people who could aid China's development with their capital and skills. Indeed, during the 1980s China actively sought the support of the overseas Chinese, for example, by returning property that had been confiscated after the 1949 revolution. Later, it supported those Chinese who sought graduate qualifications in the West. The change in attitude towards overseas Chinese paid dividends since they now invest in mainland China and provide financial resources, social and cultural networks and contacts that are of growing importance as an increasing number of Chinese go overseas – some as migrants, others on business or to study. Article 5 of China's Nationality Law states:

> Any person born abroad whose parents are both Chinese nationals or one of whose parents is a Chinese national shall have Chinese nationality. But a person whose parents are both Chinese nationals and have both settled abroad or one of whose parents is a Chinese national and has settled abroad, and who has acquired foreign nationality at birth shall not have Chinese nationality.[15]

In the nineteenth century, when European colonialism reached its height, the modern diaspora of Chinese began to meet labour shortages, for example in South Africa and in the Caribbean for the British. The devastation and loss of life caused by the Taiping rebellion led to major migration from China. The Qing Empire had to accept that many of its subjects left China to work under the colonial powers. The mid nineteenth century saw steady Chinese emigration to a range of countries, including the United States, Canada, Australia, New Zealand, Brazil, Peru, Mexico and Panama, and Europe. Leaping forward in time, between the 1950s and 1980s, Chinese who opposed the Communist regime emigrated when they could, although the government placed severe restrictions upon its citizens leaving the country. When in 1984 Britain announced the timetable for the transfer of Hong Kong to China, this set off another wave of emigration that was to be accelerated by the 1989 Tiananmen Square massacre. This fell off once the transfer had taken place in 1997.

China's renewed interest in Africa from 2000, its extensive aid programmes and search for contracts to provide it with a long-term supply of minerals set off a surge of emigration to Africa and by August 2007 there were an estimated 750,000 Chinese working or living for extended periods in Africa. There were many estimates at this time as to the number of Chinese moving to Africa (some undoubtedly exaggerated) including 200,000 to South Africa, 40,000 in Namibia[16] and 80,000 in Zambia. Other figures include 100,000 in Angola and 35,000 in Algeria. While it is clear that a major influx of Chinese into Africa has taken place over these years, many reports in both Africa and the Western media have almost certainly exaggerated the numbers, as the world comes to terms with a newly confident China on the move. What seems likely is that the move of Chinese into Africa at the present time is numerically equivalent to the move of Europeans into the continent at the time of the scramble for Africa. In the far east of Russia, the Pacific port and naval base of Vladivostok has become another target for Chinese migrants, with many attracted to the region to work in the oil developments taking place there.

The Chinese often take a long time to assimilate. In Thailand they have largely assimilated and intermarried with other compatriots already there. In Myanmar they have adapted themselves to Burmese culture although also retaining Chinese cultural affinities. In both Malaysia and Singapore the

Chinese have maintained a distinct communal identity. They have become well assimilated in the Philippines and Vietnam. Chinese migrants have played a prominent role in Southeast Asia's economic development. The following figures are revealing:

> In Indonesia ethnic Chinese make up only 3.5 per cent of the population, yet they control 73 per cent of equity in the national stock market. In Malaysia the ratio is 29 per cent of the population to 61 per cent equity; in the Philippines it is 2 per cent of the population to 50 per cent of the equity; and in Thailand it is 10 per cent of the population to 81 per cent of the equity.[17]

CHINA IN AFRICA

Much has been said about China's new role in Africa. It has offered aid without strings to supplant or at least reduce Western influence and make China an alternative partner, raising the question as to whether it is just competing with the West or essaying a new form of colonialism. Apart from aid, China's relatively sudden and massive presence in Africa is largely based upon its state-owned corporations accompanied by considerable immigrant numbers. Thus:

> Following in the wake of the establishment of Chinese businesses in Africa is a surge in immigration that has caught African communities by surprise ... The settlement of Chinese has introduced a new social dynamic to communities in urban and rural Africa.[18]

These immigrants may be Chinese labourers who came with Chinese companies or they may be semi-skilled immigrants seeking opportunities for themselves and using the cover of Chinese companies to explain their arrival. Evidence of the growing presence of Chinese immigrants is interesting.

> In South Africa, where documentation on population figures was strictly followed by the apartheid government, there were 4,000 Chinese in 1946; this rose to 10,000 in 1980 and 120,000 in 1998. By 2006, according to a variety of sources, this number had grown to between 300,000 and 400,000.

Figures for other countries in Africa appear more problematic. Thus, Nigeria had 100,000 in 2006, Ethiopia 5,000, Kenya 4,000. Namibia had none in 1980 but – a huge variation – either 4,000 or 40,000 in 2006, while Zambia, according to government figures, had 2,300 in 2006 or 80,000 according to the opposition.[19] There were an estimated 40,000 in Angola, which is a realistic figure considering China's deep involvement in that country's oil industry.

In China itself provincial and local authorities encourage emigration as a means of raising local standards of living and acquiring a source of foreign remittances, while emigration has become a real choice for people from a wide range of backgrounds across the country. As in other parts of the world, Chinese migrants appear in the role of support for the overseas Chinese, for example as retail shop owners, so a Chinese community may grow up round a construction site that has resulted from Chinese aid or direct investment. The sudden appearance of substantial numbers of Chinese immigrants across Africa over a short period of time has given rise to considerable speculation as to whether they represent a determined attempt at colonisation. Western reporting of this Chinese 'influx' tends to be sensational since nothing is said of Western migrant groups that have been in Africa for years. Moreover, Western countries, and especially the old colonial powers that have long seen Africa as being under their hegemony, resent an influx that is assisted by aid on a scale they cannot match. However, the more successful the Chinese investment in Africa turns out to be, the greater the likelihood that it will attract more Chinese migrants in the future, especially as Beijing has removed the former restrictions upon the emigration of its people.

> At an early stage, very few African observers accurately gauged the true extent of Chinese migratory flows into Africa which started in the early 1990s. Such trends were themselves a consequence of the easing of restrictions on the movement of people out of their country that the Chinese traders were among the first to exploit.[20]

What is incontrovertible is the rapid growth of the Chinese diaspora on the continent. In 2007 the total number was reckoned at 750,000 and this was seen as a reasonable estimate. Chinese traders have concentrated on poor people with small incomes. No sector is neglected, not even music. They supply poor African populations with the cheap goods they want. At the same time, the arrival in Africa of a succession of high-powered Chinese delegations over the years 2000 to 2007 indicates the importance Beijing accords to Africa, which has become an important object of China's foreign policy. The impact of this Chinese 'invasion' has by no means always been received favourably: in the long run they are liable to be regarded in much the same fashion as were former Western colonisers.

THE FUTURE

In the run-up to the Beijing Olympics of 2008 there were numerous reports in the Western press of demonstrations on behalf of Tibet and its defiance of Beijing, but though there were demonstrations in many cities round the world, those in favour of the Olympics were far larger than those against them, a fact that drew attention to the Chinese diaspora, which is long established in many countries.

> Notwithstanding the diversity of their communities – in terms of origin and length of stay – the overseas Chinese enjoy an extremely strong sense of shared identity as well as a powerful attachment to China, feelings that tend

to override regional and political differences. This affinity finds expression in many ways. The overseas Chinese have played a crucial role in China's economic growth, providing the lion's share of inward investment since the late 1970s. According to the World Bank, in 2007 China received more remittances – nearly $26bn – than any other country except India.[21]

Overseas Chinese take great pride in China's new world role.

The Chinese diaspora, however, has three characteristics that together mark it out as distinct. First, it is numerically large and spread all around the globe, from Africa to Europe, East Asia to the Americas. Second, for historical and cultural reasons, it enjoys an unusually strong identification with the Middle Kingdom. Third, China is already a global power and destined to become perhaps the most powerful country in the world.[22]

18
India, Bangladesh, Sri Lanka

In recent years the Indian government has come to see its extensive diaspora as an asset: it remits a substantial sum in foreign exchange every year; its members bring back to India enhanced skills; it represents Indian interests in the host countries; and it assists India to break into highly competitive skilled markets. There is also substantial low-skilled labour migration to the Gulf States and Malaysia; this sector of the diaspora is regarded as temporary and the government has now introduced special policies to cover these work migrants. These policies include: preparation (or briefing) before they go overseas; safeguarding their civil rights in the host countries; assistance with their remittances; and help with reintegration when they come home. Compulsory insurance has also been in effect since 2003. Important as it is, India's international migration is dwarfed by internal migration. While the numbers involved in external immigration and emigration stand at 0.5 and 0.8 per cent of the total population, the rate of internal migration stands at an estimated 4.1 per cent of the population.

India was one of the first countries to respond to the demand for low-skilled labour in the Arab States of the Gulf, following the oil boom of the mid 1970s; it has also responded to demands for low-skilled labour elsewhere, for example in Malaysia. In 2004 almost 500,000 workers were given emigration clearance for contractual employment overseas, with 90 per cent going to the Gulf. This outflow suits the government, which would like to expand it, since it takes the pressure off domestic unemployment and increases remittances.[1] India is also a major source of highly skilled migrant workers, now reckoned to number 20 million, and in 2005 the government established a new Ministry for Overseas Indian Affairs (MOIA), which will be responsible for diaspora and international labour migration issues. It must also deal with irregular or illegal migration and trafficking.

India has a long and complex migration history. During the nineteenth century Indians established communities in a range of countries across the world. This migration included the movement of contract labour from India during British rule to other parts of the Empire, most notably the Caribbean and South Africa. Subsequently, largely since 1947, skilled professionals have been attracted to North America and Europe while low-skilled workers have gone to the Gulf. As a result of political pressures, Indians already settled in East Africa (Kenya, Tanzania and Uganda) were forced to move during the 1970s because they were seen as a bar to African advancement. In the case of Uganda in 1973, President Idi Amin gave the whole Asian community 90 days in which to leave: 30,000 relocated to Britain, others to Canada, the

United States, West Germany and Sweden. During the long liberation war in Mozambique, 70,000 Indians relocated to Portugal. These movements of settled Indians came to be called secondary migration.

THE COLONIAL INDENTURED LABOUR SYSTEM

Over the last 100 years of the Empire, the British organised the system of Indian contract labour to be sent to their colonies, mainly in Africa and the Caribbean. The abolition of slavery throughout the British Empire in 1833, and the subsequent refusal of former slaves to continue working in the Caribbean sugar plantations, for example, led Britain to recruit Indians as contract or indentured labour. These labourers were sent to work in the Caribbean islands, Malaysia, Mauritius and Natal. The practice was later adopted by two other colonial powers, France and the Netherlands. By 1878, Indians were working in Guyana, Trinidad, Natal, Suriname and Fiji. At the end of the century Indians were sent to East Africa for the construction of the Mombasa to Uganda railway. Initially labourers signed up for a five-year contract. Many Indians renewed their contracts for a second term and at the conclusion of their contract time a substantial number elected to remain in the country to which they had been sent. Contract workers were treated little better than slaves. They were isolated from the local community and lived in barracks, where their lives were strictly controlled. They would be severely punished for disobedience or slackness. After much criticism, Britain abolished the indentured labour system in 1916, by which time as many as 1.5 million Indians had been shipped to these colonies.

However, a new system of labour recruitment was then developed to tap the Tamil Nadu labour surplus in south India. The managers of tea, coffee and rubber plantations or estates in Ceylon (Sri Lanka), Malaya and Burma, which all required large numbers of labourers, relied upon Indian headmen, who were licensed by the British, to recruit workers for them. These workers were regarded as outsiders and forbidden to settle or mix with local people. Such systems cast long shadows. In Sri Lanka, for example, this treatment of Tamil labour a century ago forms part of the background to the brutal civil war that finally came to an end in 2009 between the Tamil Tigers and the Sinhalese ruling class. This form of recruitment was abolished in 1938, by which time 6 million Indians had emigrated: 1.5 million to Ceylon, 2 million to Malaya and 2.5 million to Burma. In many cases Indian traders followed the labour migrants to establish small market communities to service them and, for example, they provided rural credits for these peasants in Burma, Ceylon, Malaya and East Africa. In 2009 there were approximately 1.8 million ethnic Indians in Malaysia, most of them descendants of the labour migrants. In 2004 8.4 per cent (293,000) of Singapore's population were ethnic Indians. A large influx of Indians into Fiji came to work as sugar cane cutters. These Indians now make up 37 per cent of the population and have come to be deeply resented by the ethnic Fijians, a contributory factor in the overthrow of the civil government by the military. Following coups by the army in 1987 in favour of the indigenous population, large numbers of Indians fled the country.

INTERNAL MIGRATION

Indian independence in 1947 came with the partition of British India into India and Pakistan, which led to massive migrations of Muslims from India to Pakistan and Hindus and Sikhs from Pakistan to India between 1947 and 1950. Between 12 million and 18 million people were involved in this huge movement and violence between the rival migrants led to between 200,000 and 1 million deaths. A quarter of a century later, when East Pakistan broke away from West Pakistan to form Bangladesh, some 10 million East Pakistanis, mainly Hindus, fled across the border into India to escape the war. When the fighting was over, the majority returned home, though about 35,000 remained in India.

Internal migration in search of better work opportunities involves millions of Indians, possibly as many as 20 million at any given time, most of whom will be temporary migrants working in such fields as construction, agriculture and manufacturing. This 20 million is small when compared with 120 million internal migrants in China and could be taken as a measure of India's slower rate of development. The number is likely to increase, however, as India's industrialisation gathers momentum. The movement of these internal migrants may be within a particular state or across state lines. A significant proportion of these migrants will come from socially deprived groups or from the poorest and least developed regions of the country. As in China, such migrants will encounter opposition and non-acceptance in the places where they seek work. Statistics from the National Sample Survey (1999–2000) put the number of short-term out-migrants staying away from their usual residence at 12.6 million, but this may well have been an under-estimate, as more informal estimates put the number as high as 30 million. Calculations about development and migration, whether internal or overseas, must take account of India's increasing population. Estimates range from 1.2 billion in 2010 to 1.37 billion in 2020 to 1.5 billion in 2030 to 1.59 billion in 2040 and 1.65 billion in 2050, when India's population is expected to have outstripped China's as the largest population in the world.

INDIA'S OVERSEAS DIASPORA

The Indian diaspora is 25 million strong and is the most significant foreign investor in India, with $27 billion investment in 2007.[2] The breakdown by regions of overseas Indians is as follows: Asia 36 per cent, the Gulf 19 per cent, North America 14 per cent, Africa 12 per cent, Europe 10 per cent, the Caribbean 6 per cent, Oceania 3 per cent.[3] Indians account for approximately 40 per cent of the populations in Fiji, Trinidad, Guyana and Suriname and 70 per cent of the population in Mauritius. In the United States, Canada and Britain, Indians have had a substantial economic and cultural impact, occupying senior posts in industry, commerce and politics in Britain in particular. Countries in Asia which are host to more than 100,000 overseas Indians are Myanmar (2.9 million), Malaysia (1.6 million), Sri Lanka (855,025), Nepal (583,599) and Singapore (307,000). In Africa, there are more than 100,000 overseas Indians in South Africa (1 million), Mauritius (715,756), Reunion (220,055) and Kenya (102,500). There are more than 100,000 overseas Indians in Oceania in Fiji (336,829) and Australia (190,000); in the Caribbean, in Trinidad and Tobago (500,600), Guyana (395,350) and Suriname (150,456); in North America, in the USA (1.6 million) and Canada (851,000); in Europe, in the UK (1.2) and the Netherlands (217,000); in the Gulf, in Saudi Arabia (1.5), UAE (950,000), Oman (312,000), Kuwait (295,000), Qatar (131,000), Bahrain (130,000) and Yemen (100,900). Regardless of the source for such figures, they should always be seen as approximations that depend upon a number of factors, such as the efficiency of census details in particular countries, the degree of border regulation and the number of illegal immigrants who have escaped notice by moving into the migrant underworld of people without documents.

In the early years after Indian independence in 1947, Britain was the most likely target country for migrants. The government of India considered the issuance of passports to be discretionary until 1966, when the Indian Supreme Court established the 'right to travel' as a fundamental right under the Indian constitution. This decision led to the Passports Act of 1967. In the years immediately after independence unskilled, semi-skilled and professional Indians migrated to Britain, which was experiencing a shortage of unskilled labour. Indians were also attracted to Britain because its immigration policy allowed any citizen of a Commonwealth country to live, work, vote and hold public office in Britain. Many Indian immigrants at this time came to work in Britain until the passing of the restrictive Commonwealth Immigration Acts of 1962 and 1968 made entry more difficult. Indeed, by the mid 1960s, most Indians coming to Britain were family dependants. These accounted for 75 per cent of all Indians entering Britain in 1965 and 80 per cent in 1966. The number of Indians entering Britain peaked at 23,000 in 1968. Between 1970 and 1996 an average of 5,800 Indians migrated to Britain each year. Until the 1990s, most Indian migrants to the West chose Britain as their destination, but thereafter the pattern changed and an increasing number chose Germany and Italy.

The United States became a target country for Indian migrants during the new century and a high proportion of them, with computer skills, headed for California and 'silicon valley'. Of 160,000 H-IB visas issued in 2001, 82 per cent went to Indians, mostly computer related. H-IB visas are tied to the recipient coming to work for a specific employer. The visa is valid for three years, and then renewable for a further three. Thereafter, the employer can decide whether the visa should be made permanent. In 2007 India received a third of 158,000 such visas. India's domination of computer-trained workers results from the large supply pool in India. The Indians have established a significant presence in the computer industry.

Indian immigrants were not always so welcome. From 1900 to 1930 some 8,700 Indians were registered in the United States, mainly in California, but anti-Asian legislation passed in 1917 and 1924 banned immigration from South Asia and Indians did not qualify for naturalisation or citizenship. Only after 1968 did Indian migration to the United States become increasingly important. The US 1965 Immigration Act, which came into force in 1968, abolished national origins quotas and so made it possible for highly skilled immigrants, including Indians, to gain permanent US residence and bring their families with them. The 1990 US Immigration Act (effective in 1995) introduced the H-IB visas. Between 1986 and 2005 the annual Indian influx tripled from 27,000 to 85,000 and the Indian share in total immigrant flows rose from 4.4 to 7.4 per cent.

An up-to-date picture of the Indian diaspora, in the United States, which now numbers 2.4 million, makes interesting reading.[4] Those aged 18–34 make up 33.1 per cent of the total; high school graduates account for 90.3 per cent and those with bachelor degrees 68.6 per cent, while those who have attended graduate and professional schools account for 36.5 per cent. Their average per capita income is $34,895 and the percentage of Indians falling below the poverty threshold is 8.7 per cent.[5] For years the brain drain from India was only seen as a loss to the country, but in recent years these migrants have been regarded as a long-term investment for India. Many educated Indians have chosen to emigrate because of lack of job opportunities at home. In south India, for example, they faced positive discrimination in favour of the lower castes.

Indian students now make up the largest contingent of foreigners on American university campuses, with a strong presence in IT studies. By 2007 there were 80,000 Indian students studying in the United States. In India these immigrants contribute to the expansion of India's IT sector since they place orders with them and make technology transfers. Others return to work at home or set up subsidiaries of their US companies in India. They also contribute to the Indian economy with their remittances. Since 1994 India has received more funds in the form of remittances than any country in the world, and a significant proportion comes from the US diaspora.

Like its neighbour to the south, Canada also introduced a points system for migrants in 1968, which opened the way for high-skilled Indian immigrants by assigning value to qualifications rather than to ethnic or national background. The Canadian census of 2006 recorded 443,690 foreign-born Indians in the country, equivalent to 7.2 per cent of all immigrants. The total ethnic Indian community of 963,000 included those born in Canada as well as those from East Africa, Guyana, Fiji and Trinidad. Canadian statistics also revealed that 25 per cent of the adult ethnic Indians in 2001 were university graduates, above the figure for the whole population.

The Indian migrant picture was changing fast in other parts of the world. From 1990 onwards Indian migrants spread out across Europe and were sought after for their skills; between 2000 and 2005, for example, Germany deliberately targeted IT workers from India. Australia and New Zealand also became important destinations for Indian migrants. Australia's 2006 census recorded 147,101 foreign-born migrants from India, equivalent to 3.3 per cent of all immigrants. Between 1999 and 2007 the number of Indians admitted to Australia grew by 25 per cent each year. There was a comparable increase in the Indian community in New Zealand, which had reached a total of 43,300 by 2006. These two countries attract Indian immigrants for several reasons: the English language, the educational opportunities (many students stay on after graduating), and increased family-sponsored immigration.

Low-skilled Indian workers have been attracted to the Gulf ever since the oil boom of the 1970s. They come under temporary migration schemes and work in the oil, construction and service industries. Contracts normally last for three to five years though they may renew their contracts. However, the Gulf offers little scope for family migration, permanent residence or citizenship. These migrants are regarded only as temporary labourers by the Gulf host countries. In 2008 there were about 4.5 million Indians in the Gulf of whom 70 per cent were unskilled, 20 per cent white-collar workers and 10 per cent professional.

One other group that is an increasingly important part of the diaspora is India's students. According to UNESCO, there were 51,000 overseas students in 1999 and more than 153,000 in 2007. India ranks second to China for the number of its students studying overseas. The main destination countries for students are first the United States, which accounts for more than half, followed by Australia with 16 per cent and Britain with 15 per cent. By 2008 15 per cent of all foreign students admitted to US colleges were from India, the latest estimate bringing their numbers to 95,000. Studying in Britain has been traditional for middle-class Indians. In recent years British universities have held student fairs in India to recruit students directly and at least 14 British universities have opened full-time offices in India. In 2007 Indian students accounted for 6.4 per cent of the 374,000 foreign students in Britain. The majority were enrolled in graduate programmes, the largest numbers in business studies, engineering, technology and computer science.

Indian migrants who return home bring capital, enhanced skills and sometimes are able to arrange contracts for home companies. In 1999 India introduced the Person of Indian Origin (PIO) card and then in 2005 Overseas Citizen of India card (OCI). These two designations gave emigrants practical parity with Indian citizens though they could not vote, stand for election or obtain government employment. By March 2009, India had granted 400,000 OCI cards, 43 per cent of them in the United States, and 13 per cent in Britain.

REMITTANCES

As many governments with large overseas diasporas have come to realise, these diasporas represent a number of assets for their home countries, one of which is the size of their remittances as a source of hard currency for the economy. Remittances back to India represent a significant contribution to the economy and India has become the largest recipient of migrant remittances, which have risen from $2.1 billion in 1990–91 to $52 billion in 2008. These are remittances through formal channels. Other remittances through informal channels (individuals bringing money with them on home visits for example) are undoubtedly important but impossible to quantify accurately. In 2007, remittances were equivalent to 3.3 per cent of India's GDP (as opposed to 0.7 per cent in 1990–91). Over the years 1997–2004 two-thirds of the remittances came from the United States, Canada and Europe. India has now adopted the practice of issuing diaspora bonds to raise money from a particular country's immigrants when in need of foreign exchange.[6]

According to the Indian trade group Nasscom, India is experiencing a reverse brain drain as some Indians abroad return to work at home. An estimated 30,000 technology professionals returned in 2004–5, mostly to Bangalore, Hyderabad and the suburbs of Delhi. Entry-level wages for engineers are reported to be $12,000 in India and $60,000 in Silicon Valley.[7] The development boom now taking place in India (second only to that in China) may well attract back a significant and growing number of overseas Indians whose skills will provide additional impetus to the development process. Almost 30 per cent of Indians now live in cities:

> shrinking the 600,000 villages and their agricultural way of life, as the sons and daughters of farmers leave villages in the north and east for cities in the south and west. The rural–urban migration is changing attitudes and languages, with Hindu becoming the Lingua Franca even in areas far from its dominant position in the north.[8]

INDIA'S NEIGHBOURS

The 1950 bilateral friendship treaty between India and Nepal allowed citizens of the two countries to travel and work freely across their joint border and to be treated in each country the same as native citizens. Nepalese have migrated to India since the nineteenth century, many of them to the Punjab to serve in the British Indian Army. Others went to work on the tea plantations of Assam and Darjeeling. Current estimates suggest that 1 million Nepalese work in India. These are mainly unskilled or seasonal labourers or domestic workers. According to the Nepalese census of 2001, of 584,000 Nepalese born in India, only 100,000 had registered as Indian citizens. In reverse, a majority of the settlers of south Nepali provinces are Indian citizens. India, it must be understood, is a poor country with large numbers of unemployed people. Illegal immigrants, therefore, are seen as taking away job opportunities from the citizens of the country and as increasing the burden on India, leading to higher taxes and not necessarily utilising resources in the best interests of the country.

According to the Indian census of 2001, over 6 million residents were born outside the country, 5.7 million from neighbouring countries – Bangladesh, Pakistan and Nepal. Sri Lanka and Burma accounted for a further 243,000. Only 227,000 of these immigrants were born outside the region: 28 per cent in Africa, 25 per cent in the Middle East and 20 per cent in North America, Europe and Oceania. India has a good reputation for its treatment of refugees and asylum seekers. An estimated 110,000 Tibetans live in India, as do 60,000 Afghans who fled their country following the 1979 invasion by the Soviet Union, while thousands more arrived in 1992, after the Taliban had seized power. Tamil refugees from Sri Lanka fled to India after the outbreak of civil war in 1983. Any foreigner entering India must have proper documentation or risk deportation. Given its huge development problems, India tries to restrict the number of immigrants, although it faces particular difficulties in relation to three of its neighbours – Pakistan, Bangladesh and Sri Lanka – which have been involved in conflict and, in the case of Bangladesh, rapid population increases against a background of poverty.

BANGLADESH

The new state was both poor and overcrowded and, from its inception, it witnessed a steady migration outwards of its citizens, many of them going north into the Indian state of Assam. In addition, comparatively large numbers of Bangladeshis migrated in search of work to the oil-rich Gulf, while others went to Europe, especially to Britain, and to the United States. The Indian National Security System recommended in February 2001 that, 'The massive illegal immigration poses a grave danger to our security, social harmony and economic well-being. We have compromised on all these aspects so far. It is time to say enough is enough.' Although illegal immigration from Bangladesh had been a growing problem ever since the formation of the country in 1971, by the beginning of the new century it had reached alarming proportions, while protests to the Bangladesh government had had little effect. Most of the migrants were driven by economic considerations and sought employment, better wages and comparatively better living conditions.

As cheap labour, illegal Bangladeshi immigrants are welcome as domestic workers in India. Although India and Bangladesh reached a border agreement in the 1980s, parts of the border remain un-demarcated or disputed. Meanwhile, $15 billion of Bangladeshi migrant earnings are a substantial boost to the economy and the government in Dhaka allows its nationals to migrate, since this eases the problems it faces as a result of its population explosion.[9] In a series of meetings during 2003, India urged Bangladesh to take back 'illegal immigrants' from India, then estimated to be 15 million. Speaking on 17 February 2003, President A.P.J. Abdul Kalam told a joint sitting of the upper and lower houses of the Indian parliament that, 'the problem of illegal migration from Bangladesh has assumed serious proportions and affects many states. The government is determined to take all necessary steps to check this problem.' One major decision at this time was to construct a fence along the entire 2,100 mile border between the two countries that would include the deployment of high-tech electronic surveillance equipment. A separate division to manage the border was created at this time. The concentration of Bangladeshis in Assam was of particular concern to the government: since

1990, nine militant Muslim organisations had appeared in the region, posing a security threat.

Migration flows in South Asia are an integral aspect of social-political relations, both within countries and between them. Recent surveys demonstrate that internal and international migration in Bangladesh are both on the increase. There are three forms of international migration: to Europe, North America and Australasia for settlement; to the Gulf for contract labour; and the largely illegal migration into India. Inside Bangladesh rural–urban migration is on the increase and many poor rural families depend upon remittances from a member who has migrated to an urban area in pursuit of a job.

THE BARRIER

For many years, impelled by poverty, unauthorised migrants have crossed into India where they constitute cheap labour in the informal sector as domestic helpers, construction workers, rickshaw pullers or rag pickers. However, despite their numbers, the Bangladesh government does not recognise its migrants in India officially and so provides them with no support. In 2003 the Bangladesh foreign minister said there was not a single unauthorised Bangladeshi in India. Two years earlier, in 2001, the Home Ministry in India estimated that 12 million illegal migrants from Bangladesh were residing in 17 Indian states, although in 2009 the ministry withdrew the data as unreliable. An Indian political scientist, Kamal Sadiq, estimated that the number of illegal Bangladeshis in India was between 15 million and 20 million. He based his estimates, in part, upon the growth of Muslim communities in India. He found that many Bangladeshis adopt Hindu names and obtain forged documents that give them access to subsidies and the vote. As in the United States with illegal Mexican immigrants, so in India, politicians will obtain support from illegal immigrants who have obtained the vote. Estimates may well be inaccurate, but the figures still run into millions. In April 2008 the Indian Supreme Court directed the government to take all possible steps to prevent 'illegal immigration and infiltration'. In mid 2009, the Ministry of Home Affairs reported that 2,650 km of the Indo-Bangladesh border had been fenced and that the fence would be completed by March 2010 at a total length of 3,437 km (2,100 miles).

As so often happens, the barrier has created an unforeseen problem for India. It is being constructed on Indian land, 150 yards inside the border and, when completed, will strand 65,000 Indians who live along the border in a no-man's land between the barrier and Bangladesh. 'India says it is building the fence to keep out illegal migrants and stop smuggling. But the fence does not run along the border itself ... The result for Indians ... is a disaster.'[10] These Indians, cut off from their country by the barrier, will also be cut off from the protection of Indian security guards and at the mercy of Bangladeshis, who have threatened to seize their small farms once the barrier is completed. The villagers are not being offered any compensation by the Indian government. Ironically, many of the villagers who will be cut off are the very labourers who built the fence, since it was the only work available to them. The barrier is a cause of growing tension between India and Bangladesh. Barriers such as this one do not solve problems; they create dangerous tensions.

SRI LANKA

The separatist war waged by the Tamil Tigers (Liberation Tigers of Tamil Eelam – LTTE) against the Sri Lankan government finally came to a bloody end in 2009. At the end of 2008 it was estimated to have cost 70,000 lives and forced an estimated 300,000 people to flee their homes and become internally displaced. The bitterness of the defeated Tamils has not been assuaged and problems of reconciliation are likely to dominate the country's politics for years to come. The population of 20 million, with an average per capita income of $1,540, is deeply impoverished and, at the beginning of 2009, the Central Bank decided to tap the Sri Lankan diaspora to provide an inflow of foreign funds. The financial regulator and the Ministry of Foreign Affairs would work together to leverage Sri Lanka's foreign missions to pull in foreign exchange from an estimated 1.5 million overseas migrants. The government was confident of a good response.[11] This particular approach to migrants was another indication of the importance of remittances for so many migrant-sending countries.

19
Southeast Asia

An intricate pattern of migration, much of it internal, has developed in Southeast Asia with Malaysia and Thailand acting as poles of attraction because of their greater prosperity. The economic development of the region and the rise of the Asian 'Tigers', as well as greater political stability, have contributed to a steady increase in the movement of people seeking to improve their economic fortunes. The relatively quick rebound of the region from the recession of 2008 demonstrated the underlying strength of its economies, which have recovered more quickly than after the financial crisis of 1997–8. However, the rebound remains relative and without China the recovery would have been more moderate. According to the International Organization for Migration (IOM) Southeast Asia half yearly update for East Asia and Pacific the countries of the region must resist the attraction of protectionist measures and continue to become more integrated into the global economy. They should look for growth from domestic demand rather than just relying upon an export-oriented economy. In part, of course, their full recovery will depend upon what happens in the developed economies, but they can help to safeguard their own recovery by further regional integration. The per capita incomes of these countries in 2007 were as follows:[1]

Myanmar	$935
Thailand	$3,400
Malaysia	$6,540
Brunei	$26,930
Singapore	$32,470
Vietnam	$790
Cambodia	$540
Laos	$580

Thailand's relatively well-developed economy naturally attracts economic migrants from its three poor neighbours, Cambodia, Laos and Myanmar, and many of them find employment in Thailand's agricultural, fishery, manufacturing, construction and service industries. Moreover, Thai factories have been built in border areas so as to attract and employ cheap illegal labour from its neighbours. There are estimated to be 2 million illegal migrant workers in the country. Some of these migrants come for seasonal work, while others, such as the 1.2 million Burmese with little prospect of work in their own country, will stay for extended periods if they are able to do so.

In recent times there has been little population movement in Laos although between 1975 and 1990 over 360,000 Laotians fled into Thailand and China to escape repression. The majority were resettled, some in the West, others in Thailand and China. During the 1990s, as Laos opened its economy to foreign direct investment (FDI), small numbers of Vietnamese began migrating to Laos, mainly to seek work in the construction industry. In 2005, according to estimates by the UN Population Division, the foreign population of Laos represented only 0.4 per cent (24,646) of the total population, while the main target countries for Laotian emigration were Australia, Canada, Germany, France, the Philippines, Thailand and the USA. In June 2008, Thailand deported 837 Hmong refugees to Laos, while several thousand Hmong walked out of a refugee camp in northern Thailand in protest at plans to deport them. Some 500 of these refugees (dating from 1975–9) were detained in provincial jails. Half the dwellings in the camp were burned down in the weeks before the deportations. Altogether, about 8,000 Hmong had been living in the refugee camp (Huay Nam Khao) for several years and claimed they would face persecution back in Laos. In January 2005, representatives of Cambodia, Vietnam and the UNHCR met in Hanoi to discuss the position of ethnic minorities in Cambodia, following reports of mass arrests and other ill treatment of minorities. Cambodia agreed not to host refugee camps along its border with Vietnam, while the UNHCR undertook to resettle or repatriate 700 ethnic minority Vietnamese then resident in Cambodia.

An estimated 30–40 per cent of migration flows in the region take place through unregulated channels. Malaysia and Thailand are the main targets for such illegal migrants and together they host an estimated 3 million undocumented migrants. While attempts are made to reduce the numbers of illegal migrants, both host countries depend upon these workers in such sectors as agriculture, construction and manufacturing. There is also considerable trafficking of women and children in the region by criminal organisations. The numbers trafficked range between 200,000 and 400,000 annually. As always, there are two sides to the trafficking question. Poverty, lack of education and job opportunities are behind such large-scale illegal migration, while the target countries need the cheap labour that the migrants supply. Health has become a special concern for these migrants, who end up in insanitary, overcrowded living and working environments, where they often lack any latrines or access to safe drinking water. The result is a high level of disease and malnutrition, especially among the children.

Since the 1980s, according to the UN, labour migration in East and Southeast Asia has been increasingly feminised. By the beginning of the twenty-first century, more than 2 million women were estimated to be working in the region, accounting for a third of its migrant population. Most of the women were in domestic work, sex services, private households and informal commercial sectors. Governments of receiving countries see these women merely as a work force meeting labour requirements, and show little interest in their human rights or in taking protective measures for them. The labour source countries are more concerned to increase their foreign revenues from remittances and encourage the women to migrate, while showing little interest in their overseas welfare. The transfer of foreign women within the region from the low-income economies to the high-income ones (Singapore, Malaysia, Hong Kong Special Administrative Region (SAR), Taiwan, the Republic of Korea and Japan) intensifies existing gender inequality, economic injustice and ethnic discrimination. Thus, international migration is a contradictory process that, while providing migrant women with opportunities for social mobility, also subjects them to abuse and exploitation. The majority are independent contract workers who seek employment abroad in order to supplement family incomes. The UN lists six widely recognised categories of women involved in these overseas jobs: domestic workers; entertainers (sex workers); unauthorised workers; immigrant wives; skilled workers; and workers who share an ethnic heritage with the host population, such as Japanese Brazilians in Japan or Korean Chinese in the Republic of Korea. The UN reckons that this feminised migration has increased inequality and injustice based on gender, class and nationality in Asia. At the same time, it has opened up opportunities for migrant women to increase family incomes and for Asia's growing civil society to challenge oppressive policies and practices affecting migrants.[2]

THAILAND

Historically, migration into Thailand had been insignificant. The first break in this pattern occurred during the 1920s, when large-scale immigration of Chinese into the country (fleeing chaos and the developing civil war), amounting to 70,000–140,000 a year, took place, though this was brought under control. Then, during the Franco-Indochinese war (1946–54), some 45,000 Vietnamese refugees settled in Thailand. In 1947, Thailand set an immigration quota that limited migration from any one country to 100 a year. In December 1992, the UN estimated that 63,000 refugees were living in Thailand. They represented a small proportion of the flood of over 4 million refugees who had fled Cambodia, Laos and Vietnam from 1970 onwards. About 370,000 Cambodians along the Thai–Cambodia border were repatriated over 1992–3. By 1999, the 36,000 Cambodians who fled after the political/military upheavals of 1997 were repatriated, so that three border refugee camps could be closed. In 1986, the Thai government began to forcibly repatriate many refugees from Laos. The last camp for Vietnamese refugees was closed in February 1997. In June 1998, the Thai government requested increased assistance from the UNHCR to deal with the 100,000 Karen and Karenni refugees then in eleven camps in Thailand along its border with Myanmar. During 1999, a comprehensive registration of the border population was completed in a joint Thai–UNHCR exercise.

By the new century, however, Thailand had become a major destination for economic migrants from neighbouring countries.

Thailand manages the 500,000 to 800,000 foreign migrants in the country by having periodic registrations. Thai employers may obtain six-month renewable permits for their unauthorised foreign workers by paying a fee that is about one month's wages – most employers deduct the fee from the workers' wages.[3]

There was a national registration in September–October 2001 that attracted 568,249 migrants, a re-registration in February–March for 430,074 migrants, and another registration took place in September–October 2002. The number of industries or occupations in which migrants could work was reduced, though in fact it remained extensive. Exploitation of workers, especially women and children, is not uncommon, though the Foundation for Women successfully sued a Bang Bon garment factory on behalf of Karen women, many aged under 18, and obtained a settlement of 2 million baht in August 2002. A majority of the 500,000 to 1 million migrants in Thailand are Burmese.

According to *Migration News* of April 2004, Thailand was decentralising its guest worker policies and, by 2001, employers in all sectors and provinces were allowed to register their migrants: 152,718 employers registered 568,249 migrants, of whom 85 per cent were Burmese. By 2004 Thailand was dealing with 300,000 registered migrants and 800,000 unauthorised migrants. Thailand then changed its policy, decentralising the administration of migrants and promoting economic development in the border areas of labour-sending countries. While employed under contract in Thailand, migrants are to be treated as local workers, guaranteed the same wages and benefits, and may travel in and out of Thailand. Labour-sending countries have agreed to cooperate to reduce the smuggling of migrants. The Thai government announced that it no longer needed foreign aid, and that it would be providing foreign aid and promoting investment in labour-sending areas, thus helping to stimulate development.[4]

At one level Thailand provides a safety valve for Myanmar – the source of most of its immigrants. Myanmar is ruled by a long-standing military junta whose anti-democratic stance and poor human rights record have meant that the country is subject to international trade sanctions, a fact that adversely affects employment opportunities. Moreover, many of the migrants are from ethnic minorities that do not have Burmese citizenship: such people are especially vulnerable to exploitation and abuse.

As of 2004 there were an estimated 180,000 Thais employed abroad and the government announced a target of 200,000 Thais to work abroad. The government aimed to improve their pre-departure orientation so as to increase their protection while out of the country and safeguard their remittances. An *Overview of Thai Migration* was conducted by the IOM in 2005, covering both migrants to Thailand and Thais going abroad to work.[5] Among other suggestions, the report recommended that the Thai government should adopt a five-year national social and economic migration plan. The report highlighted the following:

- Many refugees in Thailand suffer from a lack of work experience and income. They are not equipped for sustainable residence in Thailand and are frequently illegally employed.
- Although wages received by regular, authorised migrants in Thailand are often below the country's minimum wage standards, they are considerably higher than many migrants could earn in their home countries.
- The influx of migrants into Thailand will ensure there is a future demand for multicultural environments in Thai cities.
- Many Thai nationals working abroad as irregular migrants (unauthorised) initially entered countries legally and later took on irregular status once their visas had expired or changed.

Specific practical recommendations are considered:

- Improved refugee screening procedures on the Myanmar borders.
- A cheaper and simpler way to issue work permits for 1.3 million migrant workers from neighbouring countries.
- Better information about their rights for migrants and their families.
- Proactive inspections of workplaces by the Thai Ministry of Labour to ensure compliance with labour standards.
- The enforcement of counter-trafficking legislation.
- HIV and AIDS information and prevention programmes targeting mobile and difficult-to reach migrant populations, including cross-border intervention programmes.

To supplement and reinforce specific recommendations for each migrant group, the IOM report puts forward overall policy and programme recommendations, including:

- International migration to be incorporated as part of a five-year national economic and social development plan considering both population and labour force projections.
- The need for government to continue encouraging and promoting regional efforts in the development of a migration management system.
- A review of migration trends and an analysis of their social and economic impact on the country.
- The alignment of international migration policies with economic and social development.
- A wider dissemination of information on migration promoting an informal public dialogue.

These proposals are worth quoting at length because they have – or could have – a much wider application than only to Thailand.

The Thai press reported there were 668,756 registered migrants in December 2006, when the Thai government announced that these work permits could be extended for another year between 10 January and 30 June 2007. At that time unauthorised workers could register for the first time. The Thai government allows migrants from Myanmar, Cambodia and Laos to register and work legally, while their country of origin issues documents to confirm migrant identities. Thus, 760,000 Burmese who registered with the Thai Department of Employment in 2006 then had to wait for Burmese documents. At that time, Burmese who had worked at least two years in Thailand could register for another two years but would have to leave after four.[6]

SINGAPORE

The non-resident population of Singapore expanded from 3 per cent of the total population in 1970 to 19 per cent in 2000. It was Singapore policy to attract foreign manpower. In 1997, there were about 470,000 unskilled foreign workers in Singapore, comprising 80,000 from the Philippines, 70,000 from Thailand, 20,000 from Sri Lanka, and 300,000 from Malaysia, India, China and Indonesia. They worked mainly in construction, domestic and maid services, and in service, manufacturing and marine industries. These workers were in high demand because of the low wages they were prepared to accept and the reluctance of Singaporeans to fill jobs that required manual labour or shift work. State policy is to oppose long-term immigration. As of 2007 there were 80,000 foreign skilled professionals in Singapore from developed countries such as Japan, Britain, the United States and Australia while China and India are now also being targeted to attract foreign professionals.[7]

VIETNAM

A bitter legacy of the Vietnam War was the huge number of refugees, known as boat people, who fled the country in tens of thousands. During the first half of 1975, as the Republic of Vietnam collapsed, 60,000 boat people attempted to reach the ships of the US 7th Fleet. Following this first exodus, refugees sought asylum in Malaysia, Singapore, the Philippines and Hong Kong, and though these destinations were seen as temporary sanctuaries on the way to the United States or elsewhere in the West, for a majority of the refugees they became permanent homes. An estimated 5,169 people fled Vietnam in 1976 and 21,276 in 1977. Official estimates suggested that one-third of all the boat people perished at sea. There was a further mass exodus of ethnic Chinese from Vietnam following the 1979 war between Vietnam and China, with a majority of the 1.4 million ethnic Chinese who lived in the south of Vietnam fleeing the country. With between 10,000 and 15,000 refugees reaching asylum destinations every month, the Association of Southeast Asian Nations (ASEAN) declared they would no longer accept refugees unless the West guaranteed resettlement. A UN conference in Geneva that year produced pledges for the resettlement of 260,000 refugees. By 1995, 480,000 Vietnamese had been resettled in the United States and a further 260,000 elsewhere, but 840,000 under the care of the UNHCR were still in camps in Southeast Asia. These were then closed and a majority of the refugees obliged to return to Vietnam.

According to the Vietnam General Statistics Office (2005) there was a permanent increase in internal migration, especially to Ho Chi Minh City and Hanoi as well as the industrial areas surrounding these cities. Earlier, during 1994–9, 36 per cent of all intra-provincial movements were from rural to urban areas and 20 per cent were permanent moves. Every year Ho Chi Minh City receives 700,000 KT3 and KT4 migrants (KT3 is temporary registration for a period of six months and more; KT4 is temporary registration for a period of less than six months). During the period 1994–9, more than 4.5 million people in Vietnam moved residence. Over half of all migrants were aged under 25, while educated and skilled young adults were the group most likely to migrate, both internally and internationally. Women accounted for a much larger proportion of migrants in the 1990s than in the 1980s, reflecting the increased job opportunities abroad. Migrant remittances are an important source of income for many rural households. During the 1990s, the southeast and central highlands were the only two regions in Vietnam that experienced net in-migration. These regions enjoyed higher rates of expansion of market opportunities, economic diversification, jobs and services than the rest of the country.

In the present century, there has been a rise in the number of Vietnamese going abroad to work for up to two years. However, there was also a rise in reports of abuse of domestic workers in Taiwanese homes where labour laws do not apply. However, in 2006 after reports of workers being forced to work up to 18 hours a day in private homes, Taiwan strengthened protection for domestic workers. There were 71,000 legal Vietnamese migrants in Taiwan in December 2006, and another 10,000 Vietnamese 'runaways' – workers who have left the employer to whom they were assigned. Many Vietnamese pay $5,000 or more for contracts that promise 24 months of work at $400 a month, or half the $9,600 they expect to earn. However, overseas Vietnamese have clearly been a boost for the country's development. Like China and India, Vietnam has benefited from the return of those who went abroad, learned English, gained entrepreneurial experience and acquired technical skills. Foreign investors in Vietnam are led by those from Taiwan, Singapore and the US.[8]

MALAYSIA

There were 977,276 registered foreign workers in Malaysia in spring 1999; most were required to renew their work permits by 16 April that year. Irene Fernandez of Tenaganita, a migrant advocacy group, estimates that there are 2.2 million foreign workers in Malaysia, half illegal. She reports that, in some cases, employers make their workers illegal by refusing to pay the monthly levy of M$350, or about $100 for an unskilled worker. Employers sometimes tell police that the worker ran away, or that the worker is HIV-positive – such workers are deported immediately. Foreign workers who are deported with money owed them are told to collect it from their country of origin, a course of action that is rarely successful.[9]

The readiness of the newly formed Malaysia in 1965 to let Singapore break away and become an independent city state was motivated by the fear that otherwise Malaysia would be dominated by a Chinese majority. In Malaysia, overseas Chinese support equal and meritocratic treatment so that they are not discriminated against in competition for government contracts, university places and so on. But many 'Bumiputra' (native sons) Malays are opposed to such meritocracy on the grounds that Malays need to maintain some protection to retain their patrimony. The issue is highly sensitive. It is taboo for Chinese politicians to raise the issue of Bumiputra protections in parliament.

The issue of illegal immigrants in Malaysia created a political crisis in 2005. On 1 February 2005, the Malaysian government postponed for the second time a proposed crackdown on illegal immigrant workers, mainly from Indonesia and the Philippines. The mass expulsion had first been announced on 29 October 2004 and a deadline set for mid November. This was twice extended and then delayed to 1 March 2005. By the end of February, 600,000 of an estimated 800,000 to 1.5 million illegal immigrants had taken advantage of the amnesty to leave the country. These immigrants were mainly employed in low-paid 'dirty, dangerous or difficult' jobs that Malaysians were unwilling to take, but many Malaysians blamed the immigrants for the spread of violent crimes, vice and other social ills. Though many had taken advantage of the amnesty and left, thousands more went into hiding, claiming that the government's crackdown left them with no jobs to go home to, or that they were owed wages. However, the government organised 300,000 armed volunteer reservists, effectively vigilantes, to find and deport illegal migrants who had stayed behind, offering cash rewards for each illegal worker apprehended. Punishments could include heavy fines, jail sentences and whipping. However, foreign labourers without papers were offered the chance to come back if they acquired the proper documentation. Most of the illegal workers were Indonesian: the Labour Minister of Indonesia, Fahmi Idris, said that 100,000 Indonesians were refusing to leave because they were owed wages, and that his government would take legal action unless they were paid. The crackdown had been launched on 1 March but on 19 March it was reported that fewer than 3,000 illegal immigrants had been caught and that an estimated 400,000 had gone into hiding. On the same date, as though to emphasise the absurdity of the policy, the Human Resources Minister Fong Chan Ong authorised the recruitment of 100,000 Pakistani workers to fill growing labour shortages. He said the government would also seek workers from India, Sri Lanka, Nepal and Myanmar.

The crackdown in fact resulted in a substantial worker shortage in the country and by May 2005 the government had to execute a U-turn when it announced that it would allow illegal workers it had forced to flee to return on tourist visas and search for work. Work at plantations, construction sites and factories had ground to a halt. 'Illegal migrant workers made up more than 10 per cent of Malaysia's workforce. It turns out the Malaysian economy was relying on the immigrants to do menial jobs most Malaysians will not.'[10] Malaysia was further embarrassed when relatively few of those it had driven out wanted to return, while the Indonesian government was reluctant to help Malaysia entice Indonesian workers back. The bungled policy was a sharp lesson for Malaysia but it also sent a signal to a wider world about the value of low-skilled migrants, whether legal or illegal.

Malaysia is a bustling melting pot of races and religions in which Malays, Indians, Chinese and many others live together in peace and harmony. (This, at least, is the official image.) However, life for migrant workers in oil palm plantations provides a stark, contradictory reality. Malaysia is one of the largest importers of foreign labour in Asia. About 20 per cent of its workforce is comprised of migrants, mainly employed in construction, factories, palm oil plantations and domestic service. The failure of Malaysia to reform its immigration and labour policies has meant that migrant workers become prey to both abusive employers and labour agents. According to the Asia Pacific Forum on Women, Laws and Development, workers from export-oriented factories told the Forum Task Force that there was only a token response from the UN Commission on Human Rights office in Malaysia when violations of the rights of migrant workers were reported. Workers from Bangladesh, Myanmar, Indonesia and Nepal confirmed there was official collusion and deception on the part of the recruitment agencies. Many migrant workers remain indebted to the recruitment agents even when they have to leave Malaysia. Many Burmese migrant workers who have overstayed their time in Malaysia want to return to Myanmar. But, after the implementation of the crackdown policy, whoever is arrested for overstaying will be imprisoned and sentenced to corporal punishment. A new draft bill in 2007, designed to fight crime, would empower employers to detain and hold employees, a move that raised fears that the law would favour sexual or psychological abuse, especially among Indonesian domestic workers. The law would also bar migrant workers from leaving their place of work or neighbourhood and it would make employers responsible for enforcing the law and liable for any breach. Human Rights Watch attacked the legislation and expressed the hope that Indonesia, the country of origin of most migrants, would intervene to stop the law.

Domestic workers are especially subject to abuse. There are approximately 300,000, mostly Indonesian, migrant domestic workers in Malaysia, working gruelling 16 to 18 hour days, seven days a week, and earning less than US $0.25 an hour. They are excluded from key protections in Malaysia's main labour laws and thousands have filed complaints regarding sexual and psychological abuse. Nisha Varia, senior researcher on women's rights in Asia for Human Rights Watch, said: 'It's shocking that Malaysia is even considering a proposal that would give employers freedom to lock up workers.' She argued that migration had benefited both Malaysia and Indonesia by providing important services to Malaysia and income for Indonesian workers, yet, despite a long history of large migration flows, both countries lagged behind other countries in ensuring basic protections for migrant workers. However, the government did announce its intention to introduce an Online Skills Assessment System, designed to minimise conflicts. New foreign workers would have to take a half-day course in their country of origin on Malaysian law and culture before obtaining work permits.

INDONESIA

As the fourth most populous nation in the world, with a population of 225 million, as well as one of the poorest, with an average per capita income of $1,650 in 2008, Indonesia qualifies as a natural labour-surplus country. At the end of 2006, for example, an estimated 11 per cent of the work force (11.6 million) was unemployed and a further 20 per cent were under-employed. In recent years there has been increased migration of skilled people, mainly to the countries of the OECD, and these migrants are usually permanent. On a much greater scale has been the emigration of low-skilled workers seeking employment in the countries of the region, although the Middle East (the Gulf) has become a top destination for labour with 226,000 migrating there in 2004. Most legal migrants are unskilled and of these a majority are women, employed mainly as domestics in Saudi Arabia, Malaysia, Singapore and Hong Kong (Indonesia has become one of the countries of origin providing the largest numbers of migrant workers employed as household helps and caretakers). One of the driving forces of low-skilled immigration, according to the ILO, was the differential in potential earnings in 1997: labourers earned $0.28 per day in Indonesia but could earn $2 or more a day in Malaysia. And so Indonesia has become an exporter of unskilled labour to the Middle East, Malaysia and Singapore, while importing skilled labour, mainly from India and the Philippines. Labour mobility, therefore, has become an important aspect of the country's economic calculations. Further, internal migration between provinces, especially of women, has become an important aspect of the movement of people over the last 30 years, according to census data.

The largest group of expatriate Indonesians in OECD countries is to be found in the Netherlands, the former colonial power. In 2002, there were an estimated 137,485 individuals born in Indonesia living in the Netherlands and 264,100 second-generation Indonesians there as well. The fastest growing Indonesian expatriate communities are to be found in the United States, Australia, Canada and New Zealand, and the number of Indonesians born in selected developed nations in 2005 were: Australia (65,914), United States (75,370), Canada (10,660), New Zealand (4,614).[11] Australia hosts a significant number of Indonesian students (20,000 a year). Male Indonesians are the main migrants to South Korea, Taiwan and Japan. Indonesia has also become a major transit country for asylum seekers trying to reach Australia. They come mainly from Iraq and Afghanistan, travel through Thailand and Malaysia and then aim to continue through to Australia, although that country has been extremely reluctant to receive them.

Most Asian nations oppose the permanent settlement of foreigners in their countries yet substantial numbers of Indonesians have moved abroad, especially into Malaysia, which offers the advantages of both propinquity and a booming economy that needs imported labour, whether legal or illegal. The largest out-settlement of Indonesians in Asia is found in Malaysia, where the language, culture and religion are similar to those in Indonesia, making settlement there more attractive than elsewhere. It is true that migration from Indonesia into Malaysia has taken place over centuries, but only in recent times has it turned into a major movement of people. The Malaysian census of 2001 revealed that of over 1 million foreign-born people in the country, more than half came from Indonesia. Unskilled workers often become permanent settlers and this is especially the case in eastern Malaysia. However, the largest movement of temporary workers, largely unskilled, has been to the Malay Peninsula. Many of these migrants are women who work as domestic servants and are often vulnerable to exploitation. The world's second largest undocumented migration flow is that between Indonesia and Malaysia. Over the period 1990–2007 numbers increased dramatically. According to the Malaysian home minister, in 2006 there were about 600,000 undocumented migrant workers in Malaysia, most of them from Indonesia, and concentrated in low-skilled, poorly paid jobs in the plantation, timber, manufacturing and construction sectors.[12]

According to *Migration News* (2007), Indonesia aimed to increase the overseas deployment of its citizens from 450,000 to 1.5 million. Presidential Decree No. 81/2006 on the National Agency for the Placement and Protection of Indonesian Migrant Workers Abroad requires that migrants be trained before they depart; there are 246 migrant training centres in Indonesia. At one level, the government is capitalising upon its would-be migrants who must spend Rp2 million to Rp3 million to obtain the documents they require to go abroad. Legal migration is controlled by agents who recruit and place workers in overseas jobs and arrange their travel and visas. In mid 2006, the Indonesian Minister of Labour reported that there were 2.7 million Indonesians working overseas with official permission, representing 2.8 per cent of the total national work force. The government has established a directorate to improve the welfare of migrants; its officials will make regular inspection visits to work places abroad.

Indonesia has long been wary of Chinese immigrants. Ethnic Chinese in Indonesia, for example, are not allowed to educate their children in formal Chinese-language schools. In some cases, cultural markers such as Chinese calendars have been banned, while Chinese-language signs were forbidden in Indonesia until 2004. In general, emigration has not affected Indonesia as much as other Southeast Asian countries such as the Philippines partly, perhaps, because it is such a huge country that the impact of the migration problem has been limited.

THE PHILIPPINES

The Philippines were ruled by Spain as a colony for three centuries until they were brought under American control following the American-Spanish War of 1898. This was formally ended by the Treaty of Paris of 10 December 1898, when the United States paid Spain to take control of the Philippines. There followed a second war, in which Filipinos fought for independence against the Americans. Only in 1902 did the United States establish its control throughout the country, which was to remain an American colony until 1946 when it became independent.

Prior to 1946, international migration for Filipinos meant going to the United States or its Pacific dependencies. The first Filipinos to arrive in the US territory of Hawaii did so in December 1906 to work on sugar and pineapple plantations. Thereafter, there was a steady migration of Filipinos to Hawaii, California, Washington and Oregon or the salmon canneries of Alaska. It is estimated that between 1906 and 1934 a total of 120,000 Filipinos went to work in Hawaii. Since the Philippines was an American colony, its citizens were US 'nationals' and movement to the United States was regarded as internal migration. In 1934 Congress passed the Tydings-McDuttie law (Philippines Independence Act), which envisaged independence for the territory in ten years time. It therefore introduced migrant quotas for Filipinos. In 1965, the US Immigration and Nationality Act brought an end to nationality-based restrictions for migrants. Thereafter, Filipino migration to the United States increased. Similar acts passed in Canada, Australia and New Zealand opened the way for increased migration to those countries, with the result that the Philippines became one of the top ten sending countries to these traditional immigration hosts.

As of December 2004, an estimated 8.1 million Filipinos (10 per cent of the country's population) were working and residing outside the Philippines in nearly 200 countries. Although by this date the Philippines had become one of the largest emigrant countries in the world, it also attracted a modest number of immigrants and at this time there were 36,150 foreign nationals working and residing in the Philippines. Although a high proportion of would-be emigrants seek US visas, other popular destinations are situated in the Middle East, elsewhere in Asia, Europe, Africa and Oceania. Over the 30 years to 2005, a culture of migration has emerged in the Philippines and millions of Filipinos have demonstrated their willingness to work abroad. According to a 2002 survey, one in five Filipinos was prepared to emigrate. By 2005, according to other surveys, the number of Filipinos ready to emigrate was 20 per cent in July 2005 and had risen to 33 per cent by October. As one respondent to these surveys said, 'If it were only possible, I would migrate to another country and live there.'[13] The Philippines government has institutionalised the process of migration and assists migrants by regulating the recruitment agencies while also looking to safeguard the rights of overseas migrant workers. Remittances, meanwhile, have become an important annual contribution to the economy.

It was during the 1970s that the Philippines became a major migrant country. Poverty and a rapidly increasing population meant the economy could not cope and this state of affairs happened to coincide with the rising demand for low-skilled labour in the Gulf as the oil boom got under way. In 1974, therefore, the Marcos government passed the Labour Code of the Philippines, which encouraged 'temporary' work migration. At the time it was not foreseen that this process would become a permanent feature of Filipino social/political policy. By 2004, the regional distribution of land-based overseas Filipino workers was as follows: Asia 266,609; Middle East 352,314; Europe 55,116; Americas 11,692; Africa 8,485; other destinations 10,370.[14] Approximate figures at December 2004 showed there were 3.2 million permanent overseas Filipino settlers, mainly in the United States; about 3.6 million temporary labour migrants (Overseas Foreign Workers – OFWs) with 1 million in Saudi Arabia and 1.3 million illegal migrants in the United States and Malaysia. Women accounted for a majority of permanent settlers and were as prominent as men in labour migration. Since 1992 they had outnumbered male migrants, mainly as domestic workers and entertainers. Apart from the United States, the top destinations for Filipino OFWs were Hong Kong, Kuwait, Singapore, Italy, the UAE, Japan and Taiwan.

In 2001, the government of the Philippines set a target of deploying 1 million workers overseas every year, the target to be achieved by 2005. There are now more than 1,000 government-licensed recruitment agencies matching workers with foreign employers; standard placement fees are equivalent to one month's salary plus 5,000 pesos ($94). Exporting the unemployed, especially young men, relieves the pressure of unemployment at home. Government policy has been consistent: to promote migration, but only for temporary work through regulated channels. In 2000, 2.9 million OFWs were abroad under official arrangements. At the same time an estimated 1.8 million Filipinos were abroad as 'illegals' while a further 2.5 million had left to seek permanent residency elsewhere. The government plays a supporting and regulatory role for migrants. This first involves gaining access to foreign markets and is a foreign policy priority in both bilateral and regional trade negotiations. The government is not concerned to obtain permanent overseas settlement for its citizens, but sees the policy as part of its strategy to deal with unemployment at home. Most of the responsibility for recruiting workers for overseas jobs is handled by the private sector while the government retains a regulatory role to protect workers from abuse while also discouraging illegal recruitment.

Between 1990 and 2001, 'official recorded remittances alone averaged 20.3 per cent of the country's export earnings and 5.2 per cent of GNP, providing a lifeline for many families in a poor country that saw little economic growth in several of those years'.[15] For 25 years (source dated 2004) the export of temporary labour has been an explicit response to double-digit unemployment rates. The government has developed a sophisticated policy regime to promote and regulate labour emigration and the value of these emigrants has been publicly recognised. Each year the President celebrates Migrant Workers Day by awarding the 'Baygong Bayani' (modern-day hero) to 20 outstanding migrants – for sending money home. By migrating officially, migrants receive a number of subsidised benefits that include pre-migration training on social and work conditions abroad, life insurance and pension plans, and medical insurance. There have been hiccups in the migration story and, for example, in 2003 the Philippines and Indonesia jointly suspended further movement of domestic workers to Hong Kong after repeated instances of abuse of migrants had been revealed. The Overseas Workers Welfare Administration (OWWA) provides support and assistance to migrants and their families. All processes for migrants up to the point of departure are handled by the Philippines Overseas Employment Administration. The Commission on Filipinos Overseas provides services for permanent emigrants. The Philippines probably provides better and more comprehensive government support for its overseas migrants than most other emigrant countries. In April 2009, the Philippines was praised by the UN Committee on Migrant Workers as a model in the field of migration and for its robust institutional capacity to protect its citizens abroad. As its government claims, the Philippines has a clear commitment to the International Convention on the Protection of the Rights of all Migrant Workers and Members of their Families. The Philippines has been the most active advocate, in all UN fora, on the campaign to promote ratification of the Convention on Migrant Workers.

Remittances in 2004 came to $8.5 billion, were expected to reach $10 billion in 2005 (which they did) and were rising steadily, having first passed the $1 billion mark in 1990. As the World Bank reported in 2005, the Philippines was the fifth largest recipient of remittance flows after India, China, Mexico and France. Remittances provide the Philippines with a crucial source of foreign exchange. The OWWA issues an identification card to all official migrants. This is also a visa card linked to dollar or peso savings accounts in a consortium of banks. The card allows remittances to be sent at $3 or less per transaction. Remittances at the rate of $8 billion a year or more are a major addition to government finances and much more comes into the country informally. An estimated 17 per cent of Filipino families receive remittances from a family member overseas.

The success of this policy of worker migration raises important questions for the future. Is the government inflicting long-term damage upon its development projects since it is relying too much upon remittances for economic survival and neglecting home development? The Asian Development Bank released a report in November 2006, *Converting Migration Drains into Gains*, that warned the Philippines to avoid a brain drain, which it defined as emigration that leads to a fall in average income per worker. For a poor country such as the Philippines, there are no easy answers to these competing equations.

20
Southwest Asia:
The Gulf, Afghanistan, Iraq, Iran

INTRODUCTION

A World Bank report[1] on the Middle East and North Africa (MENA) examines economic integration in MENA resulting from labour mobility, which has played a major role in the region throughout its history and especially over the last 40 years. Thus, in the mid 1980s, 10 per cent of the total Egyptian labour force was employed abroad, primarily in the Gulf; 15 per cent of the Yemeni work force worked abroad; and a third of the Jordanian work force earned its living outside the country. In the present century (2005) worker remittances of all MENA countries' GDP accounted for 2.4 per cent. In Kuwait about 90 per cent of the work force was non-national and in Saudi Arabia 66 per cent. It is estimated that over the two decades 2005 to 2025 about 100 million new jobs will need to be created within MENA. Whatever national policies may be in relation to the desirability of encouraging migration, the reality is that the region as a whole depends upon a highly mobile work force. The report argues that these countries need to become more open in order to create industries and services, which can be competitive. The EU represents another aspect of this MENA labour mobility. It is to the advantage of both the EU and MENA that there should be an expansion of labour migration from MENA to the EU. The more highly educated members of the MENA work force are not necessarily the beneficiaries of worker mobility. In Egypt, for example, the unemployment level of those with secondary education is 22 per cent as opposed to 4 per cent for those with no education and 6 per cent for those with primary education. Similar statistics relate to the unemployed among those with higher or tertiary education in Algeria, Jordan and Tunisia. UN projections suggest that the EU will need an additional 1 million worker immigrants a year to maintain a constant ratio between the work force and those who retire. Work force requirements in the EU have to be balanced against social, economic, political and religious considerations and the subject of migrant incomers has become increasingly contentious. One result of tightening migration regulations is to increase illegal immigration, especially of less skilled workers. Ironically, perhaps, despite the levels of unemployment among educated workers in MENA countries, for example Morocco, migration to Europe is almost entirely confined to low-skilled labour. Worker migration from MENA countries falls into two categories: those who move from countries of high unemployment to other MENA countries such as the Gulf states in search of employment; and those who leave MENA and seek work in the EU.

THE GULF STATES

Following the OPEC (Organization of Petroleum Exporting Countries) oil boom of 1973, the oil states of the Gulf faced the question of how to deal with their huge new revenues from oil exports. In broad terms they chose three development paths: first, to build up their infrastructures; second, to invest in their industrial and agricultural sectors; and third, to improve or create new social services that covered health, education and social welfare. What amounted to a series of economic and social revolutions required extensive labour forces that the small populations of the six Gulf Cooperation Council (GCC) countries (Bahrain, Kuwait, Oman, Qatar, Saudi Arabia and the United Arab Emirates – UAE) could not meet. In 1975 their combined populations only came to 6 million and of these 4.6 million were in Saudi Arabia. Moreover, their work forces were reluctant to do, or lacked the training for many of the new tasks. As a consequence, the Gulf states adopted a policy of attracting foreign economic migrants on a major scale. Work migrants in the region rose from 1.1 million in 1975 to 5.2 million in 1990, comprising 68 per cent of the work force. The Gulf War of 1991, following Saddam Hussein's invasion of Kuwait, forced many migrants to leave, although they returned through the 1990s. In the case of the Gulf, Egypt, Jordan, North Yemen and the Palestinians sent large numbers of workers to the small Gulf states to assist the modernisation that followed the oil boom. The influx of foreign labour altered the demographic balance in the Gulf so that by 2006 the GCC countries began to adopt more restrictive migration policies in order to increase the number of their own nationals in the labour force since, in some cases, local workers made up as little as 24 per cent of the total work force. The policy has had only limited success since would-be migrants, apparently no longer wanted, have turned to illegal and sometimes more dangerous ways of entering the Gulf countries. Migrants will risk a great deal to obtain jobs in the Gulf, since they come from countries where poverty and lack of economic opportunities consign them to hopeless lifestyles, while those employed in the Gulf states, despite harsh working conditions, are able to send home remittances that are often primary sources of income to both the recipient families and also to the state, and so become a major tool in poverty reduction.

Various human rights organisations have raised questions about the harsh conditions that foreign workers have to endure. Dubai, especially, has become the second biggest building site in the world after Shanghai. Its ruling sheiks plan to turn Dubai into the commercial capital of the Middle East. 'The boom has sucked in an army of workers from India, Pakistan and Bangladesh, unskilled men who toil for years away from families to save £30 a month.'[2] While an army of British expatriates live in air-conditioned luxury:

the Asian labourers are banned from the glitzy shopping malls, new golf course, and smart restaurants. Instead they squeeze six into a dormitory room, enduring temperatures of 50C in summer and allowed to return home to see their families only once every two years. Accident rates on construction sites are high.

Most of them are housed in work camps on the city outskirts. A typical wage is 600 dirhams (£90) a month. These foreign labourers have no rights and trade unions are banned. Those who complain about poor work conditions (troublemakers) are rapidly deported. According to Human Rights Watch, many workers are exploited in conditions amounting to forced labour. Appeals for change have been largely ignored, while apologists for the system, including British companies and expatriates, defend the system from which they profit and argue that the foreign workers have come to Dubai voluntarily.

> Like their impoverished forefathers, today's Asian workers are forced to sign themselves into virtual slavery for years when they arrive in the UAE. Their rights disappear at the airport where recruitment agents confiscate their passports and visas to control them.

The Gulf states do not consider that migrants have any rights. Punishment for protest takes the form of a limited term in prison followed by deportation. Nonetheless, the GCC countries have become important poles of attraction for desperately poor economic migrants from South Asia – India, Pakistan and Bangladesh, as well as the Philippines and elsewhere. The migrants have become increasingly important to their home countries because of their remittances, which are often greater than either aid or FDI. Thus, for example, in 2007 Pakistan received $5.49 billion in official remittances, mainly from the Gulf, as opposed to $4.6 billion FDI.

In 2006, India announced new welfare measures to safeguard its overseas migrants whose value lies both in the scale of their remittances and the fact that their absence from India relieves the pressure of unemployment. By contrast, Pakistani migrants fill low-skilled jobs and so far the government of Pakistan has shown little interest in their welfare once they have left the country.[3] Many Asians who end up in the labour camps of the Gulf may have paid as much as $1,000 or more for travel costs and visas while their average wage in the Gulf is $5 to $7 a day.

Human rights groups had been worried about the treatment of migrants in the Gulf for some time before the economic recession arrived to make their condition worse. In most cases, Asian workers in the UAE fell into a vacuum of employment law and social welfare and so became the first casualties of the recession. In any case, many of them were indebted to their 'sponsors' who had purchased visas on their behalf. Without passports or identification documents (confiscated by their employers) they found themselves in a grey economy or 'no man's land'. Dubai has attracted particular attention because of its poor employment record and, though migrants are abused worldwide, this appears to be particularly the case in Dubai, where most foreign workers do jobs at the bottom of the work hierarchy. Nesrine Malik, writing in the *Guardian*, claimed:

Even in the good times, this is fertile ground for abuse. When an economy is buoyant, migrant workers supply cheap labour, which naturally gets cheaper as recession bites and re-employment options dwindle. However, this classic pattern is further exacerbated by the fact that these workers are subject to the additional restraints of debts to their employers or agents and their inability to leave the country and relocate. While abuse of cheap labour is not confined to the Middle East, the entrenched anti-immigration, anti-naturalisation policy in Arab states means these workers will never be afforded the rights of citizens irrespective of how long they have spent in the country.[4]

While international pressures have brought some changes in the Gulf – the UAE now gives workers six months rather than one month to seek alternative employment before visas are cancelled, and Bahrain has done away with its sponsorship law – it was cheap labour that underwrote much of the economic development in the Gulf.

The recession had an adverse impact upon migrant labour in the Gulf, leading among other things to demonstrations from its generally quiescent labour force against low pay, especially as the value of their pay was further reduced by the impact of inflation upon the exchange rate for their remittances. The currencies of the GCC countries are pegged to the US dollar and the weak dollar meant a slump in the value of wages. Some Indian workers are paid as little as $160 a month for a six- or seven-day week, while the average national (citizen) is paid seven times that amount.

The size of the migrant community in the six GCC countries constitutes a potentially explosive situation for the future. There are 13 million foreign workers in the GCC states, making up 37 per cent of the population. Bahrain has a population of 700,000 of whom a third are foreign workers. In Dubai, foreign workers comprise the overwhelming majority of the population, with a million-strong foreign work force living alongside a quarter of a million citizens. Any reforms of the system are likely to meet opposition from those who benefit from the repressive system. Responding to labour unrest in 2006 and 2007, the UAE Labour Minister Ali al-Kaabi acted on some of the abuses. In a region where heat exhaustion takes a daily toll, he introduced mid-day work breaks during the hot summer months and ordered one well-connected company to pay about $2 million in fines for failing to pay its workers. In a cabinet reshuffle, the minister was replaced amid speculation that he had upset powerful people.[5]

As the recession bit, the Indian government monitored the situation with regard to its migrant workers, urging them not to panic. But as migrants returned to the city of Meerut in northern India for the Muslim festival of Eid, many received text messages to tell them their jobs no longer existed and that they should not return to the Gulf. This followed the request by the property arm Dubai World for extra time to pay back debts that had become due. Although Abu Dhabi would later bail out Dubai World with a loan of $10 billion, the boom in Dubai had clearly stalled. The size of the problem for India was illustrated by the fact that the state of Kerala relied upon remittances from its workers in the Gulf for up to 22 per cent of state income since half the work force in the UAE were Malayalis. The Indian central government minister, Vayalar Ravi, said that while the Dubai World crisis would have international implications, it would not lead to large job losses for migrant workers. Nonetheless, the government was planning to announce a comprehensive package to rehabilitate those Indian workers who did return from the Gulf.[6] The concern of the minister and his desire to downplay the crisis and reassure Indian workers in the Gulf is understandable. In 2007, for example, an estimate of the remittances sent back to India put the figure at $27 billion and for some states, such as Kerala, these remittances represent a substantial part of the economy. Prior to the credit crunch, Dubai and the rest of the UAE were estimated to have a population of 6.4 million of whom 5.5 million were foreigners. More than 3 million were registered with the Ministry of Labour as workers when Dubai was still in the midst of its building boom. However, even before Dubai World asked to suspend payments on its $60 billion debt for a six-month period, the property market was collapsing, while hundreds of new building projects worth tens of billions of dollars were being mothballed. Whatever recovery is achieved, the unprecedented boom in Dubai is unlikely to return. The impact upon the migrant labour force will be profound.

AFGHANISTAN

During late 2001, there was rising concern among the country's civilian population that an American attack upon Afghanistan was imminent. This led to an increase in the number of displaced people seeking refuge in camps near the Pakistan and Iran borders. Refugee numbers rose steadily and an estimated 1.5 million people left their homes during the latter half of September. Pakistan accepted 2.5 million refugees before it restricted access to those Afghans in the border region most in need of assistance. By the end of 2001 there were some 5 million Afghan refugees in Pakistan, including some who had been there for over 20 years. There were also 2.4 million Afghan refugees in Iran. From 2002 onwards, however, more than 5 million Afghan refugees were repatriated from both Pakistan and Iran through the efforts of the UNHCR. Over the two years 2005–6, the government of Pakistan completed a registration of all Afghans living in the country. The total of registered Afghans in Pakistan as of February 2007 was 2.15 million, while there were an estimated 920,000 in Iran. In January 2008, Iran enacted tough laws to deal with refugees: illegal Afghans (not registered as refugees) could face up to five years in prison. As of March 2009, 1.7 million Afghans remained in Pakistan. They were allowed to live and work, and their children could attend school, until the end of 2012. Afghanistan was not in a position to receive all the refugees that the UNHCR was trying to repatriate, but the UNHCR managed to have a number accepted in Australia, Canada, Germany, Norway and Sweden.[7]

As the insurgency in Afghanistan deepened through 2009, the issue of refugees was overshadowed. The problem of repatriation became more difficult and is likely to remain so until an indigenous government is able to cooperate with the UNHCR. In any case, as the rural areas have become more insecure, so returning Afghan refugees have migrated to the towns, where their presence has contributed to increased poverty, unemployment and crime. After seven years of warfare, Kabul's population has tripled. At the same time internal and regional mobility has enabled families to diversify their sources of income while returning refugees have contributed to reconstruction and development by means of skills acquired in exile. However, the country's institutions and infrastructure are ill-equipped to meet the needs of repatriated families. 'The government's inability to provide for and protect its returning citizens by ensuring nationwide basic services and the rule of law has led to an increasing questioning of its legitimacy.'[8] Meanwhile, both Iran and Pakistan, the main host countries for Afghan refugees, were pressuring the UNHCR to maintain a high level of repatriation.

The prolonged refugee presence and the persistence of unchecked cross-border movements have increased Pakistan's and Iran's leverage over their neighbour. Moreover, with migrants and terrorist networks often using the same transport routes, making it difficult to distinguish insurgents from migrants, Tehran and Islamabad are inclined to seal their borders and pressure the millions of remaining Afghan refugees to return home.[9]

Afghanistan's botched 2009 elections and the subsequent assumption of the presidency by Hamid Karzai failed to ensure a stable government at a time when both the United States and Britain were contemplating withdrawal, while the inability of the government to guarantee the security of its citizens and the abiding poverty of the vast majority of the population hardly suggest that an early solution to the refugee problem will be found. In some areas, an estimated one in three people are returnees. They, like other Afghans, seek security, houses, jobs and social support. The UNHCR outlined its plans for 2010. 'The 2010 operations plan has a strengthened shelter, water and livelihoods component in order to more effectively sustain returnee reintegration in these challenging circumstances.' The main objectives of the UNHCR programme are to create a favourable protection environment, fair protection processes and see that basic needs and services are met. Under 'durable solutions' the UNHCR aims to facilitate the voluntary return of Afghans from Pakistan, Iran and other host countries, and address the longer-term reintegration needs of refugees and IDP returnees in the framework of the Afghanistan National Development Strategy (ANDS), while strengthening the government's capacity to manage and assist reintegration processes. The UNHCR set key targets for 2010 to cover housing, water supplies, transport, community-based livelihood and income-generating activities. These and other targets represent a tall order for an over-stretched organisation and their success or failure will depend upon the cooperation of a government that (at the end of 2009) had yet to establish its credibility. Voluntary repatriation will remain the preferred solution for many Afghans, though at greatly reduced levels compared with the pre-2006 period because of rising insecurity, political instability and other economic and social problems. These concerns will be heightened by intensified military operations. The UNHCR programme must be carried out against a security situation that has deteriorated since 2006.[10]

IRAQ

Although many Iraqis became refugees from Saddam Hussein's regime, both prior to 1980 and then as a result of the war with Iran over the years 1980–88, and again during the years 1991–2003, their numbers were to be hugely increased following the US invasion of March 2003 and subsequent internal strife that has characterised the country ever since. Following the 2003 invasion, an estimated 1.6–2 million Iraqis fled the country. A UNHCR report of 2006 claimed that 1.6 million Iraqis had left the country since March 2003, representing approximately 7 per cent of the population, while on 22 January 2007 the BBC gave a figure of 2 million refugees. In addition, there were an estimated 1.7 million IDPs. The figures keep changing. Thus, on 29 April 2008, the UNHCR estimated that over 4.7 million Iraqis had been displaced, with 2.7 million within Iraq and 2 million as refugees in neighbouring countries. A majority of the refugees had gone to Syria and Jordan, creating major problems for those two countries. According to UN sources an estimated 40 per cent of the Iraqi middle class have fled the country; many of them do not wish to return. In Syria, thousands of women and girl refugees have turned to prostitution to survive. Ethnic cleansing (or rather, religious cleansing) of Shiites from Sunni neighbourhoods and Sunnis from Shiite neighbourhoods has characterised much of the violence in Iraq since 2003.

Of the refugee diaspora, only a small number of Iraqis (800) have been accepted by the United States since the invasion, while Sweden has accepted about 18,000 and Australia 6,000. By December 2006 Jordan had received about 750,000 Iraqi refugees, most of them poor and unskilled, who have added to Jordan's economic problems. While Sunnis have been allowed to pursue their religion in peace Shiites have faced a degree of discrimination. In the same period, Syria received about 1 million refugees of whom half were Iraqi Christians. Up to October 2007, Syria had maintained an open-door policy towards Iraqi refugees, but then the government implemented strict visa regulations so as to limit the numbers entering the country (at one point refugees had been crossing into Syria at the rate of 5,000 a day). The new restrictions meant that only Iraqi merchants, businessmen and university professors with visas acquired through Syrian embassies could enter Syria. Egypt became a destination for Iraqi refugees during 2006. There are approximately 150,000 Iraqis in the country but, in 2007, Egypt followed Syria and imposed restrictions upon would-be immigrants.

Whatever the purpose of the Iraq War, one of its principal consequences was to spread Iraqis round the world. At the first conference on the refugee situation in April 2007, Antonio Gutteres, the chief of UNHCR, appealed to the international community for assistance. 'It is time the international community responded with genuine solidarity and aid to displaced Iraqis and to the states housing them.' Jordan and Syria, in particular, faced a growing burden even after tightening their regulations against more refugees. Other countries in the Middle East showed reluctance if not open hostility to accepting Iraqi refugees: Kuwait never admits them, while Saudi Arabia was constructing a $7 billion fortified barrier to stop refugees crossing its border. At the Geneva conference Human Rights Watch gave examples of the brutal reception that awaited refugees in the Middle East. The option of moving to safe regions within Iraq itself had become harder as 'about half' of Iraq's central and southern provinces were turning away displaced people unless they could prove they originated in the region. At the Jordan border, it had become common for officials to ask whether a new arrival was a Sunni or a Shia and to turn back the latter, while Iraqi Christians found they were particularly vulnerable. Of the two countries responsible for the invasion in the first place, the United States and Britain, the former had admitted a few refugees and promised to take 7,000 while Britain had not agreed to accept any.[11]

The movement of Iraqi refugees had become one of the largest since the Second World War, involving 4 million Iraqis, or one in seven of the population. The problem was the direct result of the US-led invasion, leading to the creation of shantytowns in Iraq and its neighbours crammed with refugees. The UNHCR, meanwhile, was facing major problems raising $100 million for relief. Part of the problem, as always with refugees, was the long-lasting nature of the Iraq War and occupation, which had induced compassion fatigue among would-be donors who had transferred their attention elsewhere. An assessment of numbers in mid 2007 showed 1.4 million refugees in Syria, 750,000 in Jordan, 200,000 in the Gulf states, 100,000 in Egypt, 54,000 in Iran, 40,000 in Lebanon, and 10,000 in Turkey, while a further 2 million Iraqis were displaced within their own country.[12] Not a great deal had changed by the end of 2009, as the Americans prepared to quit Iraq by the end of 2011. Internal violence continued and no one was willing to predict what would happen after the final withdrawal of US forces.

IRAN

Iran has not attracted a great deal of immigration, with the exception of Shia Muslims from Iraq. However, the revolution of 1979 led to an exodus of middle-class Iranians to Europe and the United States, while a substantial exodus of Shia Muslims from Iraq into Iran took place during the 1980–88 war between the two countries. At the end of 1992 there were 1.2 million Iraqi refugees in Iran and 2.8 million Afghans who had fled to Iran following the Soviet invasion at the end of 1979. In late 1993 some 53,000 refugees from Azerbaijan fled to Iran to escape Armenian occupation. There were also Kurdish refugees from northern Iraq. In 1999 statistics showed that Iran had the largest refugee population in the world. There were an estimated 1.4

million Afghans, 580,000 Iraqis and 40,000 refugees from Tajikistan, Bosnia, Eritrea and Somalia. Although there were 30 designated refugee camps, most refugees had integrated into cities and villages round the country.

Since its 1979 revolution, Iran has been much in the news, both because of its confrontation with the United States and because it has become a refugee recipient country during the first decade of the 21st century as a consequence of the wars in the two neighbouring countries of Afghanistan and Iraq. However, over its long history from the Empire of Cyrus the Great in the sixth century BCE, Persia (its name until 1934) has witnessed many phases of both immigration and emigration. Greeks, Arabs, Mongols and Turks have all left their mark. The ethnic divisions of modern Iran are Persians (51%), Azeris (24%), Gilaki and Mazandaranis (8%), Kurds (7%), Arabs (3%), Lurs (2%), Baluchs (2%) and Turkmens (2%). In the nineteenth century the followers of Baha'ism fled to the Ottoman Empire to escape persecution, while intellectuals fled the country during the agitation that led to the Constitutional Revolution of 1905–11. However, the events of 1978–9, which brought an end to the Pahlavi dynasty, prompted the largest ever emigration from Iran. From 1950 to 1979 emigration from Iran was for economic reasons and many overseas Iranians were in fact students. In the academic year 1977–8, 100,000 Iranians were studying abroad – 36,000 in the United States, the rest in Britain, West Germany, France, Austria and Italy. Following the revolution, many of these students remained in the West. In many cases, their families came to join them, while royalists who felt they would be targeted by the new regime also fled, taking substantial wealth with them. Many representatives of minorities left Iran in the years leading up to the 1979 revolution as they saw the Shah's power crumbling and there was a huge exodus after the revolution. This wave of migrants included large numbers of professionals, entrepreneurs and academics, who between them represented a substantial brain drain. According to the *Iran Times*, one in three physicians and dentists left the country after the revolution and there was an accompanying flight of capital of $30–40 billion. A further wave of emigration occurred in 1995. At the end of 2005 the UNHCR calculated that there were 39,904 Iranian refugees in Germany, 20,541 in the United States, 9,500 in Iraq, 8,044 in Britain, 6,597 in the Netherlands and 6,508 in Canada.[13]

There are no precise figures for the Iranian diaspora, whose size is estimated at anything between 2 million and 4 million. Motives for leaving Iran have been political, social and economic. At the turn of the century the ten leading destination countries for Iranian migrants (in order) were the United States (291,040), Canada (75,115), Germany (65,750), Sweden (53,982), Israel (51,300), United Kingdom (42,494), Netherlands (21,469), Australia (18,789), France (18,376) and Armenia (15,999).[14] However, the numbers of migrants in these countries are almost certainly much greater as many have gained entry illegally. The largest diaspora, in the United States, was about 330,000 in 2000 according to Census Bureau estimates. However, other estimates put the Iranian diaspora at between 691,000 and 1.2 million. The Iranian migrant communities in both the United States and Canada include a high proportion of professionals and degree holders. In the case of Sweden, the government introduced a tougher refugee policy in the 1990s and there is high unemployment among them. Overall, the Iranian diaspora is well-educated, hard-working and makes a genuine contribution to the host country. In 2006 the IMF claimed that Iran ranked highest for educated migrants leaving the country among 91 developing countries, with between 150,000 and 180,000 educated people leaving the country each year. It was also the country with the highest rate of emigration to the United States from Asia.

The loss of human capital is reckoned to be equivalent to $38 billion a year, according to the Iranian Ministry of Science. The World Bank estimated that remittances back to Iran increased from $536 million in 2000 to $1.2 billion in 2003, falling back to $1 billion in 2004. These are official figures and do not include money transferred through the *hawala* system of informal money dealers which covers over half the total of remittances.[15] Inside Iran recent decades have witnessed a sizeable movement of rural people to the towns and urban areas where 67 per cent of the population live. The Iran–Iraq War greatly contributed to this process of internal migration as millions of IDPs made their way to the towns. This internal migration also reflected the lack of investment or job opportunities in rural areas.

The revolution of 1979–80, the war with Iraq (1980–88), the enmity of the United States, which dubbed Iran a member of the 'axis of evil', its nuclear programme – which brings it into confrontation with the West and Israel – and, since his election as president at the beginning of the decade, the ready defiance by Ahmadinejad have all conspired to keep Iran in the international spotlight. At the same time, Iran has been one of the most hospitable countries towards refugees from its two embattled neighbours, Afghanistan and Iraq, even as it has qualified for the doubtful distinction of presiding over the highest rate of brain drain in the world of its own citizens. This brain drain has been a catastrophe for Iran at a time when it faces so many political and development problems. By 2006, between 150,000 and 180,000 Iranians were emigrating every year, many of them highly educated and skilled. An interesting and potentially very important by-product of this emigration has been a communications revolution through chat rooms and blog sites, with the result that Persian has become one of the most widely used languages on the internet in the world. In 2004, Reporters Without Borders claimed that internet use had grown faster in Iran since 2000 than in any other Middle Eastern country. One consequence of Western determination to isolate and if necessary punish Iran over its nuclear programme has been a relatively high level of neglect by international bodies. Thus, between 1979 and 1995, Iran spent $20 billion on looking after refugees but received almost no help from the UNHCR, which, over the same period, spent $1 billion on Afghan refugees in Pakistan but provided only $150 million for refugees in Iran. By 1999 Iran was spending $10 million a day on refugees, while the UNHCR allocated only $18 million for the year.

No other region of the world faces so many and such complicated problems relating to the movement of people, whether temporary or permanent, economic migrants or refugees, than the countries discussed above.

21
The Asian Periphery: Japan, South Korea and Australia

The three countries dealt with here – Japan, the Republic of Korea (South Korea) and Australia – each, historically, had inward-looking, exclusive policies in relation to immigration. Either they did not want immigrants at all, since they feared they would alter the homogeneous nature of their societies (Japan and South Korea) or, in the case of Australia, only wanted to admit immigrants of an acceptable racial origin, the White Australia policy. Japan had long been an exclusive society, although from the mid-nineteenth century onwards there had been a steady stream of migrants to the United States, motivated by the desire to learn Western commercial and industrial know-how so as to enable Japan to 'catch up' with the technologically advanced West. During the first half of the twentieth century until Japan's defeat at the end of the Second World War in 1945, Korea had been in a colonial relationship with Japan, a consequence of which was a sizeable Korean migrant population settled in Japan. Australia, at that time, saw itself as an outpost of the British Empire and Commonwealth, and sought to bolster its small population on a continent-sized territory by encouraging white immigration, especially after the Second World War, when it had realised how defenceless it was against a militarist Japan. However, to cope with the changing world that followed the Second World War, all three had to alter their perceptions of immigration and open their doors, however reluctantly, to immigrants who were needed to boost their economies, to support ageing populations and to accommodate the new expectations of their neighbours.

JAPAN

Japan's economic success and rapid growth after the Second World War led to greater external migration. By 1990 about 11 million Japanese had gone abroad: 80 per cent of these went as tourists, mainly to other Asian countries and North America. At the same time some 663,100 Japanese were then living abroad, of whom about 75,000 had permanent foreign residency. And 200,000 had gone abroad in 1990 for extended periods of study and research or on business assignments. This outward movement of an increasing number of Japanese was beginning to undermine the country's reputation for insularity. At the same time, the government had persistently adopted tight measures of control over immigrants, although acute labour shortages during the boom years of the 1980s resulted in many immigrants being allowed into the country on temporary or short-term contracts. In addition, many tourists to Japan outstayed their visas. However, control measures appeared ineffective in relation to clandestine Chinese immigration into Japan.

During the decade of the 1990s Japan suffered a prolonged recession or economic downturn that affected all ranks of employees. The concept of security for life offered by the big corporations had to be re-evaluated. Many Japanese firms had come to rely upon overseas recruits to do the lower-paid, unskilled jobs that indigenous workers were not prepared to take. Between 1991 and 2001 unemployment had increased from 2.1 per cent in 1991 to 3.4 per cent in 1996 to 5 per cent in 2001, yet the number of foreign workers continued to rise. In March 2002, the Ministry of Health, Labour and Welfare estimated that the number of foreign workers then in Japan numbered 710,000, equivalent to just over 1 per cent of the work force. The figure included 100,000 professionals and skilled workers as well as 54,000 with 'entertainment' visas.

In 1990 Japan adopted a policy designed to attract back to Japan what had come to be called Nikkeijin: Japanese migrants who had settled in South America, especially in Brazil and Peru. By opening its doors to Nikkeijin the government hoped to halt the growth of unauthorised immigration. The Nikkeijin from Brazil and Peru were regarded as Japanese returning home. Thus, the 1990 Immigration Control Act allowed second- and third-generation people of Japanese descent easier access to residential visas and placed no work restrictions upon them. Employers in need of additions to their work force made determined efforts to recruit these Nikkeijin and, by 2000, some 250,000 from Brazil and a further 46,000 from Peru had become resident in Japan.

In general, immigration into Japan has been small scale. From 1975 some 10,000 Indo-Chinese came to Japan as refugees. By the mid 1990s there were 1.3 million registered aliens in the country and of these 690,000 were Koreans. After the Koreans, the second largest group of registered aliens were 150,000 Chinese. Now about 42,000 foreigners are entering Japan on an annual basis to become permanent residents. However, the number of illegal aliens is probably higher.

In 2003, of 2 million foreigners in Japan, half were Korean and Chinese, many of whom belonged to long-established communities, while of the remainder, 300,000 were Nikkeijin from Brazil and Peru. Any attempt to quantify and regulate immigrants always reveals the inconsistencies of such policies. In Japan, for example, despite high unemployment, there is a range of jobs that Japanese workers will not touch and these have to be done by foreign migrants; these jobs are defined as difficult, dangerous or unpleasant. As some Brazilian Japanese workers have claimed: 'If you stay for a couple of years, you can buy a house, buy land and have capital to start a business [in Brazil].' In the years since the law was changed in 1990, Brazilian immigrants have moved on from jobs in factories to a much wider range of occupations. Immigrant workers have become a significant segment of the labour pool and provide many of the low-skilled and semi-skilled workers that the country needs. However, with the recession continuing into the new century, employment opportunities for the Nikkeijin fell and they were forced to turn to 'indirect employment', a euphemism for temporary contract work. Surveys by the Ministry of Health, Labour and Welfare revealed that foreign workers in contract jobs accounted for more than 40 per cent of the total number of foreign workers. The availability of Nikkeijin workers and their readiness to accept less than favourable working conditions has acted as a cushion for manufacturing industries in times of recession. They have proved to be a reliable source of flexible labour.

Most of the visa 'overstayers' have come from other Asian countries: Korea, China, the Philippines, Thailand, Malaysia and Iran. These are the immigrants prepared to do the jobs that others avoid. Despite being aware of the large numbers of immigrants who overstay their visas, Japan's immigration authority simply lacked the manpower to round them up for deportation and were no doubt also influenced by the fact that such workers were helping to keep firms afloat. Those who were deported were likely to be immigrants who willingly surrendered to the authorities, either because they had saved enough money for their needs back in their own countries or because they had no job and saw little chance of obtaining another. Even so, at the beginning of the new century there were an estimated 230,000 'overstayers'. Despite the official government position relating to illegal immigrants, businesses developed various strategies to survive the recession and one was to seek and use cheap foreign labour.

By the early 2000s, the policy of attracting Nikkeijin from South America had run into difficulties, since most Japanese Brazilians who had been prepared to move back to Japan had already done so and benefited from the move, while those who had remained in Brazil were doing well enough to want to stay. As a result, Japan had to turn increasingly to its neighbours in Southeast Asia and was beginning to realise that various sectors of its economy needed migrant workers despite the long-standing Japanese opposition to foreign incomers. Immigrants, for example, have become a major component of the care sector, which has been expanding for years to meet the needs of an ageing population. Current UN estimates suggest that, by 2050, Japan will have more than 33 million old people needing some form of care. Like other developed economies, Japan would like to exclude low-skilled immigrants while at the same time it looks for highly skilled foreign workers for its IT industries: companies are recruiting from India and, increasingly, from China. A further development, with uncertain implications for the future, is the exodus of Japanese companies to China, where labour is cheap: factories are established in China, while company headquarters remain in Japan.

Most important for the future, Japan has a declining population and this must become the most significant factor leading to the recruitment of more foreign workers to meet the needs of the economy. UN calculations suggest that to compensate for its declining birth rate (the country is expected to decline by 22 million to 2050) Japan will require replacement migration equivalent to 381,000 foreign workers every year to that date.

Since 1880 more than 1 million Japanese have emigrated. About 70 per cent of these migrants went to the United States or Hawaii in the years prior to the Second World War. Emigration continued after the war and was encouraged as a way of relieving population pressures upon the economy until full recovery provided more and more job opportunities at home. From the early 1970s, the number of Japanese emigrants rose again: 12,445 in 1975, 34,492 in 1985 and 82,619 in 1992. In 1999 net emigration worked out as 0.34 migrants per 1,000 of the population. At the same time there was fairly massive internal migration from the rural areas to the three major population centres of Tokyo, Osaka and Nagoya.

Japan has been criticised by the UNHCR for its attitude towards refugees and asylum seekers. In 2005, for example, the government decided to deport two Kurdish asylum seekers who had been granted refugee status by the UNHCR. The Japanese Justice Ministry claimed that the UNHCR decree was not legally binding and that the deportations had been 'conducted in precise accordance with the law'. The *Japan Times* of 21 January 2005 reported that there were no official figures available for the number of people who had been granted official refugee status in Japan in 2004, though independent sources claimed it was only 16. In 2003, just 26 people were either given refugee status or special residence permits.

The world recession that began in 2007 had a major impact upon Japan just when it might otherwise have begun to climb out of its long period in the economic doldrums. One result was the launch of a new programme that targeted the South American (Nikkeijin) immigrants who had been specifically encouraged to return to Japan since 1990. By 2009, they numbered 366,000. They were now encouraged to leave the country and return to South America. Critics denounced the programme as short-sighted, inhumane and a threat to what little progress Japan had made in opening its economy to foreign workers. Hidenori Sakanaka, director of the Japan Immigration Policy Institute, said of the policy: 'It's a disgrace. It's cold-hearted.' He added, 'And Japan is kicking itself in the foot. We might be in recession now, but it's clear it doesn't have a future without workers from overseas.' Under an emergency programme, introduced in April 2009, these Nikkeijin guest workers were offered $3,000 towards their airfare, plus $2,000 for each dependent, but they would not be able to reapply for a work visa in the future. Jiro Kawasaki, a former health minister and senior law-maker of the ruling Liberal Democratic Party, said: 'There won't be good employment opportunities for a while, so that's why we are suggesting that the Nikkei Brazilians go home.' He went on to say that the economic slump provided a good opportunity to overhaul Japan's immigration policy. 'We should stop letting unskilled workers into Japan ... I do not think that Japan should ever become a multiethnic society.'[1]

REPUBLIC OF KOREA (SOUTH KOREA)

Situated between three of Asia's giants – China, Japan and Russia – Korea was divided into North and South by the exigencies of Cold War politics, a division that has lasted for more than six decades. During the years of Japanese colonial rule from 1910 to 1945 large numbers of Koreans emigrated to settle in China, Japan and Russia, and the communities formed at that time still exist. The defeat of Japan in 1945 saw the re-emergence of an independent Korea but this was promptly divided along the 38th parallel of latitude into North Korea (communist influenced) and South Korea (Western influenced). In 1950, when the parameters of the Cold War were already in place, North Korea invaded South Korea to spark the devastating Korean War (1950–53), which, among other things, saw 10 million Koreans move from North to South. In the four decades that followed the war, South Korea raised itself from a base of destruction and poverty to become one of the Asian Tigers. Today it is an industrialised, prosperous, export-oriented country with the thirteenth largest economy in the world and an average (2009) gross national income (GNI) of US $19,690. By the early 1990s, with a low rate of unemployment and a work force that was increasingly unwilling to take on the dirtiest, most menial occupations, South Korea was forced to seek unskilled labour from elsewhere. This need for foreign labour posed an immediate political problem since South Korea prided itself on its homogeneity. The need for foreign labour had to be offset against the desire to remain ethnically pure. The only way this could be achieved was by the imposition of strict immigration policies.

Following the Asian financial crisis of 1997, the government accepted the need for temporary foreign workers to be recruited to work in certain sectors of the economy that otherwise would find survival difficult. As in Japan, despite rising unemployment, few Koreans were prepared to take the lowliest jobs. At the same time, despite general hostility to immigrants, South Korea was prepared to welcome skilled workers and allow them to reside in the country on a long-term 'temporary' basis. The real problem, as the government saw it, was how to control temporary unskilled foreign workers at the lowest levels of the economy. Paradoxically, the government developed various schemes to upgrade the skills of foreign workers. These included an Industrial Trainee Scheme, an Employment Management Scheme and an Employment Permit Scheme. These schemes to improve the lot of foreign workers were designed to regularise their position and, by enhancing their skills, make it more attractive for them to sign on officially. At the same time, employers who sought to use unskilled foreign labour had first to show that they had spent the minimum of a month trying to find a Korean worker for the job. In pursuit of foreign workers whose movements could be controlled, South Korea has entered into agreements with a number of Asian countries – the Philippines, Sri Lanka, Vietnam, Thailand, Indonesia – that are willing to supply temporary workers. These would be allowed a three-year stay and would then be obliged to leave for a year before returning for a second three-year term. These workers are not permitted to bring their families with them, a measure designed to discourage attempts to stay indefinitely in South Korea. Nonetheless, as with other immigrant receiving countries, an estimated 40 per cent of the total foreign work force in 2004 was undocumented. From the 1990s onwards, an increasing number of migrants from China, the Philippines, Indonesia, Thailand, Vietnam and Mongolia overstayed their visas.

Like Japan, South Korea does not wish to become a multi-ethnic society, but, also like Japan, its economy requires a minimum regular inflow of foreign workers. At the end of 2003, for example, there were 438,000 registered foreign workers in the country, equivalent to just under 1 per cent of the total population of 45 million. There were also many undocumented foreign workers (an estimated 289,000 in 2002), representing 70 per cent of the country's total foreign labour force. Strict migration controls make it increasingly hard for South Korean businesses to fill low-level jobs with legal temporary workers.

Historically, considerably more South Koreans have been emigrating from the country than foreigners coming into it. When in 1965 the USA opened its door to non-European migrants, South Koreans began to migrate to the USA in increasing numbers to study or to embrace a better, more prosperous lifestyle. During the 1970s and 1980s many Koreans went to the Gulf as construction workers to take advantage of the oil boom and were able to return home after a few years with substantial savings. The most popular destinations for permanent migrants from South Korea were the USA (28.4%), China (16.8%), Japan (12.6%), Canada (10%) and Australia (5.1%). Today more than 600,000 South Koreans live in China.

A particular problem for South Korea concerns refugees from North Korea. They are not regarded as refugees but as citizens of the Republic of Korea since North Korea is still seen as part of a single Korea despite the separation dating back to before the Korean War. There are believed to be between 100,000 and 300,000 North Koreans living or hiding in China. China does not see them as refugees but as illegal immigrants. The UNHCR is not allowed access to the region of China where they have settled. The government should give consideration to what might happen at a future date if the two Koreas become reunited. Almost certainly this would lead to a large movement of people from North to South.[2]

AUSTRALIA

Australia has been a major immigrant receiving country, whose continental size suggests a greater capacity to receive and absorb immigrants than is the case. Over the period 1992–3 and 2006–7 a substantial growth in immigration took place. In the former year 30,042 immigrants arrived in Australia, in the latter year 177,600, the highest level on record. The largest numbers were either skilled migrants or family reunification migrants. The spread of places of origin can be illustrated by the figures for 2004–5 when a total of 123,424 people migrated to Australia. Of these, 17,736 came from Africa, 54,804 from Asia, 21,131 from Oceania, 18,220 from the UK, 1,506 from South America and 2,369 from Eastern Europe.[3] The rate of migration into Australia continued to rise through the 2007–10 recession and an estimated 300,000 new migrants were expected to arrive in Australia in the year 2008–9.

However, in March 2009 the government announced a 14 per cent cut in the quota for permanent skilled migrants from 133,500 to 115,000 due to the recession, which threatened further cuts in immigrant quotas.

After the Second World War Australia launched a major immigration programme, which was prompted in part by the fears aroused in the war that the country might have been invaded by Japan. Australia, therefore, adopted a policy of 'populate or perish'. In the ensuing years, hundreds of thousands of displaced Europeans migrated to Australia as well as 1 million people from Britain under the Assisted Migration Scheme or £10 assisted passage scheme. The Assisted Migration Scheme was open to all Commonwealth countries and was then extended to the Netherlands and Italy. For some years after 1945 Australia operated a White Australia policy and the only qualifications required of applicants were that they were aged 45 years or less and enjoyed good health. This policy changed in 1970 when more people wished to migrate to Australia than the government could handle; consequently, all subsidies were abolished and immigration into Australia became more difficult.

By the beginning of the new century the desperate attempts of asylum seekers from Afghanistan and other troubled countries to gain entry to Australia had become a major political issue. The Liberal National Coalition under John Howard fought a successful election campaign that won strong popular support because of its proposed restrictive policy on asylum seekers. Even so, the level of immigration increased during Howard's premiership. The detention of asylum seekers became a controversial issue and there were periodic riots, hunger strikes and demonstrations. Responding to such pressures, the government closed the Woomera detention centre, while making Baxter in South Australia the main detention centre. As more asylum seekers came to Australia, the government declared that the arrival point at Melville Island was to be excised from the country's migration zone, along with many smaller islands that had always been part of Australia. Meanwhile, in return for financial aid, the Island of Nauru agreed to act as a holding centre for would-be migrants to Australia until processing had been completed. At this time such migrants came mainly from Afghanistan and Iraq. Of 300 detainees on Nauru at one point, the majority were Afghans including more than 90 children. Some of them went on a hunger strike leading the Minister for Immigration, Amanda Vanstone, to declare that they were not Australia's responsibility, a view that was confirmed by the Attorney General, Philip Ruddock. The government obtained effective cooperation from Indonesia to prevent the smuggling of people by boat to Australia and by the end of 2003 the practice appeared to have ceased. The asylum issue, which had made headline news in 2003, had virtually disappeared by 2005, when no shiploads of asylum seekers arrived. Moreover, those who had been returned to Nauru were allowed to settle in Australia on temporary protection visas. At the same time, Australia's immigration policy was moving towards one of giving priority to skilled settlers. At this time (2005), the UK had become the largest source of immigrants, followed by New Zealand, while refugees who were accepted under the new dispensation now came mainly from Sudan in Africa.

In December 2005 race riots erupted in Sydney, apparently sparked by an incident a week earlier when Lebanese youths attacked two lifeguards. Some 5,000 white men, many of them drunk, went on a rampage against people of Middle East appearance. The Prime Minister, John Howard, described the violence as 'sickening' but said 'I do not accept there is underlying racism in this country.' He went on to say:

> This nation of ours has been able to absorb millions of people from different parts of the world over a period of some 40 years and we have done so with remarkable success and in a way that has brought enormous credit to this country.[4]

However, tensions between youths of Arab and Middle Eastern descent and white Australians had been rising, linked to anti-Muslim sentiments following the 11 September 2001 terrorist attacks in the USA and the 2002 Bali bomb. Despite claims to the contrary, it was evident that significant strands of racism existed not far below the surface.

In 2006, according to the Australian Bureau of Statistics, a total of 4.9 million, or 24 per cent of the total resident population, had been born outside Australia. They ranged from 1.15 million from Britain to 48,762 from Bosnia-Herzegovina. As in other major immigrant recipient countries, the subject caused wide and often conflicting debate. Thus, Sustainable Population Australia believes that the driest inhabited continent cannot continue to sustain the present level of immigration. Another view holds that Australia is over-populated and for the country to maintain its current standard of living, it should aim for an optimum population of 10 million rather than its present 21 million, or keep to the latter figure but accept a reduced standard of living.

In April 2007 the government entered into what was described as a bizarre and illogical agreement with the USA to 'swap' refugees. The deal would see Asian people intercepted en route to Australia being flown across the world to the USA while Cuban and Haitian refugees hoping for a new life in the USA could be transplanted to Australia. The government claimed that the aim of both countries was to deter illegal immigrants by preventing them from settling in the country of their choice. Only people established as genuine refugees would be eligible for such treatment to a maximum of 400 a year. Critics either denounced the scheme as inhumane or suggested it would backfire by encouraging more rather than fewer people to embark on the dangerous ocean voyage to Australia in the hope they would then be sent to the USA. John Howard, the Prime Minister, said the agreement would drive home the point that the country would not compromise in relation to illegal immigration. The Immigration Minister, Kevin Andrews, said: 'We are concerned to ensure the integrity of our border-protection system ... It's a problem that many countries around the world share, and that's why we're trying to find regional, if not global, solutions.'[5] Later in the year the government devised tests to help newcomers 'integrate' more fully. Prospective citizens would have to demonstrate an understanding of the English language and answer 20 questions from a potential bank of 200. Anyone giving fewer than 12 correct answers would not receive a passport. A 40-page pamphlet published in August detailed these new procedures. As Kevin Andrews said of the pamphlet, 'It emphasises that those becoming a citizen in Australia have an overriding commitment to Australia, to our laws, to our values and to our community.'[6] There was a significant change in approach to immigration matters at the end of the year, when the new Labor government of Prime Minister Kevin Rudd came to power and began to dismantle the policy of its predecessor, adopting a far more humane approach towards asylum seekers, a majority of whom would no longer be detained. Mandatory detention would only apply to those who 'pose a threat to the wider community'.

Over the decade to 2007 the number of Britons migrating to Australia more than doubled and in 2006–7 23,000 arrived in the country, partly in response to an Australian recruitment drive that aimed to attract skilled workers. According to Paul Arthur, the director of the Emigration Group, a company specialising in the relocation of Britons to Australia, 'There are excellent job opportunities and the economy in Australia is booming; they need skilled traders and professionals and they prefer Brits.' His statement highlights two constants of migration: the search for skills and the preference for people of a particular ethnic group. Australia, however, did not escape the impact of the recession and in October 2008 Prime Minister Rudd said: 'As with all previous governments ... whenever we set immigration targets, we will adjust them according to economic circumstances of the day'. In February 2009, the government announced a cutback in immigration for the first time in eight years.

The Labor government gave priority to attracting immigrants with skills and new measures came into force on 1 January 2009. These included: giving priority to processing skilled immigrants; providing state and territory governments with greater scope to address their own skill needs; giving priority to people who apply without a sponsor where they have an occupation on a list of skills in critical shortage.

Australia has long given priority to maintaining a tight immigration policy.

22
Tentative Conclusions

There are always huge challenges, both social and political, to be met when migration on any scale takes place. Much migration, though by no means all of it, mirrors the interface between the rich and poor divisions of world society. The economic, social and cultural end question is how people fit into the society to which they have migrated. Do they integrate or do they become part of a multiculturally divided society? There are special connections between countries. France is the target country for migrants from much of North Africa, just as the other former colonial powers of Europe – Britain, the Netherlands Spain, and Portugal – are the destinations of choice for migrants from their one-time colonies. Any assessment of the value of migrants to their new countries must take account of age. The majority of economic migrants are aged between 21 and 35 years and thus are most able to make a positive contribution to the host country. A new factor of huge importance to migration is the development of all forms of electronic communications: television in particular has revealed the affluence of the advanced economies to would-be migrants in some of the poorest corners of the world, while it is now possible to learn from the web details of entry requirements for most countries worldwide.

A significant proportion of all migrants begin as students: they go to North America or Europe for training (and, in the process, help to boost the revenues of the universities or other institutes of learning they attend) and then are tempted to remain in the country where they have been trained. The United States, in particular, has long increased its resource of engineers and scientists by offering foreign students careers that they find difficult to refuse. It is one way in which the United States has kept ahead of its rivals, but the gain for America is a loss for the country from which the student came for his advanced education.

A number of countries have become halfway houses for migrants heading elsewhere: Mexico for Latin Americans aiming for the United States; Morocco for Africans heading for the EU; France for migrants aiming for Britain. In cases where the migrant is unable to cross the last border or frontier, he may settle for good in the halfway house. It is often asked why professionals whose services are urgently needed in their own countries will, nevertheless, migrate to rich countries. They do so, of course, for better pay, conditions and opportunities, but should not be blamed for exercising the right to move in the same way that people from the rich countries of Europe have also moved to still richer countries offering better opportunities such as the United States. Over the first decade of the present century, certain countries in Europe, such as Italy and Spain, overwhelmed by the numbers of illegal migrants to be processed, have instead granted amnesties. Yet this humane and practical approach to one aspect of the problems relating to illegal immigrants has been condemned by other EU countries, since they regard it as an invitation to yet more illegal immigration.

Economic realities are the driving force for most migration: 'going where the jobs are'. Fears of being swamped by immigrants, mainly a concern of the rich, developed economies, are always exaggerated: first, because a significant proportion of all economic migrants intend to return home after saving enough money for their needs or to meet their aspirations; and, second, if the job opportunities dry up there is no reason to remain and they either return home or seek another country where they can obtain work. Migration, in other words, is matched to work force needs. If an economy is growing it will suck in migrants, especially those who do not seek permanent residence. A controversial question concerns developed countries poaching professionals such as doctors, engineers, teachers, and nurses from poor developing countries. These personnel represent a loss to their countries of origin although this is partially compensated for by the remittances they send back to families and friends. Remittances have become a sizeable regular addition to poor countries' budgets and, over the first decade of the twenty-first century, have been worth more than the combined flow of foreign direct investment and aid to those countries. Migrant remittances have become an important economic factor for a range of poor countries and they both encourage their 'surplus' people to emigrate so as to earn and send money back while at the same time they may discourage migrants from returning home, even if they have skills that are wanted, instead preferring their remittances as an input into the economy. Some developing countries can ill afford to lose trained professionals but others, such as Indonesia or the Philippines, are relaxed about outward migration if it relieves the pressure upon the government of massive unemployment. According to UN estimates most 'natural' population increases over the period to 2050 will occur in the developing countries and these are likely to be adversely affected by the impact of globalisation and poverty that will persuade many people to migrate if they are able to do so.

Attitudes towards immigrants will be determined, at least in part, by what the individual can actually contribute to his adopted home. In most immigrant receiving countries, despite much, often mindless opposition, immigrants represent a net gain for their new country and this applies as much to unskilled as it does to professional immigrants. Countries with ageing populations and static rates of growth, where the working population becomes smaller in relation to the under 15s and over 65s, should welcome immigrants to bolster the work force. An important question for the future is how many job opportunities will be created as populations increase in size or how much will the use of advanced technology rather than extra jobs fill the gaps? At the present time a number of European countries, plus Russia and Japan, have declining populations that are also ageing, so that a contracting work force will have to support an increasing population of old people. Such countries will require replacement migration to maintain their lifestyles. These ageing populations will require carers at different levels; already, many immigrants have taken on caring roles and do them well.

Over the years 1990–2010 a huge movement of people occurred worldwide. Some were refugees, asylum seekers or internally displaced people fleeing wars or other disasters, but the majority were economic migrants seeking a better life in countries other than their own. Some hoped to settle permanently in a new country, others saw themselves as temporary migrants, trying to earn more than they could in their home country. A great deal of all movement is internal migration, which consists of an exodus from rural areas to urban areas where work and higher pay can be found. Since it opened up its economy under Deng Xiaoping, China has witnessed the greatest concentrated internal migration in history.

One negative reaction to this huge movement of people has been the construction of walls or barriers along national borders in an attempt to keep illegal migrants out or at least force them to go to recognised border crossing points where they can be checked and either provided with visas or turned back. The United States has constructed a barrier along its border with Mexico, Thailand with Myanmar, India with Bangladesh. It is doubtful that, in the long run, they will achieve much except to persuade the people they are designed to stop that the other side of the fence is preferable. Walls can be bypassed and erecting them will work as much as a challenge as a deterrent. These barriers tell us as much about the country they are designed to protect as they do about the migrants hoping to gain entry. At the beginning of 2010 Israel announced its intention of constructing fences in Sinai between its territory and Egypt to control the movement of African migrants. Each of these fences reflects a world that is only beginning to understand that globalisation is not just about finance and markets but also about people.

The benefits immigrants contribute to the society of their choice almost always outweigh the problems and negative consequences that might attend their arrival. Thus, the impact of migrants on fertility rates is advantageous to a host country, especially one suffering from an ageing or a static population, since it leads to an increase in births both among the immigrants themselves and in the host population. Some policies have both negative and positive results, while their long-term impact is difficult to assess. How far does multi-culturalism make sense as a policy as opposed to a more rigid demand that immigrants should integrate as quickly as possible to become American or British or Dutch? Most migrants, whether international or internal, move to cities. In the course of the last few years, the world has passed a turning point of huge significance: for the first time in history most people now live in towns or urban areas. The movement of large numbers in search of work to towns and cities leads inevitably to the creation of slums and shantytowns, and also promotes the creation of ghettos that attract particular nationalities or ethnic groups. In these circumstances, exploitation and abuse of immigrants, especially those who are illegal, by ruthless employers create conditions that play into the hands of criminal organisations. At the same time there has been a gradual but de facto acceptance in many countries of both the need for illegal migrants and the importance of protecting their rights.

Since the terrorist attacks upon New York and Washington on 11 September 2001 the threat of terrorism has provided another argument for limiting immigrants, especially when they are moving into Western countries from Arab or Muslim societies. Fear of terrorism, whether justified or not, has led to an increase in border and customs controls that inevitably affects would-be migrants adversely. One approach that is designed to limit the flow of migrants from poor to rich countries is to argue for a much greater provision of economic aid to developing countries so as to assist them achieve what we have come to call sustainable development. This solution, however, does not bear serious examination. In the first place, the record of aid donors has almost never lived up to expectations and the UN Millennium Development Goals, for example, simply have not been met. Second, even supposing a massive increase in aid were to be forthcoming, its effects would not deal with the poverty problem in a generation and would make little or no difference to the present rate of migration.

The psychology of those who would restrict migration is usually negative. Despite all the barriers to movement that are erected by target countries, once people decide to move, they move, and the hardships suffered by movers are a measure of their desperation. Moreover, highly qualified migrants are prepared to take menial jobs way below their qualifications as the starting point of their new lives. Too often the concern of politicians and other decision makers centres upon how to keep migrants out rather than how best to utilise their skills. Vocal anti-immigrant minorities in countries like Britain or Germany exercise a political influence out of all proportion to their importance. If they make enough noise, politicians take account of their views rather than those of the majority. And, of course, desperate migrants will put themselves outside the law by overstaying their tourist visas, by falsifying papers and creating non-existent family ties.

The importance of the race factor should not be underestimated. Many countries would prefer to maintain a homogeneous society based upon the same background and ethnic origin, but this is becoming increasingly difficult, as Japan has discovered. Closely allied to arguments about race are those pertaining to religion. The world is witnessing the revival of religions in a number of ways: Hindu extremists attacking Christians in India; the Taliban fighting to impose purity in Afghanistan; Christian and Muslim confrontations in Nigeria; Christian fundamentalists in the American Bible Belt trying to impose their views on American society as a whole – all create barriers to the acceptance of migrants. Migration has created its own group of crimes: people smuggling, fraud in the falsification and forgery of passports or visas, people trafficking, the blackmail of illegal immigrants by unscrupulous contractors and businessmen, bribery and corruption of border guards, customs officers and police.

Is it possible to globalise the world financially, economically, in terms of property ownership or control of multinational corporations, yet not globalise the movement of people – and their right to move? Generally, it is the fittest, most ambitious people who migrate in search of a better life. They leave gaps in the countries from which they emigrate and yet, by removing themselves, they also create opportunities for others, especially in countries where poverty means that employment, even if they possess professional skills, is not always available. Developed countries, while claiming to have equitable immigration policies, in fact keep out the unskilled but cream off the skilled. Despite sometimes violent antagonism to immigrants there also exist levels of ambiguity that derive from the impact they may have in particular communities or professions. Poverty is at the root of migration and this emerges clearly from an examination of the relationship between North and South, the rich world and the poor world. Wherever poverty can be eradicated many of the reasons for moving would disappear, but to expect this to occur on a worldwide basis is utopian. Massive levels of migration, fuelled by greater knowledge and cheap travel, will continue as an international political problem into the foreseeable future.

If we examine how particular countries see migration issues we find wide variations in their approach. In the Americas, the United States from its birth was an immigrant country and has always been energised by its immigrants, who have been regarded as a major source of population growth and cultural enrichment throughout its history. As always, however, there are many Americans who would like to hold back the changes that come with large numbers of immigrants, while business welcomes incomers who provide it with cheap labour. The 11 September 2001 terrorist attacks created a suspicion of would-be immigrants from Arab or Muslim countries and that is liable to last as long as what the Americans see as the 'war on terror' persists, while black immigrants now regularly reinforce the black populations in a range of US cities, although they still have to come to terms with a long and often brutal history of discrimination.

The close historical and geographical ties that bind the United States and Mexico mean that migration from Mexico to the United States, legal or illegal, falls into a special category of its own. Mexicans are changing the make-up of the United States; there are now reckoned to be 23 million of them, the majority spread through towns of the southwest in some of which Spanish has become the accepted language of the majority. Controlling the 2,000 mile border between the two countries is a thankless task, while the erection of a wall or barrier by the United States is seen as much as a challenge as it is a deterrent by migrants seeking a better life, or just a well-paid job in their rich neighbour. However Americans respond to these Mexican migrants, they are bringing about a permanent change in the ethnic composition of the country, as well as adding a Latin dimension to a predominantly Anglo-Saxon culture.

Brazil, a coming economic superpower, has witnessed huge internal migration from the rural to the urban areas and, as its wealth increases, so it is attracting migrants from its poorer South American neighbours. Historically, with Argentina and Uruguay, Brazil has seen periodic influxes of Europeans and, in the 1930s for example, a significant intake of Japanese migrants. Over recent years, however, there has been a contra-flow of South Americans to Europe, especially Spain and Italy, and Japanese Brazilians (the Nikkeijin) to Japan – immigrants or their descendants returning to their former mother countries.

Canada, like its giant neighbour to the south, has a similar history of migration and, despite its strong links to its two colonial creators, Britain and France, has become one of the most ethnically diverse countries in the world. The Caribbean Islands, small, poor, with few economic assets have long been a source of migrants heading for North America and Europe.

European attitudes towards immigrants have undergone profound changes in recent years as the EU has developed into the second great centre of economic wealth after the United States. Since 2000, Europe has become increasingly restrictive in a 'globalising' world and developed a fortress mentality that would put up barriers against those who seek a better life within this economic superpower. Europeans should not forget that, historically, they spread to all parts of the world as migrants and this applies most especially to the Portuguese, the Spanish, the Dutch, the French and the British. They may try to create a fortress to limit immigration from the poor world, but the geographical reality – the Mediterranean, Atlantic, North Sea, Baltic and huge land border with Russia and Asia – make this impossible. The temptation to turn Europe into a fortress has certain political attractions in an age when the population of the developing world is exploding, but closing the doors is a retrograde policy and doomed to fail. When the Big Bang occurred in 2004, and the EU embraced ten new member states, fears were expressed by the wealthy Western members that they would be flooded with work seekers from the former Eastern bloc countries. Now if the rich EU members could react like that towards European countries that had been invited to join the Union, it is not surprising that much greater reluctance is shown with regard to the possibility of large-scale migration from the South. The British were especially susceptible to such fears and thought they were justified when large numbers of Poles came to the country seeking work. Within a short time, however, as the recession began to bite, half these Polish work migrants returned home, illustrating by their action one of the fundamental aspects of all migration: if there are jobs available, migrants will move to them; when these dry up (as they did in Britain) the migrants will go home.

A number of European countries have virtually static populations and migrants will be needed to bolster the work force to produce the wealth needed to care for an ageing population. This is one of several problems that the EU as a whole needs to face, but as yet the EU has no central, viable immigration policy. Statements of intent, even if agreed, are put aside when the specific fears or needs of an individual country have to be addressed. The interface between 'Christian' Europe and the Muslim world necessarily affects attitudes towards immigrants from Arab or other Muslim countries. Spain, Italy, Malta and Greece have become transit countries for immigrants from the South. Both Spain and Italy, faced with large numbers of illegal migrants, solved the logistics of dealing with them by offering an amnesty.

The other EU countries to the north reacted with anger; they complained that the illegal migrants should have been sent back to the countries from which they had come whereas the amnesty meant they were free to travel north in search of work.

Libya, meanwhile, had become a principal jumping off point for Europe for migrants who had crossed the Sahara in their determination to gain access to Europe. The Europeans then proposed to a less than amenable Libya that such migrants should be put in holding camps where they could be processed. The EU also suggested that job centres for potential migrants should be set up elsewhere in Africa. Europe, despite its vaunted liberalism, was battening down and becoming increasingly hostile to African and other immigrants from the South, yet desperate boat people continued to cross the Mediterranean at great risk to their lives.

Britain, whose media and politicians sometimes behave as though it were the only country targeted by migrants, has always been both a source of migrants to many parts of the world and the recipient of immigrants and refugees through much of its history and that is as it should be. Germany has a different history. Following the end of the Second World War, millions of Germans from Russia, Central Asia and the Ukraine moved westwards, the majority ending in what became West Germany. Then, during the years of the German 'Economic Miracle' (the 1950s and 1960s) guest workers from Turkey, Spain, Italy and Portugal were invited in to provide essential labour. Those from Spain, Italy and Portugal later returned to their own countries as their economies improved, but many of the Turks remained in Germany and represent a high proportion of the Muslim minority in the country. France, with an estimated Muslim minority of 4 million to 5 million (the largest in the EU), mainly from the North African territories of Morocco, Algeria and Tunisia, is determined to maintain itself as a secular society but failed to integrate its Muslims, with the result that in November 2005 there was an explosion of anger in the suburbs of Paris and other major cities on the part of second- and third-generation immigrants who felt excluded from the mainstream of French life. Once immigrants have been accepted in any society they should not simply be treated as units of labour at the bottom of the work scale but must be educated and given opportunities to rise. If this does not happen antagonism towards an unfair state system is liable to explode in violence as it did in France. There are an estimated 20 million Muslims in the EU and their presence raises many issues: multiculturalism, emancipation of women, freedom of religion, the application of the same law to everyone – in fact, all the problems once described in relation to the United States as those of the melting pot. Some of the smallest countries in Europe, fearful of large-scale immigration, have tended to be ultra-chauvinistic in their attitudes: Denmark, some of whose politicians would keep it as homogeneously Nordic as possible, caused a furore when a newspaper published cartoons of Muhammad, while the Prefect of Thassaloniki, referring to immigrants, said, 'Greeks are born, not made.'

Turkey and Russia pose especially difficult problems for their neighbours. Turkey, a secular state since the Ataturk revolution, has sought membership of the EU since the 1960s and, though negotiations were opened in 2005, European reluctance to allow Turkey to join the club has manifested itself in an array of arguments as well as the stated opposition to its membership by both France and Poland. Germany, more cautiously despite its long connection with Turkey dating back to Bismarck's time, when the Berlin to Baghdad railway was inaugurated, is worried that the financial burden of Turkish entry would fall largely upon its shoulders. The main issues raised by the EU concern Turkey's human rights record, the sustainability of its democracy and the role of the army in public life, but the real issue is religion. The vast majority of Turkey's population of 75 million are Muslims and its entry into the EU would bring the number of Muslims in Europe up from its present 20 million to a figure not far short of 100 million. In terms of migration, Turkey is already a transit route for migrants from Asia into Europe but with entry its citizens would gain the right of free movement into the other countries of the EU.

The collapse of the Soviet Union has led to a huge movement of people: Russians migrating back into Russia from the Central Asian countries such as Kazakhstan or Uzbekistan; Tajiks leaving their poverty-stricken countries to seek work in Russia; migrants from as far east as China transiting through Russia on their way to Europe. Meanwhile, Russia fears uncontrolled Chinese migration into the sparsely populated lands of eastern Russia, while trying to persuade members of the Russian diaspora in its former Soviet republics to return home to help reverse the population decline and, above all, the need for migrants to increase a population that had fallen to 141 million in 2009. If Russia is to maintain its role as a major power situated between the EU in the West and China in the East, it needs as a matter of urgency to increase its population and to do so it must encourage inward migration.

The United States and the European Union are the two poles of attraction for Africans wanting to leave the continent; as far as the EU is concerned the most popular destination countries are Britain, France, Belgium, Spain and Italy, the former colonial powers. There is a large and growing African diaspora in Europe. There has also been an abrupt white exodus from Africa following independence in Angola and Mozambique in the mid 1970s, from Zimbabwe after 1980 and from South Africa after 1994. Many routes that are often hazardous and dangerous, from Africa to Europe, have been developed across the Sahara through Libya, Morocco and Egypt. Borders in Africa were imposed during the colonial era but have never been treated as rigid divisions, for there has always been a significant degree of cross-border mobility. Africa can least afford to lose its skilled personnel and professionals, but they are regularly enticed northwards into the EU, which snaps them up. The slave trade created a huge African diaspora in the Americas though in recent years more African migrants have been landing in the United States than in the heyday of the slave trade.

Problems from country to country vary considerably. Morocco has a substantial diaspora in the EU – mainly in Spain and France – but is also a halfway destination for migrants heading for Europe. Many of these migrants, who cannot find the money to finance the final leg of their journey, opt instead to settle in Morocco. The Horn of Africa has suffered decades of warfare – civil wars in Ethiopia, Sudan and Somalia, wars between Eritrea and Ethiopia or Ethiopia and Somalia – with the result that the region has witnessed an exodus of many hundreds of thousands of its people as migrants or refugees to other parts of Africa, Europe and the United States. There is a substantial diaspora of Nigerians to other parts of the continent, Europe and the Americas. The calamitous history of the Congo and the ethnic strife and bitterness that have characterised the histories of Burundi and Rwanda have in their turn produced a wave of refugees and migrants in Central Africa and much farther afield.

In modern times, South Africa has been an immigrant receiving country since the Dutch landed at the Cape in the middle of the seventeenth century. They then brought in Malays from their East Indian Empire. The British took the Cape from the Dutch during the Napoleonic wars and kept it when the war came to an end. To escape the British the Dutch farmers or Boers trekked into the interior and established two republics – the Orange Free State and the Transvaal – by which time they described themselves as Afrikaners. Meanwhile, major migrations had taken place among the Zulus and Xhosa, who in their turn caused widespread movement as tribes trekked to avoid the depredations of Shaka Zulu. During the last third of the nineteenth century the discovery of huge deposits of gold and diamonds led to an influx of miners and adventurers from Europe to add to the ethnic mix which has persisted to the present time. The wealth of South Africa, based upon gold, diamonds and a range of other minerals, turned it into a magnet for economic migrants from much of the continent to the north. For many Africans, seeking to escape poverty in their own countries, South Africa has been an attraction as great as Europe and estimates of illegal immigrants in the country have ranged from 3 million to 10 million, though the latter figure is excessive. Zimbabwe to the north has suffered economic collapse as well as many human rights violations under the rule of Robert Mugabe; an estimated 4 million of its people migrated into South Africa during the first decade of this century.

The rapid expansion of the Asian economies over the last 30 years has led to major migrations in the region, both country to country in search of work and internal from rural to urban areas. China has used migration as a political/economic weapon in the peripheral territories of Tibet and Xinjiang that it wants to integrate fully into the country. The official size of the Chinese worldwide diaspora is 40 million, though other estimates suggest a total figure of 60 million, equivalent to the population of Great Britain. Such a large diaspora is seen as an important political asset in Beijing. The huge expansion of Chinese activity in Africa – aid, investment and trade – has been followed by up to 1 million Chinese who have moved into the continent in recent years, leading Africans to query whether this is not a new form of imperialism. Inside China the movement of people from the rural areas to the towns has developed into the largest internal migration in history.

India also has a worldwide diaspora of about 25 million and regards it as an asset, partly because the remittances are a welcome addition to the economy and partly because its professional overseas migrants become sources of expertise and knowledge that is transmitted back to India; at the end of the first decade of the twenty-first century India was benefiting from a reverse brain drain. A different aspect of migration concerns India's relations with Bangladesh. With a population of 160 million and a per capita GNI of only $470, Bangladesh is both overcrowded and desperately poor. Global warming estimates suggest that by the middle of the present century as much as a third of its low-lying territory will have been lost to rising sea levels and that could trigger a mass migration northwards into India. Bangladeshis were crossing into India in search of work at the rate of 6,000 a week by 2006. In order to control such an influx, India has erected a 2,100-mile barrier along their joint border.

In 2005, Malaysia, one of the better economies of Southeast Asia, rounded up some 500,000 illegal immigrants, mainly from Indonesia and expelled them. Industries then complained that they could not manage without this cheap labour and the Malaysian government was obliged to do an about-face and invite those it had expelled to return. It was a bizarre episode, triggered by local antagonism to incomers, but the consequent upheaval for Malaysia's economy reinforced the argument that unskilled migrants can make valuable contributions to most economies. The Philippines has developed a unique approach to migration under which it positively encourages its citizens to migrate so as to relieve pressures upon its huge unemployment problem and to assist the economy with their remittances, which now make a substantial annual contribution to the economy.

In southwest Asia encompassing Afghanistan, Iraq, the Gulf and stretching to Israel, wars and violence have created the largest concentrations of refugees, asylum seekers and migrants in the world, while the rich oil states of the Gulf have drawn in about 10 million migrants, most of whom are unskilled labourers, for the huge construction programmes in the area.

This round-up of countries illustrates how problems related to immigrants vary widely from country to country and region to region. However, despite the fears, xenophobia and other reservations that the subject of migration raises, immigrants play a major role in world politics and the constant movement of people will not be stopped by negative policies, including the erection of protective walls, which by any standard represents a retrograde step. Migration is a universal phenomenon; it always has been and will continue to be. It may take the form of internal migration (as it is, to a large extent, in present-day China) or international migration, and, despite disasters and civil wars that create large numbers of refugees, the vast majority of movers are economic migrants seeking a better life outside their own countries. To a great extent migration mirrors the world divide between rich and poor. Migrants leave countries where their economic prospects and opportunities are not good and seek a better life in the countries to which they migrate. All too often, debates about migration ignore the fact that almost all migrants are needed in the countries to which they migrate and that they make a positive contribution to the economy and culture of their new host country. The countries which migrants choose should ask how these immigrants can make a contribution to their societies, rather than assuming that they will become an unwanted burden. Migration represents a positive world phenomenon.

NOTES

INTRODUCTION

1. See Population Division of the Department of Economic and Social Affairs of the United Nations Secretariat (2006 Revision).
2. Todd, Malcolm, *Migrants and Invaders*, p. 15, Tempus, 2001.
3. Padayachee, Vishnu (ed.), *The Development Decade?*, p. 371, HSRC Press (Cape Town), 2006.
4. Harding, Jeremy, *The Uninvited*, pp. 60–86, Profile Books, 2000, p. 100.
5. *Ibid.*
6. Sogge, David, *Give and Take: What's the Matter with Foreign Aid?*, p. 45, Zed Books, 2002.
7. Duffield, Mark, *Global Governance and the New Wars*, p. 4, Zed Books, 2001.
8. Macrae, Joanna, *Aiding Recovery*, pp. 34–8, Zed Books, 2001.
9. Cox, Robert, *Understanding Global Disorder*, p. 41, Zed Books, 1996.
10. Comeliau, Christian, *The Impasse of Modernity*, p. 102, Zed Books, 2002.
11. Houtart, François and Polet, François (eds), *The Other Davos*, p. 84, Zed Books, 2001.
12. Huntington, Samuel P., *Who Are We?*, p. 282, Free Press, 2004.
13. Blair, D., *The Daily Telegraph*, 17/03/2007.
14. *The Independent*, 19/04/2006.
15. See Mance, Henry, *One World*, hmance@gmail.com.
16. Harding, *op. cit.*, p. 63.
17. Duffield, *op. cit.*, pp. 109–10.
18. *The Independent*, 28/09/2006.
19. Harding, *op. cit.*, p. 20.
20. *The Times*, 22/09/2007.
21. Macrae, *op. cit.*, p. 34.
22. Bond, Patrick, *Looting Africa*, p. 90, Zed Books, 2006.
23. Ratha, Dilip, World Bank (web), October 2004.
24. Deparle, Jason, *New York Times*, 22/04/2007.

1. THE UNITED STATES

1. Huntington, Samuel P., *Who Are We?*, Free Press, 2004.
2. Wikipedia, 'Immigration to the United States'.
3. Williamson, Jeffry G., *The Political Economy of World Mass Migration*, AEI Press, 2005.
4. *Migration News*, April 2000, vol. 6, no. 2.
5. Babington, Charles, *Washington Post*, 25/03/2000.
6. Roberts, Sam, *New York Times*, 03/03/2005.
7. Census Bureau: Lewis Mumford Center, University of Albany.
8. See Ali Mazrui, *Islam*, James Currey, 2006.
9. *The Independent*, 11/04/2006.
10. *The Observer*, 09/04/2006.
11. *The Independent*, 11/04/2006.
12. *The Independent*, 02/05/2006.
13. Porter, Eduardo, *New York Times*, 13/05/2007.
14. Kraus, Clifford, *New York Times*, 13/05/2007.

2. MEXICO

1. Data Profiles 2002, US Census Bureau.
2. *The Independent*, 14/07/2006.
3. Maderazo, Jennifer Woodward, 'Mexico's Immigration Policy: Hypocritical?' http://vivirlatino.com/2006/06/02/mexicos-immigration-policy-hypocritical.php.
4. *New York Times*, 20/01/2008.
5. Preston, Julia, 'Multimedia', Wed. 14/05/2009.
6. Davidow, Jeffrey, President of the Institute of the Americas in La Jolla, California. Ambassador to Mexico 1998–2002, MexiData, Column 122704, Davidow, 'Immigration, the United States and Mexico'.

3. CANADA AND THE CARIBBEAN

1. The International Adult Literacy and Skills Survey (IALSS), 2005.
2. *Canada's Ethnocultural Portrait: The Changing Mosaic 2001*, Census: analysis series 2003, Statistics Canada catalogue number 96E0030XIE2001012.
3. Statistics Canada Report, *Immigration in Canada: A Portrait of the Foreign-born Population, 2006 Census*.
4. Kraus, Clifford, 'Immigrants in Canada: Have Ph.D., Must Sweep', *International Herald Tribune*, 06/06/2005.
5. Harding, Jeremy, *The Uninvited*, p. 44, Profile Books, 2000.
6. CBC, *News in Depth*, 10/02/2008.
7. *Globe and Mail*, 11/02/2009.

4. SOUTH AMERICA

1. Reid, Michael, *The Forgotten Continent*, p. 7, Yale University Press, 2007.

5. THE EUROPEAN UNION

1. *The Independent*, 19/10/2004.
2. *The Independent*, 25/10/2004.
3. Turmann, Anna, *A New European Agenda for Labour Mobility*, CEPS-ECHR Task Force Report, Brussels, April 2004.
4. *Migration News*, vol. 12, no. 2, April 2005.
5. Castle, Stephen, 'Fall in Population Threatens Economic Future of Europe', *The Independent*, 18/03/2005.
6. *The Observer*, 06/11/2005.
7. Vallely, Paul, *The Independent*, 08/11/2005.
8. *The Independent*, 20/07/2006.
9. Jain, Rajendra K. (ed.), *India and the European Union*, pp. 261–2, Radiant Publishers, 2007.
10. *The Independent*, 24/10/2007.
11. Harding, J., *The Uninvited*, pp. 68–9, Profile Books, 2000.
12. *Ibid.*, p. 67.
13. *Ibid.*, p. 56.
14. BBC, Q&A: EU Immigration Policy, 14/10/2008.
15. Brady, Hugo, *Towards a Better EU Migration Policy*, Centre for European Reform, 08/04/2009.

6. BRITAIN

1. Jain, Rajendra K. (ed.), *India and the European Union*, p. 261, Radiant Publishers, 2007.
2. Harding, J., *The Uninvited*, p. 51, Profile Books, 2000.
3. *The Independent*, 03/11/2006.
4. Jones, Harriett, *Annual Report: United Kingdom*, p. 25, Keesing's Worldwide, 2004.
5. *The Independent*, 21/10/2005.
6. *The Independent*, 09/02/2006.
7. *The Observer*, 27/08/2006.
8. *The Independent*, 30/08/2006.
9. *The Independent*, 07/04/2006.
10. *The Independent*, 02/07/2009.
11. *The Independent*, 17/03/2006.
12. *The Independent*, 19/04/2007.
13. *The Observer*, 18/01/2009.
14. Morris, Nigel, *The Independent*, 08/12/2005.
15. *The Observer*, 11/11/2005.
16. *The Observer*, 05/03/2006.
17. *The Observer*, 26/08/2007.
18. *The Observer*, 22/03/2009.

7. FRANCE AND GERMANY

1. Lichfield, John, *The Independent*, 05/11/2005.
2. *The Observer*, 06/04/2005.
3. *Ibid.*
4. Dejevsky, Mary, *The Independent*, 07/11/2005.
5. Lichfield, John, *The Independent*, 22/12/2005.
6. Bryent, Lish, 'France Tightens Immigration Requirements', Voice of America, 20 September 2007.
7. *Ibid.*
8. Von Stritzky, Johannes, 'Germany's Immigration Policy: From Refusal to Reluctance (ARI)', Real Instituto Elceno, 03/06/2009.
9. Harding, Jeremy, *The Uninvited*, Profile Books, 2000.
10. Sachsenmaier, Dominic, 'Germany Deadlocked Over Immigration Policy', Yale Global, Yale Center for the Study of Globalization, 22/08/2003.
11. *Ibid.*
12. *The Independent*, 01/06/2007.
13. 'OECD Blasts German Immigration Policy', *Deutsche Welle*, 11/09/2008.
14. Stritzky, *op. cit.*

8. SPAIN, ITALY, MALTA, GREECE

1. *The Independent*, 31/05/2005.
2. *The Independent*, 04/10/2005.
3. *The Independent*, 07/10/2005.
4. *The Observer*, 22/01/2006.
5. *The Independent*, 26/06/2007.
6. *New York Times*, 03/05/2009.
7. See Hamilton, Kimberley, 'Italy's Southern Exposure', *Migration Information Source*, May 2002; updated March 2003 with the assistance of Maia Jachimowicz.
8. *Ibid.*
9. Pastore, Ferruccio, 'Italy's Migration Contradiction', *Open Democracy*, 19/02/2004.
10. *The Independent*, 28/08/2004.

11. *The Independent*, 28/09/2004.
12. *The Independent*, 06/11/2007.
13. Popham, Peter, *The Independent*, 03/07/2009.
14. Verney, Susannah, 'Greece', in *The Annual Register 2003*, p. 88.
15. *The Independent*, 05/04/2005.
16. *Financial Mirror*, 03/12/2007.
17. UNHCR, 10/07/2009.
18. See: www.huffingtonpost.com/2009/07/13/greece-cracks-down-on-ill_n_230844.html.

9. EUROPE'S SMALL DEVELOPED STATES

1. Verkaik, Robert, *The Independent*, 27/12/2007.
2. See 'Belgium', in *Annual Review 2003*.
3. See: http://islamineurope.blogspot.com/2007/01/belgian-imarriage-immigration.html.
4. See: www.euractiv.com/en/socialeurope/belgium-legalise-25000-immigrants/article.
5. Statistics Denmark.
6. See: www.eubusiness.com/news-eu/1220245322.26.
7. *The Observer*, 30/03/2008.
8. *The Observer*, 04/05/2008.
9. *The Observer*, 04/05/2008.
10. 'Ireland – Immigration drives population increase', workpermit.com, 07/01/2008.
11. Jain, Rajendra K., *India and the European Union*, p. 200, Radiant Publishers, 2007.
12. 'Europe's Policy Defines Swiss Immigration Laws', Swissinfo.ch, 18/09/2006.
13. Vallely, Paul, *The Independent*, 07/09/2007.

10. EAST EUROPE, TURKEY

1. *A Look at Eastern European Immigration in the EU*, ECAS, 21/09/2005.
2. *The Independent*, 25/04/2006.
3. Quoted in *The Independent*, 22/08/2006.
4. *New York Times*, 03/05/2009.
5. Migration Information Source.
6. *Ibid.*
7. *The Independent*, 24/04/2008.
8. See Poptodorova, Elena, 'Bulgaria's Migration Policy', *Mediterranean Quarterly* vol. 15, no. 4, 2004, pp. 125–32.
9. See: www.romanianpassport.co.il/english/romanian-citizenship-authorities-policy/.
10. See U.S. Agency for International Development Bureau for Humanitarian Responses (BHR), Office of U.S. Foreign Disaster Assistance (OFDA), *Situation Report #1, Fiscal Year (FY) 1998*, 05/12/1997.
11. See: www.euractiv.com/en/enlargement/eu-turkey-immigration-risk-greek-democ-rac.05/08/2009.
12. Statistics taken from a BBC survey of 2005 – see BBC News Line 1, BBC News Channel.

11. RUSSIA

1. See: 'Migration into Russia', *Migration News*, vol.2, no. 4, June 1995.
2. See *The Independent*, 04/05/2006.
3. See Euromonitor, 07/08/2009.
4. Cohen, Ariel, 'Domestic Factors Driving Russia's Foreign Policy', The Heritage Foundation, 19/11/2007, Backgrounder #2084.
5. *Ibid.*
6. See Carnegie-Moscow Centre, vol. 1, issue 08, August 1999.
7. *Ibid.*

8. *Ibid.*
9. Harding, Luke, *The Observer*, 02/08/2009.

12. AFRICA AND EUROPE

1. *The Independent*, 01/08/2006.
2. *The Observer*, 19/04/2006.
3. *The Independent*, 28/05/2007.
4. *The Independent*, 28/05/2007.
5. Commission for Africa, *Our Common Future*, p. 106, quoted in Bond, Patrick, *Looting Africa*, pp. 89–90, Zed Books, 2006.
6. See Chabal, Patrick, *Africa The Politics of Suffering and Smiling*, p. 142, Zed Books, 2009.
7. *Ibid.*, p. 145.
8. See de Haas, Hein, University of Oxford – Migration Information Source (MIS) 2006.
9. *Ibid.*
10. Migration Information Service (MIS) www.migrationinformation.org is one of the best sources for detailed examinations of migration activities.
11. de Haas, Hein, Radbond University Nijwegen, 'Morocco: From Emigration Country to Africa's Migration Passage to Europe' October 2005 (MIS).

13. SUDAN AND THE HORN OF AFRICA

1. See: 'Egypt and Refugees', Wikipedia.
2. Al-Shahi, Ahmed, 'Sudan', in *Annual Register*, ProQuest, 2009.
3. *Sudan Tribune*, 20/07/2009.
4. *Sudan Tribune*, 02/08/20009.
5. See Arnold, Guy, 'Sudan', in *Civil Wars in Africa*, 2nd edn, pp. 353–361, Scarecrow Press, 2008.
6. Human Rights Watch, *War Crimes and Crimes against Humanity in the Ogaden Area*. 2008.
7. *The Observer*, 24/10/2005.
8. *The Independent*, 25/05/2006.
9. *The Independent*, 25/05/2006.
10. Darch, Colin, 'Somalia', *Annual Register*, p. 229, ProQuest 2008.

14. THE CONGO, RWANDA, BURUNDI

1. Hallett, Robin, 'Zaire', *Annual Register*, pp. 265–7, Cartermill International, 1995.
2. *The Economist*, 24/10/1998.
3. *The Independent*, 13/07/2007.
4. *Ibid.*
5. Muggah, Robert, *No Refuge: The Crisis of Refugee Militarisation in Africa*, p. 181, Zed Books, 2006.
6. Turner, Thomas, *Congo Wars: Conflict, Myth and Reality*, p. 155, Zed Books, 2009.
7. *Ibid.*, p. 153.
8. Uvin, Peter, *Life after Violence: A People's Story of Burundi*, p. 185, Zed Books, 2009.
9. Mukombozi, Bonny, *The New Times*, 15/06/2009.
10. See Files (web) 02/09/2009.
11. See Turner, *Congo Wars*, for an examination of UN performance.

15. WEST AFRICA

1. See *Encyclopaedia of the Nations*, www.nationsencyclopedia.com/.
2. See www.nigeriadiaspora.com.

3. *Ibid.*
4. *Ibid.*
5. Reported in Euronet, 10/11/2008.
6. Mason, Ernest, 'EU Opens Immigration Centre in Mali', Radio NederlandWereldomrep, 10/10/2008.
7. Bump, Micah, 'Ghana: Searching for Opportunities at Home and Abroad', *Migration Information Source*, March 2006.
8. See 'Ghana: Migration', *Encyclopaedia of the Nations*, www.nationsencyclopedia.com/.
9. Bump, 'Ghana: Searching for Opportunities at Home and Abroad'.
10. *Ibid.*
11. Buchan, James and Dovlo, Delanyo, *International Recruitment of Health Workers to the UK: A Report for DfID*, February 2004 DFID Health Systems Resource.
12. Source: République du Senegal (2004).
13. BBC 11/10/2006.
14. Fall, Salam, Interview: Naima El Moussaoui Qantara de, 2009.

16. SOUTHERN AFRICA

1. Chabal, Patrick et al., *A History of Postcolonial Lusophone Africa*, p. 187, Hurst, 2002.
2. See BBC News Online 08/11/2005.
3. *The Independent*, 03/08/2006.
4. *The Independent*, 09/08/2006.
5. *The Independent*, 24/11/2006.
6. *The Observer*, 01/07/2007.
7. Arnold, Guy, *Africa: A Modern History*, p. 335, Atlantic Books, 2005.
8. Barber, James, *Mandela's World*, p. 130, James Currey, 2004.
9. *Ibid.*, p. 135.
10. Padayachee, Vishnu, *The Development Decade?*, p. 370, HSRC Press (Capetown).
11. Harding, Jeremy, *The Uninvited*, p. 85, Profile Books, 2000.
12. *The Independent*, 13/10/2006.
13. *The Independent*, 21/05/2008.
14. *Ibid.*
15. Crush, Jonathan, Southern Africa Migration Project (SAMP), July 2008.
16. Source: The Employment Bureau of Africa (TEBA).

PART IV: ASIA

1. Overseas Development Institute, London, paper, *Migration*, 2006.
2. Awad, Ibrahim, Director, Migration Programme of the International Labour Organization.
3. Jaffrolet, Christophe, *The Emerging States*, p. 4, Hurst, 2008.

17. CHINA

1. Mende, Tibor, *China and her Shadow*, p. 208, Thames and Hudson, 1960.
2. *Ibid.*, p. 210.
3. *Ibid.*, p. 211.
4. Clegg, Jenny, *China's Global Strategy*, p. 149, Pluto Press, 2009.
5. *Ibid.*, p. 152.
6. Hutton, Will, *China: The Writing on the Wall*, p. 116, Little Brown, 2007.
7. Overseas Development Institute, London, paper, *Migration*, 2006.
8. China's National Bureau of Statistics.
9. Gao, Mobo, *The Battle for China's Past*, p. 119, Pluto Press, 2008.
10. *Ibid.*, p. 168.
11. *Ibid.*, p. 169.

12. *New York Times*, 19/07/2009.
13. *The Times*, 22/11/2008.
14. Emmott, Bill, *Rivals*, p. 23, Penguin Books, 2009.
15. See: http://en.wikipedia.org/wiki/Overseas-Chinese.
16. Politzer, Malia, 'China and Africa: Stronger Economic Ties Mean More Migration', *Migration Information Source*, August 2008.
17. See Studwell, J., *Asian Godfathers*, Atlantic Monthly Press, 2007.
18. Alden, Chris, *China in Africa*, p. 50, Zed Books, 2007.
19. *Ibid.*, p. 52.
20. Alden, Chris et al. (eds) *China Returns to Africa*, p. 130, Hurst, 2008.
21. *The Guardian*, 11/06/2009.
22. *Ibid.*

18. INDIA

1. 'Migration Issues', International Organization for Migration, 06/04/2007.
2. Jaffrolet, Christophe, *Emerging Nations*, p. 82, Hurst, 2008.
3. Source: High Level Committee on the India Diaspora (2002). Sri Lanka and Nepal: 2001 Census. The numbers are estimates of the diaspora populations including both actual migrants and descendants of migrants.
4. See: Jaffrolet, pp. 80–81.
5. Source: 2006 American Community Survey, U.S. Census Bureau.
6. See Naujoks, Daniel, *Migration Information Source*, October 2001.
7. *Migration News*, vol. 13, no. 1, 01/01/2006.
8. *Ibid.*; Rai, Santha, 'Indians Find They Can Go Home Again', *New York Times*, 26/12/2005; Waldman, Amy, 'India Accelerating: Building a Highway', *New York Times*, 4–7 December 2005.
9. See Pathania, Jioti M., 'India and Bangladesh – Migration Matrix – Reactive and not Proactive', South Asia Analysis Group, 17/03/2003, www.southasiaanalysis.org/%5Cpapers7%5Cpaper632.html.
10. *The Independent*, 12/05/2005.
11. Sunday Times, 11/01/2009.

19. SOUTHEAST ASIA

1. *Annual Register*, pp. 331 et seq., Proquest, 2009.
2. UN Research Institute for Social Development, *Policy Report on Gender and Development: 10 Years after Beijing*, Nicola Piper, Keiko Yamanaka.
3. *Migration News*, September 2002.
4. *Migration News*, April 2004.
5. Huguet, J.W., Punpuing, S.I., *Overview of Thai Migration*.
6. 'South East Asia', *Migration News*, January 2007, vol. 13, no. 1.
7. Migration, International Labour and Multicultural Policies in Singapore, 2007.
8. *Migration News*, 2007.
9. Mageswary, R., 'Malaysia: Unwanted, Migrant Workers Short-changed', Inter Press Service, 19/07/1999.
10. *The Independent*, 27/05/2005.
11. See Hugo, Graeme, 'Indonesia's Labour Looks Abroad', *Migration Information Source*, April 2007.
12. *Ibid.*
13. See Asis, Maruja M.B., 'The Philippines' Culture of Migration', *Migration Information Source*, January 2006.
14. Figures based on combined data for new hires and rehires. Accessed online, 12 September 2005.

15. O'Neil, Kevin, 'Labor Export as Government Policy: The Case of the Philippines', *Migration Information Source*, January 2004.

20. SOUTHWEST ASIA

1. Mustapha Habli, Chief Economist and Director Social and Economic Development Group MENA Region, World Bank, Brussels, 4–5 July 2005.
2. See: *The Independent*, 01/03/2005 for an account of these conditions.
3. www.qatarsucks.com/Article_Abdol—_Moghset_Bani_Kamal.
4. Malik, Mesrine, *The Guardian*, 16/11/2009.
5. BBC Online, 27/02/2008.
6. *The Independent*, 01/12/2009.
7. http://en.wikipedia.org/wiki/Afghan_refugees.
8. 'Afghanistan: What Now for Refugees?', *Asia Report* no. 175, 31 August 2009, www.crisisgroup.org/home/index.cfm?id=6290.
9. *Ibid.*
10. '2010 UNHCR Country Operations Profile – Afghanistan Working Environment', www.unhcr.org/cgi-bin/texis/vtx/page?page=49e486eb6.
11. *The Independent*, 18/04/2007.
12. *The Independent*, 30/07/2007.
13. See Hakimzadeh, S., 'Iran: A Vast Diaspora Abroad and Millions of Refugees at Home', *Migration Information Source*, September 2006, www.migrationinformation.org/feature/display.cfm?ID=424.
14. University of Sussex, 2000 Global Migrant Origin Database.
15. *Global Economic Prospects 2006; Economic Implications of Remittances and Migration*, World Bank.

21. THE ASIAN PERIPHERY

1. *New York Times*, 03/05/2009.
2. See Park, Y., 'South Korea: Balancing Labour Demand with Strict Control', *Migration Information Source*, December 2004.
3. www.migrationinformation.org/datahub/countrydatadata/country.cfm.
4. *The Independent*, 13/12/2005.
5. *The Independent*, 19/04/2007.
6. *The Independent*, 27/08/2007.

Select Bibliography

There is a vast amount of information relating to migration in all its forms to be found through the internet. Migration Information Source is possibly the most valuable internet resource. Most countries have web pages that cover their own laws and regulations concerning migration; many governments and universities have departments dealing with the subject while national census data provides valuable statistical information. The UNHCR – though in theory only concerned with refugees – provides a range of statistics and insights. Migration for many countries is a volatile political subject and for that reason is heavily covered by the press and other media, and much of the information in this book has been garnered from such sources.

Alden, Chris, *China in Africa*, Zed Books, 2007.
Alden, Chris et al., *China Returns to Africa*, Hurst, 2008.
Balisacan, A. M. and G. M. Ducanes, *Inequality in Asia: The Inter-regional Inequality Facility*, London, 2005.
Banton, Michael, *White and Coloured*, Oxford, 1959.
Barber, James, *Mandela's World*, James Currey, 2004.
Bentwich, Norman, *They Found Refuge*, Cresset, 1956.
Black, R., C. Natali and I. Skinner (2005) 'Migration and Inequality'. Equity and Development, World Development Report 2006, Background Papers, Development Research Centre on Migration, University of Sussex.
Bond, Patrick, *Looting Africa*, Zed Books, 2006.
Brook, Colin (ed.), *The Caribbean in Europe*, Frank Cass, 1986.
Chabal, Patrick, *Africa: The Politics of Suffering and Smiling*, Zed Books, 2009.
Chabal, Patrick and Jean-Pascal Daloz, *Africa Works*, James Currey, 1999.
Chabal, Patrick with David Birmingham, Joshua Forrest, Malyn Hewitt, Gerhard Eibert and Elisa Silva Andrade, *A History of Postcolonial Lusophone Africa*, Hurst, 2002.
Chauduri, Nivad, *A Passage to England*, London, 1966.
Cheyette, Brian, *Neither Black Nor White*, Thames & Hudson, 1995.
Clegg, Jenny, *China's Global Strategy: Towards a Multipolar World*, Pluto Press, 2009.
Coleman, D. A. (ed.), *Demography of Immigrant and Minority Groups in the United Kingdom*, Academic Press, 1982.
Comeliau, Christian, *The Impasse of Modernity*, Zed Books, 2002.
Crush, Jonathan – Series Editor, Migration Policy Series, No. 2, SAM Publications/Policy Series/Policy 25, 2007.
Deshingkar, P., A. Winkels, S. Akter and T. C. Thang, 'The Quality of Life of Migrants in Vietnam', paper commissioned by UNFPA, Vietnam, 2006.
Duffield, Mark, *Global Government and the New Wars*, Zed Books, 2001.
Duffy, Maureen, *England: The Making of the Myth*, Fourth Estate, 2001.
Emmott, Bill, *Rivals*, Penguin Books, 2009.
Endelman, T. M., *The Jews of Britain 1656–2000*, University of California Press, 2002.
Foot, Paul, *Immigration and Race in British Politics*, Harmondsworth, 1965.
Gao, Mobo, *The Battle for China's Past: Mao and the Cultural Revolution*, Pluto Press, 2008.
General Statistics Office, *The 2004 Migration Survey: Major Findings, Statistical Publishing House*, Hanoi, Vietnam, 2005.
GHK/IIED, *Study on Urban Poverty for the DFID China Programme*, 2004.
Grant, Bruce, *The Boat People*, Penguin, 1979.
Hannaford, Ivan, *Race*, Johns Hopkins University Press, 1996.
Harris, Nigel, *The New Untouchables: Immigrants and the New World Order*, Penguin, 1995.
Hollifield, James, *Immigrants, Markets and States*, Harvard University Press, 1992.

Houtart, François and Poret, François (eds), *The Other Davos*, Zed Books, 2001.

Huntington, Samuel P., *Who Are We? America's Great Debate*, Free Press, 2005.

Hutton, Will, *The Writing on the Wall: China and the West in the 21st Century*, Little, Brown, 2007.

Jaffrolet, Christophe (ed.), *The Emerging States: The Wellspring of a New World Order*, Hurst, 2008.

Jain, Rajendra K. (ed.), *India and the European Union*, Radiant Publishers, 2007.

Jawara, Fatoumata and Aileen Kwa, *Behind the Scenes at the WTO*, Zed Books, 2003.

Kanbur, R. and A. J. Venables, 'Spatial Inequality and Development Overview of UNU-Wider Project', 2005, http://www.arts.cornell.edu/poverty/kanbur/WIDERProjectOverview.pdf.

Kuhn, R., 'The Logic of Letting Go: Family and Individual Migration from Rural Bangladesh', Working Paper Series 00-09, August. Labor and Population Program, The RAND Institute, 2000.

Legrain, Philippe, *Immigrants: Your Country Needs Them*, Little, Brown, 2007.

MacGaffey, Janet and Remy Bazen Guissa-Ganga, *Congo–Paris; Transnational Traders on the Margins of the Law*, James Currey, 2000.

MacRae, Joanna, *Aiding Recovery*, Zed Books, 2001.

Manby, Bronwen, *Struggles for Citizenship in Africa*, Zed Books, 2009.

Mazrui, Ali A., *Islam between Globalization and Counter-Terrorism*, James Currey, 2006.

Melady, T. P., and M. B. Melady, *Uganda: The Asian Exiles*, Orbis, 1978.

Mende, Tibor, *China and Her Shadow*, Thames and Hudson, 1960.

Mercer, Claire, Ben Page and Martin Evans, *Development and the African Diaspora*, Zed Books, 2008.

Muggah, Robert, *No Refuge: The Crisis of Refugee Militarisation in Africa*, Zed Books, 2006.

Murphy, R., *How Migrant Labor is Changing Rural China*, Cambridge University Press, 2002.

Niessen, Jan et al., *Migrant Integration Policy Index*, The British Council, 2007.

Nzongola-Ntalaja, Georges, *The Congo from Leopold to Kabila*, Zed Books, 2002.

Padayachee, Vishnu (ed.), *The Development Decade?* HSRC Press, 2006.

Parekh, Bhikhu (ed.), *The Future of Multi-Ethnic Britain*, Profile, 2000.

Peterson, Scott, *Me against My Brother*, Routledge, 2000.

Phillips, Caryl, *The European Tribe*, Faber and Faber, 1987.

Phillips, Caryl, *A New World Order*, Secker and Warburg, 2001.

Phillips, Mike and Trevor Phillips, *Windrush: The Irresistible Rise of Multi-racial Britain*, Harper Collins, 1999.

Reid, Michael, *Forgotten Continent: The Battle for Latin America's Soul*, Yale University Press, 2007.

Renton, David, David Seddon and Leo Zeilig, *The Congo: Plunder and Resistance*, Zed Books, 2007.

Schulz, Michael et al., *Regionalisation in a Globalising World*, Zed Books, 2001.

Smith, T. E., *Commonwealth Migration Flows and Figures*, Macmillan, 1981.

Sogge, David, *Give and Take: What's the Matter with Foreign Aid?* Zed Books, 2002.

Stalker, Peter, *The No-nonsense Guide to International Migration*, Verso, 2001.

Studwell, J., *Asian Godfathers: Money and Power in Hong Kong and Southeast Asia*, Atlantic Monthly Press, 2007.

Todd, Malcolm, *Migrants and Invaders*, Tempus Publishing, 2001.

Turner, Thomas, *Congo Wars: Conflict, Myth and Reality*, Zed Books, 2007.

Uvin, Peter, *Life after Violence: A People's Story of Burundi*, Zed Books, 2009.

Winder, Robert, *Bloody Foreigners: The Story of Immigration to Britain*, Abacus, 2005.

Index

Compiled by Sue Carlton